W. E. WOODWARD

★ ★ ★ ★ ★ ★ ★ ★ ★

MEET
GENERAL GRANT

★ ★ ★ ★ ★ ★ ★ ★ ★

WITH TWENTY ILLUSTRATIONS

THE LITERARY GUILD OF AMERICA
1928

To My Mother

CONTENTS

I.
II.
III.
IV.
V.
VI.
VII.
VIII.
IX.
X.
XI.
XII.
XIII.
XIV.
XV.
XVI.
XVII.
XVIII.
XIX.
XX.
XXI.

CONTENTS

CHAPTER · · · PAGE

I. MEN AND HORSES 11

II. OBSESSIONS AND FANTASIES 25

III. THE UNWILLING SOLDIER 38

IV. GRANT FALLS IN LOVE 55

V. THE RESULTS OF INVENTIVE GENIUS 63

VI. GRANT THE PACIFIST 75

VII. THE ROAD TO MEXICO 85

VIII. GRANT TURNS OVER A NEW LEAF 101

IX. THE LEAN YEARS 117

X. THE OLD SOUTH 137

XI. DRIFTING INTO WAR 151

XII. GRANT LEAVES GALENA FOR THE WAR . . . 168

XIII. MEN OF PROMISE 180

XIV. GRANT AT CAIRO 190

XV. THE DOMINEERING RAWLINS APPEARS . . . 205

XVI. THE WORLD HEARS OF GRANT 215

XVII. THE SOUTH TRIES TO BE A NATION 228

XVIII. THE BATTLE OF SHILOH 245

XIX. THE NORTH AT WAR 263

XX. THE VICKSBURG ADVENTURE 282

XXI. GRANT IS MADE GENERAL-IN-CHIEF . . . 302

XXII. GRANT AND LEE 320

XXIII. THE SUNSET OF THE CONFEDERACY 333

Contents

CHAPTER		PAGE
XXIV.	THE ERA OF ANDREW JACKSON	354
XXV.	THE TURMOIL OF RECONSTRUCTION	371
XXVI.	GRANT BECOMES PRESIDENT	387
XXVII.	ADVENTURES IN HIGH FINANCE	404
XXVIII.	THE RECONSTRUCTED SOUTH	427
XXIX.	DIPLOMATIC EPISODES	441
XXX.	THE TRIP AROUND THE WORLD	457
XXXI.	THE TRAGEDY OF GRANT & WARD	478
XXXII.	THE HOUSE OF PAIN	492
	BIBLIOGRAPHY	503
	INDEX	507

ILLUSTRATIONS

Profile of President Grant . . . . *Frontispiece*

FACING PAGE

General Grant at the Age of Twenty-one 56

Grant's Parents 57

Mrs. Julia Dent Grant 128

House in which Grant Lived in St. Louis in 1859 129

Henry Ward Beecher and Harriet Beecher Stowe . . . 160

John Brown 161

Jefferson Davis 192

Abraham Lincoln 193

John A. Rawlins 224

Grant's "Unconditional Surrender" Message 225

General William Tecumseh Sherman 288

Recruiting Office in City Hall Park, New York 289

Wartime Photographs of General Grant 320

General Robert E. Lee 321

The McLean House at Appomattox 350

General Grant as President 448

Nellie Grant 449

General Grant about 1881 480

General Grant at Mt. McGregor 481

CHAPTER I

MEN AND HORSES

§ 1

JESSE ROOT GRANT, the father of Ulysses, was the kind of man who becomes grim and purposeful too early in life.

Grimness, as admirable as it seems in the biographies of great generals, is really nothing less than bad manners when acquired by any one under the age of fifty. But Jesse Grant was grim and had a purpose at the age of twenty-five. His purpose was to make money; and his grimness was the result of an argumentative disposition carried to extremes. He was not very well liked by his neighbors.

By trade he was a tanner, a humble occupation which would have given him a fairly low social status in a wealthy or long-settled community, but not at Point Pleasant, Ohio, in the 1820's. Southern Ohio was then a backwoods region; every one was poor, and society was acidly plebeian. Any assumption of elegance evoked invidious backbiting comments. Even moderately well-to-do people were few, and the culture that follows wealth had not arrived at all.

Behind Jesse Grant trailed a long American ancestry, sharply defined and easy to trace. He came of a race of Connecticut Yankees who had lived on their sorry New England farms from 1630 until poverty drove them westward a few years after the American Revolution. None of them had reached any distinction worth mentioning.

The history of these early Grants is an unbroken record of farming and procreation. They were an honest, hard-

11

working lot, slow in thought and rough in speech. To read their names and the brief records of their careers reminds one of an old-fashioned family album, or the rain-washed epitaphs on the tombstones of a quiet country churchyard. A family of thin-lipped men with long beards and strong features, sitting in the placid chambers of the dead. Beside them one sees their women, worn with toil and care . . . their meekly gentle eyes, their hair drawn back tightly, their hands lying wearily in their laps.

When Jesse Grant came to Point Pleasant around the year 1820, as the foreman of a small tannery, it was then, as it is now, a tiny place on the Ohio river, twenty-five miles east of Cincinnati. At that time the village dreamed of becoming a metropolis, and was filled with uneasy aspirations, which have long since dissolved into the past tense of hope. To-day it has a faint air of melancholy, and sits by its majestic river like a disappointed elderly man on a bench in a park; sitting there and mumbling of better years.

In 1821 Jesse Grant married Hannah Simpson, a fresh-faced, vigorous country girl who lived in a neighboring settlement. Her family had come from Pennsylvania, and her father was prosperous, considering the limitations of the time. He owned a large farm and lived in a brick house. It would appear that Jesse married above his own condition in life, for he possessed nothing but his job. But these comparisons are mere phrases, for they assert a distinction that was ignored in reality. Her people, living in their brick house, belonged, like the Grants, to the common lot of humanity.

The home to which Jesse brought his bride, and in which Ulysses was born, was in keeping with the popular idea of what a President's birthplace ought to be. It is true that it was not a log-house, but this minor defect was remedied perhaps by the fact that it contained only two rooms and was of the dry-goods-box type of architecture, without porch, veranda or trimmings. In one room Hannah Grant cooked her husband's meals at a huge fireplace which had a swinging crane or pot-hook; in the other room there was a puffy four-poster bed and some country-made chests of drawers.

In the winter the wind thrust its sharp knives through the rattling window frames and under the doors. Snow came early and stayed late. Cold corners and the smell of cooking. Rather cheerless, it seems, but Jesse and his wife had the tough vitality of youth; and besides, the hardest winter would pass in time, and then the bare forest, quivering with new life, would dress itself in shimmering green. In the woods there was the metallic ring of axes on the far-speaking air. Birds with flashing wings and the lazy gray smoke of brushwood fires. The house, so gloomy during the months of snow, lay in a crystalline sea of sunshine. The warm odors of the reviving earth drifted through the open doors and windows. Along the road came wagons creaking heavily, with dusty horses and sleepy drivers.

Hannah Grant was a self-contained woman whose words were few, who never wept and rarely smiled. We know almost as little of her as we do of Mary Ball, the mother of George Washington—and this is strange, for there are scores of people alive to-day who remember her as an old woman. Yes, they are willing enough to speak of her, but their reminiscences are of little use, consisting as they do of trivial anecdotes without thread or motivation. Evidently she never said much to any one; her life unfolds in the half-light of silent shadows. She acted like a woman who is nourishing within herself a life-long secret—but as to what that secret was, who can tell?

One of her qualities appears to have been a strange indifference to her children—to Ulysses in particular. When Ulysses was a small child he was seen by some of the neighbors crawling about among the legs of horses and swinging on their tails. There was neighborly excitement, of course, and a rush of startled women to tell Hannah Grant what her child was doing. She paid no attention to their fears and alarms, nor did she sally out to rescue her infant from his perilous position. "Trusting in God" was what the people of the community called her superb poise.

There are other informative anecdotes of this kind. At the close of the Civil War, when the name of General Grant was like a word written in the skies, to be seen by all men, Ulysses came back to his father's cottage for a brief visit. His mother appeared, in her working apron, her countenance without smile or elation. "Well, Ulysses," she said, "you've become a great man, haven't you?" With that remark she returned to her household duties.

Out of these reservations emerges the fact that Hannah Grant was a pious Methodist. Her religious faith was so profound that it carried her to the verge of an incalculable mysticism. If she had in truth a lifelong secret, locked closely in her bosom, it was perhaps the secret of her unity with God. In an older civilization she might have willingly passed her life in a convent, prostrate before an altar in the serene twilight of some medieval chapel, where she could have held herself forever apart from the ways and deeds of the world. This is, however, only a conjecture, a guess at her personality, made in the effort to reconstruct it from a handful of withered facts. That she was a good wife, a woman of piety and virtue, a person of common sense, with curious lapses into indifference and self-absorption, is all we know of her.

In the first year of her marriage, on April 27, 1822, her son Ulysses was born.

For six weeks he was without a name.

§ 2

Ulysses purrs on the tongue. A sugary name, Greek in origin, it sounded sibilant and foreign among the sturdy Johns and Alecks and Russells of the Ohio backwoods. It fell on Grant through accident, as it had been drawn by lot, and must be classified among the incorrigible verdicts of destiny.

It appears that there had been some argument over the naming of the child, and it was agreed finally to let chance decide the question. Then the assembled relatives and friends —so the story runs—wrote the names of their choice on slips of paper, folded up the slips, and drew one. It was Ulysses, the name that had been proposed by Grandmother Simpson.

Evidently the outcome was not wholly satisfactory to the masculine part of the family. Somebody who was there succeeded in tacking Hiram on in front of Ulysses, so the child was called Hiram Ulysses Grant. A virile name is Hiram, devoid of sweetness, and carrying a sense of muscular strength. No doubt it was hoped by the hard-handed tree-choppers of the family that Ulysses would fade into the obscurity of an anonymous middle initial. Futile hope. Children are known by the name their mother calls them, and Hannah called her son Ulysses, or "Lyss" for short.

Ulysses did not remember living in Point Pleasant, as his parents moved, when he was about one year old, to Georgetown in the next county.

Jesse Root Grant went at the task of dressing hides as cheerfully as if he were carving a piece of ivory. His esthetic sense was a negligible quantity, and he liked the work. He knew how to scrape the bloody lumps of flesh from the ill-smelling skins, how to prepare the bark of trees for tanning solutions, how to steep the hides in vats, how to beat the skins into hard or soft leather. To get on in business was his main idea, and he set up a tanning establishment of his own in Georgetown. He hired men and profited by their labor. With a shrewd and calculating eye he bought raw skins at a low price from befuddled yokels and sold leather at a high price to city men in an equivalent state of befuddlement. Tanning, with him, had ceased to be a trade and had become a business.

Here we have the elements of financial success. Jesse Grant might have become the Leather King of Ohio or something else equally admirable if it had not been for his disputatious cocksureness on all subjects. In supporting his ideas he was pugnacious and opinionated to the last degree. He carried pamphlets in his pockets and argued about politics with his customers, usually convincing them that they were wrong. That was a very poor thing for a business man to do.

But there were not many tanneries, and much leather was needed. Ulysses' father did not make a fortune, but he accumulated money. Before the boy had reached the age of ten Jesse had acquired a farm or two, had built a substantial house for his family, and was looked upon by the people of Georgetown as a capable and disagreeable person. His Sunday coat appeared on his back every day, and he wore gold-rimmed eye-glasses.

Ulysses was a slender boy, small for his age, but possessed of astonishing physical strength. He was fairly good-looking, with his well-shaped body, his straight nose, his blue eyes and chestnut-brown hair that persisted in being wavy despite his boyish efforts to comb it straight. A healthy lad he was, wholesome in body—but slovenly in manner.

At that time there were no free schools in Ohio, but Georgetown, like many other communities, had a subscription school —so called because the parents of the scholars subscribed various sums for the support of the teacher. In this school a Professor John D. White, for three months in a year, scattered knowledge to his pupils as one scatters crumbs to sparrows. The crumbs were poor in quality and few in number, but this meant nothing to Ulysses, whose intellectual hunger was easily satisfied. The simple curriculum consisted of reading, writing, arithmetic, and nothing else.

Professor White was good at whipping—so say the *Memoirs* written by Ulysses many years later—and the boy got his share . . . perhaps more than his share, for he was slow at answers, and his negligent appearance seemed to invite physical correction. A fresh bundle of switches was brought in every morning, and by the close of the day the switches were usually worn out. These beatings do not appear to have caused any rancor in the heart of Ulysses; or he may have had a tough skin. "I never had any hard feelings against my teacher," he wrote pensively near the close of his life, "either while attending the school, or in later years when reflecting upon my experience."

One day, after he had become famous, he remarked that he read but few lives of great men because biographers do not, as a rule, tell enough about the formative period of life; that what he wanted to know was what a man did when he was a boy. To understand a man, he continued, one must know what happened to him at home and in school, for there is where his character is formed.

That this is an excellent observation, of impeccable wisdom, every one will agree.

But when he wrote his own autobiography he devoted only eight pages out of a total of twelve hundred and sixteen to the story of his boyhood and youth up to the age of seventeen. And in these eight pages he says practically nothing about his youthful desires and feelings, nor does he mention the name of even one companion or playmate. So far as the record in his personal *Memoirs* goes he might have been brought up in a childless desert, inhabited by two or three school-teachers and a number of horses. The only reference he makes to his mother in this chapter—or, indeed, anywhere in the two volumes—is to give her name and the date of her marriage to his father.

Rear-Admiral Ammen was reared in Georgetown and went to Professor White's school with Grant. This honest old sea-dog lived to an advanced age and died amid the murmur of recollections. He might have told something of real impor-

tance about Grant's youth if he had possessed an eye for
character and a mind for remembrance, but he was unfortunately without these qualities. In his confused saga there is
a tale of Ulysses falling in the water while fishing and having
to swim out and go home in wet clothes . . . and of his love
for horses . . . and of his sluggishness of mind and body.
As to the last observation, it is worth noting that Grant himself
wrote that laziness was "my besetting sin through life."

This may be so; but I cannot see where or when he managed to exercise his vice of indolence. Certainly his life in
Georgetown was extraordinarily active. He wrote—I am referring to the *Memoirs* again: "When I was seven or eight
years of age I began hauling all the wood used in the house
and shops. I could not load it on the wagons, of course,
at the time, but I could drive, and the choppers would
load, and some one at the house unload. When about eleven
years old I was strong enough to hold a plow. From
that age until seventeen I did all the work done with horses,
such as breaking up the land, furrowing, plowing corn and
potatoes, bringing in the crops when harvested, hauling all the
wood, besides tending two or three horses, a cow or two, and
sawing wood for stoves, etc., while still attending school."

Ulysses was the oldest child in a family of six children—
three boys and three girls. After him there appeared, at intervals of three or four years, Samuel Simpson, Clara Rachel,
Virginia Paine, Orvil Lynch and Mary Frances. They all
grew up to maturity, living lives that were without the salt
of vice or the sweetening of virtue. Merely people . . .
existing.

§ 3

Ohio in those far-off days had some of the more restless
aspects of a country fair. For twenty years settlers had
poured into it like a river pouring across a broken dam. In

the year 1800 the whole state contained only forty-five thousand people; by 1820 the number had grown to nearly six hundred thousand. In another ten years the figure fell little short of a million, and Ohio stood fourth among the states in population.

It was a land of calloused hands, of lean and muscular men, of canvas-covered wagons with dry mud flaking from their wheels, of shotguns and hunting dogs, of silent women bending over the fires of cooking, with the smoke blowing in their eyes, of log-houses, of wheat growing boisterously in fields full of stumps, of Bibles and poor liquor, of sharp trades, of illiterate lawyers, of hell-fire preachers and innumerable quacks.

Everything was new. The houses were all new, the people were new, and their acquaintances and friends were new. The country had not settled down. Every farm was simply an experiment in soil and muscle, with the farmer looking wistfully toward the next county, where he thought the land might be cheaper and more fertile. This flood of newcomers paid little attention to comfort, to the building of houses, to the laying of walls and fences, because nearly everybody expected either to move on to a better place or to be in such a position of financial independence within a few years that he could build himself a really fine house.

Coarse and heavy-handed as these people were, their coming was nevertheless not a migration of peasants, but of fortune-seekers, for they were buoyant with the high tension of adventure. They were not looking merely for a home. They wanted land, money and power, and their energies fell instinctively into a social pattern that expressed these aspirations. The civilization they created was charged with a naked, muscular energy, though it was for many years without the cosmetics of grace and illusion.

The current myths of the time were the legends that enshrined the great pioneers. Stories of Daniel Boone and the stout-hearted hunters of the long trail were known from New

Hampshire to Georgia; stories of men grown in fancy to the
height of demi-gods; half-gods who lived in cabins and carved
new commonwealths out of the wilderness. The pioneer was
supposed to possess a special courage and virtue of his own.
The mirage of new lands and new careers stood on the horizon
of the American race. The conquest of nature acquired a
romanticism that is equaled only, in our day, by the golden aura
which surrounds the gospel of commercial success.

Yet, strong as was this passion for nature, it was destined
soon to pass away. By the time young Ulysses had grown
into a lad, the men and women of the Ohio settlements had
become weary of their harsh toil, and Daniel Boone's ghost
had faded through neglect into a faint, dreary wisp. A new
ideal was rising from the ground. The coming man was to
possess wit before strength, and guile before honesty. His
mission was not to work, but to befog his fellow-men and get
the better of them. The great day of the politician and the
lawyer was moving toward its dawn.

It was not long before every little backwoods county had
its flock of lawyers who served to carry on the interminable
disputes which gave raciness to life in communities afflicted
with a congenital boredom. The courthouse took the place
of a non-existent theater. Country people went to a
trial as to a picnic, taking their dinners with them. The
sayings of foxy lawyers were passed from mouth to ear around
the countryside, and a lawyer was esteemed in proportion to
his cleverness. A few sharp legal tricks—a circumventing
of known facts by quibbles of sophistry—gave a reputation
for shrewdness to its perpetrator that sometimes carried him
to the legislature, or to Congress.

Almost every young man wanted to be a lawyer, regardless
of his literacy or natural aptitude. Many a good farm-hand
was spoiled through dallying with law-books.

Despite this almost universal urge, there was no hankering
for the law in Ulysses. He was incapable of the mental sleight
of hand which a lawyer needs; not only that, he was without the
desire to acquire it. He had no talent for abstract ideas or
for village-store arguments.

He had to work too hard; much harder indeed than any
child ought to work, at tasks which were beyond his strength.
But this conception of his boyhood does not appear in his
Memoirs, and I do not suppose he ever thought of it. He
grew up to be a gawky country youth, notwithstanding his
good looks, slow at repartee and empty of bright answers.

At social gatherings he was a receding, retiring figure, with
nothing to say—but no matter; he was seldom to be found
at social gatherings, for horses occupied his interest almost
to the point of obsession. Even as a boy he was the best
horseman in Georgetown. His understanding of horses had
the easy fluency of Dr. Samuel Johnson's understanding of
Latin; he would mount a horse and master him as readily as
another boy might open a book and master its wisdom.

In this fact a discerning mind, familiar with psychological
inversions, may see the repercussion of his ineffective contact
with people. His life, like the life of every one else, was a
continuous search for power in some form. Among horses,
and in contact with physical obstacles, he found a satisfaction
which his awkwardness and slow wit kept him from finding
among his neighbors.

Once a circus with a trick pony among its attractions
came to the village. The proprietor announced that any one
who could stay on the pony's back would get a five-dollar bill.
This challenge, flaunted in the face of Georgetown's youth
and courage, brought out the awkward farm-hands, one by
one. The pony's mane had been cut off, and its bare back
was probably greased. Without saddle or bridle to hold on

to, the sheepish youths were thrown promptly. Finally Ulysses mounted the capering steed and stayed on by putting his arms around the animal's neck. The trick pony, with the ringmaster's whip cracking around its legs, gave a terrific exhibition of everything a pony can think of to get a man off his back. All to no avail; Ulysses held fast and won the money. "Why, that pony is slick as an apple," was his only comment, as—covered with dust and blushes—he backed away from the crowd.

Another adventure was with an unbroken horse which he had harnessed to a buggy and was bringing home from Kentucky. The horse ran away, and Ulysses succeeded in stopping him only on the extreme edge of an embankment where another foot of movement would have sent horse, buggy and driver all rolling to the bottom.

While the horse stood panting and trembling, the boy climbed cautiously out of the vehicle and reflected a moment, his hand on the reins. Then an idea occurred to him. He had heard that blind horses are not likely to run away, so he took out his handkerchief and tied it across the horse's eyes. Thus blindfolded, the unbroken horse became a slow-paced Dobbin and was driven home by the lad with great decorum.

These incidents may seem trivial, but they are indicative of a character which is not disturbed by physical encounters, and in which self-reliance and coolness are leading qualities.

Notwithstanding these achievements he gradually acquired the reputation of a numskull among the people of Georgetown. The handling of horses was held of small account in the back counties of southern Ohio, because it was a thing that a boy was expected to do; and his exploits fell into the desuetude that surrounds the common arts. These countrymen were tired of horses and wagons and plowing. That is why they wanted to be lawyers and merchants, and admired the Smart Aleck type of mind.

Yet, even at that, it is very strange that he made so little impression. For some reason, which has never fully come to light, he was unpopular among young people of his own age. I suspect his unpopularity was due largely to the fact that he was such poor company. He was bashful, and inept at the fluent jesting that passes for wit among boys and girls.

Among the boys of Georgetown at that time it was the conventional thing to be a successful swearer; profanity stood even higher than obscenity in the juvenile scale of excellence. Ulysses never swore and was not in the least obscene. To the end of his life he did not like to listen to off-color stories, though he had to hear a lot of them in his time. As to profanity, there is no record of his ever having exploded mildly into even a gentle "Damn."

In his later years he was curious about his own lack of desire to swear, and he said that he had no objection to swearing, but he had never wanted to do any of it himself. During the trying days of the Wilderness campaign he was heard several times to say, "Confound it!" and "Doggone it!" But at that time he was forty-two years old.

In the rasping judgment of an average boy-community such a restrained youth is generally considered a sort of male girl, and treated with ridicule. Ulysses was saved from that fate by reason of his obvious bravery and resourcefulness, so he became a mystery . . . and boys do not like other boys who have inscrutable ways.

Now and then he was the victim of a practical joke, and the people of Georgetown circulated exaggerated stories of his dullness. The village wits pretended not to be able to pronounce his strange name of Ulysses. In derision they called him "Useless" Grant. This remained his nickname until he left the village to become a cadet at West Point.

§ 5

I have an impression that he was very lonely and unhappy as a boy. He did not have any close boy or girl friends,

according to the evidence, and most of his days were passed
in the solitude of the woods or among horses. He seems not
to have cared much for his mother, nor she for him; but I
do not know why. His life was not a normal village boy's life,
though most of his biographers have assumed that it was, on
evidence which will not stand the most casual scrutiny.

There is no hint of this youthful loneliness in his *Memoirs*,
but they were written fifty years later, when he had become
one of the most distinguished men in the world, and the sorrows
of youth had dissolved into the shining aureole of a great
career. Besides, his *Memoirs* are extraordinarily objective,
and reveal almost nothing of Grant as a human being—except
by implication.

CHAPTER II

OBSESSIONS AND FANTASIES

§ 1

YOUNG GRANT had a girl's primness of manner and modesty of conduct. There was a broad streak of the feminine in his personality. He was almost half-woman, but this strain was buried in the depths of his soul; it never came to the surface, except indirectly, and he was probably not aware of it himself. I know this observation will be received with incredulity, for the conventional portrait of Grant is that of a bearded, puffy, middle-aged man who was never seen without a cigar in his mouth, whose clothes smelled of tobacco, and who was crammed full of masculine prowess.

In his youth his face was like that of a young girl's in its freshness of complexion and delicacy of outline. He was small and slender—but not fragile, for he had muscles of iron. His voice was always soft, clear and musical—though he cared nothing at all for music—and his hands had the long, tapering fingers of a woman. In the army before the Mexican War he was called the "Little Beauty" by the officers of his regiment.

His sense of physical modesty was most unusual—for a man and a soldier—and, in other respects, he was something of a prude. During the Civil War he would take his bath in his tent with the flaps carefully closed and pinned. While his bathing ritual was going on he would not admit even his own servant. The other generals at headquarters were not so finicky. Usually they stood naked in front of their tents in the early morning and had their orderlies dash buckets of water over them. Grant declared, when he was nearly sixty years old, that he had never been seen naked by any one since he had been a small boy.

Some of his biographers, feeling that there is no life without romance, have endeavored to find a ray of sweetheart sunshine in his juvenile years. Hamlin Garland writes:

> There is a whisper to be heard, also, of a little maid living in those days whose face and voice had come to be very precious to Ulysses. This boyish love was of the sweetest and daintiest type—perhaps unspoken on his part, for he feared the ridicule of his friends, and especially of his elders. It is only a tradition now—a faint odor as of pressed roses and spice-pinks.

This legend, with its faded bouquet of roses and spice-pinks, has obviously a very insecure toe-hold in history. Mr. Garland was unable to learn the name of this girl, although he went around Georgetown listening to the garrulity of old-time inhabitants.

The idea that every life must have in it the cherished fire of an early romance is an invention of novelists, and its tacit acceptance as a principle of biographical structure is a proof of the pressure of the novel on other forms of intellectual expression. As a matter of truth, large numbers of men and women reach maturity without ever having been in love; and it is not at all uncommon for people to go through their whole lives without either love or sexual experience.

It is as certain as any historical fact can be that Grant was never immersed in love in the manner of the great lovers; that he never gave himself wholly, at any time, to its ardors. With him love was a function rather than a passion.

But he did take the Georgetown girls on sleigh rides . . . loads of them at a time, boys and girls, gliding over the crisp snow under the yellow winter moon. For this service he was in great demand, for he had a sleigh and a team of his own, as well as an obliging disposition. One may see him in fancy, hunched over in the front seat, the reins in his hands, clad in his heavy coat and with a fur cap pulled down over his ears. The keen wind plays with the girls' curls and wraps. As the sleigh swings the corners the girls and boys are jumbled together, and there is bucolic jesting and laughter. Ulysses looks straight ahead, flicking the horses now and then, and replying briefly to some occasional bantering remark. This was as close as he ever got in those early days, so it seems, to the golden heart of romance.

§ 2

The fixed center of Grant's objective character was a highly developed matter-of-fact-ness. Among his contemporaries Lincoln was perhaps his most conspicuous antithesis in personality. Grant was much closer to the soil than Lincoln, despite Lincoln's extreme lowness of origin and the poverty of his early years. Lincoln looked instinctively to the dim twilight regions of the human spirit for his sense of values. The images of men and events did not fall primarily on his mind, but on the retina of his soul. He had the gift of feeling his way through life. Nevertheless, he was neither emotional nor sentimental, for he possessed the rare faculty of turning his spiritual perceptions into logical forms. That is why Lincoln's reasoning was so precise, so closely knit, and so simple . . . it came from the most primitive sources.

On the other hand, Grant's thinking ran outward, not inward, and he thought always in terms of material force. Whenever he found himself in circumstances which made it necessary for him to turn his conceptions into abstract ideas he had to readjust his mental focus with fumbling and effort. His cosmos was composed of streams of physical energy which appeared on the blank wall of perception in the form of com-

prehensible human events. When anything happened he realized that it was happening because of physical forces in
motion.

This material world was so near to him, and he was so completely in harmony with it, that he might be depicted truthfully—yet symbolically—in the posture of a man standing
eternally with a spadeful of earth in his hands.

But, after all, such a picture would be a caricature, fertile
with truth, as caricatures often are, though a caricature just
the same, for he was not a materialist all the way through.
Under the shell of his objectivity lay a repressed sensitiveness
which came to the surface in unexpected ways—as in strange
personal taboos.

One of his taboos was an aversion to firearms and to the
killing of animals.

In southern Ohio, during his youth, every man was an occasional hunter of game, whatever else his occupation happened
to be. Men gave pet names to their shotguns, and when they
met in groups they discussed the merits of their respective firearms as earnestly as a country club group of our day dis-
cusses golf balls and automobiles. Even ten-year-old boys
became expert executioners of birds and rabbits.

Ulysses, with his horror of game-hunting, must have seemed
somewhat ridiculous to that community of shotgun experts.
His aversion to shooting animals lasted all his life. He never
attempted to explain it, perhaps because he did not know there
was an explanation.

There were times, however, when he came very close to
breaking through his taboo. One of these occasions was during
the Mexican War, when his regiment was stationed in Texas.
He says in his *Memoirs:*

> Each officer carried a shot-gun, and every evening, after
> going into camp, some would go out and soon return
> with venison and wild turkeys enough for the entire camp.
> I, however, never went out, and had no occasion to fire

my gun; except, being detained over a day at Goliad, Benjamin and I concluded to go down the creek . . . and bring back a few turkeys. We had scarcely reached the edge of the timber when I heard the flutter of wings overhead, and in an instant I saw two or three turkeys flying away. These were soon followed by more. . . . All this time I stood watching the turkeys to see where they flew —with my gun on my shoulder, and never once thought of leveling it at the birds. When I had time to reflect upon the matter, I came to the conclusion that as a sportsman I was a failure, and went back to the house.

He did not want to kill animals, though he had no objection whatever to the killing of men; that is, to having them killed wholesale, in war. But even in that there was no sharp, knife-edge personal cruelty in his nature; and in some respects he was, as a soldier, unusually gentle and magnanimous.

Horace Porter, who was on Grant's staff during the whole of the 1864 campaign, says that Grant lost his temper only once during those trying months. One day the general and his staff were riding along a Virginia road in the route of the marching columns, when they came upon a teamster who was beating his horses in the face. Porter says that in the outburst which followed he realized for the first time that Grant had a temper. It is too bad, for history's sake, that he does not state exactly what his commander's words were, but he does say that there was a violent explosion of anger, and that before Grant rode away he had ordered the offending teamster to be tied to a post for six hours.

This incident is remarkable, for commanders of great armies do not pay attention, ordinarily, to petty incidents. Long before they reach war's lofty summit they have become accustomed to destruction, to burning houses, to dead and dying men. The Napoleons, the Wellingtons and the Lees disregard the wounded soldiers at their feet and fix their gaze on far horizons. Grant was a good horizon-gazer, too, but when horses were being beaten in the face, it was for him a different matter.

A few days after this episode he launched his swarm of men against the impregnable Confederate defenses at Cold Harbor. There they were shot down in a slaughter that has never had a parallel on this continent. Then for three days hundreds of desperately stricken men lay in the bullet-swept space between the lines, under the torrid sun, dying within sight of both armies, while Grant and Lee haggled over the finicky terms of a truce for taking care of the wounded.

The key to these contradictions lies in the fact that Grant was a zoöphile, an animal-lover. A strongly accentuated zoöphilism, such as an inordinate love of horses or dogs, throws the emotional nature out of balance; and those who are possessed by it are not likely to care very much for people.

In Grant's case it was probably a reflex of the attitude of Georgetown people toward him as a boy. Consider him as a sensitive child, pathetic in his hunger for love and approbation, and finding himself nicknamed "Useless" and the butt of village jokes. The companionship that he craved came only from horses . . . and among horses he had the sense of power that was of such vital necessity to him.

Somehow during his early childhood he had acquired an extraordinary inhibition against turning back when he had once started anywhere. He would not retrace his steps, if he could avoid it, even in cases where a turning back would not make the slightest difference. When he lived in New York, after his two terms as President, he still retained this lifelong taboo. It was said that he would not even reënter his house to get his umbrella after he had reached the sidewalk. Before going back he would walk around the block if there happened to be no servant in sight to send back. Of this characteristic he wrote:

> One of my superstitions had always been when I started to go anywhere, or do anything, not to turn back, or

stop until the thing intended was accomplished. I have frequently started to go to places where I had never been and to which I did not know the way, depending upon making inquiries on the road, and if I got past the place without knowing it, instead of turning back, I would go on until a road was found turning in the right direction, take that, and come in by the other side.

He calls his dislike of retracing his steps a superstition, but it had in fact the formidable dimensions of an obsession.

This peculiar and powerful trait was in full play during the Civil War, and often dominated his actions.

§ 3

He did not want to have anything to do with his father's tannery, though Jesse Grant expected his eldest son to become a tanner, as a matter of course. The *Memoirs* say, in their cool, restrained manner, "I detested the trade, preferring almost any other labor; but I was fond of agriculture, and of all employment in which horses were used."

To touch the bloody hides awakened in him a sleeping, shapeless repulsion which was made even more terrible because it had neither a form nor a name. But to be a tanner one had to scrape the hides as well as touch them. On one side of the skin the dried blood and scraps of flesh are removed by scraping; then the hide is turned over and the hair is taken off in a somewhat similar fashion.

In the beam-room of Jesse Grant's tannery the reeking skins were stretched from poles laid horizontally across the beams of the roof. A semi-dark, fetid place this was, with a musty smell of stagnant blood.

Ulysses managed to avoid the beam-room by various expedients. On occasion he would volunteer to grind the tanbark, and this would occupy his time. Outside of its monotony, the bark-grinding was not bad as a job. He had only to put the slabs of oak bark in the hopper of a machine. But this job could not be made to last long enough; the bark was soon ground, and then there was more talk of the beam-room.

However, he found to his joy that other enterprises lying close at hand would take him away from the tannery altogether. One of these was the hauling of passengers from Georgetown to the steamboat landing on the Ohio river, ten miles away. He was engaged in that, at times, before he had reached the age of eleven.

And he drove a team forty miles to Cincinnati, carrying a load of rags which he sold for fifteen dollars. A more adventurous journey was one that he made halfway across the state with passengers who were on their way to Toledo. While he was still a child he had become—in the intervals of schooling and farm work—a sort of public hack-driver around Georgetown.

In the meantime, with the passing of years, his father was growing more and more well-to-do financially. He wanted Ulysses, before he entered the tannery as his successor, to have a better education than the Georgetown school could give, and in the beginning of the winter of 1836—when the boy was fourteen—he was sent to the Seminary at Maysville, Kentucky, across the river and about twenty miles distant from Georgetown.

He attended the Maysville school only one winter, and his career there was so colorless that he was recalled with much difficulty by his fellow-pupils when the name of Grant rose like a sun some twenty years later. He was an average scholar, better in mathematics than in anything else.

In the spring of 1837 he returned to his home in Georgetown, and the tannery nudged up nearer to him and began to make inviting gestures. He was almost grown up, in his sixteenth year; and it was time for him to walk in his father's footsteps.

One day his father said to him, "Ulysses, you'll have to go into the beam-room and help me to-day." It appears that there was a shortage of workmen at the time.

Ulysses said nothing at first, but as he and his father approached the tannery, he burst out in protest. "Father," he exclaimed, "this tanning is not the kind of work I like. I'll work at it, though, if you wish me to, until I am twenty-one; but you may depend upon it, I'll never work a day longer at it after that."

Jesse Grant was a kindly parent, notwithstanding his knockdown style of polemics. He put his hand on the boy's shoulder and they stopped in the road.

"My son, I don't want you to work at it now," he declared, "if you don't like it, and don't mean to stick to it. I want you to work at whatever you like and intend to follow. Now, what do you think you would like?"

Ulysses reflected a moment, and replied: "I'd like to be a farmer, or a down-the-river trader, or get an education."

Jesse thought that he might be able to procure an appointment as a cadet in the United States Military Academy at West Point for Ulysses. "How would you like that?" he asked.

"First-rate," the boy replied.

What I have just quoted contains Jesse Grant's account of this occurrence, as he related it thirty years later. It does not agree in all respects with that of his distinguished son, who said that he heard nothing of the West Point proposal at that time, and that he objected to it when he did hear of it.

At all events, it is certain that Ulysses made a determined objection to working in the tannery; that his father humored him, and that he began at once to try to get his son into West Point, though Ulysses may not have been aware of his father's intentions.

Appointments to the Military Academy were made by Congressmen and Senators, then as now, and at that time the inspiration was usually political. Jesse Grant saw difficulty ahead of him in the matter, for the Congressman from the district—a man named Thomas L. Hamer—was a Democrat, while Jesse Grant was a Whig of violent mind who had opposed Hamer's election with invective as well as argument.

After some indecision on the part of Jesse Grant, it was obvious that there was nothing to do but to write to Congressman Hamer and beg for the appointment. This was done by the father of Ulysses in a stark naked letter, entirely devoid of cordiality or the flowery graces. No matter. Mr. Hamer was the kind of man who has a Gift for Doing the Right Thing. Sitting at Washington in the seats of the mighty and thinking of his Ohio district and the next election, he saw a politician's chance to stop the mouth of at least one rabid opponent. So his reply was gracious enough. He said that there was a vacancy from his district and that he would be delighted to give the appointment to Ulysses.

Then he picked up another sheet of paper and wrote to the War Department that his choice for the vacancy at West Point was Ulysses . . . and there his pen paused. Ulysses must have a middle name, Hamer thought, and he wondered what it was. He had always heard him called Ulysses or "Useless." But this Congressman knew his constituency, and he remembered that Jesse Grant had married Hannah Simpson. The boy's middle name must be Simpson, so the hovering pen descended and wrote Ulysses Simpson Grant.

In this manner did the insignificant Mr. Hamer contribute his mite to the history of the world.

Now the beam-room with its bloody hides glides away, hopelessly foiled and grimacing in the foggy distance, but all through Grant's life he held in his soul the residue of its receding threat. He never could eat meat that had the least drop of blood exuding from it. Steaks had to be burned to a hard crisp before he would touch them. He was the lifelong despair of cooks.

Ulysses was sent again to school to prepare for West Point —this time to another "Institute" at Ripley, which is only ten miles from Georgetown. His career there was as blank as it was at Maysville. He says in the *Memoirs:* "I was not studious in habit, and probably did not make progress enough to compensate for the outlay for board and tuition."

He was, in truth, a vegetative youth, growing up like a stolid oak. Stolid on the outside; but on the inside, and buried deep, he was all sensitiveness and feeling. At school he was devoid of banjos, songs, and gaudy clothes; and the muscular arm of Grant was not among those that stole around the waists of pretty girls.

His fear of ridicule came out in curious ways. On the eve of his departure for West Point a handy man in the village made a trunk for him. As a finishing flourish to the job the trunkmaker had put on the initials H. U. G. (for Hiram Ulysses Grant) in brass tacks. A nice touch, and the man pointed to it with pride. But H. U. G. spells "Hug," and Ulysses, in fancy, heard the cadets shouting it to one another. He was through with nicknames—to drop "Useless" and become "Hug" would never do—so the tacks had to be pulled out.

Ulysses left with mingled joy and reluctance. He had no desire to become a soldier, but he was cheered by the thought that on his way to West Point he would pass through two large cities, and would have a chance to see them. Writing of this in his day of reminiscence, he said: "Going to West Point would give me the opportunity of visiting the two great cities of the continent, Philadelphia and New York. This was enough. When these places were visited I would have been glad to have had a steamboat or railroad collision, or any other accident happen, by which I might have received a temporary injury sufficient to make me ineligible, for a time, to enter the Academy. Nothing of the kind occurred, and I had to face the music."

A relative of the Simpsons, who lived in Philadelphia, kept him at her house for a few days, which he devoted to sight-seeing. He was at that time, according to her, awkward and speech-bound. He wore a suit of butternut-colored jeans, woven on a backwoods hand loom. His shoes, she says, were rough and heavy-soled. His face was freckled; and though he had a look of strength, he seemed under-sized for his age. (He was only five feet two inches tall when he entered the Military Academy.)

It was a splendid adventure . . . this strolling about the big towns, all alone with money in his pocket. Some of the city people must have stared at him as hard as he stared at them—at his healthy, freckled face and coarse shoes and country clothes.

Though he was having a good time, he was not care-free. Beyond the buildings and the ships, beyond the glimpse of the ocean and Independence Hall and the grave of Franklin, and Broadway and Trinity Church, lay the shadow of West Point. There he would have to meet many strangers . . . the other cadets . . . the gray-clad aristocrats . . . the bright boys from everywhere . . . the learned professors. They all stood before his vision in a disquieting picture.

The time-yellowed Adjutant's register at West Point shows that he registered thereon May 29, 1839, and this is how he signed his name:

Ulysses Hiram Grant

By transposing his two names he had got rid of the menace of being called "Hug," but he did not know at that time, apparently, that his appointment to the Academy was in the name of Ulysses Simpson Grant.

There was, indeed, some little difficulty about the name. The Adjutant said that he expected a Ulysses Simpson—and

here was a Ulysses Hiram. Young Grant explained it satis-
factorily enough, but the Adjutant, tied up in red tape, declared that the papers would have to go back to Washington
to have the name changed to Ulysses Hiram.

However, the papers did not go back. Grant knew a better
method. He would, then and there, assume the name of Ulysses
Simpson, and be done with it.

His gesture of straight-line directness in this inconsequential
incident is characteristic of his entire military career. His
mind moved always in the simplest geometrical patterns. All
large problems became small ones in the distillation of his
mental processes—small in the sense that he instinctively di-
vested them of extraneous and unnecessary complications. His
ideas, such as they were, fell on their objective as a hammer
falls on an anvil.

Badeau, who served on Grant's staff for years and wrote
the history of his campaigns, said: "All his military greatness
came of the plainest possible qualities, developed to an astounding degree."

When such men are correct in their conclusions—that is,
when they have the weight of public opinion and resources
behind them—they become enormously dynamic and successful.
But when they are wrong their ideas strike like a hammer
beating water, and then their failures are egregious beyond
words.

CHAPTER III

THE UNWILLING SOLDIER

§ 1

THE seventeen-year-old Ulysses came up the Hudson to West Point, thinking of what wonderful things there are in the world. In wistful remembrance he thought, too, of the rough fields and the sinewy horses of the Ohio country that he had left behind him. There was more than a tinge of melancholy in his reflections, for the good Lord had not granted him the merciful salvation of a train wreck, and he felt that his prayers had not been answered. As the stone buildings of the West Point Military Academy showed their gray heads over the green summer of the river hills, he saw the gathering of his doom. "I had rather a dread of reaching my destination," he wrote.

§ 2

Gray-coated cadets loiter about the bulletin board at the door of the Academy guardroom. Slim young fellows, their movements graceful and fluid, they are living in a time-dimension that contains neither age nor youth. Their fresh contours have not been eroded to sharpness by the disillusion of life. Though they have ceased to be boys they have not yet become men. Their existence is happily suspended between ambition and achievement. They laugh a lot, for they are still to learn that ambition and achievement never meet.

In the throng is a vivacious youth named Sherman, slender, red-haired and blue-eyed. The world is to hear of him; and, after he has departed, his image in bronze will sit on a bronze horse and stare pensively through the changing years at the flood of new generations in New York's Fifth Avenue.

But on that day his metal steed was far away in the incredible future. He was simply young Sherman—called Bill—full of good nature and likable traits. He had queer ideas and a whimsical mind. His finger runs down the list of new cadets on the bulletin board and stops at "U. S. Grant."

"Here's U. S. Grant," he calls out. "U. S. Yes, that's what it says. What do you suppose the U. S. part of it stands for?"

"For United States!" somebody shouts. "That's what U. S. stands for. We're going to have a fellow here named after this great big United States."

"No, it doesn't," comes another voice from the crowd, "there isn't anybody named United States. It can't be. . . ."

"Well, it's Uncle Sam then," another cadet insists. "Uncle Sam Grant. That's what he is—the grandson of our good old Uncle Sam."

When Grant arrived at the Academy he found himself already named. He was "Sam" Grant, no matter how he protested; and he did not protest much. The name "Ulysses" was never heard at West Point, and does not appear when Grant is mentioned in the reminiscences of his classmates. They all knew him as Sam.

To those who attended the shrine of Mars he seemed a very unmilitary figure, not only on his first day, but for many months thereafter. His shoulders had a noticeable stoop—the result of his back-bending labor as a child; and he walked with the high-stepping clomp-clomp of a farmer on newly plowed ground. One of his fellow-cadets recollected him as "unique-appearing." Another said they all thought him "countrified." To many of them he seemed an obvious misfit.

They kept him in the awkward squad for months, and after a time he succeeded in adjusting himself crudely to his environment, though he continued for four years to be something of a trial to the tactical officers. The fact is that he possessed absolutely no native talent for soldiering—and he did not like the military profession. The molding force of West Point had to struggle here with raw material that was not adapted to its processes, and the effort was somewhat like that of trying to make an automobile engineer out of a man who wants to be a physician. Near the close of his life, after he had become West Point's most distinguished son, he wrote that when he entered the Academy he had little hope of ever getting through the course; and he had expected, if he did graduate, to resign from the army and try to get a place as a professor of mathematics in some small college.

His military career is a curious phenomenon. He never did become a soldier within the meaning that frames itself in our minds when we think of Napoleon, or Lee, or Von Moltke, or Jackson. These men were military by instinct. They loved the art of war, and studied it with the absorbing care that a mathematician gives to the study of Einstein. They looked upon a military campaign as a problem in strategy, but to Grant a campaign was a problem in mechanics. There is a profound difference in these two conceptions, which I hope to make plain when we come to the operations of the Civil War.

§ 3

Grant discovered within twenty-four hours that the scattering disorder of a Georgetown working day was at West Point nothing less than a violation of the most solemn commandments. Easy enough to learn the rules and follow them, one may say—but it was not a simple matter to a youth who had never in his life taken the trouble to fold his clothes and put them away or to keep his shoes shined.

In the battered copy of the *Regulations of the Military*

Academy for 1839 which I possess the formula for the perfect military life is given in three hundred and forty-eight numbered paragraphs. These regulations were no doubt treated with respect, but not altogether with reverence, if one may judge by the penciled comments made on the margin of the pages by the cadet who owned the book. (I do not know who this cadet was, but it was not Grant, as the handwriting is not his.)

In this gospel for young generals every contingency of existence is divined, and a rule fashioned to fit each case. Seen through such a medium, life appears as a series of mechanical reactions. Free will disappears, leading initiative by the hand, and their place is taken by a sort of military monasticism which is precise rather than harsh. One has only to thumb the book a little, dipping in here and there, to catch its spirit. Rule 187 tells what a cadet must do when he gets up in the morning. He is expected to "hang up his extra clothing, put such articles in the clothes bag as it is intended to contain, clean his candlestick or lamp, and arrange his bedding and all his other effects in the prescribed order."

There is a time for soiled clothes, and a time for religion. Rule 189 declares that "cadets shall prepare their clothes for the laundress before seven o'clock on the mornings of Sunday and Thursday," and Rule 127 says that every cadet "shall attend divine service on Sunday."

The impulse to throw things must have been rather strong among these young soldiers, for two paragraphs are given to the subject. Rule 190 states that no cadet shall "throw water from his room upon the halls or piazzas." No. 191 goes further. There we read that "no cadet shall throw anything" from the windows or doors.

Rule 181 talks about hair-cutting and tonsorial appearances. One learns that "cadets shall have their hair trimmed close, except from the crown to the forehead, which shall be neatly trimmed and dressed. Mustaches shall not be worn."

That youth of long ago who scribbled the comments on the margin wrote opposite this rule: "How can a forehead be trimmed and dressed?"

In No. 113 the drinking of liquor is absolutely prohibited; and another edict on the same page eliminates tobacco in any form from the narrow circle of pleasures. The next paragraph condemns card-playing, with a penalty of dismissal from the "service of the United States." What, then, is allowed in the way of clean, wholesome enjoyment? Chess-playing, perhaps. Napoleon was a chess-player, and chess is supposed, in some way that has never been clearly explained, to resemble the art of war. But no . . . even chess is not permitted. Rule 196 takes care of that. "No cadet shall play," it says, "at chess, backgammon, or any other game, nor keep the boards, men, or implements used in those games in his room."

Turning to another page, we find good manners the subject of discourse: "No cadet shall use any reproachful or provoking speeches or gestures to another, on pain of being confined, and of asking pardon of the party offended, in presence of his commanding officer. . . . Any cadet who shall, by any means whatever, traduce or defame another, shall be dismissed."

And there is Rule 129, with its wide-spreading implications: "The cadets are not only required to abstain from all vicious, immoral or irregular conduct, but they are enjoined on every occasion to conduct themselves with the propriety and decorum of gentlemen."

In a democratic, industrial nation the military life always bears in its heart a conscious sense of isolation and remoteness. Those who are devoted to it perceive that they are set apart, by a complex of intangible distinctions, from their fellow men.

Eventually they lose their elbow touch with the outer world.

They observe, from afar off, and as through a clouded lens, that men labor and perspire, but they do not comprehend the inspiration of achievement—nor its logic. To one who has been a military man all his life the world seems merely chaotic and unprecise—and incomprehensible. His impulse is to turn back to his own military circle and steep himself in its ideals.

At West Point one may witness this cloister type of mind being formed and fertilized. As the years go by the Academy becomes the cadet's world. Its stone walls enclose him, and the doings of men—except when they relate to war—reach him only in confused murmurs.

Grant was below the average in conduct during his whole term at the Academy, and at his graduation he stood one hundred and fifty-six in order of conduct among a total number of two hundred and twenty-three cadets in the corps. An inspection of the record shows that he was not vicious nor immoral, but merely untidy . . . and lazy. A large number of his demerits came from slovenly habits of dressing—for not brushing his clothes, for not having his coat buttoned, for spots on his garments, for not keeping his gun clean, for wearing incorrect articles of clothing. And there were a good many for being late at roll-calls. He was a heavy sleeper and was frequently reported late, or absent, at reveille . . . and he was inattentive at drill.

General J. H. Stokes, who was a cadet while Grant was at the Academy, says, "He was not particularly tidy about his dress, and he even had a certain slouchy air about him that many of the class thought unsoldierly, but he never did anything positively offensive, and, as he was always quiet and attended to his own affairs, we liked him well enough, but only in a negative way." General Stokes adds that there was nothing about Grant to indicate that he would ever be heard of; and Dr. Henry Coppée, who was also there at the time, says that Grant "exhibited but little enthusiasm for anything."

I suspect that his indifference came from fatigue. We have seen that he had been forced into an early physical maturity, that he was doing a grown man's work at the age of twelve. When he reached West Point he was probably tired through and through, though he may not have been conscious of it.

No doubt this labor strain left other and more lasting effects than fatigue. He was precocious, but his precociousness was physical, and not mental. It implied the molding of a young body to man-like attitudes and a boy's muscle to a man's work. The effect was to create an outward hard shell of maturity over a personality that was still essentially juvenile. It was a sort of congealed adolescence, and he remained in it for the greater part of his life—mature on one side and infantile on the other. In this we see the real reason for many of the surprising contradictions that appear in his career. Whenever he encountered circumstances that called for physical action he was always sure of himself, confident and at ease. But when the question before him dealt with abstractions, with ideas, or with personalities that had to be probed and weighed, then he hesitated uneasily, and his speech dripped with hazy platitudes.

In those days the military history of the Civil War lay in West Point as a child lies in its mother's womb. Among the cadets who were there during Grant's time were Longstreet, Hardee, Rosecrans, Pope, Ewell and Buckner—all of whom became famous generals, though some of them are famous only because of their defeats.

Grant was not on intimate terms of friendship with any of these young men, nor was he a prominent figure in cadet life. Even Longstreet, who in after years became his cherished friend, said that he could not remember much about Grant at West Point, though they had been there together for three years. Sherman remembered him perfectly, but Sherman had an unusually vivid sense of character and an observant eye. Rufus Ingalls roomed with Grant one year, and, of course, knew him well. Ingalls wrote long afterwards—at the time of the Civil War—that Grant took small interest in his studies, that he seldom read over a lesson more than once, and that he spent his time largely in idleness or in poring over romances.

He could not dance and had no desire to learn. It is declared as a historical fact that during his four years he never went to a dance and never entered a private house as a guest.

Swarms of fashionable girls came up from New York with their chaperones to the balls and military fêtes. Grant saw them only as one sees a far-off garden of roses. He might have met the young ladies, as the other cadets met them, but he was kept back either because he lacked interest in them, or because he distrusted his own capacity to entertain them.

Grant was neither a student nor a good mixer. His studies bored him, and he had no talent for acquiring popularity. How, then, did he spend his time? In the *Memoirs* he says:

> I could not sit in my room doing nothing. There is a fine library connected with the Academy from which cadets can get books to read in their quarters. I devoted more time to these than to the course of studies. Much of the time, I am sorry to say, was devoted to novels, but not those of a trashy sort. I read all of Bulwer's then published, Cooper's, Marryatt's, Scott's, Washington Irving's work, Lever's, and many others that I do not now remember.

During his first year as a cadet there was a bill before Congress to abolish the Military Academy. The opponents of military education declared that West Point was a breeding ground for snobbery, that it was an inefficient school and a waste of money. Grant said that he looked at the newspapers every day, hoping to read that the bill had passed, and that the Academy was to go out of existence. He adds: "It never passed, and a year later, although time hung drearily with me, I would have been sorry to have seen it succeed."

The mental picture that we get of him at this time is blowzy and unprepossessing . . . an untidy youth, with a faint suggestion of greasiness in his appearance, huddled up over the pages of a sentimental romance in a stuffy barracks room. He was consciously out of place and ill at ease. He needed nothing so much as inspiration and friendship.

And in some relations of life he was not entirely frank. In 1839, while he was anxiously waiting for Congress to put the Military Academy out of existence, he wrote a letter to a young cousin named McKinstry Griffith, in which he declared that he liked West Point a lot, and was glad to be there.

I shall quote part of this letter, not because it deals with anything of importance, but only to show his literary style at that period of his life. It is wholly out of tune with Grant's direct, sledge-hammer character—and stands as a horrible example of what rhetoric may do to a simple-hearted plowboy:

Dear Coz: I was just thinking that you would be right glad to hear from one of your relatives who is so far away as I am. So I have put away my algebra and French, and am going to tell you a long story about this prettiest of places, West Point. So far as it regards natural attractions it is decidedly the most beautiful place that I have ever seen. Here are hills and dales, rocks and river; all pleasant to look upon. From the window near I can see the Hudson—that far-famed, that beautiful river, with its bosom studded with hundreds of snowy sails.

I do not believe that he took that paragraph out of his own head. There's a guide-book air about the far-famed Hudson— "its bosom studded with hundreds of snowy sails."

Again, I look another way I can see Fort Putt, now frowning far above, a stern monument of a sterner age, which seems placed there on purpose to tell us of the glorious deeds of our fathers, and to bid us to remember their sufferings—to follow their example.

.   .   .   .

Here is the house Washington used to live in—there Kosiuscko used to walk and think of his country and of ours. Over the river we are shown the dwelling-house of Arnold—that base and heartless traitor to his country and his God. I do love the place—it seems as though I could live here forever, if my friends would only come too. You might search the wide world over and then not find a better.

.   .   .   .

On the whole I like the place very much—so much that I would not go away on any account. The fact is, if a man graduates here, he is safe for life, let him go where he will. There is much to dislike, but more to like. I mean to study hard and stay if it be possible; if I cannot, very well, the world is wide. I have now been here about four months, and have not seen a single familiar face or spoken to a single lady. I wish some of the pretty girls of Bethel were here, just so I might look at them. But fudge! Confound the girls. I have seen great men, plenty of them. Let me see: General Scott, Mr. Van Buren, Secretary of War and Navy, Washington Irving, and lots of other big bugs.

.   .   .   .

We are not only obliged to go to church, but must march there by companies. This is not republican. It is an Episcopal church. Contrary to the expectation of you and the rest of my Bethel friends, I have not been the least homesick. I would not go home on any account whatever.

Poor homesick boy! Writing bravely of the delights of West Point to keep up his courage . . . and scanning the newspapers in the hope that Congress has put an end to the whole affair.

§ 4

The curriculum covered a strange hodge-podge of war and culture. Algebra and French, the only studies prescribed for the first year, were at one end of this intellectual patchwork. With that simple beginning the course widened out, and came to a finish with a kaleidoscopic sputtering of mineralogy, geology, engineering, rhetoric, science of war, political science, moral philosophy, and the use of the sword.

English grammar was among the subjects for the second year, as well as geography and history. It appears, therefore, that a cadet had to tackle French genders and reflexive verbs before he had learned English participles. As for geography, it is not surprising to find it in the curriculum, for at that time geography was hardly ever taught in the common schools, and was generally considered a collegiate branch of knowledge.

A sort of desiccated history came and went in the second year. It must have been composed entirely of names and dates, for in those few months the cadet had to cover a course which included "a brief notice of Greece, Rome, Syria and Egypt, the Middle Ages, England, and the other European states; a brief history of the discovery and early settlement of America, and especially the history of the United States."

The course in mathematics was fairly thorough, as it began with algebra and went on up through trigonometry, analytic geometry and a part of the calculus—put down under the head of "fluxions."

And there was a little physics and chemistry, a lot of drawing, a small bite at the world's obese philosophies, and an abundance of infantry and artillery tactics. The science of war, as distinguished from drilling and tactical methods, had only a trifling part in the scheme. The course hardly touched the subject of strategy at all, and the chief effort of the institution at that time seems to have been made toward the production of drillmasters instead of generals.

It is certain that Grant was never familiar with any of the classic campaigns of Napoleon or Frederick the Great. John A. Rawlins, who knew Grant more intimately than any other man ever knew him, says that he had never read a book on strategy.

There is confirmatory evidence of the truth of this assertion in an incident that occurred after the war, when the grateful American nation was loading Grant with gifts. Philadelphia gave him a house; New York gave him one hundred thousand dollars; and Boston decided to make its present in the form of books. After the money to buy five thousand volumes had been raised one of the Boston representatives in Congress went about quietly to find out what military treatises were in the great general's library, so as to avoid duplication. Thus the donors learned, to their astonishment, that he did not own a military book of any kind.

And he says himself:

Some of our generals failed because they worked out everything by rule. . . . They were always thinking about what Napoleon would do. Unfortunately for their plans, the rebels would be thinking about something else. I don't underrate the value of military knowledge, but if men make war in slavish observances of rules, they will fail. No rules will apply to conditions of war as different as those which exist in Europe and America. Consequently, while our generals were working out problems of an ideal character, problems that would have looked well on a blackboard, practical facts were neglected. To that extent I consider remembrances of old campaigns a disadvantage.

§ 5

I have never been able to discover any sensible reason why a military education should be so thoroughly saturated with mathematics. In actual warfare there is nothing in mathematical science beyond arithmetic that is of the least value, except to engineer officers, and these are so few in number that a special education in mathematics might be provided for them without forcing every infantry officer to flounder through Descartes and Newton. It is true, indeed, that mathematics is the foundation of the science of ballistics; but, even so, artillery officers in the field are spared the torture of having to solve differential equations under a heavy fire, as printed tables of ranges and distances are thoughtfully provided by the War Department for their use. It is as simple as looking up a number in a telephone directory.

It seems better, from the standpoint of common sense, to do away with everything in mathematics higher than arithmetic in an officer's education, and devote the time thus saved to such important subjects as the relative nutritive value of different kinds of food, the structure of the human body, and the principles of sanitation and medicine.

Whatever may be the value of mathematics in an officer's education, there is no doubt that it was the salvation of Grant's class standing at West Point. It was the only subject in which he was really interested, and the only one in which his standing was good. At the close of the first year he ranked forty-ninth in French in a class of sixty members, but in mathematics he stood sixteenth.

In the second year he held the tenth place in mathematics among the fifty-three men remaining in his class. This year he stood forty-fourth in French, and forty-sixth in ethics.

There were two or three other subjects in which he showed an interest and made a fairly good standing. Engineering, for instance. During his last year he stood sixteenth in that branch of study—and in the third year he was nineteenth in drawing in a class that numbered forty-one.

His general standing at graduation was twenty-first in a class that had been reduced during the four years from seventy-six to thirty-nine.

If horsemanship had counted in class standing Grant would have graduated much nearer the top of his class. He was not only the star of the riding school, but was so far and away ahead of any one else in the management of horses that even the cavalry instructors envied him.

Let us linger here for a moment and picture the riding school on a visitors' day when Grant was the best horseman in the corps of cadets.

The interior is like that of a huge barn, dim with indecisive shadows. The floor is covered with tanbark on which the horses' feet make a sound that resembles the throbbing of soft little drums, beaten rapidly. On the walls and posts, flags and cavalry sabers are displayed—the flags draped harshly, in man-fashion, over the raw timbers. As the filtered sunlight falls on them, they glow, in the distance, like enormous red and blue jewels. A rope is stretched across the hall at one end, and behind it the visitors sit . . . gentlemen in checkered trousers and black stocks, and ladies in crinoline with saucy dish-shaped hats on their masses of piled-up hair. The ladies walk to their seats with the stately bearing of ships under full sail, and when they sit down their great skirts spread and shiver around them.

There is a polyphony of chattering overtones mingled with laughter. The young women hold delicately perfumed handkerchiefs of lace in their hands and sniff at them daintily now and then, for the air of the riding hall has in it more than a faint suggestion of a stable. The cadet escorts of these crinoline damsels sit on the edges of camp chairs, their backs as straight as boards, and point to the interesting features of the program.

At the other end of the hall a brass band suddenly explodes into martial music, but still the tanbark oval is empty, save for an occasional cavalry private, who rides in, exercising a string of led horses that trails behind him, and departs in the hangdog manner of a servant after one or two tours of the ring.

A cavalry instructor, looking like a cross between a circus ringmaster and Prince Murat, stands in the middle of the hall and tries to say something that can be heard above the noise of the band. But to no avail; his speech makes only a hoarse counterpoint in the music. Soldiers come through some indistinguishable door in the wall, bringing poles which they hold up horizontally at graduated levels.

Now a cadet, entering on horseback, canters about the oval and turns his horse in graceful pirouettes. He smiles at the visitors nonchalantly, leaps two or three hurdles and trots away, trailed by kid-glove applause and the waving of handkerchiefs.

Others follow, doing their turns with grace and precision. It has become a bit boresome—this jumping over poles—in the dust and smell of the place, and gentlemen are framing explanations for leaving early. Some of the younger girls are beginning to have vague intentions of fainting as a diversion.

The cavalry instructor motions to the band to cease playing. It stops abruptly, in the middle of a bar. There is an expectant hush; the instructor walks over to the soldiers who are holding up the pole and says something, and then he calls out, "Mr. Grant!"

The soldiers raise the pole a foot higher. A murmur flickers like a new flame among the guests. "He'll never make it in the world," says a man sententiously. A cadet in the front row turns around and looks at the man. "Won't he?" he says. "Well, you wait and see. It's Sam Grant."

Horse and man flash out of the hazy stable-shadows like a streak of light. The slovenly cadet, musty with the reading of stale romantic novels, has miraculously become a being of alertness and muscle. Riding with wild Cossack grace, he makes straight for the hurdle. The horse, as he approaches the leap, pauses for the hundredth of a second, gathers strength, and flows through the air with the sleek smoothness of water flowing over a stone. Now there is a new interest. Gloves are split with applause, ladies have decided not to faint, and gentlemen have ceased to think up excuses. Mr. Grant has encores. He must leap and turn and ride at a furious and incredible pace. The soldiers raise the pole even higher, but Grant and his horse go over it.

At last, covered with dust and sweat, they leave the ring. Cadet Grant never turns back, never smiles and never meets the admiring ladies.

§ 6

The commandant of cadets during Grant's years at the Academy was C. F. Smith, who was (I believe) a captain at that time. Smith was a soldier of great ability. He had a passionate liking for the science of war, and he knew as much about armies and soldiers as any American of that epoch could know. As commandant, he was in direct charge of the cadet corps as a military organization.

The unsoldierly Grant was, of course, under his eye, and was observed by him day by day. When the list of cadets to be appointed as corporals was read out at the end of the first year, Grant's name did not appear among them; but to the surprise of Grant—and of everybody else—the commandant made Grant a sergeant at the beginning of the third year. His appointment was the subject of much joking among the cadets. It was declared ironically that Sam Grant had been made a sergeant because he could not keep step. As a sergeant he would have to march among the file-closers and therefore would not be able to throw the column out of step by his stumbling.

The appointment to a sergeantcy turned out to be unfortunate. Grant was not much of a sergeant. At the end of a year he was dropped; I mean that he was passed over in the list of captains and lieutenants, and served the last year as a private.

West Point did not give Grant much of an education, but its moral pressure was overwhelming, and he retained an immense respect for the Academy as long as he lived. "I think West Point is the best school in the world," he told John Russell Young many years later. "I do not mean the highest grade, but the most thorough in its discipline. A boy to go through four years in West Point must have the essential elements of a strong, manly character. Lacking any of these he must fail. I hear army men say their happiest days were at West Point. I never had that experience. The most trying days of my life were those I spent there, and I never recall them with pleasure."

CHAPTER IV

GRANT FALLS IN LOVE

§ 1

ULYSSES wanted a commission in the cavalry, but he could not get it because there was no vacancy in a cavalry regiment. So the finest horseman at West Point had to be content with a second lieutenant's place in the Fourth Infantry, which at that time was stationed at Jefferson Barracks, an army post eight or ten miles below St. Louis.

On his way he stopped in Ohio to visit his parents. They lived then in Bethel, a little cross-roads village near Georgetown. Having sold his tannery, Jesse Grant had turned himself into a farmer.

Lieutenant Grant's arrival created a goggle-eyed sensation in the sleepy hamlet. Most of its inhabitants had never seen an army officer before, and did not quite know the difference between a lieutenant and a general. The rural imagination played in fantastic conceptions around his dazzling uniform, the heroic traditions of the army, and the immense learning that must be buzzing in his head after such a thorough education at West Point. If he had been a ladies' man he could have won the heart of any girl in the county; but he did not try. As a soldier taking his ease he was a philosopher of the porticos rather than a Mark Antony of the poppy fields. In the timeless afternoons he sat with the middle-aged men around the steps of the Georgetown court-house, where sticks were whittled and discourse was slow.

They did not call him "Useless" Grant any more. In their manner respect and curiosity struggled for precedence.

55

He was invited to drill the local militia company. On the day of this ceremony the whole countryside came to town and stood in glad attentiveness about the court-house square. Grant, measuring five feet eight inches in height—and very slender—looked small beside the militia officers, who had been chosen chiefly on account of size and bellowing power. All those who recalled the occasion many years afterward spoke of the resonance and clarity of his voice in giving commands. They said, too, that he was pale and nervous.

§ 2

Under the warm autumn sun Jefferson Barracks was indolently Southern. Sunny and spacious, with its wide verandas and crisp green lawns. The numerous buildings of the post were spread out like the fingers of an open hand. It had the effect of a miniature village planned by a child of generous mind. On the wide parade ground the drilling companies shrank, in the eye, to toy soldiers on a carpet of green velvet. Far away, beyond the surf of white fences, rose the stiff plumes of a horizon of pines through which the sky showed in jagged, pale-blue patches.

Life was both dull and quiet. Officers sat for endless hours on the veranda, their feet on the railing, talking of small things and playing the trumpery games that are bred in idleness.

Grant's mind was full of intentions and hopes. From his stopping place in Ohio he had written to the head of the mathematical department at West Point that he would like to teach mathematics at the Military Academy. The professor's reply was favorable, though he wrote that there was no opening at the time. This dampening statement was followed by the assurance that, when the next vacancy in an assistant professorship occurred, Grant would be considered for the place.

Out of this correspondence the young lieutenant built a

U. S. Grant
Bvt. 2d. Lt. 4th Inf'y.

GENERAL GRANT AT THE AGE OF TWENTY-ONE

JESSE ROOT GRANT

The father of General Grant. Died at Covington, Ky., June 29, 1873.

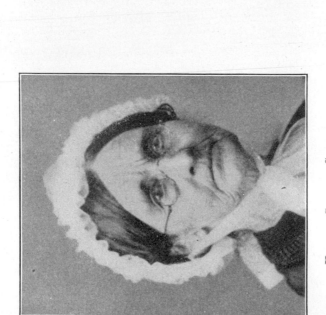

HANNAH SIMPSON-GRANT

General Grant's mother. Died at Jersey City
May 11, 1883.

Photos from the Collection of Frederick H. Meserve

daydream of himself as a teacher. He saw himself standing throughout the years by the stream of life, a half-recluse, sprinkling algebra and calculus generously upon the heads of the passing generations.

A quiet, soothing dream it was; a dream that could never come true. And it is just as well, after all. He would have been a failure as a teacher. Without the charm of personality which every successful teacher must possess, his work would have become before long an ineffective drudgery. Undistinguished and unpromoted, he would have gone laboring on for years—and then the world would have heard no more of him.

His stay at Jefferson Barracks soon came to an end. He had been there only seven months when his regiment was ordered down the Mississippi River and across western Louisiana to the Texas border.

Among Grant's classmates at West Point there had been a cadet named Frederick T. Dent. This young man was wholesome, cheerful, and beefy. His mind was almost wholly untainted by scholarship. His manners were Southern and his ambitions were few and easily satisfied. All he wanted to do at West Point was to get through, and in that desire he found a companion soul in Grant.

Frederick Dent's family lived near St. Louis, some miles from Jefferson Barracks. Young Dent himself was not stationed at the Barracks, but he arranged things so that his family invited young Lieutenant Grant to the Dent home.

Through making this simple gesture of politeness toward his classmate Frederick Dent got himself entangled in the net of history. Innumerable historical archeologists have tramped over his ruins, so to speak, with tape-line and notebook; and genealogical specialists have not failed to trace his family back through the centuries to the lords and ladies from whom all Americans have descended.

The Dents called their home "White Haven," and it is spoken of as an estate, but it was really nothing more than a farm.

They had social aspirations. Colonel Dent, the head of the family, was a hospitable person with a red face and a hearty handshake. My own desultory researches into his antecedents have not been sufficient for me to say positively whether he was a colonel by reason of military service, or merely in the way of Southern courtesy.

A family of slaveholders, the Dents were very different in manner and ideas from any one whom Grant had known as a boy in Ohio. They were not much better off than his father's family, but they possessed a gentle graciousness that would have seemed effeminate to old Jesse Grant.

In the family were five or six young people, among them a seventeen-year-old daughter named Julia, who had just finished her education at Professor Moreau's school in St. Louis. There she had been taught a little music, French, and ballroom etiquette—besides the work of the more refined among the English poets.

Grant does not appear to have met Julia Dent—so far as I have been able to learn—until the month of February, 1844. He was ordered South with his regiment in May, so whatever courting he did must have been done in three months.

I fancy that there was not much courting done by him at any time. Julia liked to ride, and she and the young lieutenant went cantering along the Missouri roads, talking probably about everything except what was on their minds. She attended some dances at the Barracks, where the wallflower Ulysses stood watching her lithe form go swinging around the room in other men's arms. He tried to keep her on horseback as much as possible.

When the regiment was sent to Louisiana Grant was away in Ohio on a short visit. Returning to Jefferson Barracks, he found that his company had departed, and the Colonel's orders were for him to follow the command immediately. Thereupon he made up his mind to propose to Miss Dent before leaving.

He tells—in the *Memoirs*—of his proposal, though from his story he left out, characteristically, all its romantic features. He says that he procured a horse and started for "White Haven." On the way he had to ford a creek which ordinarily was a mere trickle of water, but there had been a lot of rain, and the creek had become a rushing torrent.

> I struck into the stream, and in an instant the horse was swimming, and I being carried down by the current. I headed the horse towards the other bank and soon reached it, wet through and without clothes on that side of the stream. I went on, however, to my destination and borrowed a dry suit from my future brother-in-law. . . .
>
> Before I returned I mustered up courage to make known, in the most awkward manner imaginable, the discovery I had made on learning that the Fourth Infantry had been ordered away from Jefferson Barracks. The young lady afterwards admitted that she, too, although until then she had never looked upon me other than as a visitor whose company was agreeable to her, had experienced a depression of spirits she could not account for when the regiment left. Before separating it was definitely understood that at a convenient time we would join our fortunes, and not let the removal of a regiment trouble us.

In writing his *Memoirs* he avoided sentiment as if it were a deadly poison, so what I have just quoted is not the full story of his proposal to Julia.

According to Hamlin Garland, who got the story at first-hand from the folks in the neighborhood, Grant arrived at the Dent home and found the family all decked out in their best clothes and aflutter with excitement. They were about to depart to attend some neighborhood wedding. They invited Ulysses to go with them, and he rode in a buggy with Julia. On their way they came to another impetuous and overflowing creek, which had a bridge, but the water was racing, inches deep, over its planks.

"Do you think it safe, Ulysses?" the damsel inquired, fearsomely.

"Why, of course, it's safe," replied the young warrior and tamer of horses.

"Oh, I'm afraid," Julia went on, oblivious of assurance. "I'm terribly afraid."

"Now, now, don't be frightened," came from Ulysses. "I'll take care of you."

"I'm going to cling to you," she declared, "no matter what happens," and with that she clasped his arm with both her hands.

After they had got safely across Julia said, "Well, I clung to you, didn't I, Ulysses?"

"You certainly did," he replied . . . and after a moment's silence he turned to her and said: "How would you like to cling to me for the rest of your life?"

Miss Julia Dent could hardly be called beautiful. She had a slight squint in her eyes. Those who knew her declare that she was amiable, tactful and placid, but her colorless personality appears to have been without sparkle or fire. Like her parents, she was intensely Southern in spirit.

I doubt if Grant ever was much in love, in the romantic sense. Yet he was devoted to Julia Dent, in his own phlegmatic fashion. Courtship and marriage seem to have been considered by him as a sort of duty which comes up in a man's life. Very likely he felt relieved when it was settled. He could then check that performance off his list, and never bother about it again.

Colonel Dent was not informed of his daughter's engagement, nor was his consent asked, until about a year had passed. Then Lieutenant Grant came up from Louisiana to ask for Julia's hand, and receive the Colonel's blessing. The Colonel did not like it at all, and his blessing was rather skimpy. Ulysses had not impressed him as the kind of man who would rise in the world. He wanted Julia to marry some one who had the wit to make a place for himself—who was on his way to becoming a county attorney, or a Congressman, or something. He gave his consent grudgingly.

It was decided that the young people should not marry at that time. Grant had nothing but his pay as a lieutenant, and Julia was still almost a child. So they became engaged, with the wedding indefinitely deferred.

When Jesse Grant learned that his son was engaged to marry the daughter of a Southern slave-owner he was inspired by the information to make acidulous comments. This seems ungracious of him, as he had never met his future daughter-in-law, and knew nothing about her. It irritated him to think that his son was to marry into a slaveholding family; and all he heard of their so-called "estate" and semi-haughty ways increased his annoyance. He carried his dislike of the Dents into his crabbed old age. When eventually he became as deaf as a post, and could only gabble querulously without hearing the answers, still he continued to speak of "that tribe of Dents."

If absence makes the heart grow fonder, Ulysses Grant and Julia Dent must have grown fond, indeed, of each other, for they met but once in the four years that passed between their engagement and their marriage. In May, 1845, the twenty-three-year-old lover obtained a short leave of absence and went up from the camp in Louisiana to St. Louis. He was there only a few days. Most of his time was spent at the Dent home and in company with Julia. It was then that he told Colonel Dent of his intention to marry Julia.

Their attachment was undoubtedly real and a little sluggish—otherwise it could not have survived such a long separation. The emotional parsimony of Grant's character was one of his most striking traits. If he possessed any romantic qualities he managed to conceal them; and he was almost grotesquely sensitive to ridicule. Poor equipment for a lover, one must say, for ardent love-making always has an element of the comic, and a man who is in fear of making a fool of himself is hardly fitted for an amatory career.

§ 3

At quick step, with drums beating, the long blue thread of soldiers passes through the gates at Jefferson Barracks. The regiment is on its way to Louisiana, to Texas, to a land of coppery suns and burning plains. War with Mexico is to be on the next page of American history . . . and the page is turning.

The war between the United States and Mexico, if you look at it in one way, was a historical melodrama with Texas appearing on the stage as a weeping heroine, tearful and vociferous, with a shotgun concealed under her cloak. She appealed to the United States to rescue her from the Mexican dragon; but long before her rescuer appeared she had rescued herself.

If you look at it from another point of view, it was simply a case of international highway robbery, brutally frank, with Mexico as the victim.

Both of these conceptions are misleading. They are mere bubbles on the surface of events. The real cause of the Mexican War ran through our history as the Gulf Stream runs through the ocean. To understand its true significance we must go back to the last decade of the eighteenth century.

CHAPTER V

THE RESULTS OF INVENTIVE GENIUS

§ 1

IN the year 1793 a young man on a Georgia plantation tinkered with a contraption that resembled an old-fashioned music box, crudely contrived out of odd pieces of board and a wooden roller with wires projecting from it.

The young man's name was Eli Whitney, and his device was the first cotton gin. He was a Yankee, a graduate of Yale, with the clipped nasal tone of New England in his speech. Having come to Georgia with the hope of being a school teacher, he stayed with the family of the late General Greene while waiting for his school to materialize. In a letter to his father he said:

> I heard much said of the extreme difficulty of ginning cotton, that is, separating it from its seeds. There were a number of respectable gentlemen at Mrs. Greene's who all agreed that if a machine could be invented which would clean the cotton with expedition, it would be a great thing both to the country and to the inventor. I involuntarily happened to be thinking on the subject and struck out a plan of a machine in my mind. . . .

Within ten days he had made a rough model of a cotton gin. It worked so well that he gave up the idea of teaching school and devoted himself to perfecting his invention.

> I made one before I came away, which required the labor of one man to turn it and with which one man will clean

63

ten times as much cotton as he can in any other way before known and also cleanse it much better than in the usual mode.

At that period slavery was losing ground as an American institution. Many Southerners of ability and foresight were abolitionists while the Northern people had hardly begun to think of the slavery question at all. Washington, Jefferson and most of the enlightened Southern statesmen of the epoch were opposed to slavery and deplored its existence. They considered it uneconomic, and a dead drag on Southern industry. But they did not know what to do about it. Washington hoped that some form of gradual emancipation would eventually be adopted. Jefferson advocated the colonizing of the negroes in Africa, or elsewhere, and he almost succeeded in having his colonization plan incorporated into the Virginia state constitution.

Cotton-growing, which became the backbone of the slave system in the half-century that preceded the Civil War, was a negligible industry in the 1790's. Before the invention of the cotton gin the task of separating one pound of cotton from its seed required eight or ten hours of labor. A field-hand could raise about twenty-five hundred pounds of cotton in a season, on good land, but the separation of the seed and fiber would then require the work of twenty-five slaves for one hundred days. These circumstances made it impossible to produce cotton on a large scale.

Slavery was concentrated in the warm, damp lands of the seacoast, where the chief crops were rice, indigo and tobacco. In the cultivation of these products animal drudgery was worth more than intelligence.

This condition of affairs was affected profoundly by the new method of ginning cotton. The immense uncleared regions back of the coast became available for cotton planting, and it was found that a negro was worth as much in a cotton field as in a rice swamp. Within five years after Whitney had puttered over his contrivance, the entire South blazed with the energy of new lands and new fortunes. White cotton fields appeared on the red soil of the upland counties.

The movement from the coast to the upland regions was equaled by that from east to west. Planters from the Carolinas carried small armies of slaves to the rich young lands of Mississippi. Slavery ran like a tidal wave across the Gulf states.

Whitney's invention was the most momentous achievement of a single individual that has ever occurred on the American continent. It made cotton one of the great agricultural products of the United States. It put fresh life into the languid institution of slavery, perpetuated the slave system, and created a new Southern aristocracy. Without the cotton gin, there can be hardly a doubt that the Civil War would not have happened. Slavery would have died peaceably of economic anemia. The Southern states would have done away with it on their own initiative.

In the historical background of Grant's career Whitney and his cotton gin are gigantic figures. In a genealogy that is almost Biblical in its directness we may say that Grant came from the Civil War; the Civil War came from cotton; and cotton came from Eli Whitney.

§ 2

The production of cotton by slave labor, as it was generally carried on, was wasteful in the extreme. Most of the planters were shiftless and unbusinesslike. They seldom used fertilizers and hardly any attempt was made, by rotation of crops, or otherwise, to maintain the productivity of the soil, for land was abundant and cheap. The planter would have his slaves clear the ground in a haphazard fashion, plant cotton on it for a few years—until it was worn out and full of gullies—and then clear new fields. There were, of course, exceptions to this general rule.

In the bright glow of cotton-made fortunes the Southern idea of emancipating the negro slowly faded to a shadow. But what of the North? Long before the Revolution it had been found that negroes were not worth their keep on Northern farms, and so slavery gradually disappeared, but there was no emphatic feeling against it in the great mass of Northern people. The opposition to slavery was kept alive by small groups of intelligentsia, or reformers, who were disliked by their neighbors. In Northern communities they held about the same place in popular esteem that is occupied to-day by radical socialists and communists.

The first definite crystallization of Northern antagonism to slavery was not moral, but political, and was brought about by the intense ambition of the Southern leaders to maintain control of the national government. They created a Southern oligarchy in Congress which was so nearly airtight that hardly any measure proposed by a Northern Congressman—unless it happened to be entirely without bearing on Southern affairs— could get itself passed.

The Southern theory of gradual emancipation died, but it died hard, and echoes of it were heard for many years. It is surprising to learn that even as late as 1826 there were one hundred and three emancipation societies in the Southern states. Free negroes were considered citizens in North Carolina, and voted in that state until 1835, when a new state constitution deprived them of the franchise. Many wealthy Southerners followed the example of George Washington and left provision in their wills for the freeing of their slaves.

Owing to this and other causes the number of free negroes in the South was greatly increased. In 1840 nearly ten per cent of all Southern negroes were free. These freedmen were much restricted in their activities by municipal laws, but in the mass of documents on the subject one comes across many cases of free negroes who had become well-to-do tradesmen and farmers.

In the Northern states, especially in the cities, free negroes were so unpopular with the working people that they had great difficulty in getting along. Even at the height of the Abolition excitement, in the late fifties, when the colored race was drenched in the tears of Northern sympathy, a negro could hardly get a job in New York City. The white working-man considered the negro as a competitor who would work for lower wages than a white man and live on a scale below the white man's standard.

§ 3

The political resentment that was developed by the haughty attitude of the Southern clique in Congress was accentuated by a difference in outlook and general conception of things between the North and South.

There was hardly any flow of population between the two sections, which were geographically so near together, but so far apart in sentiment. Lack of contact and exchange of ideas brought about innumerable misunderstandings, and men were already learning to hate one another for no more substantial reason than that they lived in different latitudes and faced different problems. In fact, two civilizations were growing up, side by side, both of them narrow and sharp at the edges . . . and in 1819 they had their first head-on collision over the admission of Missouri as a state. The citizens of Missouri wanted to bring their territory into the Union as a slave state, and they were supported by all the Southern representatives in Congress. The North, in its desire to limit the slavery area, bitterly opposed the admission of Missouri unless its state constitution prohibited the ownership of slaves within its borders. For the first time thousands of easy-going people realized that the country was already divided into two sections with modes of thought that were utterly antagonistic to one another.

There was talk of disunion, of secession, of forming two nations—and in these secession projects the North was not in the least behind the South.   Up to the beginning of the Civil War a large and influential body of opinion in every part of the country considered secession as an inalienable right of any state.   For the sake of truth it is well to make a point of this general attitude, for in the ordinary school history it appears that secession was an unheard-of and astonishing idea concocted by Southern slave-owners, and that it came like lightning from a clear sky in 1860.   Such a conception is wholly misleading.   Secession had been discussed for fifty years before it occurred, and almost every state in the Union had threatened to secede at one time or another.   During the War of 1812 there was a strong movement among the New Englanders to form a separate nation of the New England states; and the Connecticut legislature resolved that "the state of Connecticut is a free, sovereign and independent state; that the United States are a confederacy of states; that we are a confederated and not a consolidated republic."

When the Constitution was formed in 1787 the states were so fearful of any infringement of their rights that the makers of the Constitution purposely left the relations of the states to the central authority of the Union in vague indetermination.

As the Constitution was constructed, it was open to two conflicting interpretations, both of them legitimate and reasonable.   One might argue that the United States was intended by its founders to be a league instead of a nation; and a plausible case could be made from the wording of the Constitution itself . . . an association of independent republics that had voluntarily surrendered some of their inherent rights for the good of all.   The national government was held to be an agent with limited powers, and not a sovereign.   But, according to this school of thought, the delegation of power to the central agency was not necessarily permanent; any state might resume its status as a free nation whenever it desired to do so. This is the essence of the doctrine of states' rights, briefly stated, as it was conceived before the Civil War.

The other and opposing theory begins with a different set of assumptions. Those who made it their political gospel point to the first sentence of the Constitution, wherein is written: "We, the people of the United States, in order to form a more perfect Union . . ." and they contended that the Constitution made the American people an indissoluble nation—that its authority came from the people of the country and not from the states.

In the debates over the admission of Missouri these conflicting ideas came out in their most corrosive form, but there were enough even-tempered men to put a conciliatory measure through Congress. A sort of gentlemen's agreement, known in history as the Missouri Compromise.

It was decided by the terms of the Compromise that Missouri should come into the Union as a slave state, but thereafter—and this is the core of the matter—slavery was to be debarred from all territory situated west of the Mississippi River and north of the 36° 30′ parallel of latitude, which is the southern border line of the state of Missouri.

The country was divided by the Missouri Compromise into two opposing parts. A neat piece of anatomical dissection. Imaginary lines, parallels of latitude, freedom on one side of a chalk mark and slavery on the other. The clever statesmen who concocted this measure did not realize that they themselves were laying the foundation for a civil war; that they were dividing the nation into two countries instead of welding it into one.

Nevertheless, the Missouri Compromise was generally accepted at the time as a solution of the problem. For many years thereafter slavery was hardly mentioned in Congress, except in minor rhetorical skirmishes. But silence in Con-

gress did not keep people, including Congressmen, from thinking of it. It became the skeleton in the Congressional closet.
Adroit Southern leaders managed to sidetrack the subject
as a critical issue, but these Southern gentlemen were like men
sitting on the safety valve of a throbbing steam boiler; they
had to use all their strength to hold it down, and were always
in danger from an explosion.

The Missouri Compromise lasted for a generation, but it
was repealed in 1854. It was unconstitutional, anyway,
though this important question was not decided until after its
existence was over.

§ 4

Then came, in 1836, the revolt of Texas from Mexico . . .
and the slavery skeleton came out of the closet. It never went
back. From then until the Civil War slavery was an important
issue in national politics.

The Texans, who were settlers of American origin, won their
independence from Mexico after a short and sanguinary conflict, but the Mexican government refused to confirm the treaty
of peace in which their independence was granted, so they remained a virtually independent republic without the consent
of Mexico. In 1837 their independence was recognized by
the United States.

The Texans never could have won if they had not been
supplied with arms and volunteers through the unofficial con-
nivance of the Jackson administration at Washington. A
Texas war debt grew up and expanded marvelously. It was
represented by bonds and scrip, or deeds to lands on the
immense cattle-raising plains. Nearly all this debt was held
by American financiers.

The next thing in the list of events was a campaign of
propaganda for the annexation of Texas to the United States.
This movement was inspired by Southern statesmen, aided

powerfully by the financial interests of the North that had got control of most of the depreciated Texas bonds.

The Missouri Compromise effectually prevented the expansion of slavery in any direction except toward the South and West. Unless Texas could be annexed it was obvious that the South would, in a few years, have to take a back seat in national affairs. The Southern advocates of annexation hoped to make four new states of Texas, which would give them eight additional Senators.

The opponents of slavery—the intelligentsia and reformers of the North—came defiantly to the combat. William Lloyd Garrison, the leading abolitionist of the time, called upon the Northern states to secede from the Union if Texas with its slaves was admitted. William E. Channing declared, "I now ask whether as a people we are prepared to seize on a neighboring territory to the end of extending slavery? I ask whether as a people we can stand forth in the sight of God, in the sight of nations, and adopt this atrocious policy. Sooner perish! Sooner our name be blotted from the record of nations!"

In the face of so much clamor the annexation program lay down and seemed to die. But its quiescence was a sham. Behind the scenes there was no cessation in activity. Public speeches gave way to whispered conferences. Texas bonds and land scrip appeared miraculously in thousands of pockets. Charles and Mary Beard say, in their *Rise of American Civilization:*

> In New York City, for example, three land companies, organized to buy claims of doubtful validity, had issued stocks to a gullible public. . . . In a word, the independence of Texas, the admission of Texas to the Union, and the confirmation of acquired land rights were essential to realizing the inflated hopes founded on an immense volume of paper scattered around through the United States.

The full program of the annexationists was not limited to the acquisition of Texas. It was far more ambitious, and was divulged to only a few. A war with Mexico was to be provoked, and in the end the whole of the Mexican republic was to come under American rule. There was much talk of "Manifest Destiny" and the "onward march of civilization." With Mexico in the Union, and carved up into numerous slave states, the balance of power would be in Southern hands for a long time to come.

In spite of all these shrewd manipulations it looked as if Texas was about to be turned away like an uninvited guest. But there were other things to be done. The annexationists had a trump card hidden away. When the uproar against annexation was at its loudest pitch this little trump gave them comfort, and they would take a peep at it now and then. Finally, they slid it unobtrusively on the table.

Suppose Great Britain should take over Texas as a part of the flourishing British empire? What then? England needed cotton, and Texas seemed likely to become the greatest cotton-producing region in the world. There was the Monroe Doctrine, of course, but would it apply if an American nation should voluntarily put itself under the protection of a European power? Texas was a free and independent republic, despite Mexico's claims, and might dispose of herself as she pleased.

Hints were passed to representatives of the Texan republic, and they began some vague conversations with British agents. The London government was afraid of the proposition. Very likely the Queen's ministers realized the true inwardness of the situation, and saw that they were being used as a cat's-paw by the annexationists. The proposal was kept warm, however, and the news of it was allowed to filter out. A small but influential party in the North began to declare that it would be better to admit Texas, after all, rather than let such a rich domain come under British influence.

In the autumn of 1844 the question of annexation was one of the chief issues of the presidential campaign. The Democrats made "Manifest Destiny" the corner stone of their political philosophy for the moment. What possible objection could there be to admitting Texas? And as a slave state. Was not slavery recognized by the United States Constitution? And was it not a part of American civilization, like Plymouth Rock and the Baptist religion? As for the Mexicans, what had they to say about it that a white man ought to listen to? A lot of yellow-skinned half-breeds and god-knows-what mixture of Spaniards and Indians, presuming to lay down boundary lines and claim this and that as their territory. They had no right to any territory. If the American nation possessed the right spirit it would go down to Mexico, conquer the whole lazy tribe, and take civilization and slavery to that part of the continent.

So ran the minds of the annexationists as the presidential election approached.

James K. Polk, an insignificant Tennessee politician, who was almost unknown to the American people, was nominated by the Democrats because he had written a strong letter in favor of immediate annexation. His career had been so colorless that nobody knew anything against him, and the Democrats managed to elect him.

The results of the election cheered the annexationists wonderfully, and started a rise in the value of the cheap Texas bonds. But there was Congress still to reckon with, for although the annexationists had a majority of both the Senate and the House they were not strong enough in the Senate to get a treaty of annexation ratified, as a treaty requires a two-thirds vote. After thinking it over awhile the leaders of the annexation party tore up the proposed treaty with Texas, and decided to do the job with a joint resolution, which needs only a majority of both Houses.

The joint resolution went through, but only by a bare

majority. The efforts of the administration were aided by a vast crowd of lobbyists.

§ 5

With Texas in the Union, protected by the powerful United States, the whole contention with Mexico should have soon come to an end. But the larger scheme of Mexican conquest was still in the background, and something had to be done in that direction. It was necessary to find a cause for a quarrel with Mexico . . . and this necessary cause was quickly discovered.

Turn to the map of Texas in your atlas, and you will see the small river Nueces running into the Gulf of Mexico, about one hundred and twenty miles north of the Rio Grande. The Mexicans claimed that the southern border of Texas was the Nueces, while the Texans declared that their territory extended to the Rio Grande. This insignificant strip of land was made the pretext for war. The conflict was begun by American troops moving into the Nueces region and occupying it.

CHAPTER VI

GRANT THE PACIFIST

§ 1

GRANT'S regiment went into camp on the western edge of Louisiana, near the town of Natchitoches, and remained there for more than a year. Life was almost without incident, though Ulysses wrote that he retained very agreeable recollections of his stay. The poker games among the officers were agreeable, to be sure. They played for very small stakes; in the course of three or four hours Grant would win or lose a trifling sum, measured not in dollars but in cents.

The troops stationed on the Texan border were pompously called the "Army of Observation." A better name, although it would not have been so soothing to national hypocrisy, would have been the "Army of Provocation," for its purpose was to goad Mexico into a conflict. Every one from commander down to drummer boy knew that war with Mexico was just around the corner, and the spirit of elation in the camp overcame the long weariness of waiting.

The officers of the Army of Observation, with the exception of Lieutenant Grant, and perhaps a few others, were all for war, and the order which came in July, 1845, for the Fourth Infantry to proceed to New Orleans, and later, to Corpus Christi, Texas, was received with joy.

At the bottom of his heart Grant was a pacifist . . . not only then, but throughout his life. In the 1840's pacifism as a principle was unknown. The best minds in the world were still magnetized by the Napoleonic conception of military power as a substitute for ideas. As a substitute for justice,

75

too. The spiritual and economic diseases that fester under the skin of the conqueror had not yet been traced to their true cause. The conqueror still vainly imagined that he was made stronger, and not weaker, by his victories.

In such a world atmosphere there was no place for any considerable body of pacifist opinion to form; but there were individual pacifists, and Grant was one of them, although he never called himself anything of the kind.

A striking evidence of his instinctive pacifism was his often expressed dislike of armies and fighting. When he was on his tour around the world the Crown Prince of Germany invited him to attend a military review. Grant accepted the invitation, but in commenting on the review he said to Bismarck:

> The truth is I am more of a farmer than a soldier. I take little or no interest in military affairs, and, although I entered the army thirty-five years ago and have been in two wars, in Mexico as a young lieutenant, and later, I never went into the army without regret and never retired without pleasure.

At Versailles the French government conducted him, with an escort, as a distinguished guest to the famous gallery of war paintings in the palace. "I tried to enjoy the pictures," he said, "but found them only disgusting. . . . I never saw a war picture that was pleasant," he added.

One does not have to go very deep into his personality to observe his aversion to war, yet his mind was so foggy in all its abstract conceptions that he was never able to form for himself any sharply defined theory of pacifism. He had no formula for doing away with warfare in civilized countries. The Civil War, he thought, "was necessary"—to use his own expression, but he took part in it only because he was a graduate of West Point, and he considered it his duty, though a disagreeable one.

In reflecting upon the various aspects of his character we encounter this strain of pacifism as it appears in many forms, but at the same time we know that he was a material-minded man whose energy ran instinctively into physical action. How then shall we reconcile such a liking for applied force with an underlying pacifist philosophy?

My opinion is that his mind was that of a mechanic or engineer, rather than that of a soldier. He was constructive by nature—a builder and worker in material forms. The military academy started him on a soldier's career, and he lacked the initiative to abandon it before its routine had become a crystallized habit. We shall see further on that his greatest victory—that of Vicksburg—was not so much a feat of strategy as it was of mechanics and transportation.

In the Mexican War he had not only his pacifist inclinations to overcome, but also his feeling that the war was utterly unjust. On this subject he said:

> With a soldier the flag is paramount. I know the struggle with my conscience during the Mexican War. I have never altogether forgiven myself for going into that. I had very strong opinions on the subject. I do not think there was ever a more wicked war than that waged by the United States on Mexico. I thought so at the time, when I was a youngster, only I had not moral courage enough to resign. . . . I considered my supreme duty was to my flag. I had a horror of the Mexican War, and I have always believed that it was on our part most unjust. . . . Texas had no claim beyond the Nueces River, and yet we pushed on to the Rio Grande and crossed it.

§ 2

Corpus Christi was in the forties a tiny Mexican hamlet lying asleep under the high-arching sky. You will find it on your map, a dot at the mouth of the Nueces River. In September, 1845, the bright blue Gulf before Corpus Christi was speckled with ships. The American transport fleet had arrived from New Orleans, and Manifest Destiny—which had worn so long the dull garments of a political phrase—began to strut around in a head-dress of gleaming bayonets.

The few Mexican inhabitants of Corpus Christi were tremendously excited by the sudden appearance of Manifest Destiny in their midst. Nobody in the village had ever possessed more than five dollars in cash, but they had chickens, tobacco and liquor to sell. In twenty-four hours the place had turned itself into a bazaar; and in a month modest fortunes had been acquired from the conquering Nordics.

The Army of Occupation, as the expeditionary force was called, was under the command of General Zachary Taylor. Its total effectives were less than three thousand men, all of them regulars. They were good troops, but too few in number for a decisive invasion of Mexico. Besides, the two countries were still at peace with one another. President Polk could not call for volunteers until a state of war existed, and the American case was morally so weak that it would never do for American troops to be the aggressors. So Taylor's army sat down at Corpus Christi and waited six months for something to happen.

To amuse themselves during the wet Texas winter, when the sky dripped all day and the ocean roared on the beach, the officers organized an amateur dramatic company, and built a small theater. Money was spent for costumes, which were sent from New Orleans. There Grant appeared as an actor for the first and only time in his career. He took a part in Shakespeare's *Othello*—not as the dusky Moor or Iago or a Venetian Gentleman, but in the sweetly feminine rôle of Desdemona. He wore one of the great bell-like skirts of ancient Venice and carried a fan, very likely, as the rôle calls for such a costume. I know it sounds incredible, this appearance of Ulysses as the lisping daughter of Brabantio, but it is a fact.

As an actor he was a failure. General Longstreet, who, as a young officer, was also in the company, says that Lieutenant

Porter, who played Othello, "protested that male heroines could not support the character nor give sentiment to the hero, so we sent over to New Orleans and secured Mrs. Hart, who was popular with the garrisons in Florida. Then all went well, and life through the winter was gay." (Mrs. Hart was a well-known professional actress of the time.)

To a mind slightly tinged with cynicism it does seem that the whole affair was contrived for the purpose of getting Mrs. Hart to Corpus Christi . . . but maybe not.

In his *Memoirs* he devotes twenty-five pages to his stay with the regiment at Corpus Christi. This account, which was written by him nearly forty years afterward, is luminously revealing as to the nature of his outlook on life. He begins by telling of the arrival of the transports in Corpus Christi bay. Then he relates the story of what was supposed to be a mutiny of the sailors on board one of the transports, which he thinks was no mutiny at all, but only a little row where all concerned said "damn your eyes" with excessive reiteration. Grant was only a spectator. The next episode has to do with his falling over the side of the ship into the water . . . no harm done.

He goes on to describe briefly the Army of Occupation. After that he writes of the price of mules . . . eight dollars apiece . . . herds of wild horses on the plains . . . lots of game in the country, too . . . then comes the story of his futile turkey hunt that I have given in an earlier chapter. . . . Howling of wolves on the prairie . . . thought there were a dozen, but all the noise was made by one wolf.

On the next page we come again to the subject of mules. He tells how they are branded with a hot iron and broken to harness . . . three pages of that. Then, he remembers a mule that ran away but reappeared for awhile every day at feeding time. He remarks that mules and horses were too cheap to let a runaway bother one. . . . He purchased a number of wild horses at three dollars apiece, and for awhile he owned more horses than he had ever possessed before. But his horses all ran away together. Jokes about it. . . . "Yes; I heard Grant lost five or six dollars' worth of horses the other day," said General Taylor's adjutant-general, and everybody had a laugh.

His account has no vivid touches; no shafts of light play through its words. It is as matter-of-fact as the weekly report of a traveling shoe salesman; but then one does not expect either generals or shoe salesmen to write like poets. When he wrote his *Memoirs* he was in his last days, and very ill. That fact, however, would hardly change the character of his recollections.

§ 3

The Polk administration endeavored for months to irritate the Mexicans to the point of beginning hostilities, but without success until April, 1846. In March Taylor was ordered to advance across the Nueces strip to the Rio Grande. Corpus Christi was abandoned, and the army marched southward over ground claimed by Mexico. On the Rio Grande, opposite the Mexican town of Matamoras, the Americans built a fort. They were within a few hundred yards of the Mexican army; things began to look warlike, indeed.

General Taylor's new sea-base was at Point Isabel, a place on the coast some twenty miles north of the Rio Grande. He was afraid that the Mexicans would cross the river in force and seize his supplies on the coast, so he left a few men in the fort and marched the larger part of his army to Point Isabel for the purpose of bringing back food and ammunition. The Mexicans thought he was retreating, and pursued him. The American column had reached Point Isabel and was on its way back when it encountered the Mexicans.

The two armies met at a place called Palo Alto on May 8, 1846. This was the first battle of the Mexican War . . . and the first time that Grant ever heard the sound of a bullet going on its way. It is indeed a disconcerting sound, but Grant stood it without flinching. He said later that he had been too busy to be afraid.

The Mexicans were badly beaten at Palo Alto, and retreated during the night to Resaca de la Palma—a few miles farther south. Taylor's column pursued them, and defeated them again the next day.

Grant wrote a long letter home immediately afterward. It was a hurried epistle, full of misspelled words.

> During the days fight I scarsely thought of the probability of being touched myself (although 9 lb. shots were whistling all round) until near the close of the evening a shot struck the ranks a little ways in front of me and nocked one man's head off, nocked the under jaw of Capt. Page entirely away and brought several others to the ground. Although Capt. Page received so terrible a wound he is recovering from it. The under jaw is gone to the wind pipe and the tongue hangs down upon the throat. He will never be able to speak or to eat.

After the second day's fight—the one at Resaca de la Palma —he wrote:

> Here they made a stand. The fight was a pel Mel affair evry body for himself. The Capparel is so dense that you may be within five feet of a person and not know it. Our troops rushed forward with shouts of victory and would kill and drive away the Mexicans from every piece of Artillery they could get their eyes upon. The Mexicans stood this hot work for over two hours but with a great loss. When they did retreat there was such a panic among them that they only thought of safty in flight.

As a result of this two-days' battle the Mexicans abandoned Matamoras, which was occupied immediately by Taylor's army.

There it remained all through the hot summer of 1846, doing nothing, and awaiting the regiments of volunteers that were being raised in the states.

We must linger here a moment and take a good look at General Zachary Taylor, for the reason that he became, in a sense, a sort of life-pattern for Grant. Taylor was not a West Point man. The young officer had never seen a soldier of high rank who resembled Taylor in the least. His military superiors at West Point and in the army had all been rigid men, precise and spotless, who said yea and nay in voices that were as smooth as milk and as cold as ice. Taylor was not of their breed. He wore the coat of a private soldier, carelessly thrown on his back, and his boots were muddy. He had a large heart and a burry manner. When he did not like people he got angry about it, and his mouth filled with hot words. "Dirty in person, uneducated, eccentric, he was yet a great natural leader of men and exceedingly popular with his soldiers," H. J. Eckenrode says of him. "He blundered into victories in an amazing way, and all of his battles were victories. . . . Rough and practical, Taylor had a natural distaste for West Point fastidiousness and airiness. . . ."

Among the volunteer regiments was one from Mississippi commanded by Jefferson Davis, a lean, gray-eyed, sensitive man of intellectual habits. His first wife had been General Taylor's daughter. As a member of Congress Davis had spoken ardently in favor of the annexation of Texas, and of expansion at the expense of Mexico. Though he had entered the House of Representatives only the year before the Mexican War began he had already made a name for himself as a leading champion of slavery and states' rights.

Taylor and Davis were related by marriage, but they were a thousand miles apart in mental quality. Davis was a logician —a keen and brilliant sophist. In his mind everything was kept bright and shining, and in its proper place, like the tools in a neat carpenter's chest. Taylor, on the other hand, was almost illiterate. He was moved by obscure emotions and was disorderly in his intellectual gestures. Davis was stubbornly opinionated; he had the narrow outlook that often goes with a high culture. His father-in-law was stubborn, too, but his stubbornness came from prejudice and ignorance.

Taylor's soldiers called him "Old Rough and Ready," and the nickname fitted him perfectly. He was always ready—and usually rough.

Grant's admiration for him glows in the following paragraphs from the *Memoirs:*

> General Taylor was not an officer to trouble the administration much with his demands, but was inclined to do the best he could with the means given him. He felt his responsibility as going no further. If he had thought that he was sent to perform an impossibility with the means given him, he would probably have informed the authorities of his opinion and left them to determine what should be done. If the judgment was against him he would have gone on and done the best he could with the means at hand without parading his grievances before the public. No soldier could face either danger or responsibility more calmly than he. These are qualities more rarely found than genius or physical courage.
>
> General Taylor never made any great show or parade, either of uniform or retinue. In dress he was possibly too plain, rarely wearing anything in the field to indicate his rank, or even that he was an officer. . . .

That is Grant's picture of Zachary Taylor—and in it Grant unconsciously drew a portrait of himself, as he was during the Civil War. In Taylor he saw a slouchy man who was also a general. If Taylor could win battles sitting sideways on his horse, his coat unbuttoned, and a cigar in his mouth, why could not another man do as well?

§ 4

Now the American army, increased by a horde of disorderly volunteers, pours out of Matamoras and goes streaming southward into Mexico. The country is an ocean of sand on which the thorny desert shrubs seem to float like tangled wreckage. A glowing copper sun throws its heat on men and animals with the brutal carelessness of a maniac scattering coals of fire. Tongues are silent in the ranks. The only sounds are the crunch of feet and the click of metal. It is the hour of remorse and fantasy.

Besides the startled gray-green lizards, all spine and venom, the only moving creatures in this blazing land are sunburned men in sombreros who hang about the army's flanks and shoot down stragglers.

CHAPTER VII

THE ROAD TO MEXICO

§ 1

LIEUTENANT GRANT was assigned to duty as quarter-master of his regiment. His job was to conduct the wagon train, pack up and move tents and blankets, pots and pans; and to issue supplies. It was a by-path that led away from military renown. The only quartermasters that are spoken of in an army are the unsuccessful ones. To be a success in this position an officer must be unobtrusive as well as efficient, like a butler in a well-ordered household.

It was desperately hard work in Mexico in the month of August, 1846. Loose sand and prickly cactus conspired with Mexican mules and overloaded wagons to make the daily moving of the regiment's housekeeping a nightmare to any one who had charge of it. Grant was, in effect, the regimental drudge. He went through his exasperating duties with the cool patience that characterized him fifteen years later in the Civil War, but he was not insensitive to the annoyances of his position. "I am not aware of ever having used a profane expletive in my life," he wrote, "but I would have the charity to excuse those who may have done so, if they were in charge of a train of Mexican pack mules. . . ."

That his name is not mentioned even once by any of the diary-keepers and memoir-writers among the officers who were engaged in the Mexican War is an interesting fact. If anything at all was written about him at the time by these gossips it has eluded a rather vigorous search. The army was small, and all the regular officers must have known one another, yet

Grant did not make a sufficient impression on any of them to get himself discussed in their reminiscences, which are, in most cases, well sprinkled with names.

Perhaps this may be partly accounted for by his position as quartermaster, which kept him usually in the rear of the column. A carelessly dressed, taciturn officer, he seldom appeared at social gatherings.

Besides his natural lack of aptitude for the jesting by-play that goes on among officers in the field, there was another reason for his solitude. Whisky was humming in his soul; he had begun to use liquor in Mexico, and he was always a solitary drinker. When he was under the influence of liquor he was morose and downcast. This trait would doubtless give him a certain isolation, and keep him out of the company of more joyous, rollicking officers.

Excessive liquor drinking is a result of personal maladjustment. Men drink because they are dissatisfied, though they are often unaware of the causes of their unhappiness. They drink because they are defeated in the sphere of psychic desire; because they are inhibited; because they are engaged in doing something that they do not want to do.

Freud says: "Under the influence of alcohol the adult again becomes a child who derives pleasure from the free disposal of his mental stream without being restricted by the pressure of logic."

In some respects Grant never got over being a boy. He was forced to become a man too quickly—a man on the outside—but his adolescence lay always under the surface. We shall see it coming out later, in unexpected ways . . . in his naïve business dealings . . . in his immature judgment of men. Liquor-drinking probably released the boy that was in him.

But it is entirely plausible to believe that his bitter distaste for the military life started him in the drinking habit. We shall not understand his character at all unless we conceive him constantly as a pacifist. Yet his pacifism was chiefly subconscious, and can be observed only by its outcropping implications. Externally, he was throughout his whole life greatly influenced by the people around him. He was continually doing and saying things because these were the things to do at the time, although they were not in accord with his inner life. The fact that he detested war—and especially the Mexican War—did not prevent him from being a good soldier. He went into it from a sense of duty, and did his best.

§ 2

Taylor's army moved southward down the long axis of the land of Mexico. If the plan of campaign was to pierce the country sufficiently deep to take its capital, it was very foolishly conceived, for the distance from the Rio Grande to Mexico City is six hundred and fifty miles.

But it appears that the Polk administration did not really contemplate any such complicated operations. It was believed by the President and his advisers that if Mexico were invaded from the north the Mexicans would quit fighting after they had lost one or two battles.

In September Taylor's army arrived before Monterey, a stone-built city of sixteen thousand inhabitants, after having marched two hundred miles from Matamoras. The place was taken by the Americans in a series of desperate attacks. Men fought in the streets and on the flat roofs of the houses.

Grant's place was in the rear of the army with the wagon trains, but he did not remain there long. The sharp rattle of gunfire came back to the distant teamsters' camp like the popping of firecrackers, and the entire quartermaster's department stood on a little hill, looking and listening. After a while Grant turned over the command to a subordinate and rode to the scene of battle. Before the day was over he distinguished himself by a helter-skelter ride through bullet-swept streets to bring up a supply of ammunition.

His exploit was talked about for a few days and then forgotten. There were so many daring ventures in men's memories that a perilous ride could not hold the attention very long.

One result of the battle of Monterey was to add stature and muscle to the infantile Zachary Taylor myth, which was already thriving in the nursery of heroes. Songs in praise of "Old Rough and Ready" were bawled in streets and barrooms, and much liquor was drunk to the continuation of his good health. Astute people who spoke in whispers and communicated gossip as if they were revealing the Egyptian mysteries predicted that the next President's name would begin with a T.

The war had been conceived by the Democrats, and the Democratic administration was not at all pleased with the soaring fame of Taylor, popular hero of the Whigs.

President Polk reflected moodily on this turn of fate, and resolved to do something that would divert public attention from Taylor and his achievements. If he had been a shrewd statesman he could have turned Taylor's victories to the advantage of his administration, but he was a second-rate politician, simmering in jealousy, and the scheme he evolved for putting Taylor on the shelf was simply a cheap political trick.

At the beginning of the war both General Taylor and General Winfield Scott had proposed to invade Mexico by the way of Vera Cruz. The distance from the sea to the Mexican capital is about two hundred and sixty miles by that route, against six hundred miles, or more, by the route across the Texas border. It was the only sound strategic plan, but Polk had disregarded it because he did not think it necessary. The war would come to an end in a short time, anyway, he thought, so why go to the trouble of sending an army by sea to Vera Cruz?

Now the idea was revived, and General Scott was selected by Polk to command the new expedition. Taylor was left in command in northern Mexico, but two-thirds of his troops were ordered back to Matamoras, to take ship there for Vera Cruz. Among the regiments that marched back was the Fourth Infantry, with Grant and his train of wagons toiling along in its rear.

Everybody realized that Taylor had been neatly shelved. The war's line of force had been changed in direction abruptly, and Taylor was supposed to be henceforth only a spectator.

But the unexpected is the essence of all history . . . and the unexpected happened.

A letter to Taylor in which the new plan of campaign was set forth fell into the hands of Santa Anna—the Mexican commander-in-chief—through the capture of a messenger. All at once Santa Anna had the key to the situation. He saw that the real fighting was to take place between Vera Cruz and Mexico City, and not in the north. He knew that Taylor had barely five thousand men at Monterey, while the Mexican army in front of him had grown to fifteen thousand. Scott had not yet arrived at Vera Cruz, and could not possibly land there for some time. Santa Anna made up his mind to crush Taylor at once, and then swing his army a thousand miles south, by forced marches, to face Scott when he reached Vera Cruz. This brilliant plan had a touch of strategic genius, and it would have succeeded if Santa Anna's army had not been composed of such wretchedly poor human material. His soldiers were half-breed conscripts, driven to the army in gangs. They had no interest in the war, nor much conception of what it was about.

With this rag-tag army he met Taylor at Buena Vista, not far from Monterey, and there occurred the most hotly contested battle of the war, in which the Americans lost one-fifth of their number in killed and wounded. But the Mexican loss was even greater. Santa Anna's army was terribly beaten, notwithstanding its immense numerical superiority.

Taylor was the outstanding hero of the great day at Buena

Vista, but Jefferson Davis also won renown. At a critical moment the Mexicans had attempted to break through the American line. Davis formed his regiment in the shape of a triangle, open at the wide end, and received their onslaught in the hollow part of his V-shaped formation. The Mexican assault wilted under a fire that came from both sides as well as from the front.

The events that led to the battle of Buena Vista provide a fine example of the futility of human foresight. The administration had carefully insulated Zachary Taylor, and had done it so shrewdly that nobody could pick any flaws in the technique of the operation. Then, unexpectedly, at the moment of his official decapitation, he won the most dramatic battle of the war, and became a living image of spectacular success.

The country went mad with enthusiasm when it learned that five thousand Americans had beaten fifteen thousand Mexicans. The war grew enormously in favor, even among those who were opposed to it on principle at the start. It did not seem possible that anything so successful could be wrong. Manifest Destiny was a high-riding star.

The long arm of Buena Vista reaches far into history. It made Zachary Taylor a President of the United States; and it was unquestionably a deciding factor in the deliberations of the Confederate Congress when that body elected Jefferson Davis to the leadership of the Confederacy.

Through his single military exploit Davis acquired an absurdly exaggerated reputation. As its echoes came back to him he began to look upon himself as a great strategist, though he was, in fact, no strategist at all, and his military opinions were usually faulty. The ghost of Buena Vista hovered over the bloody Confederate battlefields, interfering with the plans of able commanders, and contributing eventually to the many causes that led the Confederacy to its downfall.

§ 3

We shall now leave Old Rough and Ready, with the wreath of laurel on his brow, and turn to Winfield Scott and his army.

The American expedition landed among the sand dunes of Vera Cruz with the bands blaring out "Yankee Doodle" as the troops floundered through the surf. The Mexican army, such as it was, stayed behind the walls of the town and made romantic resolutions to die in the last ditch. Across the level sea lands the Americans heard the clamorous ringing of church bells, calling the inhabitants to arms and prayer. Santa Anna, though beaten at Buena Vista, was coming hot-foot from the north. If the commander at Vera Cruz could only hold out until his chief arrived the Mexicans would have Scott between two fires.

But neither prayers nor arms were of avail; the Mexicans could not keep up a resistance long enough for Santa Anna to get there. On March 27, 1847, the town surrendered after Scott had battered his way through the walls. Despite the fierce resolutions hardly anybody died in the last ditch, though a few misguided patriots fired from second-story windows after the surrender and were shot for their excess of zeal.

Grant was there, with his mules and wagons, on the sandy plain where the army camped. He took no part in the military operations. The time of the siege was spent by him in getting supplies from the vessels and organizing the domestic arrangements of the Fourth Infantry for the march to Mexico City.

Scott left a small garrison to hold the forts in the harbor and got away from Vera Cruz as quickly as he could, for the yellow fever season was coming on. He had less than twelve thousand men, and though more volunteer regiments were on their way, he was too much afraid of pestilence to wait for them.

To reach Mexico City he had to march uphill for more than two hundred miles, until the army stood eleven thousand feet above the sea. The campaign was like a series of hand-to-hand fights on a stair-case, the Mexicans retreating slowly up the stairs as the Americans advanced.

The Mexican War was a grubby affair, without a trace of sentiment, and singularly lacking in chivalrous gestures. The American officers quarreled continually over promotions. Many of them almost forgot the war in the contemplation of their own small destinies. It is the only war in our history that did not inspire a swarm of romantic novels. As soon as it was over the American people tried to forget it, and they have been trying ever since.

Yet there is no gainsaying the fact that Scott's march to the City of Mexico was daring in conception. He had less than twelve thousand men, and there were seven million people in Mexico. This was emphasized in Santa Anna's impassioned, patriotic addresses to the Mexican people. "We can crush them by weight of numbers," he declared in effect. "There is only a handful of them, while we are millions." Scott's army was not crushed by weight of numbers because the people of the country were virtually serfs who hated the ruling classes even more than they disliked the Americans.

The volunteers in the American army—and they composed the larger part of it—appear to have been undisciplined and out of hand. They not only pillaged the Mexican villages, but outraged women and shot down non-combatants on the most trivial pretexts. "Their conduct," Captain E. Kirby Smith wrote, "towards the poor inhabitants has been horrible, and their coming is dreaded like death in every village in Mexico."

Everything possible was done by Scott and his officers to put an end to this riotous disorder, but without success. Strange as it may seem, considerable numbers of the American troops deserted and went over to the Mexican side. These desertions were symptomatic of the disorder that saturated the volunteer force of Scott's army, and were perhaps a sign of the soldiers' rebellion against the discipline that he attempted to enforce.

The whole of the renowned San Patricio battalion in Santa Anna's army was composed of American deserters. Grant says that many of the best artillerists deserted. Some of these deserters, taken on the battlefield with arms in their hands, were hanged or whipped.

It was a campaign of engineers, and one that required their most expert skill. Scott's chief of engineers was Robert E. Lee, a forty-year-old Virginia captain who loved war and had become highly proficient in its technique. After graduating with honor at West Point he had married Miss Mary Custis, the daughter of George Washington's stepson, and his deportment reflected the chivalrous traditions of the Washington and Lee families.

At Cerro Gordo, a mountain pass about fifty miles from Vera Cruz, Lee's abilities came sharply into use. This pass was so thoroughly commanded by Mexican artillery that even the daring Scott stood before it in blank frustration. If there had been a possibility of success the army would have fought its way through, but how can men march for miles along a a winding mountain road that is swept from one end to the other by cannon fire? At the further end there would have been no army left, except a few hysterical survivors without unity or strength. The real difficulty of the situation lay in the fact that there was apparently no way to get at the Mexicans. Their batteries were posted on ledges of rock halfway up a mountain side. Before them was a slope that troops could not climb under fire, and the bleak scarp of the mountain rose behind them.

While Scott fumbled with his pile of maps, looking for another road, Captain Lee studied the contour of the mountain and came to the conclusion that the steep slope in the rear of the Mexican position could be scaled. He was allowed to make the attempt, so while some desultory firing was kept up in front to distract Santa Anna's attention, Lee hauled the American artillery to the crest of the mountain that commanded the Mexican camp. Long ropes were attached to the guns, and hundreds of men, clinging to rocks and trees, dragged them up the acclivity, foot by foot. It was like lifting tons of coal up the sloping roof of a house.

Next morning the Mexicans saw the American artillery established on the mountain top in their rear. Shells began to fall with precision into the Mexican position. The rout of Santa Anna's army was pitiable. He lost all his artillery and most of his supplies, including his own personal baggage, and escaped capture himself only by sliding down a ravine on the back of a mule.

The credit for this victory belonged distinctly to Captain Lee. Scott recommended him for promotion, and referred to him as "gallant and indefatigable."

There was no more really serious fighting until the Americans reached the City of Mexico, though there were numerous skirmishes—called battles—in which the Americans easily drove off their assailants. The conflict ceased to be a war and became a raid.

The army arrived at the crest of the lofty rim of Mexico valley in September, 1847. From the bold encircling hills Scott and his army looked down on the glittering white city of the Montezumas. They stood where Cortez and his fighting crew of Spaniards had stood more than three hundred years before.

There is not a place in the world better situated for defense. The city is surrounded by a natural rampart of mountains. The road from the sea level writhes in fantastic zigzags among peaks and plateaus. At every turn there are natural defensive positions of great strength.

The country immediately adjacent to the City of Mexico consists chiefly of marshes which are spanned by causeways. These were easy to defend. It looked for a time as if the

place could not be taken without an enormous loss of men,
but Captain Lee and his engineers distinguished themselves
again by finding a practicable road over lava beds which were
supposed to be impassable. In this way the Mexicans were
flanked out of most of their forts, and the Americans drew close
under the city walls.

On his way back from a reconnoissance of the Mexican defenses Captain Lee reined his horse among the wagons and
chatted for awhile with Lieutenant Grant. One may see, in
fancy, the young, freckled quartermaster, in his rumpled uniform, standing by the horse's side and looking up into Lee's
face. How startled they would have been if the veil of the
future had lifted for even one blazing instant, and they had
seen themselves bound together eternally in the pages of
history.

Now there came a week or two of confused fighting which
sprawls in wriggly red and black lines all over the campaign
maps. Every stone wall had its defenders. Men entrenched
themselves on house-tops and turned the pillars of an aqueduct
into a barricade. For a time one can make neither head nor
tail of it, but after awhile names of places appear, hazily in-
distinct, like electric signs gleaming through a fog . . . Con-
treras, Churubusco, Molino del Rey, Chapultepec . . . all of
them milestones to mark the triumphal route of the Americans.

Grant left his mules munching their hay quietly in the rear
under the care of his teamsters while he took himself to the
front and joined his regiment.

In the assault on Molino del Rey he showed himself to be
courageous and cool under most trying conditions. Molino
del Rey—or "the mill of the king"—was a long stone building
filled with Mexican riflemen. The engagement became extremely
mixed, as the building was taken and lost three or four times
in the course of an hour, and the Americans and Mexicans
mingled with swords and bayonets in a bloody hand-to-hand
struggle. It was here that Grant saved the life of Frederick

Dent, his future brother-in-law, whom he found lying wounded and helpless in the midst of the fighting.

A few days later, in the final struggle for the city gates, Grant performed a feat of mechanical ingenuity that was characteristic of him and typical of his entire military career. It was merely an exhibition of common sense, but common sense is a quality that is so seldom used in warfare that it attracts immediate attention whenever it appears.

A church with a broad, square steeple stood just outside the walls of the city. Grant borrowed a howitzer from an artillery unit, and, with the aid of a few soldiers, succeeded in getting it up the stone stairs and into the steeple. The priest stood at the door in his black cassock, with a crucifix in his hand, and protested against the desecration of his church. Grant told him, through an interpreter, that such matters had no weight in warfare, and ordered his men to bring up the gun. It was a difficult job, for it was found necessary to unbolt the gun from its carriage and take it up the narrow staircase in pieces. When it was once there he set it up again and opened fire on the Mexican troops inside the city.

The fire from the steeple was so damaging to the enemy that General Worth sent for Grant to compliment him on its effectiveness. Worth's messenger to the young man in the steeple was Lieutenant J. C. Pemberton. (Sixteen years later this same Pemberton—then a general in the Confederate service—surrendered Vicksburg to Grant.)

On September 14, 1847, Scott's army entered the city, and the Mexican War was at an end.

According to the terms of the peace treaty Mexico had to give up all her territory north of the Rio Grande, including California, Arizona, New Mexico, and the entire Southwest, as well as her claim on Texas. In area this amounted to more than half the Mexican republic. On the other hand, the American government paid the Mexicans fifteen millions of dollars in order that the Mexican commissioners should not appear wholly empty-handed before their people.

The imposing imperialistic idea of seizing the whole of Mexico was assassinated in cold blood by David Wilmot, an insignificant Congressman from Pennsylvania. He rose in his seat on a memorable day when a bill appropriating money for the war was being discussed, and proposed an amendment, now known as the Wilmot Proviso. He moved that slavery should be forever barred from all territory taken from Mexico as a result of the war. This Proviso did not apply to Texas, of course, as that state was already in the Union.

Wilmot's motives were not clear. He was a Democrat, but his Proviso was certainly in direct opposition to Democratic policy, and was probably proposed without consultation with his party leaders.

What about the Missouri Compromise of 1820? The prevailing but rather uneasy myth was that the famous Compromise had settled the problem of slavery for once and all, yet here was Wilmot opening the controversy again, as casually as one opens a door to let an undesirable cat into the house. The Southern Democrats and their friends had certainly taken it for granted that the Missouri Compromise line along the 36° 30′ parallel would be continued to the Pacific Ocean. That would have divided California into two parts, with the southern section a slave state.

The irrepressible Wilmot prowls for a flickering instant among the Mexican débris. He is a man without a future or a past, and lives in history only as the author of the Proviso. He had no right to be on the stage at all—so his party leaders thought—when abler men were in charge of things.

But there he was, and his Proviso came to a vote. Notwithstanding the Missouri Compromise and the "gentlemen's agreement," the Wilmot Proviso turned out to be a popular measure in Congress. It was defeated, but only by the smallest of margins. The vote on it showed the temper of the country.

No use now to talk about gobbling up the whole of Mexico. Even the Democrats would have opposed such a measure, for what would be the use of eight or ten new Mexican states with slavery forever debarred from them?

At any rate, the pro-slavery party had Texas. That was something—and its leaders hoped to get California, or a part of it, admitted to the Union as a slave state. So caucuses were held, and small portions of comfort were passed around while David Wilmot was admonished earnestly, and finally sent back into obscurity.

§ 4

During the eight months that Grant stayed in Mexico City he became friendly with some of the American and English residents, learned a little Spanish, and ran a bakery for the benefit of the regimental fund.

He made a commercial success of the bakery—a notable achievement, for it was the only success in business that he ever had in his life. "I rented a bakery in the city," he wrote. "Hired bakers—Mexicans—bought fuel and whatever was necessary, and I also got a contract from the chief commissary of the army for baking a large amount of hard bread. In two months I made more money for the fund than my pay amounted to during the entire war."

Bull-fighting was a national sport, and officers and soldiers attended the fights in large numbers. Curiosity led Grant to see one bull-fight, but only one. He wrote: "The sight to me was sickening. I could not see how human beings could enjoy the sufferings of beasts, and often of men, as they seemed to do on these occasions." Several bulls were killed in the ring and he saw a horse gored to death. "I confess that I felt sorry to see the cruelty to the bull and the horse. I did not stay for the conclusion of the performance; but while I did stay, there was not a bull killed in the prescribed way."

What did he do besides running the bakery and attending

to his duties as quartermaster? Did he spend his time in making acquaintances? In exploring the surrounding country? In reading books? Did he get drunk? Did he visit the bagnios with the other officers and acquire a Mexican mistress?

As to the last question, we may be allowed a strong presumption that he never even thought of a Mexican mistress, for we know that he was a thorough puritan by temperament. The repression of his sexual impulse, combined with loneliness and an aversion to army life, fertilized the taste for liquor that he had acquired during the campaign. In Mexico City he was rather pathetically lost among the flashing gayeties of the army of occupation . . . a solitary drinker . . . and the record of his life falls away into a few discursive notes about mountain-climbing and bull-fights. At this time he was a silent, moody officer, engaged in a war that he thought rapacious and unjust.

There was no latent joy in Grant's life; none that is discoverable. He was devoid of that lyrical quality of soul which causes a man to have pleasure in his own perceptions, in the feel and texture of living. His emotions were buried, but not dead; they were buried alive.

In history he exists only in events. Whenever we think of him there is a simultaneous mental picture of something being done. Washington, too, was a doer, but his personality glowed like a bright, cold flame. If the Revolutionary War had never occurred Washington would have been, nevertheless, a stately country gentleman with an aura of power and dignity. But if there had been no Civil War what could we say of Grant?

In considering his liquor drinking, we should not forget that practically all the officers and soldiers in Scott's army were drinkers. Intoxication was a custom of the time, and was not looked upon as a fault, unless it was carried to excess. The officers' messes were always supplied with liquor, and officers who did not drink at all were supposed to be strange and perverse creatures.

Before Scott's troops had left Mexico, and the echoes of the war were still in the air, gold was discovered in California. Within four years the gold supply of the world was quadrupled, and as this so-called precious metal ran through the veins of commerce, an extraordinary transformation took place in the economic structure of the American nation.

In a few years the New York banks were full of California gold. It was used to construct railroads, to augment the size of manufacturing establishments, to acquire mortgages, to control labor, and to manipulate the prices of farm products. It led to a prosperity that was temporary and fictitious, for though the abundance of money had the effect of raising the wages of labor, it increased the price of all the necessaries of life at the same time. In the end the working man and the farmer found themselves but little better off than they had been before.

The entire gold output of California did not add as much as a dollar's worth of real wealth to the world. Its effect was to give power to the individuals and groups that got control of it. Its chief result was to fasten capitalism on the world by providing the financial mechanism through which capitalism maintains its authority; and, in America, it laid the foundations of the huge personal fortunes which grew into full flower during the Civil War and in the decade that followed it.

Very little of the gold from this new El Dorado found its way into Southern banks, or Southern industries, and the slave states began to feel acutely the economic preponderance of the North.

CHAPTER VIII

GRANT TURNS OVER A NEW LEAF

§ 1

NOW we see our dusty young officer coming back from Mexico as a brevet captain, with favorable mention in the reports of his brigade and regimental commanders. But these commendations lacked the exclusiveness that carries distinction. A great many officers had been cited with honor, and a long list of brevet promotions had been made. The brevet rank made no change in Grant's actual status as an officer, nor did it give him an increase in pay.

Besides his phantom promotion, Ulysses had brought back a few interesting trinkets, a fleet-footed gray horse, and a pleasant-faced, empty-headed peon servant named Gregory. He had also brought back the liquor habit. It had settled down in his silent personality with the ease of a careless family moving into a wide house. The curios were soon given away, the gray horse was raffled off, Gregory returned to Mexico, but the drinking habit remained.

In August, 1848, he went to St. Louis; and, on the twenty-second of that month, he married Miss Julia Dent. The wedding was a joyous occasion, with laughing, fiddling and dancing. Some one diverted the company with a slow-rhythmed Spanish dance to the clacking of castanets and the stamping of feet; and a huge wedding cake was sliced with an officer's sword.

Among the attendants was Lieutenant James Longstreet, then one of Grant's intimate friends. A stolid, thick-set, young South Carolinian was Longstreet, with bluish-gray eyes and a

101

quiet manner . . . another Grant. He was to become the best fighting general in the Confederate army, and Lee's right-hand man.

One may imagine Grant and Longstreet attempting feminine repartee with the fashionable young ladies who thronged about the bride . . . girls in billowing skirts, with unspoken thoughts in their eyes and a honeyed Southern drawl on their tongues. There was much to eat and drink, and the better-looking of the Dent slaves, dressed in servant's finery and carrying trays in their hands, moved like dark living statues among the guests.

None of the Grant family was present at the wedding, but Ulysses' parents and relatives met Julia when the newly-married couple stopped in Ohio on their way to his post at Sackett's Harbor, New York. These harsh Ohio folks liked her; she was pleasant, graceful and possessed the flexible art of making friends. Even her father-in-law forgot for awhile that she belonged to a slave-owning tribe.

Sackett's Harbor is on Lake Ontario, and, in the winter, is one of the coldest places in the eastern part of the United States. The Southern bride looked out on a landscape that made her think of the frosting on a cake; it was glittering white, and still, save when the wind rattled the icy branches of the trees. She made the best of her crowded little nook in the married officers' quarters. Rooms almost as nude as negro cabins, painted in harsh and depressing tones and filled with the stale odor of long-burning fires.

It is characteristic of Grant that he always did, under any circumstances, what an ordinary man would do, unless the doing happened to be sidetracked by one of his deep inhibitions. His history is a record of obvious decisions. We should not be surprised, then, to learn that he joined the Sons of Temperance at Sackett's Harbor. Any ordinary young man, newly married, with a gnawing urge for liquor, but full to bursting with good resolutions, would do just that. He was, indeed, one of the organizers of the local lodge.

So, like any other plain-thinking young husband, who wants to be respectable and stand well with his wife, he joined the temperance society and discoursed on the evils of rum. "There is no safety from ruin by liquor," he declared at that time, "except by abstaining from it altogether."

His daily existence at Sackett's Harbor was as blank as a bowl of water. He was the kind of man whose life becomes readily set and standardized, and whose days run into identical patterns. The historian, gazing into the crystal ball of the past, can see nothing there but checker games, and a swift horse being driven with a sleigh over the crackling snow. He had no close friends among the officers, and if he wrote any letters they are buried in the heart of some uncommunicative letter file.

In the early spring of 1849 the Grants were transferred to Detroit, where the regiment had its headquarters. For about a year they lived in a small wooden house on Fort Street, East—between Russell and Rivard Streets. It was in a neighborhood inhabited by laboring people, from which circumstance we may infer that Grant was living on his small salary as an officer.

In Detroit Grant bought a little black mare from a horseman named Cicotte. He paid two hundred dollars for her, on condition that she could pace a mile in 2:55. She made the mile, with Grant and Cicotte riding in a buggy behind her. Thereafter, Albert D. Richardson says, "Everybody knew the appearance of Sam Grant in a cutter in winter or a buggy in summer, flying along after his Cicotte mare." She ran races, and won them, to Grant's delight.

He had hardly anything to do—an intelligent soldier clerk ran the quartermaster's office. So under the strain of blank idleness the Sackett's Harbor temperance pledge was worn threadbare and eventually forgotten.

On Jefferson Avenue, near the corner of Woodward Avenue, in what is now the downtown district of Detroit, the sutler's store of the post was located. It was full of the things that soldiers think they need. Grant and other officers turned it into a kind of lounging room. In one of the dusky corners in the back of the store stood a barrel of whisky. The hospitable proprietor invited the officers to serve themselves. The barrel was always miraculously replenished, and the tin cup which was used for drinking was constantly in use. Liquor was cheap in those days.

The officers talked about Clay, Webster and Calhoun, and the debates in Congress; about Indians and Mexicans and California gold; about the niggardly pay of army officers and the general meanness of the government; about Scott's novels and the acting of Edwin Forrest, and the size of skirts and the pugnacity of bulldogs. Grant would sit with his legs crossed, looking gravely at the voluble faces, and speaking a sentence now and then.

He was the best listener and the most silent man in the world when he was in uncongenial company, but when he had sympathetic people about him he would talk for hours on end. Horace Porter, who served on his staff during the last year of the Civil War, said that Grant was far from reticent and "had the ability to impart a peculiar charm to any topic." His charm was the allure of common sense. He was as remote from any kind of bookish theory as a man could possibly be, but he had a seeing eye and a prodigious memory. Occasionally, when the topic of discussion was about something of which he had a first-hand knowledge, he would make a remark that was startling in its depth and clarity. But these occasions were rare. Most of his conversational wisdom consisted of platitudes worn as thin as ancient dimes.

It must have required a good deal of "peculiar charm" to explain to Julia his lapse from the eternally binding temperance pledge, which had been uttered with such solemnity at Sackett's Harbor. Whatever he said when he appeared at home, in the dusk of the evening, in a condition that implied a close contact with liquor, remains a lamentable hiatus in history. His own explanation, and the back-and-forth conversation between him and his wife, would probably be more illuminating as to his personality—and certainly more interesting—than his description of the battle of Shiloh.

At this time there was a dry-goods merchant in Detroit named Zachariah Chandler. This rising young man was so busy making money that he neglected to remove the glassy ice from the sidewalk in front of his house. Army officers, going home from the sutler's store in the late hours, would slip and fall on this mantrap, which was doubtless hard to traverse even in daylight and when one was sober. Grant fell one night and hurt himself severely. Thereupon he swore out a complaint against Chandler, and had him brought into court.

Chandler conducted his own case with wonderful vituperation. He declared that the officers were all idle loafers, doing nothing and living on the community. Turning to Grant and his officer friends, he said: "If you soldiers would keep sober, perhaps you would not fall on people's pavements and hurt your legs." The jury brought in a verdict against Chandler and assessed him six cents as damages.

Years afterward Grant, as President of the United States, made this same aggressive Chandler his Secretary of the Interior. The Detroit merchant had gone into politics and had reached the Senate long before Grant had become a national figure. The resounding row about the icy sidewalk was the first thing that occurred to both of them when they met again in Washington, but they succeeded in laughing it off. One fancies that considerable laughing was required.

In the spring of 1850 Julia Grant went to her father's home in St. Louis to give birth to her first child, who was called Frederick Dent, after his uncle. Why she did not remain in Detroit, with her husband, for her lying-in, I do not know, but I presume that the house on Fort Street was too small and uncomfortable. The young couple was poor; Grant had nothing but his pay as a lieutenant, and was borrowing money from time to time.

While Julia was in St. Louis Grant and Captain Gore, an army friend, lived together in a cottage on Jefferson Avenue, where the rent was two hundred and fifty dollars a year. Their landlord was a teacher who had served in the army himself, and he liked army people. The rented cottage stood directly behind the landlord's house, and he saw the two officers every day. Yet Grant moved about so unobtrusively, and had so little to say, that his teacher-landlord soon forgot his name. One day in 1862, when the country was excited over Grant's success at Fort Donelson, and the name of "Unconditional Surrender" Grant was in every newspaper and on every tongue, his former landlord accidentally discovered "U. S. Grant" scratched with a diamond ring on a pane of glass in the cottage—and he recalled then that the national hero had been one of his tenants, though he could not remember how he had looked, or anything he had said.

Julia returned to Detroit late in 1850; and in June, 1851, the headquarters of the Fourth Infantry was changed to Sackett's Harbor, and the Grants returned there to live.

They appeared again in their old quarters, but now the snows had gone, and the little village made a picture of green lawns and white cottages beside the smiling blue water of the lake. There were June roses with bees thrumming about them. Mrs. Grant sat on the little veranda of their house and played with her baby as with a doll, in the manner of young mothers.

This pleasant life did not last long. In the early summer of 1852 the regiment was ordered to the Pacific Coast. The route was by the Isthmus of Panama, and was beset by disease and danger. The Grants decided that Julia had better not attempt it, so she went back to her father's house with her child, and Ulysses journeyed to California alone.

It was two years before he saw his wife again; and when he

returned from the Pacific Coast he was penniless, in disgrace, and no longer an officer in the army.

§ 2

While Grant was getting married, and trading horses, and taking temperance pledges, "Old Rough and Ready" Taylor had been elected President of the United States. The Whig Convention that nominated him was so dazed by hero worship that it adjourned without devising a party platform, and Taylor was pushed into the presidential office simply as a man and war hero. He was a citizen of Louisiana, a Southerner born and bred, and the owner of three hundred slaves. That appeared to make him safe enough, even to the pro-slavery Democrats, but in the end he turned out to be bitterly disappointing to his Southern friends.

He had been for years in command of troops on the western plains, and was out of touch with urban civilization. He had managed to divest himself of ideas, and existed in a state of mental nudity, as simple and direct in habit as an Indian. His sense of curiosity was small; it did not seem probable that he would ever learn anything about statecraft, diplomacy, or the functions of civil government. He was about as well fitted to be the head of this nation as any chance captain of a whaling vessel.

As President of the United States Taylor had to have opinions, and there were plenty of keen-minded Southern gentlemen ready to supply them. But he developed bad political habits. He produced startling ideas from somewhere in the esoteric recesses of his own mind. And that was not all . . . he began to stroll about the intellectual regions of the anti-slavery party and pick up notions that were lying around.

Even before his inauguration he acquired a disturbing admiration for William H. Seward, the anti-slavery Senator from New York, and pocketed a large collection of Seward's views.

"The people of the North need have no apprehension of the further extension of slavery," he declared . . . and in these words Southerners heard the undertone of Seward's voice.

Did the Northern people at that period really object to slavery in the Southern states—and if so, why? Or was it merely talk?

If we cut through all superficial appearances, to the heart of the matter, we find that the anti-slavery party was small in numbers and loud in voice. The great majority of Northerners was sentimentally opposed to slavery in the South, as a theory—but the theory was rather feeble, and in actual reality they had no objection to it at all, though there was a vast amount of anti-slavery propaganda, and the use of words by the million.

The abolitionists never won an election. Lincoln was elected on a platform which was bitterly fought by the more determined among the abolitionists because it did not call for an immediate ending of slavery.

Among the comfortable, moneyed classes in the North—who are supposed to form public opinion—the term "abolitionist," right up to the beginning of the war, was one of opprobrium, and meant anything from fool to bandit.

Yet slavery has been so highly dramatized by novelists and historians that it is generally accepted without question as the sole cause of the Civil War. This was not so, in fact. The war was brought about by many interlocking causes, and one may reasonably doubt if slavery was the principal one. But it was a convenient handle for the manipulation of motives that were more profound and more obscure, and we see it weaving in and out of the texture of events like a dark stripe in a garment.

It ought to be an axiom of history that economic issues are the inspiring motives behind all moral attitudes. The story of mankind, in its broader sense, is nothing but a record of the successive adjustments of social status to economic facts. Sometimes these adjustments are leisurely and slow in movement, and society adapts itself by almost imperceptible degrees to new forms of existence. At other times they are projected with a high initial velocity because their explosive elements are too powerful to be controlled. In that case history records a war or a revolution. The fundamental difference between social evolution and war is simply a matter of their respective rates of speed.

One does not have to dig long into the cluttered soil that surrounds the slavery controversy before unearthing several packages of dynamite; and the largest of them all is labeled Protective Tariff.

While the South had remained an agricultural region, dozing through the years in its placid cotton fields, the North had turned its energies toward manufacturing. In the course of time the brisk spirit of Yankee enterprise had developed many industrial communities of wealth and importance in the Northeastern states. Then came the railroads, which meant cheap and quick transportation, and a prodigious widening of markets. Factories grew larger, and the factory system expanded towards the West. This flow of dynamic energy hardly touched the South. The slave states continued to purchase practically everything that could not be grown on their own soil; and the two sections gradually assumed a new set of relations towards each other—that of merchant and customer; maker and wearer; creditor and debtor.

The Northern manufacturers needed protection against European competition—or thought they did—so the policy of setting up a tariff wall around their industries became a cardinal article of their political creed. The higher the tariff, the more profit they could make on their goods, and the Southern states constituted an enormous field for the sale of manufactured articles. Southerners, on the contrary, wanted to buy in the cheapest market. They had only cotton to sell, and that had no protection, and required none, for the slave states produced most of the cotton used throughout the world. Why, therefore—they reasoned—should the Northern factory owner be aided by a tariff? The Southern planter knew very well that he could buy more with his cotton in Europe than in the tariff-protected North. He was opposed to any kind or degree of tariff—except, perhaps, the small duties required to produce enough revenue to carry on the national government.

The nature of this conflict is clear, and it becomes more sharply defined in perspective when we remember that the South had managed for many years to dominate the national government. Most of the Presidents had been Southern men, and a compact group in Congress had usually been able to maintain a hold on affairs. Their group was so strong, indeed, that they slashed the tariff to pieces by sharp reductions on several occasions in the years preceding the Civil War. This destructive attitude toward tariff protection aroused the manufacturing interests that controlled public sentiment in the Northern states. Dr. Charles A. Beard says, "Many an orator who might have forgiven the South for maintaining a servile labor system could not forgive it for its low tariff doctrines and its opposition to centralized finance."

In the slave states pamphlets showing how much the South lost each year through the operation of the tariff were in vigorous circulation.

With these facts in mind one may see plainly how the slavery and tariff questions became merged into one confused entanglement. The Northern industrialists saw that they would have to capture the national administration if they were ever to put through their higher tariff program. But they could never control Congress if new slave states were allowed to spring up in the Western territories. They were not opposed to slavery, but to its extension.

It was, in effect, a fight to the death between the nascent money capitalism of the North and the feudal slave capitalism of the South—and in the course of the struggle the anti-slavery movement was adopted by a powerful political group that had its own views in mind. Abolition propaganda was the sentimental vehicle for reaching the masses of people.

§ 3

The main issue in President Taylor's time concerned the status of slavery in the new territory that had been taken from Mexico. A practical solution—and one that occurred immediately to those who were indifferent to everything except peace—was to run the Missouri Compromise line straight on westward to the Pacific. Two states might have been made of California, and the slavery party would have got New Mexico and Arizona, but not much else.

Strange to say, this solution, despite its practicality, did not appeal to either the North or the South. The die-hards among the slavery party, led by the aged John C. Calhoun and the young Jefferson Davis, maintained that Congress had no right to prohibit slavery anywhere, under any circumstances; that slaves were a species of property and that slave-owning had all the time-honored rights that surround and protect any kind of legal ownership.

They were diametrically opposed by a Northern group which demanded the total exclusion of slavery from all the territories. They, too, had an excellent precedent for their attitude, for Thomas Jefferson—himself a Virginian and a slave-owner—had succeeded, through his Ordinance of 1787, in getting slavery excluded forever from the territory then called the Northwest, and which now comprises the states of Ohio, Indiana, Michigan, Illinois and Wisconsin.

Others thought that each territory, as it reached the stature of a state and applied for admission to the Union, should decide the matter for itself.

This four-cornered argument was still wrapped in the coils of rhetoric when the young territory of California created a

sensation by forming its own constitution, and inserting a
clause in that document which prohibited slavery in California
forever. To the amazement of the Southern leaders there
had not been a single vote in the constitutional convention in
favor of slavery. Southerners had been in the convention, too.
. . . Southerners who had gone to California in the days of
the gold rush. They had voted against slavery the same as the
Yankees.

This incident was a profound moral defeat for the South.
There could be no longer any thought of extending the Missouri Compromise line to the Pacific. The South saw the iron
ring of hostile states closing about it.

Under these rather trying circumstances the Southern idea
of states' rights became so crammed with sultry emotions that
it threatened to burst. There was unlimited talk of secession,
but nothing came of it, for the suave compromisers were still
doing business. Under the leadership of Henry Clay the renowned Compromise of 1850 was patched together. It was
intended to distribute favors, like all compromises, but it gave
considerably more to the North than it gave to the South.

California was to be admitted as a free state, in the first
place. Next, slave-trading in the District of Columbia was
forbidden, though slavery was still to continue there. Both of
these provisions were distinct victories for the Pro-Tariff,
Anti-Slavery North.

Then came a little sugar—but not much—to sweeten the
bitter taste in Southern mouths. No action was to be taken
by Congress on the question of slavery in the territories of
New Mexico, Arizona and Utah. This was a concession without value, as those territories were not adapted to slave labor
in any event. And finally . . . Congress was to devise a
more effective law for the capture and return to their masters
of fugitive negroes who had escaped to the North.

The outstanding defect of the Compromise of 1850 was
that, while it was conceived with the best intentions, it did not

get down to the root of the dissension that was dividing the North and South. It was like a meal poultice laid over a cancer. It dealt with the limitations of slave territory on one hand, and the rights of slaveholders on the other, when it should have dealt with the economic system of the nation. It was the work of politicians instead of statesmen. They made it their business not to cure, but to soothe.

Though it was nothing but a patchwork of inessentials the Compromise of 1850 was accepted cheerfully at first by most of the American people. They were bored by the stream of heavy affirmations, and wanted to think of other things. For a brief spell the North and South fraternized like two suspicious bulldogs that have decided to be amiable, come what may.

The first break in this superficial harmony came—and it was not long in coming—over the application of the clause in the Compromise which applied to fugitive slaves. There had always been a thin trickle of escaping negroes from the border states. In the early days they were taken up, as a rule, and returned to their masters without much being said about it. But in the 1840's the small but dynamic abolition group organized a network of its members in Ohio and other states for the purpose of aiding negro fugitives from the South. If a runaway slave from Virginia or Kentucky managed to get across the border he was fed and secreted by abolitionists, who passed him from one house to another until he reached Canada, or some other safe refuge. This organization was called the "Underground Railroad." These activities—one must understand—were illegal, even in the free states, as they were in violation of the Fugitive Slave Act of 1793, passed by Congress in Washington's time. The efforts to recapture slaves and defeat the Underground Railroad's operations often led to disorder and bloodshed.

To remedy this state of affairs the Fugitive Slave clause was put in the Compromise of 1850. In carrying out the

Compromise a most extraordinary law was enacted by Congress. The rendition of fugitives was put in the hands of the United States marshals, but the supposed slave was not given a chance to have a jury trial, or any appeal to the courts. All the slave-owner had to do was to submit an affidavit to the effect that the negro belonged to him, and take possession. This could be done through an agent or attorney; the owner of the slave was not even required to make a personal appearance.

One may readily imagine the enormous abuses that would cluster around such a savage and stupid law. Northern negroes who had never been slaves at all might conceivably be taken South and sold on the claim of some passing stranger, or a fancied resemblance to an escaped slave might imperil a negro's freedom.

But, after all, the practical effect of the Fugitive Slave law was approximately zero, for it became a dead letter throughout the North. Upon the appearance of a slave-catcher in any free community everybody would try to keep him from accomplishing his errand. In three years less than fifty negroes had been taken, in the whole of the Northern states, under the provisions of the act.

The net result of the law was to augment the anti-slavery feeling in the free states. Most of them proceeded to enact Personal Liberty laws which annulled, in effect, the act of Congress. The Vermont legislature, for example, produced a defiant Personal Liberty law which directed the state's attorneys to serve as free counsel for alleged fugitives, and made it a penal offense to seize a free negro with the intent to enslave him. This pugnacious Vermont act also contained a clause to the effect that any negro within the state was to be considered a free man, regardless of his status elsewhere.

One is astonished at the small number of negroes who did escape, even with the help of the abolitionists. Their number was so small, indeed, as to appear negligible, and it is not exactly clear why the Southern states expressed such indignation. In 1850 only 1,011 slaves ran away to the North, and ten years later, in 1860, the number had diminished to 803. It is entirely probable that the total, in twenty years, was less than fifteen thousand—while there were three million slaves in the Southern states.

The explosive element in the situation lay, not in the money value of the fugitive slaves, but in the active threat against the whole institution of slavery. One of the historic results of this agitation was to bring slavery forward as the chief national issue, and to obscure the underlying financial and economic problems. In other words, the slavery question was swiftly becoming a moral as well as a political controversy; it was spreading from a small group of reformers outward through the mass of people; and the growing capitalism of the North was getting ready to adopt the "Down with Slavery" slogan as a means of acquiring control of the national government.

§ 4

During these years Grant's political opinions were drifting away from the abolitionist ideas of his father and moving toward the pro-slavery, Democratic notions of the Dent family. His habitual indecision in the field of intellectual conceptions kept him from being plainly either one thing or the other. He was not an eager student of large affairs, nor the kind of man who seizes a newspaper and, devouring its contents, talks about it all day. He had horses to talk about, and the doings at the post, and his reminiscences of the Mexican War.

Yet if we are to place him at all, at this period of his life, we must include him among the Democrats. He voted in only one presidential election. That was in 1856, and his choice for President was James Buchanan, the Democratic nominee. He wrote:

It was evident to my mind that the election of a Republican President in 1856 meant the secession of all the slave states, and rebellion. Under these circumstances I preferred the success of a candidate whose election would prevent or postpone secession. . . . I therefore voted for James Buchanan for President.

During the Civil War, on August 3, 1862, he wrote to his father, "I have no hobby of my own with regard to the negro, either to effect his freedom or to continue his bondage." But his wife owned slaves, and kept on owning them while the Civil War was being fought.

CHAPTER IX

THE LEAN YEARS

§ 1

IN the slack years that followed Grant's return from Mexico we see him drifting into a sort of frowzy stagnation. Within the narrow frame of his life-picture we can discern nothing but horses, the taproom scenes of a sutler's store, some piddling work about a quartermaster's office, and a wife and baby; all of them the pursuits and interests of a rural youth who had miraculously become an army officer.

He was weighed down by the lethargy of those who find themselves out of place. He was easy-going and indolent, but beneath his indolence there was ambition and energy which had no outlet. He was stirred into action only by external circumstances. No; circumstance is not a strong enough word. What he needed was not a circumstance but a predicament. He was at his best in the midst of dire confusion. He mounted to fame on a ladder of desperate situations.

A distressing predicament occurred while the Fourth Infantry was crossing the Isthmus of Panama on its way to the Pacific Coast. This was in the summer of 1852. The contractor who was expected to furnish mules at the railway's end could not get them. He threw up his contract, and the regiment—without means of transportation—sat down in the tropic jungle and waited while the colonel wondered what he ought to do. In a few days cholera ran through the regiment like fire in a field of dry corn; and men began to die.

Then the stodgy quartermaster came to the front. He managed somehow to get together a few mules and a gang of

117

climate-hardened natives. The regiment, under the inspiration of Grant's energy, struggled to its feet. The sick men and the soldiers' wives were put on mules, while the rest of the regiment started out on foot. There were children, too, in the expedition; they were carried on the backs of natives.

The command got across the Isthmus, but it was a pilgrimage of agony . . . delirious men by the score; lost squads who could not keep up; and pale-faced stragglers who wanted nothing in the world but to lie down and die. In one day thirty-seven men died, and altogether the regiment lost about one-fourth of its personnel. Without Grant's resourcefulness the loss would have been much larger. His "great activity and efficiency were generally recognized," says one of his biographers—but apparently not by the War Department. There was no official commendation of his work. The only thing that happened was a silly, red tape inquiry into the circumstances of the march. Later in the year we find him writing a letter from California in reply to an official demand from the Department to explain why some of the government's property had been lost or abandoned on the Isthmus.

For two years he was on the Pacific Coast; first at Fort Vancouver, on the Columbia River, near Portland, Oregon—which was then a village inhabited by shaggy pioneers—and afterwards at Fort Humboldt, in northern California. His duties at Fort Vancouver, translated into commercial terms, were simply those of a shipping clerk. He received supplies and distributed them. Fort Vancouver was the distributing point for more remote posts in the interior. But most of Grant's work was done by soldier subordinates, and he spent his time riding horses and moodily hating the army and all its works. One who knew him there said, "He was one of the kindest and best men I ever knew. He seemed to be always sad; that is, he never seemed jovial and hearty, like most of the officers."

In August, 1853, he was made a captain in the line, and

was sent to Fort Humboldt to command a company. He had the lounging habit, as we have seen, and as soon as he got to Fort Humboldt he looked about to find a good lounging place. There was a good one in the near-by village of Eureka, at the store of a man named Ryan. This person was an odd character, and the chief man of the neighborhood. He ran a store and a sawmill, besides acting as a surveyor, preacher, bartender, Indian trader and general arranger of things.

A barrel of whisky always stood on tap in Ryan's store. It must have reminded Grant of the old days in Detroit. But the scene was different. As he sat on the store's wooden porch he could look down the squalid, muddy little street and fill his eyes with the dreariness of pioneer life. Men in checkered shirts and fur caps, with pistols in their belts; Indian squaws begging or peddling; tied horses stamping at their hitching posts. The forest closed sharp and hard around the unpainted, flimsy houses—and, despite the tinkling of banjos and hoarse, carousing songs, the air held the brooding sadness that strikes deep in the soul of man.

Some enterprising historical society ought to mark the site of Ryan's store with a memorial tablet, for it was on that spot —or thereabouts—that Grant drank himself out of the army.

But, one may ask, why commemorate an event so foreign to lofty historical traditions?

The reason is that if Grant had not drunk himself out of the army he would probably never have had a chance to command more than a regiment during the Civil War. When the war began the regular army, with all its trained officers, was stupidly kept together by the government. The states were expected to drill and equip their volunteers as well as they could without technical supervision. Everybody with military experience was in demand in the volunteer forces. Grant's chance came because he was a West Pointer, and out of the army.

If the circumstance which led to that result is not worth a tablet—then what is?

§ 2

In the inside pocket of his faded blue uniform coat Captain Grant carried a package of time-worn letters. When his coat was buttoned they made a bulging rectangle on his chest. Letters from Julia, all of them. Their endearments clothed his loneliness with a soft warmth. At times he would take them out, smooth their creases on his knee, and reread them. Once he went about the post showing a letter-sheet with the inky print of a baby's hand on it . . . the hand of Ulysses, Jr., his second son, whom he had never seen.

On the verge of heartbreak with homesickness and hatred of the army, his inner life slowly became a gray emptiness, like a rugged landscape covered with fog. Glibness of speech, combined with a sharp introspective egotism, might have saved him, for men who can talk for hours on end about themselves are able to endure any amount of desolation. But he was too inarticulate, and too shy, to be relieved by any such mental catharsis, so he sat gloomily staring into space. It was only when liquor was in his veins that he became sociable and told stories of the Mexican War and showed the near-by settlers how to tame horses.

As Captain Grant grew melancholy and inattentive, Colonel Robert Buchanan's eyes lingered on him. Regimental commanders like officers who are jolly and red-faced, whose clothes are always neat, who laugh loudly and swear heartily. They give tone to a regiment and make things hum. But what can one do with an officer who wears a soiled uniform, speaks in monosyllables and neglects his work?

Moody as he was, there were hilarious moments. On one occasion—according to local tradition—he went dashing through the village, driving three horses tandem, with a string of three buggies, tied together, whirling and bouncing along after him. He must have stayed at Ryan's store a long time that day.

The colonel began to think that Grant was, perhaps, not fitted for a military career . . . that the whole thing was a mistake. Anyway, he had his regiment to consider . . . nothing breaks down the morale of a military command like inefficient and drunken officers. The colonel spoke to the captain about his drinking habits, and Grant wrote out his resignation and placed it in the colonel's hands, with the understanding that it was not to be forwarded to the War Department if he stopped drinking.

His resolutions were excellent, but they did not last long. One day he was so intoxicated while paying off his men that the whole regiment noticed it, and he made himself a little ridiculous. Then and there the colonel washed his hands of the captain and vowed never to try to reform anybody else. The resignation was drawn out of its envelope, dated to take effect on July 31, 1854—and Grant found himself out of the army, out of money, out of a job, and a long way from home.

A quartermaster in San Francisco lent him enough money to pay his passage to New York, where he arrived with a few dollars in his pocket; and there he was stuck, for he did not have the railroad fare to get to his father's home in Ohio. In this seedy condition he went to see Captain Simon B. Buckner, a classmate, who was stationed in New York, on recruiting service. Captain Buckner advanced the money for his expenses while he waited for a remittance from his father.

(We shall hear of Captain Buckner again. He became General Buckner in the Confederate service, and commanded at Fort Donelson, which Grant captured in 1862, with fifteen thousand prisoners, including General Buckner.)

I think Grant felt a relief at getting out of the army, though he was crestfallen because of his summary dismissal—for his resignation amounted to nothing else. On leaving Fort Humboldt he said to a friend: "Whoever hears of me in ten years will hear of a well-to-do Missouri farmer."

"Whoever hears of me in ten years." In ten years he commanded half a million men, and through fire and smoke was battering the Southern Confederacy to its doom.

Among the five hundred thousand men was his former regimental commander, Colonel Buchanan, a model soldier who never got drunk. He stood far down in the list of brigadier-generals.

§ 3

It was a sorry home-coming. Old Jesse Grant was mortified at his son's failure, and went around clenching his hands, and beating the air with gestures. He wrote to Jefferson Davis, the Secretary of War at that time, and begged him to take Ulysses back in the army. "I never wished him to leave the servis," Jesse wrote. "I think after spending so much time to qualify himself for the army and spending so many years in the servis, he will be poorly qualified for the pursuits of private life."

It was the sort of letter that one might write about a boy who had been dismissed from school. Old Jesse did not realize that his son had grown up. To this pleading letter the War Department replied that nothing could be done, as the resignation had already been accepted, and the episode was closed.

Colonel Dent let his son-in-law have eighty acres of land near St. Louis, and Grant's career as a Missouri farmer began. It was a rather discouraging start. He called his farm "Hardscrabble," in anticipation of the hard times he expected to have there—and it must be said that he was not deceived by his expectations. The land had no house on it, and Grant had no money to build a house, or to buy cattle, or even to live while he was tilling the soil. He applied to his father for aid, but Jesse's hard fist had shut tight.

For a year the Grants lived with Julia's family, while

Ulysses cleared the land and put in his first crop. To obtain spending money he would cut firewood, load it on a wagon and take it to St. Louis for sale. Years afterward, while he was President, there were many people in St. Louis who remembered him well. They said he sat perched on his wagon in a worn blue army coat. Stoop-shouldered, bearded, and streaked with country mud, he looked much older than he was.

In the summer of 1855 he built a log cabin on his farm, felling the trees and dressing the timber himself. When the time for raising the house arrived, the neighbors came and helped, and it was put up in a couple of days. Grant worked hard, plowing in the field and hoeing corn like any hired farmhand, but he was utterly lacking in the penny-gripping instinct that poor people must have to make a financial success of anything.

In the meantime Julia was supplying him with children—four in all. The first of these was Frederick, who was born in St. Louis in 1850, before his father left for California. Then came Ulysses, Jr. (called "Buck" as a nickname), who arrived in 1852, while Grant was on the Isthmus of Panama; Nellie, the only daughter, who was born in 1855; and Jesse Root, the youngest, born in 1858.

The farm was a failure. He was not able to make a living as a farmer, and his father had to lend him about two thousand dollars in numerous small sums during the four years he was engaged in trying to make the farm pay.

In the fall of 1858 he sold his live stock and farming utensils at auction and paid a few of his debts with the money. When he left "Hardscrabble" he was in debt, and poorer than he had been when he came out of the army. He was thirty-six years old, a confirmed failure in life, and with a growing family to look after. His hands were hard and his shoulders bent with toil. Defeat was written large all over him.

Then came the Boggs episode.

Henry Boggs was in business as a real estate agent. He

had known the Dents a long time, and had been present at
Grant's wedding.   Colonel Dent persuaded Boggs to take
his son-in-law into the little firm as a partner.   He knew so
many people, especially army officers, said the persuasive
Colonel Dent, that he ought to be able to find purchasers for
houses.   It seems that Boggs was not enthusiastic over the
partnership, but he finally consented, and the firm of Boggs &
Grant began business on January 1, 1859.

There were many things that Grant could not do, and for
which he was totally unfitted by nature.   Near the top of the
list one must put the real estate business.   The urbanity, the
polite wheedling, the shrewd sizing up of other people's pocketbooks, the capacity to gloss over obvious defects in the habita-
tions of men . . . none of these existed in Grant's arsenal of
ability.

He realized his own unfitness, but he had to have a job, so
he went into the partnership and tried to do his best.   He
rented a house in a poor neighborhood for himself, at twenty-
five dollars a month, and brought Julia and the children to
the city.

His failure was pathetic, for he labored early and late,
and hoped that diligence would take the place of business sense
—which it never does.   Among the many incidents of this
period is one concerning a Mr. White.   This gentleman wanted
to buy a house, and Captain Grant tried to sell him one.   The
sale was almost made, when it fell through because some other
real estate man got to Mr. White and sold him a different
house.   White met Grant on the street, and after the usual
handshaking and polite discussion of health and politics, Mr.
White said, "By the way, Captain, I think I shall not be able
to take the house for the present, and I intended to see you
about it."

One of White's friends, who was with him at the time, said
that Grant's face quivered with disappointment, and he turned
away silently like a stricken man.

Boggs looked moodier every day as Grant came into the office. In fancy one can see the former captain walking softly about the place, eagerly working on the ledgers, sending out bills, and trying to make himself useful while he realized in his heart that he was not wanted.

In the fall of 1859 Boggs came out flatly and told him that they had better separate. The partnership broke up, and Grant was again out of a job. The position of county engineer was vacant, and he tried to get himself appointed to the place. With his letter to the county commissioners he submitted a number of recommendations from citizens of St. Louis. "I have made no effort to get a large number of names, nor the names of persons with whom I am not personally acquainted," he wrote. This, too, was a wasted effort. Three of the five county commissioners were Republicans, and Grant was a Democrat—so the appointment went to another man.

Now he was on the crumbling edge of desperation, and he went about St. Louis borrowing small sums of money. Some of his acquaintances would cross the street to avoid him, when they saw him coming. In exploring this period of his life one comes to feel that he was completely disoriented, like a man suffering from shell shock. Haunted by remorse and melancholy memories, he tramped into one office after another, asking for impossible jobs, and growing shabbier every day.

"He had no exalted opinion of himself at any time," said Mrs. Boggs, the widow of his former partner, when she spoke of him many years later, "but in those days he was almost in despair. He walked the streets looking for something to do. He was actually the most obscure man in St. Louis. Nobody took any notice of him."

His wife owned two slaves—house servants they were—and Grant tried to sell them, or hire them out to increase the family income, but did not succeed. The details of this attempt at slave-huckstering are as dim as the words of a letter which somebody has attempted to erase. The incorrigible

eulogists who have had Grant's career in hand for two generations have tried to forget that Julia ever owned slaves, fearing,
perhaps, that some slight smudge of discredit might appear
on her husband's reputation. Such an attitude is absurd. At
that time there was no social stigma attached to slavery in
Missouri. It was a recognized institution, and many excellent
people owned negroes.

§ 4

In these years, while Grant was smothered by the difficulty
of making a living, the American nation was facing such a
fierce political gale that it could not do much more than stand
still and hold its hat on its head. The older statesmen, who
had guided national affairs for so many years, were falling
like solemn ancient oaks that have outlived their time. And the
newer men who followed them did not inherit their suavity
and benevolence. Congress became an arena for clamorous
verbal combats.

The Whig party, which had handsomely met every critical
situation by never doing anything definite, had been drowned
in the rising tide of new issues. Its lifeless body lay on the
beach of politics, unburied and almost forgotten.

The national controversy over slavery had acquired an
enormous momentum. As it swept through the political sky it
drew into its gravitational field all the minor parties as well
as various powerful but carefully veiled financial ambitions.

There were vain attempts to enforce the Fugitive Slave
law; new and ineffective measures of sectional adjustment;
peace offerings and shotgun fights. There was a row over
Kansas which shattered the Missouri Compromise of 1820, that
had been held sacrosanct for a generation. Although the
whole Kansas region was north of the Missouri Compromise
line it was finally agreed that the settlers of that territory
should decide whether they wanted a slave or a free state.

This was in itself a direct incitement to local civil war, and it led to midnight murders and pitched battles between the slavery and free-state settlers.

Lord Brougham once said that the American Constitution is not worth the paper it is written on—or words to that effect —for the reason that dead men's hands could never stop an urgent living impulse when it got under way. The abolition movement was to prove that Lord Brougham knew human nature very well. The right of slavery was recognized by the Constitution; but in the 1850's Senator Seward, of New York, declared that there is a "higher law than the Constitution"— and his words resounded through that tempestuous decade.

Not long after Seward had discovered that there is a higher law than the Constitution, William Lloyd Garrison celebrated the discovery by burning the Constitution in public.

Channing says in his *History of the United States* (Vol. VI, p. 180): "Ever since 1841 William Lloyd Garrison and the ultra anti-slavery people—the abolitionists—had argued for separation from the slave states. In 1842 Garrison declared that the repeal of the Union was the measure of one's patriotism and piety."

At the head of his newspaper, *The Liberator*, Garrison carried this blazing dictum: "No Union with slaveholders. The United States Constitution is a covenant with death, and an agreement with hell."

Garrison is one of the strangest figures in American history. His flaming spirit, as one sees it down the years, glows like a lamp at the end of a dark corridor. He was to the abolition movement what Paul of Tarsus was to Christianity. A penniless Boston printer, a common man without much education, he succeeded nevertheless in moving the hearts of men and women who had never seen a slave. He possessed the dramatic power that springs from fervor and intensity. In the first issue of *The Liberator* he wrote: "I will be as hard as truth and as uncompromising as justice . . . I am in earnest—I will not equivocate . . . I will not excuse—I will not retreat a single inch—and I will be heard."

But Garrison's newspaper hurt business in Boston; it annoyed the Southern trade. In his early years every effort short of murder was made to suppress him. His office was raided; his presses were destroyed; he was dragged through the streets of Boston with a rope around his neck. He lived on husks of bread that he might have the money to buy ink and paper; and he went about the country organizing Anti-Slavery societies, regardless of threats and mobs.

Garrison urged the immediate emancipation of all slaves without any compensation. To him the negro was a man and a brother. The Southern arguments that the African belonged to an inferior race . . . was a savage . . . a child in mentality . . . had no bone in his nose . . . semi-anthropoid ape . . . and that slavery is sanctioned by the Bible as well as by the United States Constitution . . . all these struck Garrison as a feather strikes a slab of granite. And he was deaf to the contention that cotton could not be produced without slave labor. "Then let's not raise any more cotton," was his reply, "if it has to be grown by a race in bondage." In short, he was a visionary, an impractical person, of tremendous courage and conviction, engaged in a death grapple with a highly practical problem.

Yet he believed in non-resistance. He was opposed to liberating slaves by force. It was through the onrush of moral ideas that he wanted to abolish the slave system.

Garrison and his friends could never exchange ideas with the advocates of slavery because the opposing sides lived on different planes of existence, and neither of them knew what the other was talking about . . . nor did either of them ever try to find out. To the Southern mind Garrison was an instigator of slave insurrections; they thought he wanted the negroes to murder the Southern whites in their beds. The

MRS. JULIA DENT GRANT

This photograph of General Grant's wife was made during the Civil War.

House in which Grant Lived in St. Louis in 1859

Georgia legislature offered a reward of five thousand dollars for his arrest and conviction.

Books and newspapers containing anti-slavery arguments were seized at Southern post-offices and burned by local committees. There was, of course, no legal sanction for such interference with the delivery of the mail. The Southerners met the resentment that it aroused in the North with the story of how the Fugitive Slave law had been rendered unavailing by abolition mobs.

Garrison was a character from the New Testament, translated into the modern world. Such men always attract followers, because they symbolize feelings that lie deep in the soul of man. *The Liberator* grew in circulation and influence, and men of high standing—among them, Wendell Phillips and Theodore Parker and William Ellery Channing—became Garrison's friends.

But a great many people, mostly among the cultured and well-to-do, disliked him to the end. He was crude, harsh, and wholly lacking in the social amenities. Henry Ward Beecher— an abolitionist himself—said that Garrison was "one of the most unfortunate of all leaders for the best development of anti-slavery feeling."

§ 5

The abolition crusade, seething in its narrow bowl, bubbled over into literature and began to touch the conscience of the great middle class. Mrs. Harriet Beecher Stowe made a far-rippling splash in the world when she wrote *Uncle Tom's Cabin*, a novel dealing with the lives of slaves. "Tranced, surrounded by her family, she had begun without premonition or plan, breaking into ecstasies of tears and sobbing as she wrote."

In her way Mrs. Stowe was as strange a being as Garrison. She was the wife of a professor of theology in Cincinnati. Her husband, whom she called her "poor rabbi," was a moon-struck student of Chaldean and Assyrian lore. He had visions, and saw troops of spirits walking at his side. Mrs. Stowe also appears to have had hallucinations. She heard her dead children playing guitars. Her sad, dreamy life was circumscribed by the sharp circle of genteel poverty. She had day-dreams of a literary career, of a life of generous affluence, of Europe, of the storied ruins of the past . . . fancies which were interrupted by the changing of her children's diapers and the incessant darning of stockings.

She was stirred to write *Uncle Tom's Cabin* by letters from her relatives in Boston telling of the injustice of the Fugitive Slave law. It was written at a kitchen table, in the intervals of cooking and housekeeping. As preparation for her work she had read abolition pamphlets and Garrison's newspaper. She had never been in the South, had no knowledge whatever of slavery, and was wholly ignorant of the negro mentality.

Her novel is a well-meaning and sentimental picture of slavery as she thought it was. It has hardly anything to do with reality; yet, after all, there is not a single one of its incidents that was impossible. For example: Simon Legree, one of her characters, makes a practice of beating his slaves to death for the fun of it. At that time field-hands cost about one thousand dollars apiece. Would the owner of a blooded horse, worth a thousand dollars, be likely to beat it to death, just to see it die? Preposterous, certainly—but as preposterous as it is, such a thing might occur. Drunken men and half-insane sadists sometimes do even worse.

She depicted slaves as being systematically worked to death in swamps. Mrs. Stowe did not know that for twenty years before the Civil War Irishmen were hired by the day to dig ditches and drain swamps on Southern plantations, as the slave-owners of the time considered their negroes too valuable to do that sort of work. A slave might catch malarial fever and die, leaving his master with a loss of a thousand dollars or so;

while if the hired Irishman got sick he was paid off and allowed
to shift for himself.

Her description of slavery is a generalization drawn from
the bizarre rarities of human nature. Yet, despite this serious
defect, *Uncle Tom's Cabin* is well written . . . moving . . .
vivid . . . and with a plastic feel of life about it. Upon the
Northern mind, tuned to alertness by twenty years of Garrison
and the abolitionists, Mrs. Stowe's novel fell like a burst of
dazzling light. Now one might know all! Here was reality;
here was truth. Eliza and Uncle Tom, the kind-hearted Mrs.
Shelby and her husband, Simon Legree, Little Eva and the
soft, exotic St. Clares—these were not political notions nor
moral principles. They were people. Folks. Cruel villains,
warm hands, shining faces, bitter sneers, gay laughter. Anti-
slavery propaganda had become a great, nation-wide melodrama.

Uncle Tom's Cabin was the best-selling book of its day . . .
three hundred thousand copies during the first year . . . and
Mrs. Stowe found herself a distinguished literary woman. "God
wrote it," she declared in an awe-struck whisper.

Garrison and Harriet Beecher Stowe were voices of the
tempest and the dawn. They spoke from the battlements of a
lofty certitude. Their moral confidence carried conviction;
they touched the heart of the great mass of humanity.

And the heart of humanity was not all they touched. Astute
Northern politicians, contemplating ways and means for getting hold of the national government, saw in this popular emotional outburst the raw material for a new party that would
unite all the anti-slavery elements then swinging at loose ends.
In 1854 the Republican party was organized. It swallowed
the small abolition group at one gulp. Within a year it was
strong enough to control many of the Northern states.

There was no abolition plank in the Republican platform,
and the anti-slavery group within the party had to content
itself with a declaration that slavery ought not to be ex-

tended beyond the Southern states. The shrewd directing minds of the party cared more for control than they cared for abolition. They were willing to have the South keep its slaves if they could direct the national government, and have their own way with the currency, the public lands and the tariff.

§ 6

An intangible feeling of disquiet existed among the American people. It came to the surface sometimes in new and fantastic literary movements, in schemes for regenerating the world, in strange religions—like Mormonism; but more often it appeared in liquor-drinking and fighting. The easy amiability of an earlier day had disappeared; a coarse, irascible vulgarity simmered beneath a thin crust of good manners. Members of Congress were often seen maudlin drunk; they even attempted to make speeches in the halls of legislation while their tongues were tangled.

Daniel Webster was a drunkard. . . . I mean that he appeared frequently in public places in a state of intoxication. Yet Webster was not in any sense an imitation statesman; he was a real one—a man of profound intellect and breadth of view. But sometimes his mind was sadly befogged by Madeira wine. On one occasion he was down on the program for a speech on the tariff. (I take this incident from Perley's *Reminiscences*.) Just before the time came for him to rise those around him observed that he could hardly hold two ideas together. Webster insisted on getting up, anyway. A friend sat behind him to prompt him. The prompter said, "Tariff, tariff," in a loud whisper as Webster stood wavering on his feet. Webster began:

"The tariff, gentlemen. is a subject requiring the profound attention of the statesman. American industry,

gentlemen, must be . . ." (*nods a little*). Prompter:
"*National debt.*" Webster: "And, gentlemen, there's the
national debt—it should be paid (*loud cheers which
arouse the speaker*); yes, gentlemen, it should be paid
(*cheers*), and I'll be hanged if it shan't be—(*taking out
his pocketbook*)—I'll pay it myself! How much is it?"
This last question was asked of a gentleman near him
with drunken seriousness, and, coupled with the recollection of the well-known impecuniosity of Webster's pocketbook, it excited roars of laughter.

In that epoch a good many things excited roars of laughter. Vindictiveness was relieved by a sort of hearty, humorous gusto. A Rabelaisian spirit mingled with Puritan ideals,
and the result was marvelous to contemplate.

Physical beatings were in fashion, and these personal encounters occurred usually before a crowd of vociferous spectators. Sedate, bearded men in somber black clothes rolled
about in the mud, pummelling each other. The Hon. Albert
Rust, an Arkansas Congressman, gave Mr. Horace Greeley,
editor of the New York *Tribune*, a public whipping in the
streets of Washington—and for sometime thereafter Mr.
Greeley went about his journalistic duties with an armed de-
fender at his heels. "Extra Billy" Smith, a member of Congress from Virginia, attempted to chastise Mr. Douglas Wallach, but Mr. Wallach succeeded in getting Mr. Smith's thumb
in his mouth. The fight came to an end when Mr. Smith
bellowed, "Let go my thumb; you're chawing it to the bone."

A California Congressman named Herbert shot and killed
a waiter in a Washington restaurant. Mr. Herbert entered
the restaurant, so he said, in a pleasant frame of mind, gave
his order, and perused the news of the day for about an hour.
Then he spoke to the waiter and remonstrated about the
delay. There was more waiting, more expostulation on the
part of Mr. Herbert, and some insolence on the part of the
waiter. Eventually the food came, served in the wrong order

—and with cold coffee. Upon realizing what a mess had been made of his luncheon, Mr. Herbert killed the waiter. He had to make a stiff fight to keep from going to the penitentiary, but it was universally agreed by observers that the service in restaurants thereafter was greatly improved.

During a debate in the House of Representatives Mr. Keitt, of South Carolina, called Mr. Crow, of Pennsylvania, "a Black Republican puppy." A fist fight, in which a dozen members engaged, followed this critical observation. Mr. Covode, of Pennsylvania, tried to brain a Southern gentleman with a cuspidor. Mr. Cadwallader Washburne seized Mr. Barksdale, of Mississippi, by the hair, but Mr. Barksdale wore a wig which came off in Mr. Washburne's hand. Upon the restoration of peace the wig was returned, with faint apologies.

The assault on Charles Sumner by Preston Brooks, of South Carolina, caused immense indignation throughout the North. Mr. Sumner, champion of the abolitionists in the Senate, had a scholarly manner and a vitriolic tongue. He wrapped vituperation in classical literary phrases—and was considered a very irritating person even by those who supported him politically.

One day Mr. Sumner spent an hour or two of the Senate's time in a verbal castigation of the aged Senator Butler, of South Carolina. In return Mr. Brooks, who was a member of the House and a relative of Senator Butler, decided to give Mr. Sumner a beating. He appeared in the Senate chamber, soon after the adjournment for the day, armed with a gold-headed cane, and attacked Mr. Sumner, who was sitting at his desk writing a letter. In attempting to rise Mr. Sumner wrenched the desk loose from its iron fastenings and gave himself an injury to his spine which incapacitated him for several years.

A number of Southern Senators, standing near by, witnessed this assault but they made no move to stop it. After it was over a page picked up the gold head of Brooks' broken cane, lying on the floor. "Mr. Brooks, don't you want this piece of your cane?" he said. Brooks took the gold head out of the boy's hand, put it in his pocket, and walked away silently.

An effort to expel Brooks from the House failed by a few votes. He resigned shortly afterwards, and was unanimously reëlected by his constituency.

Although this assault made Sumner an invalid, its effect on his assailant was even worse. Brooks was a man of culture, bred as a gentleman, and his soul wilted under the denunciation and the charges of cowardice that blazed in the Northern press. He said that he had expected Sumner to defend himself. While the Northern newspapers were calling him a cowardly assassin, Southerners were sending him gold-headed canes by the score. He fell ill, and lay in bed watching the canes arrive. "I shall go down in history as a bully," he sighed wearily . . . then he turned his face to the wall and died.

§ 7

These things were holding the attention of the American people while the insignificant Captain Grant—who was destined to inherit the accumulated power of the anti-slavery movement—walked alone in his land of despair.

Something had to be done for him; that was certain, for he was visibly going to pieces, and in a short time he and his family would be without anything to eat.

One wonders why the Dents did not come to his aid with ready cash, or some kind of job. The reason, I surmise, is that they had already done a good deal for him, and probably felt that they should not be called upon to do any more. For awhile he had been an overseer on Colonel Dent's plantation, but he made pets of all the animals and was not firm enough with the negroes to get much work out of them.

Old Jesse Grant, basking in the ease of his sixty years at Covington, Kentucky, bestirred himself when Ulysses borrowed railroad fare and went to see him. Some years before his retirement he had set up Ulysses' two younger brothers in a leather business at Galena, Illinois. Both of these sons, Orvil and Simpson, were cast in the mold of small-town tradesmen . . . eager, sharp, unromantic and coarse-grained. Their business was growing, and the idea occurred to their father that they might take Ulysses in the store as an assistant, and they did.

Grant's position in the Galena store was humiliating. He knew nothing about the leather goods business, and was under the tutelage of his younger brothers, who assumed from the start that he was an incompetent and had to be carried on the pay-roll as an object of family charity. His salary was eight hundred dollars a year.

"He was courteous and popular with all who met him on business," Albert D. Richardson says, "but never sought acquaintances. He was a very poor salesman, could not chaffer, and did not always know the price of an article. So, whenever a difficult or an important customer was to be dealt with, Orvil, Simpson, or one of the clerks took him in charge." A resident of Galena who knew Grant said that "he had not more than three intimates in the whole town."

He was at the bottom of his pit, a forlorn figure, a man who dared not think of the future, and who had lost the bright pictures of his day-dreams.

CHAPTER X

THE OLD SOUTH

§ 1

THE connection between the Southern people and Grant's career is so close that one thinks of it as a kind of mystic fatalism. He married a Southern woman; a Louisiana general—Zachary Taylor—was his military ideal; and he became one of the shining stars of American history through the rebellion of the slave states.

For sixteen years, from the outbreak of the Civil War until the close of his second Presidential term, he was occupied continually with Southern affairs . . . in fighting Southern men, in conquering Southern states, and in endeavoring to reconstruct their governments.

§ 2

It was the fate of Southern civilization to be entangled in anachronisms that had to be continually defended. As its panorama unfurls we see that the Southern mind, in the generation before the Civil War, was peculiarly unreceptive to ideas and deficient in intellectual metabolism. Its horizon was limited by the necessity of maintaining the hopelessly out-of-date institution of slavery in the face of a moving world.

But if the Southern mind was closed to mental innovations, the Southern heart was still open to emotions, and it throbbed with an urgent romanticism. The flame and sweep of noble legends, the spirit of great traditions, profoundly affected even the small events of daily life, though these high traditions were often nothing more than pure fiction. The men and women of the time clothed themselves in the heroic stanzas of Byron's poetry, and lived imaginary lives. William Gilmore Simms, the greatest of Southern novelists, found his inspiration in the romances of Sir Walter Scott. In Simms' novels the haughty but magnanimous Scotch lairds were transformed into South Carolina cotton-planting squires. Generous impulses, young cavaliers, blushing damsels, dog-like devotion, the clash of steel and the jovial triumph of right over wrong are all thrown pell-mell on his huge canvas. His works are high-toned melodramas. He represented the spirit of his age; he portrayed the old South as the old South saw itself.

In this atmosphere of romantic make-believe there grew up an aristocracy that possessed all the virtues, and most of the faults, of the ill-fated Bourbons. One feels quivering in the air the punctilio of rigid manners and the stately poise of a society that believes in its own superiority.

But the distillation of these qualities was too strongly acid. They crystallized into set rules, devoid of spontaneity. Social formulas which had ceased to live, and had no sap in their marrow, still continued to exist in petrified shapes as hard as metal.

Woman was enshrined in Southern tradition, as she has always been in civilizations saturated with chivalrous ideals. And the Southern woman of high degree was placed on such a lofty eminence that she was scarcely approachable as a human being. It was understood that a woman's name should be mentioned only twice in a newspaper; once at her marriage, and again at her death . . . called her demise. If it happened to appear in print on many other occasions some unlucky editor was in danger of a horse-whipping.

A personal touchiness on all sides set limits to intellectual controversy. Where there was so much humorless dignity arguments could seldom be carried to their ultimate conclusion for fear of giving offense. Pistols for two gleamed distantly at the far end of logic. The newspapers of the time were loaded with apologies and explanations, with intricate satires, with delicately veiled criticisms.

In the subconsciousness of Southern thought slavery was always on the defensive, even at the moment of its most potent security. It was apologetic in the early years of the nineteenth century, but its back stiffened under attacks. In the South itself, where there should have been frankness—if anywhere—about such an important institution, the topic of slavery was packed with moral evasions. It was generally asserted by the defenders of slavery that negroes would not work at all if they were free, regardless of the fact that 238,000 free negroes were actually at work in the Southern states in 1850; and some of them had done so well that they had built up modest fortunes and owned slaves themselves.

There were curious inconsistencies in the social atmosphere. For example, a gentleman might buy negroes from a slave-trader, or sell them to him, but the slave-trader himself was looked upon as a social pariah. The subject of slave-trading was tabooed in polite society. When it had to be discussed at all, its least repulsive profile was looked at for a brief instant—and then it was led back to the closet of social skeletons.

Southern civilization was an oligarchy, with the whole of the legislative machinery in the hands of the great slave-owners and their intellectual dependents. It duplicated, in a way, the money capitalism of the North; but slave capitalism was a far more rigid and inflexible state of society. The emphasis of merit was placed on breeding—on family—on associations—rather than on culture or ability. The families of the plantation aristocrats went over their genealogies daily, refreshing their memories, and fingering the generations as good Catholics finger the beads of a rosary. Everybody who amounted to anything had descended from somebody who had amounted to something.

Undemocratic—and a little foolish, one may say—and so it was. But with this high sense of personal value there was a collateral strain of uprightness. Pride and honesty went hand in hand. Men who are living up to great traditions do not stoop to theft and lying, nor to shifty financial dealings.

The lofty though somewhat quixotic sense of honor among the ruling class was carried into public office. Governmental functions were honestly administered. The tricky, money-making office-holder had not yet appeared on the scene; peculation was so rare that it was almost non-existent.

The genius of the South was sterile, though it is true that the higher classes among the Southern oligarchy were cultured people. There was no lack of Latin and Greek. Here and there learned botanists puttered over their dried specimens, and produced dry treatises; and there were essays on optics and the campaigns of Hannibal. But the whole civilization lacked creative imagination. It did not have the propulsive power that sends ideas flying outside the orbit of the age. It never produced an Emerson, nor a Robert Fulton, nor a Walt Whitman, nor a Rockefeller. It gave hardly anything to the world in the way of fresh and vivid thought, and it asked nothing of the world but to be let alone.

§ 3

In the decade before the Civil War the cost of supporting a prime field-hand was not more than one hundred and fifty dollars a year, even if his food as well as his clothes had to be bought for cash. In Phillips' authoritative work on negro slavery we find an itemized estimate of the cost of maintenance of slaves owned by the Charleston and Savannah railroad. These calculations are business-like; they include the cost of life insurance (for slave-owners usually insured their negroes) as well as interest at seven per cent on the capital invested. Other items are: Twenty dollars a year for clothing, fifteen dollars for corn, tobacco and molasses, fifteen dollars for tools and repairs (these slaves worked on a railroad and needed tools), one dollar for physician's fees, and ten dollars for overseer's wages.

From other reliable documents—such as plantation account-books—we may learn what it cost to support a slave on a farm, where he raised his own meat and bread. Consider the income and expense account of the James H. Hammond plantation in South Carolina. Mr. Hammond owned one hundred and forty-seven slaves; and in the year under consideration—which was in the 1830's—the total cash outlay for maintenance was $3,696.98—or about twenty-five dollars apiece. Five hundred dollars of this amount went to the overseer as his salary. Most of the cash expense was for clothing. I do not find anything, in this case, set down for insurance or depreciation.

Turning to the other side of the Hammond ledger we learn that the gross income for the year was $11,491.86. Deducting the cost of maintenance as given above, the net profit from the plantation for that year was $7,794.88. The capital invested in land, live stock and negroes was given at $92,000. We should take it for granted that the time of the owner— acting as manager—was worth something. Let us say $5,000 a year, and this amount should be deducted from the net profit. That leaves $2,794.88 as the return on an investment of more than $90,000—or about three per cent.

Of course, there were exceptionally large profits here and there, as there are in all industries. Some cotton planters, favorably situated on land of unusual fertility, had large incomes; but, taking the South as a whole, just before the Civil War, there were very few large fortunes—comparable to the wealth of the North—and not many large incomes.

The floating capital of the South went into the purchase of

negroes, while the financial resources of the North were invested in buildings, factories, machinery and railroads. At the beginning of the Civil War the people of Massachusetts had on deposit in their banks more money than the total deposits of all the seceding states. The profits of the cotton-planters disappeared like water thrown on dry sand. There was no inherent economic necessity to buy negroes; they were already there, on the ground; if they had been free they might have been hired instead of being bought.

Entangled with these questions was the fact that the South paid tribute to Northern manufacturers on virtually every commodity that could not be grown on Southern soil. Shoes came from Massachusetts, hats from Connecticut, books from New York, plows from Pennsylvania, chinaware from New Jersey, knives from somewhere else. The Northern industrialist or importer, aided by a protective tariff, drew a profit from the South on everything from children's dolls to candlesticks.

Slavery as an economic institution would have been on a firmer basis if every white man—or even most white men— had owned one or more slaves. But three-fourths of the white families possessed no slaves at all. In other words, the majority of the Southern people had no direct interest in slavery, and in actual operation the slave system worked greatly to their disadvantage.

In 1860 there were 384,000 slave-owners in the fifteen slave states. The total white population amounted to 8,000,000 people, or approximately 1,600,000 families. Less than a fourth of the white families owned all the slaves and controlled the mechanism of government and finance. It is evident that slavery was not only sectional by geographical limitation, but also that in the South itself it was a class institution. Small farmers who were not able to purchase slaves—and they formed the bulk of the agricultural population—could not live decently in competition with this enormous organization of black pauper labor.

Under these circumstances an illiterate race of white peasants came into being in the heart of slave civilization. There was no place for them in the social structure. Long before the Civil War the downward pull of economic forces had brought them almost to the negro's level.

The mechanics, carpenters, bricklayers and other working men of the towns were hardly any better off than the poor white farmers. Slaves trained in the mechanical trades were hired out by their owners at low wages. The competing white mechanic had to accept the same rate of pay or find himself out of work.

In Charleston in 1848 there were one hundred and twenty slave carpenters against one hundred and nineteen whites engaged in the same occupation; forty slave blacksmiths and fifty-one whites; sixty-eight slave bricklayers and sixty whites; sixteen slave painters and eighteen whites. As we run down the long list of mechanical occupations we find slaves represented in every trade; there were even five slaves set down as printers, thirty-six as tailors, fifty as pilots and sailors, three as bookbinders, and thirty-nine as bakers. The services of a fairly competent negro craftsman were sold for about twenty-five or thirty dollars a month in the late fifties.

With a vast body of servile strike-breakers at hand labor unions were impossible, and white labor found itself continually defeated in its attempt to get higher pay or better conditions of employment.

Manual labor came to be looked upon as degrading. To work with one's hands brought one down to the social status of the negro . . . or so men thought. The entire social body was poisoned by this deadly virus. Workmen were ashamed of being workmen. People who had no need of slaves saved money and bought them, in order to attain the social status that accompanied slave-ownership.

§ 4

It was impossible to defend slave industrialism with reasons that were intelligible to the civilized world. Not only the Northern states, but indeed the whole of civilization had outgrown the idea of negro slavery. There was a moral repugnance to the thought of one man owning another, as a horse is owned, that could not be overcome by any amount of argument.

In vain the Southern defenders of their "peculiar institution," as they called it, declared that the negro—half savage and half child—was better off as a slave than he would be as a free man faced with the responsibility of looking out for himself in an intricate commercial society. They pointed out that the slave system forced the negro into regular and abstemious habits, that it taught him cleanliness, that it gave him a religion, that it kept him in health, that it provided him with useful employment, that it cared for him in his old age, that it took a race of African savages and civilized them.

This was all true, but it dealt entirely with physical facts, while the basic evil of slavery was not physical but spiritual. It lay in the subjection of the will of one race to the will of another race—an unnatural, perverse relationship which has nothing to do with material well-being.

In its physical aspects slavery was much worse in theory than it was in practice. The slave laws which put almost unlimited power in the hands of the master were devised to meet remote possibilities. Social custom and public opinion constituted the real code. A slave-owner could starve his people almost to death and remain within the law. He could whip them unmercifully day after day; he could take little children away from their mothers and sell them; he could use for immoral purposes any negro woman whom he happened to own. All these brutalities were possible, but they occurred very seldom. Men who were cruel to their slaves found themselves in bad repute. Their families were ostracized, they had difficulty in getting the financial assistance of banks, they found it impossible to buy negroes from their neighbors. The intangible forces of decent society were arrayed against the brutal master; yet, at the same time, the institution of slavery was defended with an amazing venom. Abolitionists who attempted to speak before Southern audiences were mobbed.

Slaves were not whipped very much, and on many plantations there were no whippings at all. In one case, mentioned by Mrs. Roger A. Pryor in her *Reminiscences of Peace and War*, the master made lazy negroes stand at attention before him while he read long passages from Homer in the original Greek. This man was probably a humorist with a classical turn of mind. In numerous instances the punishment was left to the slaves themselves. The Brierfield plantation of Jefferson Davis, in Mississippi, was conducted on that principle. Davis instituted a form of self-government for his negroes. A recalcitrant slave was brought before a court of his own color, and if found without an excuse for his disobedience or laziness he was sentenced to be whipped by another slave, or put on a starvation diet.

There were cruel people in the South, as there are everywhere, but they were exceptions. The ante-bellum Southerners were a kindly people on the whole. Their boundless romanticism struggled continually with the sordid circumstances that surrounded them. One hears of families that were eaten literally out of house and home by their negroes. The average cotton-planter thought of himself as a benevolent patriarch, with his family and his slaves around him . . . like a medieval baron at the head of his barony . . . and the slaves ranked in his affection just below the members of his family.

The master's affection was reciprocated by the slave. I know this fact has been obscured by the diatribes against slavery, and has been neglected by historians, but we must accept it as true, nevertheless, unless we disregard the evidence of innumerable witnesses.

During the Civil War, when the white men were away from home in the Confederate army, the slaves took care of the white women and children. At that time there were nearly a million adult males among the Southern negroes. They could have destroyed most of the Southern population in a single day; they could have put an end to the Confederacy between sunrise and sunset. It was not lack of courage that kept them from revolt. The theory that the negro is a coward has no foundation; experience has shown that he has about the same supply of physical courage that God has given the other races. He did not rise and make himself free during the Civil War because he cared more for his white folks than he did for freedom. If this had not been so the paltry little statistics of the Underground Railroad would have been swollen to gigantic proportions. Instead of eight hundred slaves escaping in one year we would find that there were eighty thousand.

The negro subtly invaded the Southern soul. The experience of mankind shows that in all slave civilizations the master eventually succumbs, morally and spiritually, to those who are held in bondage—if the system is continued long enough. This process was going on in the ante-bellum South. The negro's influence on the civilization where he was held in bondage was intangible, but powerful. Faded remnants of it exist even to-day, although the terrific shock of the Civil War tore the two races apart and created a new and sharp antagonism.

I cannot find any evidence that slavery did the negro permanent harm. It was only a passing phase of his social evolution. It made a civilized being of him in a shorter time than any savage race was ever civilized before.

But it did the Southern white man a great deal of harm. It was he who was poisoned by its false ideals, and dazzled by the tinsel of its shallow opulence, and dragged back to the Middle Ages by its spiritual and economic degeneration.

§ 5

There was a Russian air of sharp contrast about this serf-pervaded society.

Here are the somber dwellings of the poor—ramshackle, unpainted houses—standing in the bare fields—in the slashing November rains; these are pictures which we have seen in Tolstoi, in Andreyeff, in Gorky. The poor folk . . . we have seen their counterparts in Russia on the flat, colorless lands . . . men and women with chalky faces; people with lank frames and leaden eyes.

And there are the homes of the wealthy . . . lofty mansions glittering white among the glossy-green magnolias.

At the ballroom door stands a girl in her wide-spreading silk dress, her feet tapping impatiently to the rhythm of the music. Her glistening black hair is brushed tightly back and caught in a coil behind, her long earrings of amethyst flash in the reflected light. We hear her mellow Southern voice, and see the gentle swaying of her painted fan of ivory and silk. She might be Varvara Pavlovna Korobyne in Turgenev's *Nest of Nobles*.

The young man who advances to meet her is both stately and graceful. A wide black stock is wound around his neck; his broadcloth coat narrows at the waist and flares out again below. His face is flawless in contour; he is so highly bred that he is almost insolent in the perfection of his manners. Before offering the lady his arm he kisses the tips of her fingers. We know him, too; he strikes a responsive chord in our memory; he has come straight from the pages of Gogol's *Dead Souls*.

§ 6

In 1857 a book against slavery appeared that caused more indignation in the South than *Uncle Tom's Cabin*. Its author was Hinton Rowan Helper, a North Carolinian, and the title of his book was *The Impending Crisis in the South*. Mr. Helper was a poor white who had educated himself; his point of view was that of the Southerner who did not own slaves.

The Impending Crisis is crammed with figures, and arguments based on statistics. It is an economic study of the effect of slavery on the Southern states in general, and on the non-slave-owning white man in particular. His theme was that the Southern white man was being ruined by slavery. It was a literary work of intellectual power, entirely bare of sentimentalism, with every argument supported by facts.

Helper did not care anything at all for the negro; he was occupied wholly with the welfare of the white man, and he was convinced that white men, as a class, could not prosper as long as slavery continued to exist.

He held up to scorn the slave-owner's dictum that "Cotton is king," and proceeded to prove by census statistics that the hay produced in the North had a larger money value than the cotton crop, with tobacco, rice and several other Southern agricultural products thrown in. He points out that the hay crop of the free states in 1850 was worth $331,000,000— which was four times the value of all the cotton grown in the South.

That slavery, through its inefficiency, depreciated the value of everything it touched, was one of his chief arguments. To illustrate this point he showed that the real and personal property of New York state was worth more than all the property, including slaves, in Virginia, North Carolina, Tennessee, Missouri, Arkansas, Florida and Texas.

His devastating analysis continued in a consideration of land values. Let us compare New Jersey and South Carolina, he said. In South Carolina the seventeen million acres of land assessed for taxation were valued at about twenty-three million dollars, or $1.32 an acre. In New Jersey, the five million acres assessed for taxation were worth more than one hundred and fifty million dollars, or $28.76 an acre. The reason . . . slavery . . . according to Mr. Helper. The cotton-planters of the South, he asserted, did not clear a net profit of as much as one per cent annually on their invested capital.

One would naturally think that such a book, backed by statistics, would have been considered a notable contribution to the economic literature of the day, but it was not looked upon in any such light in the slave states. Bonfires were made of it, and any man caught reading it was in danger of being mobbed. This truculent attitude was the result of Mr. Helper's conclusions rather than his statistics. He wrote that the non-slave-holding whites among the Southern people themselves ought to take the matter in hand, cast the slave-owning aristocrats from the seats of power and force them to pay, by means of special taxation, for the ruin they had brought upon the South.

The Impending Crisis had a huge circulation. Within three years about a million copies had been either sold or given away. The time-stained copy that I own was originally bought by an E. M. Davis, of 55 Bank Street (New York City, I presume), and he had presented it to some one else. On the fly-leaf Mr. Davis pasted a printed slip which throws some light on the vigor of the anti-slavery propaganda. Mr. Davis said on this slip:

> I have bought 500 copies of *The Impending Crisis in the South* for gratuitous distribution. I can circulate judiciously ten times that number. If you are disposed to coöperate, be kind enough to send, without delay, the names, with post-office addresses, of any parties you would like the book sent to, and such amount of funds as you feel justified in contributing. If you hesitate to aid me, read the book anyway, and then write me afterwards. Promptness is of importance.

Public opinion in North Carolina—meaning the opinion of the oligarchy—was not in the least bit favorable to Mr.

Helper. His former neighbors were not impressed by the fact that *The Impending Crisis* was a "best-seller," or that Mr. Helper was the only North Carolinian in the history of the state who had ever written a book that had sold to the extent of a million copies. After his reverberating literary success, the North Carolinians did not put any wreaths on his head, but they threatened to put tar and feathers on his back if he ever returned to his native state.

The North, as well as the South, had its weak spots. We find Southern publicists harping on the long hours of labor in Northern factories, on the indigent poor, and on the homeless children that roamed in crowds through the streets and alleys of New York City.

The living conditions of the laboring people in some of the Northern cities was indeed deplorable. Of the homeless children in New York, Denis Tilden Lynch says in his *"Boss" Tweed:* "Harriet Beecher Stowe did not have to seek among the blacks for a Topsy. She could have found her in any one of the hundreds of little girls of six to ten years of age, who swept the crossings of the principal streets of New York. These children, in ragged dress and pinched face, broom in one hand, and the other extended, depended for their living on the chance coins bestowed on them by those whose boots were kept clean through their exertions."

There were more than ten thousand of these abandoned children in New York City alone. They grew up like wild animals. Their lairs were dry goods boxes and disused cellars. Compared with their hunted and starved lives the existence of a black slave child on a Southern plantation was a paradise.

CHAPTER XI

DRIFTING INTO WAR

§ 1

HENRY WARD BEECHER held a slave auction in his Brooklyn church, just to show his congregation what slave-trading actually was. He had managed to get possession of a lovely octoroon slave girl, with long golden hair flowing down her back. In all outward appearances she was as white—or even whiter—than the crowd which jammed the church. The auction was a grotesque caricature of reality. Beautiful young slave women of this description—and there were very few of them in existence—were never auctioned off at all in the South. They became rich men's mistresses, wore Parisian clothes, and had carriages and servants of their own. The members of the church bid briskly for the girl. The auction was illegal, of course, in New York state, and was understood to be merely a dramatic entertainment. The girl was set free at once, and the money that was bid for her went to support the anti-slavery crusade.

Funds were raised by public subscription in the Northern states to send armed abolitionist settlers to Kansas. Emerson descended from his Nirvana of philosophic calm to say that "it is impossible to be a gentleman and not be an abolitionist." Garrison was no longer dragged about the streets of Boston with a rope around his neck. Highly respectable people invited him to their houses, and he became a popular hero.

The swelling fury of the North was fully met by the indignation of the South. Northern travelers in the Southern

151

latitudes were carefully watched, and some of them were searched to be sure that they were not laden with abolition pamphlets. Southern postmasters refused to deliver the New York *Tribune* to its subscribers. The papers came back scribbled over with invectives.

Robert Toombs, of Georgia, who was considered the leading Southern statesman of the time, made pro-slavery speeches which spluttered with such fiery anger that he got his words twisted. He declared that he "would rather see the whole country the cemetery of freedom than the habitation of slaves." He meant, of course, that the threatened invasion of states' rights would reduce the Southern white man to a negligible position in national affairs when he spoke of "habitation of slaves."

§ 2

The abolitionists did not have everything their own way, by any means. In 1857 Chief Justice Taney, of the United States Supreme Court, handed down the celebrated Dred Scott Decision—a blow which dazed the anti-slavery party, and sent it reeling about the political arena.

Judge Taney and a majority of the associate justices ruled that "the right of property in a slave is distinctly and expressly affirmed in the Constitution." The court decided that the Ordinance of 1787, the Missouri Compromise, the Compromise of 1850—and every other legislative act which had for its object the restriction of slavery to geographical limits —were unconstitutional and void. Never before in the history of the United States had such a sweeping and cataclysmic decision come from its supreme tribunal.

It might seem, in the light of this momentous legal opinion, that the slavery party had won every point at issue; and that there were not to be any free states. It appeared that the only way to get rid of slavery—other than by the voluntary action of the slave states—was to amend the United States Constitution.

The anti-slavery party was nonplussed for a while, and lost its bearings. Talk of secession of the North from the Union bubbled around Boston. A secession convention was called to meet at Worcester, but before the time came for its meeting a nation-wide financial panic occupied the attention of the country, and the convention never assembled. Justice Taney was the subject of unlimited abuse in the Northern press, and the Supreme Court was frankly described as a contemptible political organism. Yet, now that seventy years have passed and the passions of ante-bellum strife have dissolved, the best legal opinion is that the Court's decision was perfectly sound, and in accordance with the Constitution. Taney could not have taken any other stand without being false to his oath to uphold the fundamental law.

The Republican party soon pulled itself together, picked up the shattered pieces of its program, and went ahead. Notwithstanding the Supreme Court's decision, the Northern states, through their legislatures, continued to put obstacles in the way of slave-owning within their borders, and the abolitionists (as well as the Southern Democrats) still continued to send rifles to Kansas, where a local war was going on. There one saw, from a distance, whirling figures covered with dust and blood. The Kansas struggle was as savage as Indian warfare, and was made up of midnight massacres, house-burning and secret murders. Both the pro-slavery party and the abolitionists in Kansas were guilty of the most ghastly atrocities. It is one of the ironies of history that the Southern effort to capture that wheat-growing prairie land was a mistake from start to finish. Kansas was no place for slaves. The climate was too cold, and slave labor lacked the intelligence to grow wheat successfully. Even if Kansas had been given bodily to the slave power without a struggle it never would have become a slave state.

From these tumbling phantasms a tall, hard-faced old man emerged, with a rifle in his hand, and stood for a moment in the beating light of public attention before he passed into history. This man was John Brown, an abolitionist fanatic of the hysteroid or neurotic type. In Kansas he had murdered pro-slavery men in cold blood, and was known all over the country for his connection with the Pottawatomie massacre, where five men were dragged from their beds at night and butchered with ancient army cutlasses without having a chance to defend themselves. John Brown was a sadist—a slayer by instinct—an egocentric with a conviction of his own superiority which was so dominating that it cut the air around him like a knife.

This extraordinary desperado was religious to the point of mania. Before his killings—and after them—he would read the Psalms of David to his family in a loud, sonorous voice. Religion, cruelty, and a saintly mildness of manner mingled grotesquely in his personality. He loved little children, and would sit holding them on his knees for hours at a time. He was moved to tears by music, wept when Schubert's "Serenade" was played, and "rose with tears in his eyes."

Whenever I see his picture it brings to my mind Pazzi's statue of Savonarola that stands in the Palazzo Vecchio in Florence. There we behold the rapt countenance, the stony cold eyes and the lean jaws of the martyr . . . but if John Brown had the Florentine's talent for martyrdom, it was mixed profoundly with the cruel motivation that distinguished the founders of the Spanish Inquisition.

His life story is pitted with dark recesses—gaps of silence and dimly drawn events—for he was always doing something or other in secret. Before he went to Kansas he had been a lifelong ne'er-do-well, and had spent most of his time in evading his creditors, in quarrels over dubious land titles, and in promoting fantastic financial projects which left his backers in a state of sharp suspicion.

Among his imperative desires was a love of dramatic situa-. tions. He belonged to the race of men and women who are willing to do anything, believe anything, or suffer anything, if by so doing they may appear for awhile in a conspicuous rôle.

Into his half-insane mind there came an idea that he might instigate single-handed a slave rebellion that would put an end to slavery and make John Brown himself one of the great heroes of history. Emotions of grandeur, of compassion, of revenge, of blood-lust, flickered through his thoughts. His plan, at first, was to furnish arms to escaped slaves, take command of them, and establish a military stronghold in the heart of the Southern Appalachians. Then, as more slaves joined him they would be supplied with arms—contributed by Northern abolitionists—and a chain of mountain fortresses, held by negroes, could be extended farther into the South.

This seems to have been his idea at the beginning, but he changed it after awhile into a more grandiose conception—that of an independent free negro republic, with himself at its head. At any rate, that is what I make of his scheme after a pro-longed study of the documents. He went to Canada in 1858 and held a secret convention of about a dozen white followers and thirty-four negroes. This convention adopted a "Pro-visional Constitution and Ordinance for the People of the United States." A provisional Congress met—in secret—and elected Brown commander-in-chief. This Congress consisted of only two members, both colored men.

John Brown's next move was to try to seize the government arsenal at Harpers Ferry, Virginia. That was to be the dis-tributing point for arms, and the geographical nucleus of the negro revolution. The arsenal, which contained enough arms and ammunition to supply a small army, was defended by only two watchmen.

Before he was ready to make his attack nearly a year was

spent in preparation. About the middle of 1859 he rented an abandoned farm in Maryland, six miles north of the arsenal, and used this isolated place as a point of observation. Here he collected twenty-one followers—sixteen white men and five negroes—and hired an ex-soldier to drill them into military form. Funds to keep this force in being were supplied by a group of bitter abolitionists to whom Brown confided his plan. He wrote to his son from Boston:

> My call here has met with a most hearty response, so that I feel assured of at least tolerable success. . . . All has been effected by a quiet meeting of a few choice friends, it being scarcely known that I have been in the city.

Garrison, who still held to his policy of non-resistance, was not among the abolitionists who gave the "hearty response," though he knew what Brown proposed to do. And the response of Dr. Samuel G. Howe, another stern, dyed-in-the-wool abolitionist, was a little chilly. Dr. Howe had recently made a trip to South Carolina, where he had been royally entertained by Wade Hampton, and had left Hampton's Millwood estate laden with presents and good wishes. When he realized that Brown's scheme included the eventual massacre of the slave-owning population, including the delightful Hamptons, he advised that the whole idea be dropped . . . but he did not communicate his objections to anybody outside the little circle of abolitionists.

During the night of October 16, 1859, Brown and his followers appeared at Harpers Ferry and seized the town's fire-engine house—a brick building which could be easily fortified. The first man killed—as the irony of Fate would have it—was a free negro who attempted to run when Brown's men ordered him to halt. Soon afterward the mayor of Harpers Ferry was killed by a stray shot from the engine house as he was approaching the place, unarmed, for a parley with Brown.

The village was struck with terror. The mayor's body lay in the street for hours, as no one wanted to go within range of the fire from Brown's stronghold. The bartender of the local hotel did manage, however, to get within range and was captured by Brown.

In the meantime a detached expedition, which had been sent by the raiders to round up the local planters, returned with Colonel Lewis Washington and fourteen of his slaves. Brown held them as prisoners in the engine house. The scion of the great Washington family sat down in grumpy discomfort on the fire engine and waited to see what would happen. The expedition also brought back George Washington's sword, a family heirloom, which Brown promptly buckled around his own lean body.

Breakfast time had arrived, but there was nothing to eat in the engine house, as Brown had forgotten the commissary department in planning his campaign. After some palaver he agreed to let the bartender go if the hotel would supply breakfast for forty men. The hotel gladly agreed; the barroom was packed with thirsty and excited citizens; it looked as if it were going to be a big drinking day. So ham and eggs came across the street, and the bartender was set free.

As the day wore on it became evident that the negroes had no intention of rallying to the cause of freedom. Even Colonel Washington's slaves, held in the engine house, refused to take up arms. But the neighborhood militia began to appear in numbers, and by noon bullets were flying. Brown's two sons were wounded (one died during the night), and several of his men were killed. One who attempted to escape by swimming the river clung exhausted to a rock in the middle of the stream and was riddled by a hundred bullets. Another, pursued through the streets, ran into the hotel and took refuge in the parlor. When the crowd burst in, the hotel proprietor's daughter, who had never seen the man before, sat in his lap and put her arms around his neck to save him from lynching.

The crowd recoiled out of respect for Southern womanhood, but eventually they got the man out of the hotel, by some device, and shot him on the railroad bridge. His body was thrown in the river and went rolling down stream, leaving a red streak in the water.

Late in the evening of the 17th a detachment of marines came up from Washington under the command of Colonel Robert E. Lee, of General Scott's staff. Next morning a flag of truce from Colonel Lee went gingerly toward the engine house, and Brown said, "I prefer to die just here," in reply to the summons to surrender. Within an hour the door was battered down and Brown and his men were taken prisoners.

The old man was kept in jail two weeks and then brought in court charged with treason, conspiring with slaves to rebel, and murder. Harpers Ferry became the center of the American universe. Lawyers traveled from Boston and Cleveland to defend John Brown and troops came from Richmond to hold the place under martial law and prevent any attempts to effect his release. Newspaper correspondents crowded the little hotel. Governor Wise of Virginia visited the prisoner with the hope of finding out who were his accomplices. He refused to tell. At his trial, which was a fair one, his bearing was one of great courage and dignity. He gloried in the renown that was winging its way over the wires to every hamlet in the country.

He was found guilty on all counts and hanged. On a bright, clear December morning he rode to the scaffold in a wagon that contained his coffin. There is a well-known painting in existence which depicts him stopping a moment at the jail door to kiss a negro child. Pure myth. The contemporary reports of his execution prove that there was not a negro within half a mile of him. He was surrounded by soldiers.

"This is a beautiful country," he remarked to the sheriff as they sat in the wagon and his eyes swept over the blue Piedmont hills.

"You are a game man, Captain Brown," said Mr. Sadler.

"Yes," he said, "I was so trained up; it was one of the lessons of my mother; but it is hard to part from friends, though newly made."

"You are more cheerful than I am, Captain Brown," was the reply.

"Yes," said he, "I ought to be."

As he stood on the gallows, with the rope around his neck, and a white cap over his eyes, the sheriff said: "Captain Brown, you are not standing on the drop. Will you come forward?"

"I can't see, gentlemen," was his reply in a firm voice, "you must lead me."

So died old John Brown—and his death thundered and reverberated through the length and breadth of the American nation. The abolitionists now had a martyr to hold up before the unthinking, sentimental millions of the North. On the other hand, the South felt that its worst suspicions were founded in truth. Southerners, almost to a man, believed that the entire North was behind John Brown, that the abolitionists carried the North with them; and that an immense servile insurrection had been narrowly averted. But this was not so. There was nobody in the Brown plot except himself and about a dozen visionaries.

§ 3

It became almost impossible to carry on the ordinary routine of business in the houses of Congress because of the flaming anger that lay under the surface of things. Mild little arguments over matters of small import would suddenly flare into volcanic outbursts. I shall quote a page or two from Rhodes (*History of the United States*, Vol. II, pp. 393, 394) as an illustration of the fist-and-dagger attitude of the North and South.

In Committee of the Whole, Lovejoy had the floor and proceeded to make an anti-slavery speech. "Slave-holding," he asserted, "is worse than robbing, than piracy, than polygamy. . . . The principle of enslaving human beings because they are inferior . . . is the doctrine of Democrats, and the doctrine of devils as well; and there is no place in the universe outside the five points of hell and the Democratic party where the practice and prevalence of such doctrines would not be a disgrace."

As Lovejoy spoke, his manner as boisterous as his words were vehement, he advanced into the area and occupied the space fronting the Democratic benches. Pryor, of Virginia, left his seat, moved quickly towards Lovejoy, and with a gesture full of menace, exclaimed, in a voice of anger: "The gentleman from Illinois shall not approach this side of the House, shaking his fists and talking in the way he has talked. It is bad enough to be compelled to sit here and hear him utter his treasonable and insulting language; but he *shall not*, sir, come upon this side of the House shaking his fist in our faces."

Potter, of Wisconsin, stepped towards Pryor and shouted: "We listened to gentlemen on the other side for eight weeks, when they denounced the members upon this side with violent and offensive language. We listened to them quietly and heard them through. And now, sir, this side *shall* be heard, let the consequences be what they may."

"The point of order I make," replied Pryor, "is that the gentleman shall speak from his seat; but, sir, he *shall not* come upon this side shaking his fist in our faces and talking in the style he has talked."

"You are doing the same thing," cried Potter.

"You shall not come upon this side of the House," said Barksdale, of Mississippi, menacingly to the face of Lovejoy.

"Nobody can intimidate me," uttered Lovejoy, with a loud voice.

And now thirty or forty members had gathered in the

HENRY WARD BEECHER AND HARRIET BEECHER STOWE

JOHN BROWN

He is usually shown wearing a beard, but during most
of his life he was clean-shaven. He grew a beard in
1859 for the purpose of disguising himself.

area around Lovejoy and Pryor, shouting and gesticulating. The confusion was great; men trembled with excitement and passion; rage distorted many faces; it seemed as if the long-dreaded moment of a bloody encounter on the floor of the House had come. Above the din might be heard the voice of Potter, saying, "I do not believe that side of the House can say *where* a member shall speak, and they shall not say it"; also the cries of a member from Mississippi and a member from Kentucky insisting that Lovejoy could not speak on their side, "let the consequences be what they will."

"My colleague shall speak," said Kellogg. The chairman of the committee, having in vain tried to preserve order, called the speaker to the chair and reported the disorder to the House. The speaker begged gentlemen to respect the authority of the House and take their seats.

"Order that black-hearted scoundrel and nigger-stealing thief to take his seat, and this side of the House will do it," shouted Barksdale. The efforts of the speaker were at last successful; order was restored, the chairman of the committee resumed the chair, and Lovejoy went on. The speech was interspersed with remarks from Barksdale, calling Lovejoy "an infamous, perjured villain," "a perjured negro-thief," and from another Mississippi member terming him a "mean, despicable wretch."

Nothing daunted Lovejoy. "You shed the blood of my brother on the banks of the Mississippi twenty years ago," he cried to the Southerners, "and what then? I am here to-day, thank God, to vindicate the principles baptized in his blood. . . . But I cannot go into a slave State," he continued, "and open my lips in regard to the question of slavery . . ."

"No," interrupted a Virginia member, "we would hang you higher than Haman."

"The meanest slave in the South is your superior," cried Barksdale.

Lovejoy was, however, permitted to finish his speech,

and for a few days the story of his bearding the slaveholders in the representatives' hall of the nation filled the
North.

These are figures half-drowned in shadow. Gesticulating
hands and ferocious faces are seen in a welter of smothered
light. We are haunted by their animalism and their hate.

§ 4

The presidential campaign of 1860 was the most important
political contest in American history.

The Democrats, split asunder by a row within their party,
nominated two candidates for President. The nominee of the
Northern wing was Stephen A. Douglas, of Illinois, an extremely clever politician whose enormous capacity for wrong
thinking was equaled by his shrewd plausibility. He thought
that the question of slavery in the territories should be settled
by the inhabitants of each territory. This conception of
"popular sovereignty" had been embodied by him in the famous
Kansas-Nebraska bill, a fatuous measure which had brought on
the Kansas civil war.

The Southern Democrats nominated John C. Breckenridge,
of Kentucky, who was at that time the vice-president of the
United States in the Buchanan administration. He and his
party contended that Congress not only had no right to prohibit slavery in any of the territories, but that it was the duty
of Congress to protect the slave-owner and his property rights
anywhere within the United States.

The Republican party nominated Abraham Lincoln, an Illinois lawyer who had served in Congress, and who had been
defeated by Douglas as a candidate for the Senate in 1856.
Though he had been beaten by Douglas he had made a national
reputation for himself in the Lincoln-Douglas joint debates.
The Republicans maintained that slavery should be restricted

to the Southern states, that it should be kept out of the territories and free states. Their platform was intended to nullify, in effect, the decision of the Supreme Court.

Lincoln said, in a speech at Charleston, Illinois, in 1858:

> I am not now, nor ever have been in favor of bringing about in any way the social or political equality of the white and black races. . . . There is a physical difference between the white and the black races which will forever forbid the two races living together on social or political equality. There must be a position of superior and inferior, and *I am in favor of assigning the superior position to the white man.*

These opinions did not suit the ultra-abolitionists, but most of them voted with the Republican party.

There was a fourth candidate—John Bell, of Tennessee—whose party consisted of the remnants of the once powerful Whigs, and the tag ends of other vanished political organisms.

The Republican platform was carefully devised to consolidate the Northern vote. It said nothing about abolition (many influential Republicans were not abolitionists), and it distinctly accepted the theory that slaves are property. As to states' rights, the Republican platform conceded, "The inviolable rights of each state to order and control its own domestic institutions." But it proposed to keep slavery out of the territories. It had a protective tariff plank, which was obviously put in to satisfy the manufacturers of the Eastern states. Then it had something to say about the distribution of the public lands, and urged the passage of a free homestead law. This last was intended as a net to catch the votes of the working people of the North.

Lincoln was elected, though he received considerably less than a majority of the total number of votes cast. Douglas and Breckenridge got, between them, 2,223,000 votes—and, of these, 1,375,000 were for Douglas. Bell was the choice of

590,000 voters, and Lincoln's supporters numbered 1,866,000. The Democrats outnumbered the Republicans, and could have won if their whole strength had centered on Douglas.

It is plainly evident, from a consideration of these figures, that Abraham Lincoln was not the choice of the American people. There was, indeed, no choice expressed by the popular vote, though the Republicans carried enough states of large population—such as New York, Pennsylvania and Ohio—to give Lincoln one hundred and eighty electoral votes against seventy-two for the other three candidates.

Lincoln did not get a single vote in the eleven slave states that seceded. His record in that region is a blank; if any citizen voted for him the vote was not counted.

§ 5

Grant did not vote at the election of 1860; he had not lived in Galena long enough to qualify as a voter. But he appears to have been a Douglas Democrat. He says, in reference to the fact that he could not vote: "I was really glad of this at the time, for my pledges would have compelled me to vote for Stephen A. Douglas, who had no possible chance of election."

During the campaign Grant heard Lincoln speak, and seems to have been converted to the Republican view of things. I say "seems," for his statement of the matter is so loose and vague that it is difficult to grasp what he meant. At any rate, Lincoln, whom he saw and heard from a distance—as a spectator in a crowd—made a great impression on him.

The election of Lincoln led to the secession of South Carolina and ten other slave states.

President Buchanan was at a party in Washington when the news of South Carolina's secession arrived. An aging but handsome President in a brightly lighted room, with a swarm of young girls around him. He liked the adulation that youth pays to distinction. Through an arched doorway came the quick music of an old-fashioned dance, and the click-click of heels on the floor.

Outside, in the entrance hall, a commotion arose. "Go and see what it is," the President said to one of his attendant ladies. In the hall she found Congressman Keitt, of South Carolina, capering about with a telegram held high over his head. "I feel like a boy let out of school," he shouted. "South Carolina has seceded."

The girl made her way back to the President's side. "South Carolina has seceded," she said quietly. The President's face seemed to get years older in a moment. "Please—some one—won't some one call my carriage," he murmured in a husky voice that was but little above a whisper. "I must go."

But Southerners were not unanimous on the matter of secession. Hot-headed Congressmen might dance around with telegrams in their hands, yet a very considerable minority of the Southern people was not in sympathy with them. I am not referring now to the common man, whose opinion was not asked or given—and who, in most cases, had no opinion—but to the influential leaders. Among the opponents of secession was Alexander H. Stephens, who afterward became vice-president of the Confederate States. Mr. Stephens said in 1860:

> The seceders intended from the beginning to rule or ruin, and when they find they cannot rule, they will then ruin. They have about enough power for this purpose; not much more; and I doubt not but they will use it. Envy, hate, jealousy, spite—these made war in heaven, which made devils of angels, and the same passions will make devils of men. The secession movement was instigated by nothing but bad passions.

In Tennessee the people of the state voted against a secession convention by a majority of twelve thousand, and it was only by the most frantic bullying that the secession program could be put through. It was found, in North Carolina, when the convention assembled that only thirty-eight delegates out of one hundred-and-twenty were in favor of secession; but there, too, the secession leaders succeeded in overriding a timid majority.

§ 6

The gaunt, homely Lincoln stood on a flag-draped stand in front of the half-finished Capitol. As he read his inaugural address in a mumbling, hesitating voice the March wind caught up his words and sent them flying over the heads of the turbulent crowd that had come to see the first Republican President sworn into office. He said:

> I have no purpose directly or indirectly to interfere with the institution of slavery in the States where it exists. I believe I have no lawful right to do so, and I have no inclination to do so.

Lincoln was an indecisive, vacillating half-mystic who had become, through the inscrutable alchemy of life, a shrewd politician. He has been so glorified by historians, and so completely surrounded by an all-embracing reverence, that the Lincoln who was known to his contemporaries has disappeared altogether. The accepted picture of him is so different from the actual Lincoln that his own mother would not recognize it. He is even more of a fiction than George Washington—and that is saying a great deal.

He cared as little for the Constitution and its limitations as any Communist of to-day. In this he fitted in perfectly with the temper of the American people—for hardly anybody ever has taken the Constitution seriously, despite all the learned hypocrisy and patriotic orations about its sanctity.

The most surprising of all the Lincoln myths is, I think,

the one which makes him appear deeply religious. All the substantial evidence leads one to a directly contrary opinion. W. H. Herndon, who was Lincoln's law partner, says:

In 1835 Mr. Lincoln wrote a book on infidelity and intended to have it published but Hill, believing that if the book should be published it would kill Lincoln as a politician, threw it into a stove and it went up in smoke and ashes before Lincoln could seize it.

When Mr. Lincoln became a candidate for the Legislature he was accused of being an infidel and he never denied it. He was accused of saying Jesus was not the Son of God, and he never denied it.

And Ward H. Lamon, who was Lincoln's closest friend, in commenting on this statement said, "Not until after Mr. Lincoln's death were any of these facts denied."

Dennis Hanks, a first cousin of Lincoln, declared that Abe would stand in front of the backwoods meeting houses in his early days and make fun of the preacher. "He frequently reproduced the sermon with a nasal twang, rolling his eyes, and all sorts of droll aggravations [exaggerations?], to the great delight of the wild fellows assembled. Sometimes he broke out with stories passably humorous and invariably vulgar."

CHAPTER XII

GRANT LEAVES GALENA FOR THE WAR

§ 1

THE South confronted the North with the insolence of poetry defying prose. The new Confederate States government began its life in a cloud of romantic prophecies. Everybody believed that "Cotton is King" —a phrase that Southern men shouted to each other as they went their ways. Think of it! There were four hundred thousand cotton factory operatives in England alone. They would all be out of work and starving if the stream of cotton should stop . . . and the Confederate States had the power to stop it. England and France must soon recognize the Confederacy. The world could not afford to let the cotton-planting South be ruined.

These were mere dreams, but the leading minds of the Confederacy considered them facts.

The high intelligence of the South at the breaking out of the war was provincial in its limitations, deficient in economic knowledge, and almost entirely ignorant of the motivating forces of the modern world. The Confederate Government stopped the exportation of cotton absolutely. The purpose of this measure was to force England to recognize the new government, but the English mill-owners had cotton enough already to keep their factories going for a year. The last thing in the world that English cotton-spinners wanted at that time was to have the cotton trade opened again. They were making fortunes hand over fist, as the price of raw cotton went up day by day—together with the price of cotton cloth—while the wages of labor remained at a standstill. There was no scarcity of cotton in England until 1862. During the latter part of 1861 cargoes of cotton were actually sent back from England and sold in New York.

The Confederate States copied the United States Constitution bodily and took it for their own, with a few interpolated clauses. One of these added clauses made property in slaves a constitutional right, but the importation of African negroes was forbidden. The levying of a tariff "to promote or foster any branch of industry," or for any other purpose except to provide revenue, was declared unconstitutional.

In the center of things sat Jefferson Davis, President of the Confederate States, "a slight, light figure, little exceeding middle height," holding himself erect and straight in his chair. "He was dressed in a rustic suit of slate-colored stuff," says W. H. Russell, correspondent of the London *Times*, "with a black silk handkerchief around his neck; his manner is plain, and rather reserved and drastic; his head is well-formed, with a fine full forehead, square and high. . . . The expression of his face is anxious; he has a very haggard, careworn, and pain-drawn look, though no trace of anything but the utmost confidence and the greatest decision could be detected in his conversation."

Davis was a scholarly, bookish man who appears to have learned everything he knew in a library, although he had been in public life for more than twenty years, and had met almost everybody of importance in the United States. He believed in the power of words; of phrases; in sharp, subtle interpretations of the simplest social phenomena. He was the kind of man who thinks that when a problem is once solved on paper the job is nearly done. He reminds me of Charles Sumner in many ways. Both Davis and Sumner were idealists—or visionaries, I should say—and both of them played with words as if words were things. They were both incurable neurotics, moody and irritable, and both were men of culture.

In the presence of Jefferson Davis one became hypnotized by the high and noble quality of his mind. He dealt habitually in philosophical generalizations, pleasant to contemplate, but rather remote from the sweat and worry of life. His ideas were the regurgitations of ancient thought, put in precise and elegant form. He could talk with a fiery and cultured earnestness on almost any subject: On Homer, on loggerhead turtles, on astronomy, on Roman law, on cowhides, on the Italian poets, on the American Revolution; yet everything he said seemed to be rigid, definite and settled for good. In his mind there was neither flexibility nor humor. He did not argue with people; he gave them information and set them right. He possessed

> "All things except success, all honesty
> Except the ultimate honesty of the earth,
> All talents but the genius of the sun."

No wonder he looked careworn in the early spring of 1861, for the secession movement was holding together by the thinnest of threads, and threatened to go to pieces at any time, notwithstanding the confident assertions of its leaders. Lincoln, who understood the common mind far better than Davis, or any other public man of the time, said: "It may well be questioned whether there is to-day a majority of the legally qualified voters of any state, except perhaps South Carolina, in favor of disunion. There is much reason to believe that the Union men are the majority in many, if not in every other one, of the so-called seceded states." Virginia, North Carolina, Tennessee and Arkansas had not yet left the Union. In Louisiana the question of secession had been put to a popular vote, and on this show-down it had a majority of only three thousand . . . twenty thousand for secession and seventeen thousand against it. In Alabama and Georgia the secession leaders had not dared to risk the issue by a vote of the people. Those states were taken out of the Union by conventions which were skillfully manipulated.

§ 2

The confusion of ideas and impulses in the South was equaled by the hysterical state of the North in the face of actual secession.

The abolitionists, or most of them, thought that nothing at all ought to be done to bring back the seceded states. They felt that the Northern people should thank God that secession had helped the Union to get rid of slavery. Horace Greeley wrote ponderously in the New York *Tribune* that secession was justifiable, and that he was glad the slave states were saying good-by. Wendell Phillips delivered an impassioned, erratic speech in which he declared that a war against the South could end only in disaster. The people of the North would not fight, he said, and the only result of a war would be the conquest of the North by the South, with slavery fastened on the country forever.

New York City was a center of disunion sentiment. Its mayor, Fernando Wood, proposed in black and white that, in case of hostilities, the metropolis should dissociate itself from the Union and become a free and neutral city. The bankers and politicians whom W. H. Russell met in New York on his arrival from England held similar views. "They told me," he wrote in the London *Times*, "that the majority of the people of New York, and all the respectable people, were disgusted at the election of such a fellow as Lincoln to be President, and would back the Southern states if it came to a split."

Lincoln had, at this time, only one plank in his personal platform; he was for the preservation of the Union. He said, "If I could save the Union by emancipating all the slaves I would do so; if I could save it by emancipating none of them

I would do it; if I could save it by emancipating some and not others, I would do that too."

That sounds plain and forthright; it might have been made the basis of a get-together program. But as a statesman Lincoln was extremely inept during the early part of his administration. He was inexperienced in statecraft and was surrounded by people whom he did not know. At that period—and later even after he had learned the business of being President—he was hesitating and evasive. He liked to express himself indirectly and by roundabout methods. His favorite method of conveying an idea was to relate an anecdote that included what he wanted to say, but left him uncommitted to anything definite.

I do not mean to imply that he was two-faced or hypocritical; he was far too great a man to be a hypocrite. The essential feature of his character is that he was not a leader of men, but a highly sensitive reflector of public opinion. Whenever he felt that he had public opinion at his back his indecisiveness vanished.

Jesse Macy, in his *Political Parties in the United States*, sums up Lincoln's character admirably. He says:

> Lincoln was thoroughly original and peculiar in his genuine and controlling belief in democracy. Thousands before him had professed to believe in it, tens of thousands had hoped that the democratic theory would prove the correct one, millions had traditionally accepted the name of democrat, but few indeed had been the men who really believed in democracy as did Abraham Lincoln. . . . The mature, ripened political judgment of the people he accepted as absolutely final. In that type of democracy in which Lincoln believed, what the people actually think becomes for the statesman the ultimate determining fact.

His most outstanding defect was his inability to dominate, to take command, to make his voice be heard from the sky.

Before he could do anything effective he had to wait for public opinion to crystallize. If he had been a born leader of men like Lenin or Mussolini it is possible that he might have saved the Union without a civil war. Lincoln did not have a leader's capacity at that time. He had no definite plan. Hesitating and afraid to move, he talked in vague abstractions about saving the Union, and refused to receive the Confederate commissioners for fear that such an act on his part would be considered a tacit recognition of the Confederate States.

In these finicky questions of the hour he was often at fault, but how clear and vital was his foresight in its larger range! To preserve the Union at all costs . . . an idea that was in line with the progress of the world, with the future of humanity. Is there a single ex-Confederate living to-day, or the descendant of one, who thinks that the United States ought to be two nations instead of one?

On the other hand, the new-born Confederate States was almost on the point of disintegration. "You'll have to sprinkle blood in the faces of the people of Alabama," said a prominent citizen of that state to Jefferson Davis, "or Alabama will be out of the Confederacy in ten days."

Eventually Jefferson Davis and his cabinet, sitting uneasily in a jungle of conjecture, decided to do a little blood-sprinkling. The Lincoln government had refused to give up Fort Sumter, in Charleston harbor, and it was held precariously by seventy-odd men under Major Robert Anderson. It was on Confederate territory, said Davis and his advisers, so why not fire on it, force its surrender, and prove to the world that the Southern Confederacy has the vitality to act and the stamina to carry things through, regardless of consequences?

It seemed to the intelligence of the South that there could be nothing whatever for the Northern people to fight about. They wanted to get rid of slavery. Well, they had got rid of it. The Confederate States had no intention of invading Northern territory, nor of interfering in Northern affairs.

Then, what motive was there to induce Northern men to risk their lives? Of course, the idea of preserving the Union, there was that . . . but would men fight for such a cloudy abstraction? Could the uncouth Lincoln drag a whole nation into war on such a flimsy pretext?

In this, as in all wars, most of the actual fighting was done by poor people who had nothing at stake and who would not benefit in any way from its outcome. Or, as Grant himself said, "When wars come, they fall upon the many, the producing class, who are the sufferers." What conceivable difference could it make to a mechanic in Philadelphia or New Haven if slavery existed in fifteen states of the Union? Brotherhood of man, we may say at a guess; maybe that was the Northern working man's reason for going into the war. Not at all—there was no brotherhood idea in it. Northern laborers detested the negro; they would not work with him when he came to the North; they kept him out of all the well-paid jobs; they wanted him to remain in the South.

But if the white man of the North had little or nothing to fight about, what shall we say of the Southern poor whites who poured out their blood so lavishly on a hundred battlefields that slavery might be perpetuated? The laboring man of the South was already reduced nearly to the negro's level through illiteracy and peasant poverty, and even the slaves called him "po' white trash." If it seems incredible that he should have taken up arms to maintain such a state of affairs, we must remember that society is a living fabric held together by the connective tissue of tradition, heritage and association. The people in a community are bound to one another by invisible ropes.

§ 3

The bombardment of Fort Sumter, which began on April 12, 1861, was a theatrical episode. Though thousands of shells curved beautifully in the sky, and the houses of Charleston trembled with the thunder of the guns, not a man on either side was killed or wounded.

There came very near being one casualty, however. A Confederate officer who went with others to the fort in a rowboat to demand its surrender saw a bottle on Major Anderson's desk and thought it contained brandy, but what it actually held was some kind of medicinal poison. The officer, elated doubtless by the situation, took a good long drink. Meanwhile the wooden buildings in the fort were burning, the entire place was filled with acrid smoke, and there was some fear that the magazine would explode. Eventually the fire was extinguished, the officer's stomach was pumped out, the fort surrendered, and Major Anderson was rowed over to Confederate headquarters to dine with General Beauregard.

That night in Charleston there were cheering mobs . . . brass bands . . . champagne . . . sonorous speeches from balconies . . . beautiful ladies waving hands to a street full of bayonets . . . souvenirs . . . palmetto cockades . . . crowded barrooms. All night the urgent, overflowing wires carried the news to cities and towns in every part of the country.

The Charleston newspapers compared the event to the Boston Tea Party; but the Northern editors thought it resembled more closely the treason of Benedict Arnold.

Next day the Northern states blossomed into flags and loyal resolutions. Stores were closed; people covered the fronts of their houses with the Star Spangled Banner; and the newspapers, appearing in special editions, spread a hundred insane rumors. Mayor Wood, of New York City, sensing the turn of the tide, hurriedly composed a proclamation of "ringing and sturdy patriotism." If his patriotism had been a little more ringing and sturdy a few weeks before he might have helped to avert the Civil War.

Then came a stream of refugees—Northerners who had been in Charleston at the time of the bombardment. Disheveled, wild-eyed people who talked as fast as they could and expanded their stories with each repetition. One of them whose tale appeared in the New York *Herald* declared that he was in a Confederate battery and witnessed the terrible execution that Fort Sumter's guns had done among the Confederates. He said that he saw twenty-nine dead men. Another eyewitness furnished even more agreeable testimony to the readers of the New York *Tribune*. He said he stood on a wharf and saw the dead brought in. There were two hundred of them . . . that is, he counted up to two hundred and then had to catch the train for New York.

These lies seem rather dull, I know, when compared with the great inspirational lies of the World War. But they were good for their day, and as the Civil War progressed the art of lying improved and became better organized.

One of the favorite Southern lies was that Hannibal Hamlin, vice-president in the Lincoln administration, was a negro. In the first year of the war it was freely used by Confederate orators to encourage the enlistment of poor whites in the Southern army.

A Northern lie of great potency was that the Southern troops butchered their prisoners. Many officers in the Northern army helped to circulate this falsehood for the reason that a considerable proportion of the soldiers in the Northern armies were foreigners—mainly German and Irish—who had enlisted for pay. These foreign-born troops cared little or nothing about the issues behind the war, and there was a feeling among the officers that they allowed themselves to be too easily captured. So they were told that the Confederates were bloodthirsty villains who carried bowie knives for the purpose of cutting their prisoners' throats.

The Kentucky soldiers in the Confederate army spread a wonderful fable which survives even to this day. They said that Abraham Lincoln was an illegitimate half-brother of Jefferson Davis. According to the story Davis's father—well-to-do

Kentucky planter—ran across poor Nancy Hanks, Lincoln's mother, seduced her and begat Abraham Lincoln. Since the war this yarn has been run down to the last raveling of its thread, and there is not the smallest trace of probability in it. But millions believed it during the Civil War, and thousands still believe it.

The attack on Fort Sumter did what the Confederate leaders expected it to do. It unified the South; but it also unified the North.

The lagging states of Virginia, Tennessee, Arkansas and North Carolina seceded. Maryland attempted to secede, and would have gone out of the Union forthwith if the Lincoln government had not put the entire state legislature under arrest. Missouri was counted on absolutely by the Confederates, but to their surprise the Union sentiment turned out to be too strong. The Kentuckians tried to play the impossible rôle of neutrals.

The eleven states that formed the Confederacy made up a solid block of territory that was enormous in size. From the Potomac river it ran southwestward sixteen hundred miles to the Mexican border.

§ 4

Now the grim Fates are no longer absorbed in casting their malign magic about Ulysses. Their dry whispering has come to an end. They have turned Grant's somber page and are poring over other tortured destinies.

Along the roads of the Future come the shimmering bearers of Good Fortune, with wreaths on their brows and laurel trailing in their hands.

But Grant knows it not; the trumpet of a new day has not yet sounded in his ears. The sunlight touches the hills, and the swift runners are on their way, while he sits fingering the buttons of his threadbare coat.

§ 5

Grant thought, like nearly everybody else, that the war would be over in three months. The whole affair was so far removed from common sense, so fantastic even to those who were taking part in it, that men could not bring themselves to a realization of its disastrous magnitude. Grant wrote to his father on May 6, 1861: "My own opinion is that this war will be but of short duration . . . a few decisive victories in some of the Southern parts will send the secession army howling, and the leaders in the rebellion will flee the country. . . . Negroes will depreciate so rapidly in value that nobody will want to own them." Then he added this interesting comment:

The negro will never disturb this country again. The worst that is to be apprehended for him is now: he may revolt and cause more destruction than any Northern man, except it be the ultra-abolitionist, wants to see. A Northern army may be required in the next ninety days to go South to suppress a negro insurrection.

In a week or two after the fall of Sumter we find Grant drilling the Galena volunteers—a crowd of husky youths who called themselves the Jo Daviess Guards. He drifted into this duty; he was by nature a drifter. He had drifted into West Point, drifted into the army, drifted out of it, drifted in and out of half a dozen hopeless occupations. He drilled the local company because they asked him to . . . and they asked him because there was nobody else to do it. He was the only man in Galena who had the training of a regular army officer. One wonders why he was not made captain of the company, and his own explanation is not very satisfactory. The officers of volunteer companies—at the beginning of the war—were elected by the soldiers. He says in his *Memoirs:* "I declined the captaincy before the balloting, but announced that I would aid the company in every way I could and would be found in the service in some position if there should be a war."

I am sure that he did decline the captaincy before the balloting commenced; and I am equally sure that the reason he declined to be a candidate was because he thought he would not be elected. He was known in Galena as a broken-down man who was loose about money obligations and who drank too much. I do not think that this reputation was justified, for I know how easily bad reputations are acquired in small towns. He was out of luck and poor; he was convicted on his appearance of the unpardonable crime of poverty. Besides, it was known in Galena that he was held in contempt by his up-and-coming brothers of the leather store.

He drilled the company, taught the officers their duties, and showed the patriotic women how to make uniforms for the young men. He was in hourly demand . . . people running to him to ask how to do this and that.

But the honor and adulation went to others. When the Jo Daviess Guards departed for Springfield, to be turned over to the state authorities, there was a tremendous stir in Galena —blaring music and nodding plumes. Grant went with the company to Springfield, but the captain whom he had taught was in command. Grant tagged along behind the company unnoticed, in his worn citizen's clothes, a grip-sack in his hand and a pipe in his mouth.

In the light of history what a dramatic spectacle that was! The pompous captain and his bright company, the men with bouquets in their gun-barrels . . . the clapping of hands and the waving of handkerchiefs . . . the rippling flags and the cheering. And behind this flash of color comes the common-looking man who is destined to command all the armies, to end the war, to be President of the United States, and to make Galena itself a place that is mentioned in books.

CHAPTER XIII

MEN OF PROMISE

§ 1

IN the anxious days of 1861 the American nation turned to its Men of Promise. There were many of them. General George B. McClellan, a scientific soldier who was right up to the mark in military scholarship, was a man of promise. The American people hugged him to their breast. The newspapers said that with McClellan in the saddle the back of the rebellion would be broken in a few months. He was more popular than Lincoln—and he possessed all the technique of war. People nicknamed him "The Little Napoleon."

The trouble with McClellan was that, although he knew all about soldiering, he was not made by nature to be a soldier. He knew how to organize armies, how to make friends with his men and how to plan campaigns, but he could not win battles. He could do everything else about war except just that. He was like a man who understands everything about an automobile from radiator to differential, yet cannot drive one. To win battles a man must have something of the rowdy at the bottom of his nature. He must be willing to mix things up generally, to have dead men and destruction on every side. McClellan could not bear the sight of dead men, or bloody men, and that put him at a disadvantage.

The most promising of all the men of promise was Colonel Robert E. Lee of Virginia. He was considered the coming soldier of that era. Every one looked upon him as the natural successor to the aged General Scott. His father had been one of George Washington's trusted lieutenants, and Lee himself had married Martha Washington's great-granddaughter.

When Virginia seceded Colonel Lee walked into Scott's office and resigned his commission.

"But . . ." General Scott stammered, astonished . . . and behind this *but* there were other *buts*, and a torrent of reasons why Lee ought to remain in the Union army. He was an emancipationist, and had long ago liberated his own slaves. He did not believe in slavery, and said that if he had the power he would free every slave in the South if such an act would prevent the war. The name he gave to secession was "anarchy." Yet there he was, going into the Confederate service, and destined to become the South's great general. "I cannot take up arms against my own state," he said.

This attitude of narrow patriotism had a thousand counterparts. Consider William Tecumseh Sherman, for example. He was a native of Ohio, but when the war began he was the commandant of the state military academy of Louisiana. He was opposed to abolition. In December, 1859, he wrote, "I would not if I could abolish or modify slavery," and we find him writing—on July 10, 1860:

> All the Congresses on earth can't make the negro anything else than what he is; he must be subject to the white man, or he must amalgamate or be destroyed. Two such races cannot live in harmony save as master and slave.

On July 31, 1862, he was still of the opinion that negroes ought to be slaves. "When negroes are liberated either they or their masters must perish," he wrote. "They cannot exist together except in their present relation." Nevertheless, Sherman promptly gave up his Louisiana job, went back to Ohio and entered the Union army. Next to Grant, he accomplished more than any other Union general in conquering the Confederacy.

When we contemplate these contradictions, we find ourselves

wondering if there is really any sense in the world, or is it—as John Adams thought it was—merely a large lunatic asylum?

§ 2

A great mind and a fine soul are unnecessary baggage among the qualities that go into the making of a successful general. War is an anachronism in the modern world, a survival from primitive society. It has no more place in the complex modern social structure than a dinosaur has in a drawing room. The most successful generals are primitive men, whose opinions on everything outside of war and soldiers are often—and, indeed, generally—extremely naïve and childish.

Breadth of vision in a highly placed military man is usually fatal to its possessor's reputation. Cultured men, such as McClellan and Beauregard—men with fine and delicate minds —generally fall down somewhere on the road to military fame. They know too much, and they are too compassionate, too thoughtful and too sympathetic. They lack the knock-down energy, the heat, the obstinacy, that are necessary to success in war.

Grant, like Lee and Sherman, was fitted by nature and temperament for meeting the problems of actual warfare, though he did not cut much of a figure on dress parade. And he was not considered one of the men of promise in the early months of 1861. He was so unpromising, indeed, that he had considerable difficulty in getting into service at all, despite the frantic demand for trained officers.

With a letter of introduction in his hand he worked his way through the jostling crowd that surrounded the governor's office at Springfield. Grant hoped to have a talk with the governor, and offer his services to the state, but he might as well have expected to make himself heard in a cyclone. The place was full—day after day, of nervous and aggressive office-seekers, tobacco-chewers, and men with flasks in their pockets.

Grant had made up his mind to go back to Galena when the governor, who had met him once, saw him standing dejectedly in a hotel lobby. "Come to my office to-morrow, Captain Grant," said the governor, "and maybe I can find something for you to do."

It was very disappointing to Grant, the work that the governor found for him to do. He was set at the task of ruling forms in the adjutant-general's office. Any neat-handed lad of sixteen could have done it just as well.

In the meantime, the governor was distributing military commissions right and left to men who knew nothing whatever about army organization. These untrained officers got in the habit of coming to Grant and asking him what to do. He became a sort of military encyclopedia in the state-house.

Years after the war he told the Duke of Cambridge that he volunteered only because of a sense of duty. The government had educated him, and he thought that he owed it some return for his education. "I never liked service in the army. I did not wish to go to West Point. My father had to use his authority to make me go," he continued. "I never went into a battle willingly or with enthusiasm, and I never want to command another army."

In following the impulse of duty he wrote to the War Department at Washington early in 1861, stated who he was, and said that he thought himself competent to command a regiment, "if the President in his judgment should see fit to intrust one to me."

There was no reply to this letter. After the war it was found among a mass of miscellaneous papers in the Adjutant-General's office. Probably no one in authority ever saw it.

A drill-master was needed at Camp Yates, near Springfield. Governor Yates thought of the meek-looking man who sat ruling forms in his office, so Grant went out to the camp and tried to teach military habits to a crowd of disorderly recruits.

He did well at it . . . so well that reports came back to the governor of the drill-master's excellent work.

But he made a rather sorry figure on the parade ground, as he had no uniform, nor the money to buy one. The only mark of military distinction about him was a rusty cavalry saber strapped around his waist. He had found this sword among the discarded articles in the state arsenal.

About the middle of May he was sent by the governor to muster in a new regiment at Mattoon—a small town near the center of the state. This regiment—the Twenty-first Illinois Volunteers—had been handled so incompetently that it was degenerating into an armed mob. Its overlord was Colonel Goode, a military adventurer of the swashbuckler kind, who had a habit of calling sentinels off their posts to drink whisky with him. Grant stayed with the regiment a few days, did whatever he could to improve its discipline, and made a great impression on the junior officers.

Now he is back in Springfield; the mustering in of the volunteers has been done; the forms are all ruled, and there is nothing else for Captain Grant to do. He is once more out of a job. The Civil War is beginning; troops are moving to the front, and the forlorn Grant is only a spectator standing on the street and watching them go by. "It is strange," he said to a friend, "that a man of my experience and education cannot secure a command."

He was at the end of his money, too. Julia remained in the little house in Galena with her four children, living on grudging subsidies advanced by Grant's brothers at the leather store.

About the middle of June he went to visit his father, who lived at Covington, in Kentucky, just across the Ohio river from Cincinnati. His object was to borrow money; also probably to get his father to use some political influence in his behalf. But the old man was testy and irritable, and inclined to let Ulysses shift for himself.

While he was at Covington it occurred to Grant that there

might be a place for him on General McClellan's staff, so he crossed over to Cincinnati, where McClellan's headquarters were at that time, and sat for several days—hours on end—waiting for the great man to see him. He had known McClellan at West Point and in Mexico. But the general was always out, or busy, or something, so Grant finally gave up the attempt.

Meanwhile things were happening at Springfield. The officers of the Twenty-first Illinois had come to the conclusion that they would not serve under the blustering Colonel Goode, and a committee of officers had gone to the governor with most serious back-biting intentions. They said they would resign if they could not have a better colonel.

"But he's the best colonel I've got," said Governor Yates. "Whom shall I appoint in his place?"

Somebody suggested Captain Grant, and most of the officers agreed with the suggestion. "It shall be Captain Grant," the governor decided, and a telegram was sent immediately to Covington inviting Grant to come back with the rank of colonel of volunteers.

When Grant took command the regiment had become so rowdy and insubordinate that it was a terror to the citizens in the neighborhood. General John E. Smith wrote:

> I shall never forget the scene when his men first saw him. Grant was dressed in citizen's clothes, an old coat worn out at the elbows, and a badly damaged hat. His men, though ragged and barefooted themselves, had formed a high estimate of what a colonel should be, and when Grant walked in among them, they began making fun of him. . . . One of them, to show off to the others, got behind his back and commenced sparring at him, and while he was doing this another gave him such a push that he hit Grant between the shoulders.

"They're an unruly lot," one of the governor's aides remarked. "Do you think you can manage them?"

"Oh, yes, I think I can manage them," Grant replied in his quiet, even tone.

Within a week he had scraped off the regiment's hard crust, and found that there was nothing underneath but a lot of good-natured farm youths, full of high spirits and a little rough. He began to enforce discipline, and camp life took on some of the pleasant amenities of a Sunday School picnic. The men spoke to one another politely without calling on Jesus Christ or using double-damned oaths. They even saluted the officers now and then. That had been brought about in a week; in a month he had a model regiment.

How was it done? The method was simple; Grant's ways were invariably simple ways. He reformed this rough regiment by being rougher than any other man in it. Men who started disorderly rows were picked up by the scruff of their necks and thrown pell-mell into the guard-house. Those who used insolent language to their officers were tied to posts and kept tied up all day. One day the morning roll-call was an hour late; the men got up as they pleased. That day Grant stopped all rations; there was no breakfast, dinner or supper.

The regimental "bad man"—known by his nickname of "Mexico"—swaggered drunk before the commander's tent, and dared anybody to touch him. Grant had him tied up to a post. "For every minute I stand here I'll have an ounce of your blood," the boisterous "Mexico" shouted at his colonel. Grant turned around and said to a sergeant, "Put a gag in that man's mouth." This was done. When the time came to let "Mexico" loose, Colonel Grant untied him with his own hands. "Now salute me and go to your quarters," he said. "Mexico" saluted mournfully and walked away without a word.

Straightening out the regiment was not such a hard job for Grant, but there was a tougher problem on his hands. How in the world was he to get a uniform, and a horse? Officers were supposed to furnish their own equipment; they were supposed to have some financial resources. Grant was penniless. How could he insist on his officers appearing properly dressed if he were not properly dressed himself? His father, always deaf and always thinking of money, became very deaf when his son asked him for a loan of a few hundred dollars. As for his brothers, they thought they had already done enough.

Still there remained Colonel Dent, his father-in-law. Oh, it was no use to approach him. That irate Southern gentleman was so full of rage that he did not want to look on Grant's face. He considered him a renegade, a traitor, and other things saturated with opprobrium, because Grant had gone into the Union army. "Don't talk to me about this Federal son-in-law of mine," Colonel Dent exclaimed—according to John Fenton Long. "There shall always be a plate on my table for Julia, but none for him."

Grant became a sort of social problem . . . Grant and his uniform. For two or three weeks he had to let his lieutenant-colonel conduct the regimental dress parades, for Grant possessed neither a uniform nor a horse. This was embarrassing, and subjected him to some ill-natured ridicule. Finally a Galena business man named E. A. Collins came forward and advanced enough money to purchase his equipment.

§ 3

The epic quality in Grant's career was slow in rhythm . . . heavy, sluggish . . . and without any gleam of sentimental heroism. Patrick Henry smote his breast and said, "Give me liberty or give me death"—and the world pauses to contemplate the scene. Napoleon stood on the bridge at Arcola, a heroic figure entirely surrounded by sizzling bullets.

Grant does nothing of the kind. He passes in and out among the ranks of his command, seeing that the men keep their guns clean, that they are supplied with rations and clothes, and that they are drilled with precision. He has nothing special to say; the great beating light of advertisement falls on other men, yet the tide of his career is beginning to turn. But its course is almost imperceptible in movement, like the gradual rising of the water-line on a beach.

We see him marching his command across Illinois into Missouri in search of a particularly obnoxious rebel named Colonel Thomas Harris. This Confederate colonel and his men were considered terrific fighters, though from contemporary newspaper accounts it appears that they expended most of their energy in robbing hen-roosts. Grant said in his *Memoirs*—

> As we approached the brow of the hill from which it was expected we could see Harris's camp, and possibly find his men ready formed to meet us, my heart kept getting higher and higher until it felt to me as though it was in my throat. I would have given anything then to have been back in Illinois, but I had not the moral courage to halt and consider what to do; I kept right on. When we reached a point from which the valley below was in full view I halted. The place where Harris had been encamped a few days before was still there, and the marks of a recent encampment were plainly visible, but the troops were gone. My heart resumed its place. It occurred to me at once that Harris had been as much afraid of me as I had been of him. This was a view of the question that I had never taken before; but it was one I never forgot afterwards. From that event to the close of the war, I never experienced trepidation upon confronting an enemy, though I always felt more or less anxiety. I never forgot that he had as much reason to fear my forces as I had his.

For weeks Grant's regiment wandered over the harsh Missouri roads, looking for vanishing Confederates and never finding any. Much shoe leather was worn out, but the experience did the regiment a lot of good. It helped Grant, too. He said that it was in Missouri that he learned how to handle a regiment in the field.

He might have remained in Missouri for the rest of the war,

as many officers did, engaged in bandit-hunting and inconsequential skirmishes, if the kindly Fates had not set his feet in the path that leads to glory.

Success is the product of ability multiplied by circumstance. Grant was an able soldier, but who can doubt that there were others, perhaps many others, in the Union army who were as able as he? Their careers were frittered away inconspicuously, chasing snipers in Missouri, perhaps, or drilling recruits in training camps. They never encountered the right combination of circumstances.

Grant himself said with becoming modesty: "There are many men who would have done better than I did under the circumstances in which I found myself."

While Grant was marching aimlessly through Missouri Lincoln and his cabinet were creating brigadier-generals by the dozen. These appointments were made amid the clamor of political squabbles. Mr. Elihu B. Washburne, Congressman from the northwest corner of Illinois, insisted that at least one brigadier-general ought to come from his district. He was a shrewd politician who did not want his constituents to get an impression that he had gone to sleep in Washington. That is how it happened that Grant read one day in a St. Louis newspaper that he had been made a brigadier-general.

In later years Washburne basked comfortably in the light of Grant's renown, and claimed all the credit for bringing him to the front. And Grant himself wrote to thank Washburne "for the part you have taken in giving me my present position. I think I see your hand in it. . . ."

CHAPTER XIV

GRANT AT CAIRO

§ 1

WITH this step upward in the world Grant entered a wider field of action. He had permanent head-quarters of his own at Cairo, in Illinois, and a hazily defined territory or district. His headquarters were at the Cairo Hotel, which W. H. Russell, correspondent of the London *Times*, described as "almost untenable by reason of heat and flies."

The streets and barrooms were filled with crowds of soldiers who did not know what to do with themselves. Innumerable vendors of food and trinkets had stands on the populous cor-ners—selling fried catfish, sweetish, sickly looking little cakes, and souvenirs of one kind or another. There was a holiday air about the camp, as there was about the war everywhere during its first six months.

Grant's immediate superior was Major-General John C. Frémont, in command of the department of the Missouri, with headquarters at St. Louis. Frémont was a romantic, addle-headed person who had lived for years in the show window of celebrity. He was an exhibitionist, an actor by temperament who had never happened to get on the stage.

When it came to a question of common sense Frémont's mind was as empty as a drum . . . yet he had his points. His popular title of "Pathfinder" had come to him on account of his daring explorations in the Far West. It was said that he had placed the Stars and Stripes on the highest peak of the Rockies, though unfortunately there were no motion pictures at the time to send the scene careering down the ages. Grant said of him:

> Frémont had as much state as a sovereign and was as difficult to approach. He sat in a room in full uniform with his maps before him. When you went in he would point out one line or another in a mysterious manner, never asking you to take a seat. You left without the least idea of what he meant or what he wanted you to do.

The second day after Grant assumed command at Cairo he decided to undertake a military operation . . . to occupy Paducah on the Kentucky side of the Ohio river, about forty miles above Cairo. If you are not familiar with the geography of the Ohio-Kentucky region a look at the map will show you the importance of Paducah. The Tennessee river and the Cumberland river both flow into the Ohio at or near the town. These large rivers rise far southward in Tennessee and Alabama.

It was plain to the Confederate military authorities that Union gunboats, with an army trailing behind them, might readily penetrate into the heart of Tennessee—even to Nashville, its capital city—if the Tennessee and Cumberland were not strongly fortified and defended. Consequently, they had constructed two well-made and heavily-armed forts—Fort Henry on the Tennessee and Fort Donelson on the Cumberland—at about the place where the state line separates Kentucky from Tennessee.

Then it occurred to the Confederates that as an additional defense they ought to occupy and fortify Paducah, so as to command the mouths of both rivers. A Confederate military force was on the way to Paducah when Grant decided to get there first—so he telegraphed to Frémont for permission. No reply was received. Nevertheless he put his troops on board the fleet of river steamers lying at the Cairo wharves, and later the same day he wired again to Frémont: "Unless I hear from you to the contrary, I shall move on Paducah to-night." Then he sat down and waited until nearly midnight, while his capering soldier boys played leap frog on the steamers' decks.

"I will take Paducah if I lose my commission by it," he said, and the darkened fleet moved slowly upstream.

Paducah was taken on the morning of September 6th without firing a shot. The storekeepers had closed their shops, fearful of pillage, and the streets were deserted. The citizens were at home, busily employed in hauling down the Confederate flags that were flying over the town when Grant's steamers came up the river.

The first thing Grant did was to issue a proclamation that was a perfect specimen of good sense. Here are some extracts from it:

> To the Citizens of Paducah: I have come among you, not as an enemy, but as your friend and fellow-citizen; not to injure or annoy you, but to respect the rights and defend and enforce the right of all loyal citizens. An enemy in rebellion against our common government has taken possession of and planted its guns upon the soil of Kentucky and fired upon our flag. . . . I am here to defend you against this enemy. . . . I have nothing to do with opinions. I deal only with armed rebellion and its aiders and abettors. You can pursue your usual avocations without fear or hindrance. . . .

When Lincoln read this proclamation, a few days later, he said: "The man who can write like that is fitted to command in the West."

It was a time of proclamations. Almost every general who could hold a pen felt the urge to proclaim something or other —but very few of these proclamations were as sensible as Grant's.

ABRAHAM LINCOLN

A copy of a photograph made on April 10, 1865, by Alexander Gardner, of Washington. This is Lincoln's last picture—a face of infinite suffering and pathos.

The negative was accidentally broken, and only one print was made from it.

JEFFERSON DAVIS
From a photograph made about the beginning of the Civil War

With Frémont the proclaiming habit attained the dimensions of a vice. He proclaimed this and that, and eventually he contrived to proclaim himself into a serious mess. On the last day of August, 1861, he issued a proclamation in which he took over, in effect, the functions of government. "Circumstances in my judgment," he proclaimed, "of sufficient urgency, render it necessary that the commanding general of this department should assume the administrative powers of the state."

Following this wholesale assumption he continued in paragraphs that grew in intensity. In one of them he liberated all the slaves in Missouri who were owned by people suspected of treasonable tendencies. Next, he ordered that any man—not a Federal soldier—caught with arms in his hands should be shot; and he wound up the proclamation by confiscating all the property "real and personal" of Confederates living in Missouri.

Lincoln and his cabinet were aghast when this foolish document appeared in their midst. They had been petting the border states as one pets an irritable friend . . . there were thousands of slave-owners in the Union army . . . and here, all at once, Frémont destroys the administration's policy.

A special messenger, with a letter from Lincoln, was sent to Frémont. The President asked him to withdraw the proclamation. Frémont replied, in substance, "No, you can withdraw it if you want to, but over my head."

So Lincoln removed him from command, the sensation died away, and Frémont became a political and military has-been.

Had Frémont been an able general and a wise administrator, the glowing light of his sun might have blotted out Grant's pale star. Grant would have been known only as one of Frémont's subordinates, and the credit for his victories in 1862 would have been shared—or perhaps absorbed—by the romantic Pathfinder.

§ 2

The nation went to war with gayety and boasting. Civilized white men were to kill one another like tribes of savages, and the American people was to be drenched in blood for four years, but an observer who did not know what it was all about might have thought the regiments going to the front were on their way to a carnival. They carried innumerable mascots—eagles, goats, dogs, and so on, as well as all sorts of flags.

The Confederate troops were particularly joyous. The volunteer companies gave their organizations such fierce names as "Tigers," "Wild Cats," "Lions," and "Scorpions," and for the first few months these rowdy aggregations were almost entirely beyond control. One regiment from Mississippi or Alabama—I forget which—carried a coffin at the head of its column, with the inscription: "This is for Abe Lincoln. We will bring him back in it."

Some of the Northern volunteers carried coffins, too—for Jefferson Davis. A Wisconsin regiment had no flag, but brought in its place a large and impressive American eagle, perched on a pole. This fighting bird took delight in battles. When the firing began it would rise in the air and soar over the field, uttering weird cries.

Like soldiers everywhere, both the Northern and Confederate troops sang songs from morning till night. One of the favorite Union songs was "John Brown's Body." It had a slow movement and a rich melody:

> John Brown's body lies a-mouldering in the grave,
> John Brown's body lies a-mouldering in the grave,
> John Brown's body lies a-mouldering in the grave,
> His soul is marching on!

Chorus—Glory! Glory Hallelujah!
Glory! Glory Hallelujah!
Glory! Glory Hallelujah!
His soul is marching on.

It was an interminable song, getting longer and longer as the war went on. One of its stanzas had to do with the President of the Confederacy:

We'll hang Jeff Davis to a sour apple tree,
As we go marching on.

Why they wanted to hang the gentleman to an apple tree in preference to other trees, and to a sour one, has never been made clear.

Among the patriotic songs of the day was "The Battle-Cry of Freedom," by George Frederick Root. It was more popular toward the end of the war than "John Brown's Body." It was a fierce, shouting chant, and ran like this:

Yes, we'll rally round the flag, boys, we'll rally once again,
Shouting the battle-cry of freedom,
We'll rally from the hillside, we'll gather from the plain,
Shouting the battle-cry of freedom.

Chorus—The Union forever, hurrah! boys, hurrah,
Down with the traitor, up with the star,
While we rally round the flag, boys, rally once
again,
Shouting the battle-cry of freedom.

The celebrated "Marching Through Georgia" is erroneously classed among the Civil War songs, but it was, in fact, written at the very end of the war, and not sung by the soldiers at all.

The best-known of the Southern songs is "Dixie," which is supposed to have been written by a New Englander named Albert Pike, who had settled in the South.

Equally popular at the South was "The Bonnie Blue Flag."

In wording, it expressed political philosophy as well as enthusiasm:

> We are a band of brothers, and native to the soil,
> Fighting for the property we gained by honest toil;
> And when our rights were threatened, the cry rose
>   near and far;
> Hurrah for the Bonnie Blue Flag that bears a single
>   star!

Chorus:

> Hurrah! hurrah! for the Bonnie Blue Flag that bears
>   a single star.
> As long as the Union was faithful to her trust,
> Like friends and like brothers, kind were we and just;
> But now when Northern treachery attempts our
>   rights to mar,
> We hoist on high the Bonnie Blue Flag that bears a
>   single star.

> First, gallant South Carolina nobly made the stand;
> Then came Alabama, who took her by the hand;
> Next, quickly, Mississippi, Georgia and Florida—
> All raised the flag, the Bonnie Blue Flag that bears
>   a single star.

§ 3

At the beginning of the war the fighting was localized in a dozen areas. Neither side had any conception of grand strategy. Without direction or purpose, the country had simply drifted into a civil war. Most people thought it would all end in talk. Lincoln called for 75,000 volunteers to serve only ninety days, as the general expectation was that the fighting would be over in that time.

The South possessed many natural advantages which partially offset, in a military sense, the preponderance of the

North in men and resources. Its immense self-sustaining territory was one of them. There was no vital point in the Confederate system; it had no heart; there was no place to thrust a fatal dagger. New Orleans, the largest and richest city in the Confederacy, and its greatest seaport, was captured by the Union fleet early in 1862, but the war ran right on for three years. Even if Richmond had been taken by McClellan at the same time it would not have made much difference.

The certainty of the Confederate food supply was another favorable circumstance. It was impossible to starve out the rebellious states by even the most rigid blockade as long as there were between three and four million slaves on Southern plantations. The ring of warships and bayonets deprived the people of many things to which they had been accustomed—such as coffee, spices, medicines, and nearly all manufactured articles—but the supply of basic foods could not be touched. At the end of the war there was actually more meat and bread in the Southern states than there had ever been before. The armies, and the people in the cities, were occasionally—or often—in a state of semi-starvation, but this was due to bad management and lack of transportation, and not to a lack of food in the country.

But, after all, the essential feature of the military situation was that the South was decidedly inferior in wealth and population to the North. The chance of Southern success was certain to diminish as the war was prolonged and the economic and numerical superiority of the North became gradually effective.

The population of the Confederacy at the beginning of the war was approximately 8,700,000—and of this total 3,600,000 were negroes, which leaves a Confederate white population of 5,100,000.

The best expert opinion is that there were about a million white men of military age in the Confederate States at the beginning of the war. To this sum should be added the young men who reached the age of service during the four years of the war. These are estimated at 120,000—that is, three per cent of the original total matured each year. We have here, then, an aggregate of 1,120,000 available; but we should subtract a considerable percentage—say, thirty per cent—to allow for physical disability, and for detachment on services in civil life necessary for the maintenance of society. Take off thirty per cent from 1,120,000 and you have a remainder of 784,000.

And then we must consider the half-Confederate border states. There were in the Southern armies 238 regiments from states that were nominally in the Union, such as Kentucky and Missouri, and these regiments had a strength—according to the most reliable figures—of 125,000 men. Add 125,000 to 784,000, and the total is 909,000. That would seem to have been the highest possible military power of the Confederacy.

The enlistment figures are very deceptive, for many men enlisted for short periods only, and some were enrolled three or four times. A large number of conscripted men deserted almost immediately. The only practicable method of estimating the military strength of either the Southern or Northern armies is to consider the actual number of men under arms and ready for duty on a definite date. The largest number of men on the Confederate rolls was in January, 1864, when the Southern armies had a combined strength—on paper—of 472,781 men. But of these nearly half were absent, with or without leave. General Marcus J. Wright, who made a most thorough research into this subject, said that the Confederate army was larger in June, 1862, in actual fighting strength, than at any other time. There were then approximately 340,000 men present, under arms, and ready for service. From that time the number diminished steadily until the close of the war. The number that was surrendered in 1865 and given paroles by the Union generals is known exactly; it was 174,223. But the Confederate war department estimated in September, 1864—seven months before the surrender —that there were 800,000 white males between the ages of fifteen and fifty in the seven states east of the Mississippi river. This number was subject to a deduction of 250,000—boys between fifteen and seventeen, and the physically unfit—which left a total of 550,000 who might have been brought into military service at that time.

It is clearly demonstrable, from these figures, that the South never put its full man-power in the field at any time during the war. The last-man-in-the-last-ditch conception of the Confederate defense which has been so long cherished by sentimental Southern writers is historically untenable, and out of tune with the facts.

General Lee's own letters confirm this judgment. He wrote: "Our people have not been earnest enough, have thought too much of themselves and their ease, and instead of turning out to a man, have been content to nurse themselves and their dimes. . . ."

A large section of the Southern people was opposed to the war from the start. Before the conflict came to an end their opposition grew exceedingly active. They deserted in huge numbers, evaded conscription, and organized themselves into bands to fight the enrolling officers.

The states that were distinctly Northern—not counting the border states of Kentucky, Maryland and Missouri—had a population of 18,907,000 in 1860. Half the population of these border states—say, 1,500,000—should be added to this total to obtain a correct idea of Northern man-power. The aggregate is about 20,400,000. The number of men of military age at the beginning of the war was about 4,000,000.

The Union had control of the sea, and this was an immense factor in the Southern defeat. The North could send its wheat to Europe and receive arms and other supplies in exchange. After the first year the Federal navy was strong enough to set up a blockade of the Southern ports which greatly restricted the importation of supplies.

§ 4

The Confederates attempted the impossible task of defending all points of their immense territory. The effect of this policy was to scatter their forces, and they were beaten in detail, and everywhere. Jefferson Davis was a cautious man, fearful of defeat, and afraid to take large risks. Caution is excellent in its place, though it was the last thing in the world that the Confederate States needed. Davis occupied himself with little local wars, shifting small driblets of men from one place to another.

The Confederate leaders understood clearly that the North was superior in weight of men and metal. The statesmen among them relied—for a time, at least—on the intervention of England and France, and when that hope faded they dreamed of a Democratic victory at the North in the Presidential election of 1864. They thought they could make peace with the Democrats and gain their independence.

The Confederate generals pinned their faith on the fighting quality of the Southern soldier. That was Lee's hope, and he held to it from beginning to end. The Northerner was a good fighting man, too, but my impression is that the Confederates, on the whole, were better soldiers. In numerous instances the Confederates gained victories over forces that were much superior in numbers; notably at Chancellorsville, where Lee and Jackson, with 57,000 men, defeated decisively a Union army of 97,000 men under Hooker. I do not know of any important engagement—except at Fort Donelson— where a Union army won against a numerically superior force of Confederates. And at Fort Donelson, Grant's army, smaller than that of the Confederates at the beginning, was larger at the end, because of the arrival of reënforcements.

The Confederate high command never did anything with its full strength. There was a continual puttering. Consider Lee's invasion of Pennsylvania in 1863. He took 75,000 men with him, a force that was wholly inadequate. There was at that time a Southern army in Tennessee, another one facing Grant at Vicksburg, another one in Mississippi under Johnston, besides a large number of men in forts and garrisons, yet the Confederate war department declared that Lee carried with him all the men who could be spared.

Lee, with his 75,000 men, encountered Meade at Gettysburg. Meade's army was stronger than Lee's in numbers, and it had the advantage of position. Lee was defeated, with heavy loss. If his army had been a little larger, if he had been reinforced by 50,000 of the men then in Southern garrisons, there is hardly a doubt that he would have smashed Meade hands down.

The reader may consider me presumptuous for criticizing the plans of able men who were on the ground and actually facing the conditions that existed at the time. But this attitude of dissection and criticism is precisely the correct one for a historian to take. The vision of even the most capable men who are contemporary to events is always and necessarily limited. They have not yet had time to organize the immediate past, and the future is unknown to them.

On the other hand, the historian, in looking back over the past, is in a position to observe the ultimate results of actions. History, therefore, to be worth the paper it consumes, must be a work of analysis and comment; and many a biographer who does not possess the qualities of leadership himself can nevertheless point out clearly the errors of those who were the leaders of a previous generation.

§ 5

At first the Union army and navy merely nibbled at the Confederacy, taking a bite here and there, but these nibblings were without a centralized purpose; they had no unity of pattern.

The navy did a good deal of nibbling. It captured Port Royal, a deep-water harbor on the South Carolina coast, and fortified the place; and it managed to secure Hatteras Island, off the coast of North Carolina. These were important ventures, because the occupation of such strategic points on the Southern coast kept the Confederate authorities in doubt and suspense. At any time a large Union army might have been landed at Port Royal, for the Union had full command of the sea, and this would have given an entirely different aspect to the military situation.

Lincoln and his cabinet were obsessed by the idea of capturing Richmond. One may truthfully call it an obsession, for the capture of Richmond as a place was not worth the effort. It was not in any sense an established national capital. The departments of the Confederate government camped in temporary headquarters, in buildings hastily adapted to their use. The Tredegar Iron Works, which were to the South what the Krupp works were to Germany, were located there, but after all the Tredegar concern supplied only a small portion of the arms used in the Confederate army.

As it finally did happen, the war was actually brought to a close when Richmond was taken, but one event was not the result of the other. It was merely a coincidence. The war came to an end because Sherman had broken the Confederacy in two in his march through Georgia and the Carolinas; and because Grant in 1863 had fought his way down the Mississippi, and had opened it under Union control from its source to its mouth.

The great and winning strategy of the war was created by Grant, yet it was hardly a conscious act of creation. It was a product of circumstances, and came to him instinctively. Grant's immense military ability arose from the fact that he had the vision to see the war in its larger and simpler aspects. In his mind the successful conduct of the war implied only two modes of action. One was to defeat the Confederate armies, and the other was to cut the Confederacy into separate and isolated pieces. He knew that as long as the Southern armies existed there was no use in occupying towns or places, unless such occupation would interrupt the enemy's communications or deprive his armies of sustenance. To him the war was not a war of positions, but a war of movement. We shall see him moving continually, and always toward the armies of the enemy.

As early as May, 1861, he sent to President Lincoln, through Governor Yates, a suggestion that the main attack on the Confederacy should be along the line of the Mississippi.

This piece of ordinary common sense did not find much encouragement at that time among the strategists at Washington. Yet any one may readily see that the Union possession of the great river throughout its entire length would not only isolate Texas, Arkansas and part of Louisiana from the rest of the Confederate States, but it would also provide a base for an army of invasion that might start from the Mississippi at any point and proceed eastward across the states of Mississippi, Alabama and Georgia.

Grant's success in the Mississippi basin gradually caused the Lincoln administration to realize that the Eastern campaigns had been not much more than dramatic spectacles—enacted at an enormous cost of men and money—and that the Confederacy was being broken up by the Union victories on the Mississippi. The total effect of the Union campaigns in Virginia—until Grant took command there in 1864—was merely to hold a considerable portion of the Confederate army in front of Richmond. To that extent the prolonged Union effort in Virginia had a military value. It kept the best Confederate generals and the best troops away from the Mississippi.

This situation was highly favorable to Grant's personal career. In the West he was confronted by the lesser Confederate generals, and by inferior, poorly disciplined troops. There was no Southern general in the Western region who could reach to the height of Lee's elbow; and, of course, none of the stature of Stonewall Jackson.

CHAPTER XV

THE DOMINEERING RAWLINS APPEARS

§ 1

GRANT was lucky in having over him a superior officer as inefficient as Frémont, and he was even more fortunate in having on his staff, and continually at his elbow, a young man named John A. Rawlins. As soon as Grant received his commission as brigadier-general he made Rawlins the adjutant of his brigade. Rawlins, who was then under thirty, was without military training of any kind, even in the militia.

He was a swarthy, black-eyed person, with hair as dark and wiry as an Indian's. Grant had known him only a few months. They had met for the first time in Galena, where Rawlins was the attorney for the Grants' leather store.

He was emotional in temperament, and had made a local reputation for himself as an expert jury lawyer. In turning over the musty reminiscences of the time one reads a lot about Rawlins' "flashing black eyes" and his "quivering muscles." He was in deadly earnest in everything he undertook. In his hours of relaxation he used to recite Burns' poem *A Man's a Man for a' That*. Those who heard him said that his rendition of the poem, and the thrill of his fine, sonorous voice, "lingered long in the memory." How he would have loved to intone: "My head is bloody but unbowed . . . it matters not how strait the gate, how charged with punishments the scroll, I am the master of my fate, I am the captain of my soul." It is a pity that Rawlins had passed away to another world before Henley wrote these lines.

205

He was entirely the captain of his own soul, and of any other souls that happened to be near at hand. With all his emotion he was a domineering person, and a slave to duty. He had rules, and lived up to them . . . dry, ascetic rules. The first of them was never to indulge in whisky, beer, wine or any other alcoholic beverage. He preached against the demon rum to all who would listen, and he frequently said that he would rather see a friend of his drink a glass of poison than a glass of whisky.

§ 2

But why did the military Grant ever think of putting this very unmilitary person on his staff? And why was the whisky-loving, unsystematic Grant attracted by a teetotaler who was punctual, precise and abstemious to the verge of fanaticism?

I cannot answer these questions with certainty, but perhaps they answer themselves. Grant knew his own failings. It may have been that he wanted Rawlins at his side to help him overcome them. It takes a great deal of brazen self-assurance for a man to get drunk under the frown of a cold-water prohibitionist.

In his *Memoirs* Grant merely states that he appointed Rawlins, but does not say what his reasons were. He wrote:

> He [Rawlins] was an able man, possessed of great firmness, and could say "no" so emphatically to a request which he thought should not be granted that the person he was addressing would understand at once that there was no use of pressing the matter.

Further on he says, "General Rawlins was a very useful officer in other ways than this."

Among these other unspecified ways of usefulness was that of being the keeper of Grant's conscience. One of the first things that Rawlins did upon arriving at his post was to get a pledge from Grant that he would stop drinking liquor. Nevertheless, Grant did drink, forgetful of the pledge, now and then; and there were occasions when he seems to have been quite drunk.

But this, after all, was Rawlins' minor rôle. He was a great deal more than an accusing forefinger. He was an inspirer, an energizer. He had a catalytic quality about him, like those curious chemical substances which cause other chemicals to combine without taking any part in the combination themselves. General James H. Wilson says:

> It was Rawlins, more than any other man, who aroused Grant's sensibilities and gave his actions that prompt, aggressive and unrelenting character which so distinguished them. In fact, it has been frequently and truthfully said that the two together constituted a military character of great simplicity, force and singleness of purpose, which has passed into history under the name of Grant.

Rawlins was extremely aggressive, and without much consideration for others. Charles A. Dana, who was the official observer of the War Department with Grant's army at the siege of Vicksburg, wrote of him: "He bossed everything at Grant's headquarters. He had very little respect for persons, and a rough style of conversation. I have heard him curse at Grant when, according to his judgment, the general was doing something that he thought he had better not do. . . . Without him Grant would not have been the same man."

Grant had a profound affection for his cantankerous subordinate, though his favorable opinion of Rawlins was no higher than Rawlins' opinion of himself. There was some elusive, indefinable quality in him that makes one think of Grant's father —of old Jesse Root Grant. Rawlins was fully as cocksure and as dogmatic as the elder Grant. He was a disputatious doctrinaire, over-emphatic and unafraid.

When the new brigade adjutant reached Cairo in September, 1861, the papers belonging to the brigade headquarters, says one observer, were "blowing about the streets or lying on the floor of Grant's office." It was Grant's habit, when he received a letter or a report to read it and thrust it in his pocket. In time the pockets of his blue, unbuttoned coat—stuffed with documents—came to resemble queer, distended blisters. Then he would empty out everything incontinently on a table, or throw the letters and papers into whatever receptacle was near at hand.

This was all straightened out by Captain Rawlins. With one eye on the office files, and the other on Grant's conduct, he started his military career, learning army organization by scraps, here and there.

Adam Badeau, who was Grant's military secretary, told Henry Adams (*Education of Henry Adams*, p. 264) that no one except himself and Rawlins ever understood Grant. He said, according to Adams:

> Grant appeared as an intermittent energy, immensely powerful when awake, but passive and plastic in repose. For stretches of time his mind seemed torpid. Rawlins and the others would systematically talk their ideas into it, for weeks, not directly, but by discussion among themselves, in his presence. In the end, he would announce the idea as his own, without seeming conscious of the discussion; and would give the orders to carry it out with all the energy that belonged to his nature. They could never measure his character or be sure when he would act. They could never follow a mental process in his thought. They were not sure that he did think.

The key to that word picture is, I believe, in the admission that "they could never follow a mental process in his thought." Grant's military ideas were his own—so I think—but the encouragement of Rawlins, and of Badeau, perhaps, inspired and energized him into carrying them out.

§ 3

Twenty miles below Cairo the Confederates had fortified both banks of the Mississippi. On the left bank they had erected a huge defensive work called Fort Columbus. It was the western end of the chain of forts that they had set up across the state of Kentucky.

On the right bank, opposite Columbus, at Belmont in Missouri, there was a Confederate camp, protected by an abatis of felled trees.

Now General Frémont, who had not yet been removed by President Lincoln, comes into our story again. He was attempting to drive the Confederates from Missouri, and he feared that they would be reënforced by Southern troops from Columbus and Belmont. So he instructed Grant to move down the river and "make a demonstration" against the Confederate position. Making a demonstration is a military term which means hovering about an enemy's position in force without bringing on a serious engagement.

According to Frémont's instructions Grant gathered up about three thousand men, put them on steamers and moved down the Mississippi. This was early in November, 1861. When the flotilla was a few miles above the Confederate forts Grant made up his mind to attack Belmont, instead of merely threatening it. He wrote:

> I had no orders which contemplated an attack by the national troops, nor did I intend anything of the kind when I started out from Cairo; but after we started I saw that the officers and men were elated at the prospect of at last having the opportunity of doing what they had volunteered to do—fight the enemies of their country. I did not see how I could maintain discipline, or retain the

confidence of my command, if we should return to Cairo without an effort to do something.

The Belmont adventure came within a hair's breadth of being Grant's undoing at the moment when his great career was at its sunrise. He landed his troops on the Missouri side, a few miles above Belmont, and marched down through cornfields and underbrush toward the Confederate position.

It was a disorganized fight, full of cheering, yelling and smoke. None of the troops on either side had ever been under fire before. Grant's men wasted a cartload of ammunition by firing blindly in the general direction of the enemy before they could see a single Confederate. But they carried everything before them in a spirited charge, and drove the Confederates out of their camp.

Then there was a scene of boisterous joy. The stalwart young men who composed Grant's command swarmed through the enemy's deserted camp, seizing the spoils—such as they were—and giving themselves up to clamorous exultation. The officers, too, assisted in these celebrations. Some of them dashed here and there on horseback and made patriotic speeches about their glorious cause and the wonderful achievements of the day. Whisky bottles were passed around freely. A few slain Southerners, in their coarse gray clothes, lay staring upward with dead eyes. Many of the men of Grant's command thought the war already over—that they had settled the whole thing.

It would have been quite all right if the Confederates had been really beaten, but they were not defeated at all. At that moment they were reforming their lines at the water's edge, under the cover of the river bank. Across the river, in plain sight, stood the massive earthworks and batteries of Fort Columbus. Southern officers on that side had watched the skirmish through their field glasses. They loaded two steamers full of men and started them across the river. A field battery had been captured with the camp. "Some of my men," Grant wrote, "were engaged in firing from captured guns at empty steamers down the river, out of range, cheering at every shot. I tried to get them to turn their guns upon the loaded steamers above and not so far away. My efforts were in vain."

The scattered Confederate regiments hidden under the river bank succeeded in pulling themselves together. They started off at a swift march to get between the Union steamers and Grant's exuberant troops. Grant saw this movement, but he could not get his men away from the camp. Finally he told Rawlins to have the camp set afire; and staff officers ran with flaming torches from one tent to another.

Then all of a sudden a sort of panic came upon the soldiers. "We're surrounded," they shouted, and joy dissolved instantly into sudden dismay. "Surrounded . . . what are we going to do now?" The clutter of spoils, blankets, frying pans, Confederate caps, and what not, fell from disillusioned hands and rattled on the ground.

"If we are surrounded," Grant said coolly to his startled officers, "we'll cut our way out just as we cut our way in."

They did, but it was a close shave. The disorganized mass of breathless men got to their steamers just ahead of their Confederate pursuers, and went aboard pell-mell. Grant himself was the last man to arrive. When he reached the river bank the gang planks had been taken in and the paddle wheels were beating the yellow water into foam.

Grant went into a cabin and lay down on a sofa to rest, but he was there only a moment. He got up almost immediately to see what was happening on deck. As he rose a musket ball cut cleanly through the boat's wooden side and splintered the head of the sofa where he had been lying.

And still we waste ink and paper in trying to prove that there is no such thing as luck!

Now Frémont goes; Lincoln has dropped him, and Major-General H. W. Halleck arrives at St. Louis to take his place. He summoned Grant to headquarters to discuss affairs.

Halleck was called "Old Brains" because of his look of owlish wisdom. He was, in reality, a large emptiness surrounded by an education. Military history was his specialty. He had a contempt for generals who did not know what had happened at the battle of Austerlitz. Grant had not the faintest notion of what had taken place at Austerlitz, but his hand lingered over the map of Kentucky and Tennessee. "Here," he said to Halleck, "are the Tennessee and Cumberland rivers." His finger traced them from the Ohio southward across the two states.

"Right here at the border line of Kentucky and Tennessee," he continued, "these rivers, running northward and parallel to each other, are only twelve miles apart. On the Tennessee river at this spot the enemy has Fort Henry—and due east, twelve miles away—where you see the town of Dover on the Cumberland river, he has a strongly garrisoned fort called Fort Donelson. We can put an army on a fleet of steamers, protected by gunboats, and go right up the Tennessee river to Fort Henry. I think we can take that fort in a few days; then we'll march our army across the twelve miles of land and besiege Fort Donelson."

"Yes," said Halleck dryly. He was thinking of the great subtle campaigns of the past and was bored.

"With Donelson and Henry in our hands," Grant went on, "there is nothing to prevent us from going straight to the heart of Tennessee—to Nashville, on the Cumberland river—and as far as Muscle Shoals, on the Tennessee river. Here's Muscle Shoals; you see it's on the edge of northern Alabama. When we get there we can cut the Memphis and Charleston railway, which is the enemy's main line of communication between the east and west."

Halleck turned away without making any comment, and

began to look over the papers on his desks. Grant says "I was cut short as if my plan was preposterous."

His interview with Halleck lasted about ten minutes, and left him depressed and uncertain of himself. He spent the rest of his day or two in St. Louis in looking up his acquaintances, and in paying debts. He visited his wife's family, and found the Dents more hospitable than he had expected. The Southern cause did not seem so glorious to them as it had a few months before, and they were becoming reconciled to their son-in-law. His rise had been rapid—and was not a member of their own family, Frederick Dent, Jr., also in the Union army? Under such circumstances political theory usually disappears and sentiment takes its place.

Those who had known Grant in the days of his wood-peddling and real estate ventures were a little dazed by seeing him in a brigadier-general's uniform. "Who would have dreamed of that man ever being a general?" some one said. "I knew he'd do something big," Mrs. Boggs replied. She was the wife of Boggs, the real estate man. "I knew he would be a great man some day, if he ever got a chance."

§ 4

At the close of the jovial Christmas season we find Rawlins writing frantically to Congressman Washburne. Subject: General Grant's Drinking Habits. Date: December 30, 1861. Word has reached Washington that Grant is drinking heavily, but Rawlins, who ought to know, denies everything. Nothing but gossip. He says—in part:

I will answer your inquiry fully and frankly, but first I would say unequivocally and emphatically that the statement that General Grant is drinking very hard is utterly untrue and could have originated only in malice. When I came to Cairo, General Grant was as he is to-day, a strictly total abstinence man, and I have been informed

by those who knew him well, that such has been his habit
for the last five or six years.

If he really believed that Grant had not done any drinking
"for the last five or six years" he was undoubtedly misinformed.
The total abstinence was not so completely total, after all,
as the quoted paragraph above would lead one to believe, for
Rawlins says further on that a gentleman had given Grant
a case of champagne as a present, and that the general had
drunk a few glasses, "but on neither occasion did he drink
enough to in any manner affect him." He refers Washburne
to a number of gentlemen, giving their names and standing in
the world, and asks the Congressman to inquire of them. He
wants to nail the lie to the mast of contumely, once and for all:

Have no fears; General Grant by bad habits or conduct
will never disgrace himself or you, whom he knows and
feels to be his best and warmest friend (whose unexpected
kindness toward him he will never forget and hopes some
time to be able to repay). But I say to you frankly, and I
pledge you my word for it, that should General Grant at
any time become an intemperate man or an habitual
drunkard, I will notify you immediately, will ask to be
removed from duty on his staff (kind as he has been to
me), or resign my commission.

CHAPTER XVI

THE WORLD HEARS OF GRANT

§ 1

HALLECK was a desk general. Like many intellectual men, he was fearful of his own ideas . . . afraid to put them to the test. He knew as well as Grant that Fort Henry and Fort Donelson were strategic points of great importance, but he did not think a campaign against them was feasible. That—and bad manners—accounts for his turning away coldly while Grant was outlining a plan for taking these forts.

Grant, on the contrary, was a doer rather than a thinker. Action was the essence of his military system. After the rebuff from Halleck he talked with Flag Officer Foote, who commanded the gunboat flotilla on the Mississippi, and persuaded Foote—who loved action as much as Grant himself—to join him in approaching Halleck again with a proposal for an expedition against the Confederate forts.

With the army and the navy both pulling at his coat-tails General Halleck finally agreed to the expedition against Fort Henry.

§ 2

Smoke came up the Tennessee river like an advancing black wall on the morning of February 6, 1862. The river steamers burned pitch pine under their boilers, and at a distance they made one think of a house afire. Behind the gunboats came the transports, crowded with the seventeen thousand men of Grant's army.

215

While the land forces were being put on shore three miles below the fort, Foote advanced with his vessels and opened fire. There had been a rise in the river and the ground near the fort was covered with water. Long before the troops could flounder across the half-drowned land and get within striking distance the gunboats had shot the fort to pieces, and the Stars and Stripes was flying over the place.

Grant and his staff rode into the captured works at about three o'clock in the afternoon. They found only seventy-eight prisoners. The remainder of the garrison, 2,600 in number, had been sent over to Fort Donelson before the fort surrendered. Captain Jesse Taylor, of the Confederate army, wrote:

> Here I first saw General Grant, who impressed me, at the time, as a modest, amiable, kind-hearted but resolute man. While we were at headquarters an officer came in to report that he had not as yet found any papers giving information of our forces, and, to save him further looking, I informed him that I had destroyed all the papers bearing on the subject, at which he seemed very wroth, fussily demanding, "By what authority?" Did I not know that I laid myself open to punishment, etc., etc.? Before I could reply fully, General Grant quietly broke in with, "I would be very much surprised and mortified if one of my subordinate officers should allow information which he could destroy to fall into the hands of the enemy."

"Fort Henry is ours," Grant wired Halleck; "the gunboats silenced the batteries before the investment was completed," and he added: "I shall take and destroy Fort Donelson on the 8th and return to Fort Henry."

This message sounded like news that required three cheers and a day's celebration to do it justice, but Halleck wired back that Grant should remain where he was, strengthen the defenses of Fort Henry, and await reënforcements.

Grant either disobeyed orders or did not receive this message in time—I do not know which—for he was soon on his way toward Fort Donelson. He did not take and destroy it on the 8th; the roads were too deep in mud for the troops to move, although there was a distance of only twelve miles to travel.

His army began to march on the 12th, and on the 13th he had 17,000 men in front of the formidable nest of trenches that the Confederates had established on the Cumberland river. They had more than 20,000 men in Fort Donelson. Ninety miles distant—to the east—the Confederate commander of that military district, Albert Sidney Johnston, had his headquarters at Bowling Green, with 14,000 men.

As soon as Fort Donelson was threatened General Johnston abandoned Bowling Green, but instead of going to the relief of Donelson he marched straight to Nashville. Perhaps the reason for his movement was that he thought the fort strong enough to stand up against Grant, without his assistance.

Fort Donelson, with its outlying rifle pits and redans, covered a large area. It was in the shape of a half-circle, with the flat side resting against the river. The terrain was extremely irregular—broken by hills and gorges. The work was strong and extremely difficult to approach, as its front was protected by entanglements of felled trees.

The investment of a fortified position by a besieging force smaller in numbers than the troops occupying the works is considered by competent authorities to be foolhardy in the extreme. But the foolhardiness of any military venture depends on the circumstances. In this instance Grant thought the circumstances were in his favor. He had only 17,000 men at first, though reënforcements arrived in a day or two which raised his effectives to 27,000.

The garrison in Fort Donelson was commanded by General John B. Floyd, who had been the secretary of war in Buchanan's cabinet. At that time he was under indictment in

Washington for embezzlement of public funds while at the head of the War Department. He was not guilty of this charge —the money had been taken by a subordinate—but it lay heavily on his mind.

Floyd had also been accused in the Northern press, and in Congress, of having sent large quantities of arms from Northern arsenals to the South when war became imminent and while he was in the President's cabinet. This accusation was also without a vestige of truth. It is discussed at length by Rhodes (Vol. III, p. 125) and by Channing (Vol. VI, p. 285). I give these authorities, in order that any one who loves details may look them up.

Instead of being favored in the way of arms and ammunition, the Southern arsenals had actually less than their proper quota at the outbreak of the war.

Floyd was wholly lacking in initiative and inspiration. The second in command, General Gideon J. Pillow, was even worse as a commander of men. Pillow was an irascible, supercilious know-it-all to whom it was impossible to give advice, or even to impart information. The third general in the fort was Simon B. Buckner. Perhaps you will recall him. He was in Grant's class at West Point—and it was he who had lent Grant the money to pay his hotel bills in New York when Grant was on his way home, in disgrace, from the Pacific Coast in 1854.

During the 13th the Federals extended their works around Donelson, and the Confederates behaved as if they were paralyzed.

On the same day Grant, acting with the urgent immediacy that characterized all his movements, made an attack on the fort. Not much was gained at that time, and the attack was renewed on the 14th. Then Foote's gunboats came up the river and engaged the fort's heavy batteries. All day long the sonorous tom-tom of the brazen guns echoed among the hills. The gunboats got the worst of it. Some of them were put out of action, and Flag Officer Foote was wounded.

It began to snow on the 14th. By nightfall the sleet was falling so thickly that it was not possible to recognize a man at a distance of ten feet. The thermometer touched ten degrees below zero during the night. The wind came from the west; it drove the crackling sleet before it in lines that were almost horizontal. Imagine the condition of Grant's army. The men had no tents, and they lay in blankets on the icy ground. It was impossible to cook food, to make coffee, to light a fire, in such a driving storm. Grant and his staff spent the night in a ramshackle farm-house, lying on the floor.

But if Grant's army was in bad shape, that of the Confederates was worse. They had no overcoats, and not many blankets. Men were frozen to death in both armies.

During the night the Confederate generals moved the greater part of their men and artillery from the right to the left of their position, as they had determined to make an effort to break through the Federal lines at daybreak. This movement of troops was unknown to Grant and his officers, and unsuspected. The artillery and heavy wagon trains were taken from the Confederate front in the howling storm without a sound having reached the Union outposts.

Before daybreak on the 15th a messenger came to Grant from Flag Officer Foote. The old seaman wrote that he was wounded and could not get about—would Grant be good enough to come on board his flagship and confer with him?

About the time Grant reached Foote's battered gunboat in the dim light of a wintry sunrise, with sleet still flying in the air, the Confederates began to smash their way through McClernand's division, which stood opposite them on the extreme right of the Federal position. The ground was covered with ice, and the wind of the subsiding blizzard cut like a knife. The men's hands were so numb that they could hardly load their muskets. The shrill Confederate yell rang through the icy woods, and then came the sharp crack of rifle fire and the booming of the heavy guns.

That Grant did not hear the firing is one of the inexplicable facts of history. He was only three miles away, and the roar of artillery sounded far down the river. His detractors have asserted that he smoked cigars and drank whisky in Foote's comfortable cabin until after midday, and they hint that he was drunk while aboard the flagship. On the other hand, his friends declare that he remained with Foote only two hours, and was back on shore at nine o'clock. That is Badeau's statement. But the weight of evidence leads to the conclusion that he did not return until past noon. General Lew Wallace says, "About three o'clock General Grant rode up the hill." He was absent from the battlefield while the Confederates were breaking through his lines, but the assertion that he was drunk seems to me to be pretty flimsy, for he was certainly sober, and unusually clear-headed, when he appeared on shore. Besides, Flag Officer Foote was a teetotaler of the bitterest brand. He would not allow any kind of intoxicating liquor on his vessels.

The Confederate attack tore McClernand's division to pieces. The Confederate soldiers looked grotesque with blankets and old pieces of cloth tied about them in place of overcoats, but they fought like demons. By nine o'clock the road was open, the Federal army was demoralized, and the whole Confederate garrison could have escaped. But now Floyd's asininity comes to the front. He thought that the whole of Grant's army was in retreat, and he sent silly pæans of triumph by telegraph to Richmond and Nashville. In Richmond the church bells were rung, and joyful crowds surged through the streets.

Having come to the conclusion that the enemy was defeated, Floyd—disregarding the decision of his own council of war— decided to remain on the ground. With that the last hope of saving the Confederate army disappeared.

When Grant came ashore he was met by excited, pale-faced

messengers who told him what had happened. As he rode
along his lines on his cream-colored horse he saw soldiers standing in groups, out of line, out of position . . . standing in
panicky little knots of men. There was a feeling of defeat
in the air. The generals crowded around him. "The position
on the right must be retaken at once," Grant said. In his hand
was an unlighted cigar which Foote had given him.

"There are some prisoners here," some one said, "and they
have three days' rations in their knapsacks."

"Are you sure?" Grant asked alertly.

"Absolutely. Here is one of the knapsacks." Grant looked
over the fried bacon and bread.

"Yes, their men are carrying three days' food," was his
comment. "Now I know for certain that they are trying to
cut their way out." Until then the true nature of the Confederate attack was not known. "They are trying to get
away," he continued, "so most of their army must be massed
at the left of their position. On the right of the works here"
—he pointed toward the tangle of trenches in front of him
—"there can't possibly be many men, so let's strike them right
here."

General C. F. Smith's command was ordered to advance.
Smith was a much older man than Grant. It was he who was
the commandant of cadets at West Point while Grant was
there, and at Donelson he served under his former pupil. The
charge into the Confederate works was magnificent. By sunset all the Confederate outer trenches were in Grant's hands,
and McClernand's broken lines had closed up. Floyd had
thrown away the chance of victory, and as the cold winter night
fell on the scene the Union ring of men and iron held the fort
firmly in its grip.

Now a council convenes at Floyd's headquarters . . . long,
earnest and somber. There was nothing to do but to surrender
the fort—so it seemed. It was known by the Confederate council that there were two steamers coming down the river about

daybreak, and Floyd announced that he was going to escape on them, if possible, with two regiments of Virginians. In other words, he intended to leave his own command in the lurch, and get away. Pillow said he was going, too, and thus the command fell on General Buckner. As soon as the steamers arrived Floyd and Pillow piled in them with as many men as they could hold, and departed.

§ 3

Grant was asleep in a negro shanty when a flag of truce came. Buckner wrote suggesting an armistice until noon, and "the appointment of commissioners to agree upon terms of capitulation." Grant's reply was destined to become as famous in American history as Nelson's signaled message to his fleet at Trafalgar. He sent this to Buckner:

> Yours of this date proposing armistice, and appointment of commissioners to settle terms of capitulation is just received. No terms except an unconditional and immediate surrender can be accepted. I propose to move immediately upon your works.

Buckner replied that he was compelled, "notwithstanding the brilliant success of the Confederate arms yesterday, to accept the ungenerous and unchivalrous terms which you propose."

Rather disagreeable tone all around, but it was only on paper. Within a few hours Grant and Buckner were sitting together, like old comrades again, at Buckner's headquarters, while nearly 15,000 dejected prisoners marched by and laid down their arms.

Thousands of intelligent people at the North had already come to the conclusion that nothing would come out of the war but expense and a loss of men—with Southern independence in the end—and the news of this astounding victory fell on their drooping hopes like rain on a sun-parched field.

The newspapers were filled with praise of Grant. As I turn their ragged files I catch an echo of the resounding roar of exultation that swept over the country.

Who was this Grant, who could win battles so casually; who could capture an entire army in the course of an afternoon? A Western general with U. S. as the initials of his name. What does U. S. stand for? For "Unconditional Surrender" some newspaper suggested humorously, and this struck the fancy of the American nation. For months he was known as Unconditional Surrender Grant, and "I propose to move immediately upon your works" became the motto of the Union army.

Fantastic sketches of Grant's life—made up by journalists to satisfy the public demand—appeared in the newspaper columns by the side of dispatches from the war. There were pictures of him, too, drawn from imagination or hearsay.

One effect of the victory was to give Grant the cigar habit. He said to General Horace Porter, years after the war:

> I had been a light smoker previous to the attack on Donelson. . . . In the accounts published in the papers I was represented as smoking a cigar in the midst of the conflict; and many persons, thinking, no doubt, that tobacco was my chief solace, sent me boxes of the choicest brands. . . . As many as ten thousand were soon received. I gave away all I could get rid of, but having such a quantity on hand I naturally smoked more than I would have done under ordinary circumstances, and I have continued the habit ever since.

A few days after the surrender of Donelson Grant was made a major-general by Congress, and was appointed to the command of the military department of Western Tennessee.

What a wonderful change for the better had occurred in his fortunes in the short space of twelve months! In February, 1861, he was a slipshod clerk in a Galena leather store, selling hides to saddle-makers and cobblers. There he had passed his spare time in the back of the shop, playing cards with the town loafers. He was considered a "has-been," a man who had had his chance at West Point and in the army, and had failed.

Now, in February, 1862, he is a major-general with the most brilliant victory of the year-old war to his credit. On the horizon there is the gleam of bayonets . . . and the silhouettes of marching men. He commands thousands of them —they are a moving, dynamic power under his hand, like a horse beneath its rider. His name appears in the far-away capitals of Europe; men are thinking of him; the President of the United States smiles as he fingers the terse reports of things accomplished.

§ 4

Let us consider the military results of the capture of Fort Henry and Fort Donelson.

In a direct line about seventy miles southeast of Donelson is Nashville, the capital of the state of Tennessee, and—in 1862—one of the most important supply depots of the Confederacy. I have already said that General Albert Sidney Johnston, the commander of all the Southern troops in that region, abandoned his position in Kentucky when Donelson was threatened. If he had gone directly to the relief of Fort Donelson it is highly probable that he would have saved the situation. It is even possible that, by so doing, he would have caught Grant between two fires, and might have crushed the Union army.

But he was not equal to the emergency. He sent his 14,000 men scurrying to Nashville, and was there when Donelson surrendered. His move was an unpardonable strategic error. Then he appears to have been seized by a sort of panic, and ordered Nashville to be evacuated, and the bridge across the Cumberland destroyed. The Union general Buell had followed

Hd Qrs, Army in the Field
Camp near Donelson, Feby 16ᵗʰ 1862

Gen. S. B. Buckner,
Confed. Army,

     Sir; Yours of this date proposing Armistice, and appointment of Commissioners, to settle terms of Capitulation is just received. No terms except an unconditional and immediate surrender can be accepted.

     I propose to move immediately upon your works. I Am Sir; very respectfully
your obt. Sert.
U. S. Grant
Brig Genl

GRANT'S "UNCONDITIONAL SURRENDER" MESSAGE SENT TO GENERAL
BUCKNER AT FORT DONELSON

John A. Rawlins

on his heels from Kentucky, and was in Nashville as soon as the Confederates departed. Johnston lost the whole of central Tennessee without striking a blow.

So Nashville has fallen, and Fort Columbus—that Confederate Gibraltar on the Mississippi—has fallen, too. It was impossible to hold Columbus with Grant in its rear at Donelson. The Confederates are out of Kentucky, and their line has sagged back to the heart of Tennessee.

These movements are profoundly significant; they foreshadow the eventual breaking down of the Confederacy.

But Grant is in trouble again, despite his resounding fame. He falls into trouble easily. He went up to Nashville to see how things stood, as he considered that place within his undefined department of Western Tennessee.

In the meantime Halleck wired to McClellan, who was in command of all the Union armies:

> I have had no communication from Grant all week. He left his command without my authority and went to Nashville. . . . Satisfied with his victory, he sits and enjoys it without regard to the future. I am worn out and tired with his neglect and inefficiency. General Smith is almost the only officer equal to the emergency.

The next day Halleck received this message rrom McClellan: "Generals must observe discipline as well as private soldiers. Do not hesitate to arrest him at once, if the good of the service requires it, and place General Smith in command."

Halleck, who seems to have been Grant's special kill-joy, wired back to McClellan:

> A rumor has just reached me that since the taking of Fort Donelson, General Grant has resumed his former bad habits. If so, it will account for his neglect of my often repeated orders. I do not deem it advisable to

arrest him at present, but have placed General C. F. Smith in command of the expedition up the Tennessee. I think Smith will restore order and discipline.

Grant came back to Fort Donelson in a few days and found a telegram from Halleck which read: "You will place General C. F. Smith in command of the expedition, and remain yourself at Fort Henry. Why do you not obey my orders to report strength and positions of your command?" Grant wept when he received this message and passed it sadly around for his staff to read.

It took some time to get all this straightened out. As to the charge that he had left his department without permission, Grant could only assert that he thought Nashville was in his department. It is true that his men were riotous and undisciplined—for a few days, at any rate, while celebrating their victory. He declared that he had wired Halleck daily, but through some break in the telegraph connection his messages had not reached their destination.

After awhile the whole affair was dropped and Halleck retracted his accusations. "As he acted from a praiseworthy although mistaken zeal for the public service in going to Nashville and leaving his command," he wrote to the War Department, "I respectfully recommend that no further notice be taken of it."

I have no doubt that Halleck was Grant's enemy at this time; he disliked him as a person. There may have been some slipshod dereliction of duty on Grant's part. I do not know whether there was or not—there is not sufficient evidence to be sure—but Halleck thought there was, and came to the conclusion that it was a good opportunity to get rid of Grant altogether. His plan failed, I think, because public opinion was so strongly in favor of Grant that Halleck did not dare to press his charges to a conclusion.

§ 5

From all this emerges one certain fact—and that is that Grant had no powerful friends at court. He was not in favor with the Halleck clique; McClellan was indifferent to him; Lincoln and his cabinet knew almost nothing about him. His rise came from military achievements which were too substantial to be disregarded.

CHAPTER XVII

THE SOUTH TRIES TO BE A NATION

§ 1

A DRIPPING sky, heavy with rain, covered Richmond like a gray tent on Washington's Birthday of the year 1862. It was Jefferson Davis' inaugural day. Until then he had been a provisional president, but now he was to begin his regular term of six years.

Davis stood under an awning by the side of the equestrian statue of George Washington, on the public square before the Virginia state capitol, and spoke his inaugural address to a crowd of rain-sleek umbrellas. The cold, precise voice of Davis rang out over the multitude and carried on to the crowded windows of the houses across the square. His words were sharp and metallic, like pieces of steel wire cut into even lengths. But there was no warmth in them, because there was no warmth in Davis himself. A patriot of the deepest dye, he would have given his life gladly for the ideals he represented. Yet, somehow, with all his deep conviction, he lacked the power to inspire, to electrify, to enthuse.

In words that were without wings Davis made it clear that the South did not consider itself in rebellion, except technically. The feeling in the Confederate States was that the North had departed from the ideals of our Revolutionary forefathers, and that the sacred duty of preserving them had fallen upon the Southern people. He predicted that the financial strain of carrying on the war would wreck the North.

Even before his inauguration Davis had lost most of his popularity. He was destined to lose all of it before the end of the war. Though he was censured bitterly by his Southern contemporaries, history will deal more kindly with him, for his task was really one of superhuman size.

In April, 1861, after the fall of Fort Sumter, Davis called for 100,000 volunteers, and 366,000 men responded. The whole Southern population bubbled with anticipation of the great adventure. Even those who had opposed secession volunteered by the thousands. There were not arms enough for such a large number of men, and most of them had to be sent back home.

The Confederate patriotism of most of the poor whites soon dissolved, and left nothing in its place but a sense of dull resistance to the whole enterprise. The war had turned out not to be a picnic, or a free trip to Virginia with a little shooting at frightened Yankees. To the surprise of many Southerners the North had poured forth men who would fight, and tales of misery and slaughter were related at Southern firesides.

In January, 1862, the Confederates had 318,000 men on their muster rolls, but this was not enough, and volunteering had almost come to an end. In April of that year the Confederate Congress passed its first conscription act. All able-bodied white men between the ages of 18 and 35 were made subject to the draft.

The conscription act had a supplement which consisted entirely of exemptions. Druggists were declared exempt, and thereafter any passer-by in a Southern town would come across grocery stores or hardware stores, with a tiny shelf of drugs in some remote corner . . . an exempt druggist.

Teachers were exempt if they taught at least twenty pupils. Schools sprang up in nervous haste throughout the South, and Education proceeded on her stately progress with a sprightlier step. Many teachers hired poor children to attend their schools. Blacksmiths were exempt, and so were telegraph operators, and wagon-makers, and railroad workers, and printers and public officials and factory owners. Bids of thousands of dollars were offered for clerical positions under the new government.

But the poverty-bitten small white farmer, laboring on his twenty barren acres, was not exempt. Although he owned no slaves, and would never have the means to buy any, he was expected to fight for slavery and independence . . . and man is such a fighting animal by nature, that many thousands of these men, who had nothing whatever to gain by the war, did fight heroically for the Confederacy for four years.

There was one category of exemptions which was the source of extreme bitterness. This was known colloquially as "the twenty-nigger law." Any owner of twenty slaves was allowed to claim exemption on the ground that he had to remain at home and look after his negroes. The practical effect of this provision was to exempt the wealthy, though it must be understood that many rich men—slave-owners, merchants and bankers—were in the war from its beginning to its end. They went in voluntarily, and endured all its hardships, from a sense of patriotism.

There was General Wade Hampton, of South Carolina, for example. He was one of the richest men in the South at the beginning of the war. He raised a body of cavalry, called Hampton's Legion, and equipped it at his own expense. The cost of putting it in the field was about a million dollars.

When the Federals approached his Mississippi plantation, where 4,700 bales of cotton were stored, he telegraphed from the army in Virginia to burn the cotton, which was worth approximately $1,200,000 in gold. General Hampton came out of the war without a cent of money, or a home to live in.

W. L. Fleming, in his *Civil War and Reconstruction in Alabama*, tells an interesting story of a planter who owned nineteen negroes, and was summoned before the draft board. He was an able-bodied man, it seems, of conscript age, and was ordered to the war. He went around the countryside frantically trying to procure another slave, but he was an unpopular person, and nobody in the neighborhood would help him out. Just as the enrolling officers came to get him a black woman on his plantation gave birth to a child, which made him an owner of twenty negroes. The military retired, foiled and browbeaten, while the relieved gentleman sat down on his veranda to enjoy his whisky and tobacco.

The unpopularity of the "twenty-nigger" law forced the Confederate Congress to amend it eventually so that it covered only plantations owned by single women, minors and imbeciles. On each of such plantations one white man was exempted.

The employment of substitutes was allowed, provided the men thus vicariously sent to the front were not themselves subject to the draft. This means that the substitutes had to be over thirty-five years of age, or under eighteen—or foreigners. As the war went on, and the condition of the South grew more desperate, the conscription age was raised, and finally every white man between seventeen and fifty was made subject to military service. Large sums were paid for substitutes, sometimes enough to enrich a poor family.

(The substitute system flourished at the North, too, and even more vigorously than at the South.)

Poor men could not afford to hire substitutes, and the sight of well-to-do men staying at home while substitutes took their places greatly increased the reluctance of the poor to serve. J. B. Jones—chief clerk of the Confederate war department —wrote in his always interesting *Diary*, on November 29, 1863: "The rich have contrived to get out, or keep out, and there are not enough poor men to win our independence."

The Southern woods were full of draft-evaders and deserters. They were currently known as "outliers," because they stayed away from their homes—where the enrolling officers might have found them—and had camps of their own. In time they developed an animal-like ferocity, and would shoot at a member of the local conscription board as readily as they would shoot at a rabbit. In northern Alabama eight thousand of them banded together and defeated the Confederate cavalry that was sent against them. In North Carolina a mob of draft-evaders raised the Union flag, drove away the Home Guards, and took possession of things generally. The Bureau of Conscription declared that, in the last year of the war, the number of deserters amounted to approximately one hundred thousand.

A. B. Moore, in his *Conscription and Conflict in the Confederacy,* quotes a vivid, rakish letter which was written by a deserting conscript to President Davis. It is dated at "Headquarters Scalp-Hunters, Camp Chowan, N.C.":

EXCELLENCY DAVIS: It is with feelings of undeveloped pleasure that an affectionate conscript intrusts this sheet of confiscated paper to the tender mercies of a Confederate States mail-carrier, addressed as it shall be to yourself, O Jeff, Red Jacket of the Gulf and Chief of the Six Nations—more or less. . . . To you, O Czar of all Chivalry and Khan of Cotton Tartary! he appeals for the privilege of seeking, on his own hook, a land less free—a home among the hyenas of the North. . . .

It is with intense and multifariously proud satisfaction that he gazes for the last time upon our holy flag—that symbol and sign of an adored trinity, cotton, niggers and chivalry. . . .

Elevated by their sufferings and suffrages to the highest office in the gift of the great and exceeding free people, you have held your position without a change of base, or purpose of any sort, through weary months, of war and want, and woe; and though every conscript would unite with the thousands of loyal and true men in the South in a grand old grief at your downfall, so too will they sink under the calamity of an exquisite joy when you shall have reached that eminent meridian whence all progress is perpendicular.

And now, bastard President of a political abortion, farewell. . . .

(Signed)   Norm. Harrold, of Ashe County, N.C.

This conscript expressed unquestionably the feelings of thousands of the poorer class, especially those living in the hill country, where there was not much cotton grown and slaves were few.

General Lee said that although he regretted "the sad necessity" of shooting deserters, he thought they ought to be shot, for the good of the service, and they were actually shot in batches in all the Southern armies.

Had patriotism disappeared? By no means. A large number of people was opposed to the war, perhaps a majority of Southern voters, and the deserters and draft-evaders were a multitude, but Southern patriots formed the main strength of the army, and they fought for four years with a fortitude that is unexcelled in the annals of history. There were not enough of them . . . that was all.

§ 2

Richmond seethed with the chaos of new aspirations. Before the war it had been a sleepy town where men sat quietly in the sun and drawled away the long afternoons. All of a sudden it had become a jangling, brazen city of light and color. People poured into it as water pours into a pitcher, until it was full of humanity, and overflowing. The hotels were jammed to the doors, and every other decent-looking house was filled with boarders. Swarms of men and women who wanted something drifted through the streets. Here one might see newly-made officers, conscious of their uniforms, strolling about and waiting for orders that would send them to the front, and there were wounded men from the battlefields, white-faced, stumbling awkwardly on crutches. Cat-eyed gamblers stood in groups before the barrooms, looking for easy money.

In the jostling crowds there were anxious men with documents in their hands, waiting for somebody in authority to sign them; and befrilled and jaunty prostitutes, wearing flaring skirts and saucy little hats which sat insecurely on their coils of piled-up hair; and Confederate congressmen, rotund and heavy, clad in black broadcloth, with heavy gold seals on their watch chains; and pale, careworn mothers—shawls on their shoulders and silk mitts on their hands—hoping for a sight of their beloved boys; and cotton speculators, Union spies, perfumed dandies, young girls, obsequious slaves, and hordes of newspaper men.

Through this noisy tumult ran squalid little newsboys, their hands full of printed sheets. Every one read the papers as intently as if they contained magic formulas, though they usually had nothing in them but rumors which sounded like the literary creations of a madhouse. France had decided to ally herself with the Confederacy—it was in the newspapers and must be true. The French were sending a fleet of war vessels to Charleston to break the blockade; McClellan had been killed by a stray bullet, and his army was in retreat; the Northern people were about to impeach Lincoln and remove him from the presidency; Grant had been made a prisoner—he was to be brought to Richmond that very day; a new gun that would kill a hundred Yankees at every shot had been made for the Confederacy in England and was soon to come through the blockade.

After absorbing such bright and glorious news men drifted into the cheerful barrooms, drank toasts and clasped hands. There they thought well of the world. The white-jacketed bartenders stirred about and set drinks before their eager customers. When the time came to pay huge rolls of yellow bills appeared. Before the end of the war men carried bundles of almost worthless paper money in every pocket.

The Confederate treasury went on a paper basis in February, 1861. It never issued any metallic coin. The poorly engraved treasury notes—easily counterfeited if counterfeiting had been worth while—carried on their face a promise of redemption within six months after the establishment of peace. For a few months this paper money was at par—until July, 1861—and then it began to sink in value. By September of 1862 a Confederate paper dollar was worth fifty cents in gold; by August of 1863, twelve Confederate dollars were exchanged for a dollar of real money; and a year later the ratio was twenty to one—in other words, by the middle of 1864 a Confederate dollar was worth five cents. From that time, on to the end, the decline was precipitous, and in January, 1865, the dollar was worth two cents.

Prices rose enormously, of course, but in proportion their rise was not as rapid as the decline in the value of money. People who had money could get more for it than ever before. An Englishman who lived at the Spottswood Hotel in Richmond in 1864 wrote that he was paying twenty dollars a day for his room and board, and that he had never lived so inexpensively in his life, as the cost of his living was equal to only three shillings daily in English money.

In 1864 the Oriental restaurant at Richmond was one of the celebrated eating places of the city. Its bill of fare is interesting. Among its items one finds nearly everything that appears on the menu of a good restaurant of New York to-day, even coffee at three dollars a cup—and coffee was indeed a scarce article in the South in wartime. The price of three dollars a cup figures out about fifteen cents in actual money. Ham and eggs cost three dollars and a half a portion, and champagne fifty dollars a quart.

The financial hardships of the war in the South fell chiefly on the salaried people of the towns and cities. There was always something to eat on the farms, and a kind of makeshift clothing, but as commodities rose in price those who

lived on salaries could hardly buy food enough to keep themselves alive.

On February 21, 1864, J. B. Jones wrote in his *Diary*:
"I know my ribs stick out, being covered by skin only, for the
want of sufficient food; and this is the case with many thousands of non-producers, while there is enough for all if it were
equally distributed."

His salary as chief clerk of the war department was raised
in March of that year, but his remarks were still full of gloom:
"My income," he wrote, "including Custis's [his son, also a
government clerk] is now $600 a month, or $7200 per an-
num; but we are still poor, with flour at $300 a barrel; meal,
$50 per bushel; and even fresh fish at five dollars per pound."
On March 18th he wrote: "My daughter's cat is staggering
to-day for want of animal food. Sometimes I fancy I stagger
myself. We do not average two ounces of meat daily." And
a month later he says: "To-day Custis's parrot, which has
accompanied the family in all their flight, and, it seems, will
never die, stole the cook's ounce of fat meat and gobbled it up
before it could be taken from him. He is permitted to set at
one corner of the table, and has lately acquired a fondness for
meat. The old cat goes staggering from debility, though
Fannie often gives him her share. We see neither rats nor
mice about the premises now. This is famine."

Jones went to church regularly, though he was ashamed of
his clothes. One Sunday he wrote sadly, on coming home from
church: "Every Sunday I see how shabby my clothes have
become, as every one else, almost, has a good suit in reserve.
During the week all are shabby, and hence it is not noticeable.
The wonder is that we are not naked, after wearing the same
garments three or four years . . . the rascals who make money
by the war fare sumptuously, and have their good things in
this world."

The Jones family had, nevertheless, a tiny celebration on
one salary day around the middle of 1864: "Custis resolved on

a little indulgence. So he had a couple of small saucers of ice-cream—one for his mother, costing $6; a quarter of a pound of coffee and two pounds of sugar, $25; and to-day a rice pudding, two pounds of rice, $5; one pound of sugar, $10; two quarts of milk, $5; total $51."

The cat died at last, a victim of the war. "My daughter's large cat died last night under the cherry tree," wrote the hungry department clerk, "and was buried this morning under a rose bush. I sympathize with Fannie in the grief natural on such an occasion; but really, the death of the cat in such times as these is a great relief to me, as he was maintained at a cost of not less than $200 per annum."

President Davis held a public reception, and the Joneses went. They were astounded at the fine clothes of the ladies, and the air of splendor. "I cannot imagine how they continue to dress so magnificently . . . the statures of the men, and the beauty and grace of the ladies, surpass any I have seen elsewhere, in America or Europe." Many of the ladies—he says—were in mourning for those slain in battle.

This diarist prayed daily for Southern victory, but his patriotism was mingled with civic indignation. He was greatly depressed and went home in a blue humor when some one in authority showed him a government warehouse crammed to the roof with barrels of flour and sides of bacon—enough to feed the city of Richmond for months.

On April 3, 1863, there was a noisy bread riot in Richmond. It seems to have been the spontaneous uprising of several thousand women—wives of mechanics and soldiers. They raided the bakeries, smashing windows and showcases, and taking all the bread in sight. Then the women proceeded toward the government warehouses. The mayor had the riot act read, but the famished wives were not in a mood for listening.

President Davis was summoned from his study, where he was no doubt meditating on the high problems of statecraft.

He mounted a wagon and appealed to the women to disperse. "You say you are hungry and have no money," he said to them. "Here is all I have; it is not much, but take it." He threw whatever money he had in his pocket—a few dollars— out into the crowd with a statesman-like gesture. "We do not desire to injure any one," he continued, "but this lawlessness must stop. I will give you five minutes to disperse; otherwise you will be fired on."

Thereupon the women and children went away, their arms full of bread that they had taken from the ravished bakeries.

The deeply religious quality of the Confederate people was one of their most striking characteristics. Eckenrode says: "Perhaps nowhere in the world were there so many people who believed that dancing and theater-going were cardinal sins as in the South. Lee's army was made up of Baptists, Methodists and Presbyterians; it was the most religious army since Cromwell's time. Revivals were its favorite recreation."

Many Confederate companies and regiments invariably knelt in prayer before going into battle. There were thousands of preachers in the army, serving not only as chaplains, but as officers and even as privates in the ranks. Stonewall Jackson was a religious fanatic; Lee was a moral, God-fearing Episcopalian; General Polk had been a bishop before he became a general; and even Stuart—the rollicking cavalry leader—who carried a professional banjo-player named Sweeney around with him, was a pious teetotaler. His chief relaxation was in listening to Sweeney play the banjo.

The only downright, outspoken sinner among the generals was Jubal A. Early, and his principal vice appears to have been nothing more than a fluent talent for profanity.

§ 3

The Confederate States had no financial policy in the true sense of the term. Its statesmen were inexperienced in high finance, and by the middle of the war their fiscal scheme was simply a tangled mass of figures and unwarranted assumptions.

The cash receipts from taxation and customs duties were pathetically insignificant in comparison with the immense outlay which the government was called on to make—in fact, taxation was neglected during the first two years of the war, so far as the central government was concerned, but before the end something, though not much, was realized from what was known as "the tax in kind." This was a tax levied in the form of agricultural produce; the tax collectors received hams, corn, eggs and cattle in place of money.

The government paid its expenses by issuing unlimited quantities of paper money, and by floating two or three small bond issues at a high rate of interest. The bonds—the domestic issues—were paid for in cotton, and in that manner the Confederate government accumulated about 400,000 bales of cotton which it hoped to dispose of in Europe at some later time.

Besides the domestic loans, there was one bond issue which was handled abroad by the Paris banking house of Erlanger et Compagnie—a French concern, though most of the bonds were sold in England.

The story of this Confederate foreign loan presents an extraordinary picture of sinuous finance slithering in and out through more doors than there are in a mystery drama.

One of the Erlangers—a Parisian dandy, with a shrewd sense of money, who looked as if he had been born in one of Balzac's novels—came to Richmond and conferred with Davis and the cabinet. A plan evolved. The Confederate States was to authorize a $15,000,000 bond issue which was to be sold in Europe by the Erlanger firm. The bonds were to bear interest—payable in gold or its equivalent—at the rate of seven per cent; and the tangible security behind the issue was to be the cotton owned by the Confederate government and stored in various warehouses in the Southern states. The bonds might be exchanged at any time within six months after peace between the North and South for cotton at a stated price of sixpence a pound.

As cotton was then selling in Great Britain at twenty-five pence a pound the bonds—on their face—would appear to be attractive investments if . . . but the Ifs were numerous and very self-assertive. In the first place the Confederate States might lose the war. In that case the United States government would undoubtedly confiscate the cotton, and the bondholders would be left with nothing but some pieces of crinkly paper in their hands. In the next place, the cotton was in the Southern states and not in Europe. Another point to be considered was that the price of cotton would probably fall immediately after the war was over, and the ports were opened.

The terms of the contract are interesting. The Erlangers agreed to guarantee a minimum of 77 for the bonds, and they were to get—as their profit—the difference between 77 and the actual selling price. In addition they were to be paid a commission of five per cent on the total receipts from the sale. The most that the Confederate government could expect, therefore, was approximately seventy-three dollars for every hundred dollars of face value of the loan.

The issue was a success. The loan was oversubscribed three times in the London market within two days after it was announced. This was in March, 1863. The bonds were sold at 90 per cent of their face value to the public. The Erlangers made a profit of thirteen dollars on every hundred dollars' worth of bonds, besides their five per cent commission. Most of the subscribers were under the impression that the cotton would be secure, even if the Confederacy should be defeated. A press campaign had accomplished that much. In a week or two the price of the bonds went up to 95½, which was the highest mark they ever reached.

Then a reaction set in. The price of the bonds fell steadily, day after day. The Confederate commissioners in Europe were in a state of dismay, and they allowed the Erlangers to persuade them into making a new arrangement. This supplementary agreement was intended to keep up the price in the hope of sustaining Confederate credit abroad. The Confederate commissioners allowed the Erlangers to draw on funds in their possession—the money obtained from the sale of the bonds—and use it in buying back the bonds whenever the price sagged below ninety. In short, after the Confederate commissioners had got the proceeds of the loan they turned right around and began to spend it by taking back the securities they had just sold. Their connection with the price-raising manipulation was kept a secret. The Erlangers were supposed by the public to be buying for investors.

The greater part of the funds that the loan had produced was squandered in trying to keep up the market price of the bonds. It seems to us now—as a moral certainty—that the Erlangers themselves were bearing down the market. They were evidently playing the game both ways, forcing down the price of the bonds, then buying them on their own account, and reselling them to the Confederate government.

In the final accounting the Confederate commissioners in Europe appear to have received a little more than $6,000,000 as the net proceeds of the $15,000,000 loan. This amount was expended principally in building Confederate war vessels at British ship yards (most of which never reached their destination, nor were of any service in the war), and in subsidizing European newspapers.

In July, 1863, after the news of the Confederate defeat at Gettysburg and Grant's capture of Vicksburg had reached London, the bonds went down to 65, and in December of that year they were down to 37.

All this is illuminating in view of the fact that the Confederate government would have had ample means to finance itself abroad if it had shipped its cotton crop to Europe in 1861. At that time the blockade was a mere form—the United

States did not have enough vessels to close the Southern ports —and virtually the whole of the cotton surplus could have been taken out of the country. In Europe it might have been held in warehouses, and sold gradually at high prices.

§ 4

Notwithstanding the desperate poverty that pervaded the Southern states during the war many sharp-minded people managed to acquire fortunes. There was the illicit business of trading with the enemy, for instance. All up and down the Mississippi, and around every port occupied by Union troops, Southern cotton speculators bought cotton at ten or twelve cents a pound and resold it for fifty cents a pound in gold to buyers for Northern mills. They made the trade pay both ways. They delivered cotton to the enemy at a large profit, which they invested in things needed in the South, such as salt, medicines, and manufactured goods. Their tremendous paper fortunes sometimes—or often—were used to purchase land and buildings. After the war, although Confederate money was worthless, the land that had been purchased with it still remained.

The makers of war supplies, as well as their middlemen and agents, grew fat and pompous. J. R. Anderson & Co., of Richmond, owners of the Tredegar Iron Works, chief munition plant of the Confederacy, became so wealthy that they did not know what to do with their accumulated profits. A paper mill earned 575 per cent in dividends during the war, and a woolen factory paid $530,000 on an invested capital of $200,-000. Other business concerns had large earnings.

The railroads wore themselves out in hauling troops and supplies, but while the war lasted they made enough to turn over large sums to their stockholders. The South Carolina Railroad Company paid sixteen per cent annually on its capital stock—it had never paid more than seven per cent before the war—and most Southern railway companies did equally well.

These commercial activities, as profitable as they were, can be considered, however, as only small money-changing when compared to the trade of blockade-running. There, indeed, was a princely business. The blockade-runners were swift steamers, usually sky blue in color, though some of them were camouflaged by schemes of bizarre painting. They could out-steam the Federal cruisers, and in a stern chase they quickly melted away into a thin smear of smoke on the horizon. The hazardous part of their voyages was in getting in and out of the harbors, but they managed to evade the blockading fleets by entering and leaving on dark nights. They took out cotton and brought in supplies. The profits were so large that a blockade-runner was expected to pay its own cost in two trips. Everything that came after a couple of ventures was pure profit, and some of them made many voyages. It has been suspected, since the war, that there was collusion between some of the officers of the blockading squadrons and the blockade-runners. Theodore D. Jervey, of Charleston, who has made a special study of this phase of the war, writes that among the stockholders of the companies operating blockade-runners were a number of New York people.

One of the leading concerns engaged in blockade-running was John Frasier & Company, of Charleston. By the end of 1862 this enterprise had earned a net profit of twenty million dollars—Confederate currency—worth at that time about four or five millions in gold.

Despite the incessant blockade-running the whole population—rich and poor—suffered privations that make a long and rather queer list. There was no manufactory of window glass in the South, for example, so when a window pane was once broken, it was out for good. Whitelaw Reid, who made a trip through the Southern states immediately after the war, wrote that he did not see a single whole window in any train in which he rode. The glass had all been broken, and boards had been nailed across the windows.

In some parts of the South pins were not procurable at all, and sharp thorns were used in their places. Buttons could not be had. In country districts persimmon seeds, with holes bored in them, were used in place of buttons. J. B. Jones wails in his *Diary* of the difficulty of keeping his clothes on his body. Poor people made coffee out of parched peas, and shoes were constructed weirdly of wooden soles and canvas tops. The breakage of a cup or a plate was a family catastrophe; crockery was almost ungettable at any price. There was a permanent shortage of wool, for the South was not a sheep-raising region, and carpets were taken off the floors and cut up into blankets. Sometimes they were used to make overcoats. It must have been interesting to see men going about with flowered carpet overcoats on their backs.

It was under these circumstances that the South carried on the war. At first there was an appalling deficiency of muskets, ammunition and artillery, but munition factories were established here and there, and large supplies of the most improved patterns of firearms ran past the blockade. At the end of the war the Confederates—destitute of many things—were better armed than the Northern troops.

CHAPTER XVIII

THE BATTLE OF SHILOH

§ 1

GRANT'S trouble with Halleck was over, for a time, but the Army of the Tennessee—as his command was called—had gone on its way without him. He had stood on the river bank and seen it depart, with its accompanying fleet of gunboats, up the Tennessee river, moving southward under General C. F. Smith. As the bright bayonets faded on the horizon, and the gunboats became a plume of smoke in the sky, Grant turned back to the half-deserted barracks of Fort Henry. There he sat miserably for more than two weeks, reading newspapers down to their last shred of rumor, as idle men do; reading newspapers, smoking cigars and trying not to drink liquor.

When word finally came from Halleck for him to rejoin his command the army was then at Pittsburg Landing on the Tennessee river. This place is about one hundred miles directly south of Fort Henry, and is almost exactly on the border line between Tennessee and Mississippi. At that time the Landing was nothing but a steamboat wharf and a log-house, on the west side of the river, with a steep bluff rising above it. Some two or three miles from Pittsburg Landing, in the woods, was a stark little Methodist meeting-house called Shiloh church. The battle of Shiloh gets its name from this church.

Grant's army—under Smith's command—had marched across the state of Tennessee without serious opposition. General Albert Sidney Johnston had retired before it, gathering up new regiments and brigades of Confederates as he went.

245

Nashville had been abandoned; all of central Tennessee was open to the Union army.

But on the border of Mississippi Johnston had decided to make a stand. In the agitated states of the lower South it was a critical time for the Confederate cause; it looked as if the Federals might go straight on to the Gulf unless they could be decisively beaten. General Beauregard, one of the best of the Southern tacticians, was sent out from Richmond to be Johnston's second in command. The governors of the neighboring states made unusual exertions to reënforce the Confederate army. New troops, raw in experience but eager for battle, came splashing along the half-liquid roads and entered Johnston's camp with the bands playing "Dixie" or "The Bonnie Blue Flag."

§ 2

The geography of the region is simple. Its most prominent feature is the Tennessee river, flowing northward, a muddy stream navigable for light draft steamboats. When one walks ashore at Pittsburg Landing, on the river's west bank, and climbs the bluff, one finds an undulating plateau, which in 1862 was covered with woods and small clearings. It was a puzzling sort of place, with hardly any roads. I went over the ground sixty years after the battle, and I carried away an impression of trees and blue sky, all in a jumble.

North of Pittsburg Landing, and five miles distant, is Crump's Landing, also on the west bank—and it, too, was at that time merely a place for steamboats to pause a moment.

The main body of Grant's army—about 33,000 men—was at Pittsburg Landing when he resumed command of it on March 17, 1862. But, in addition, there were about 5,000 men under General Lew Wallace—the author of *Ben Hur*—at Crump's Landing, separated from the rest of the army by five miles of bad roads and a creek which, at times, was impassable on account of floods.

Grant took up his headquarters at Savannah, on the other side of the river, and nine miles from the main body of his army. He went back and forth every day in a river steamer, going to work in the morning like a New York suburbanite, and coming home in the evening.

There is no satisfactory explanation as to why Grant did not remain with his army all the time, night and day.

General D. C. Buell, at the head of some twenty thousand men, was marching down from Nashville to reënforce Grant; and Grant says in his *Memoirs* that he went to Savannah every night so that he might meet Buell there.

This explanation hardly seems plausible, for it appears, as a matter of ordinary common sense, that the place for him to await Buell was at the Landing, where his army was. He was at Savannah only at night; suppose Buell had arrived during the day-time?

Grant was completely deceived by the Confederates. He virtually admits it himself in his account of the battle, for he declared that he had no idea they would take the offensive; he expected to attack them. And, feeling secure in that conception of the state of affairs, he considered himself justified, perhaps, in leaving the army every night and sleeping comfortably in a dry, well-kept house.

§ 3

Twenty miles southwest of Pittsburg Landing is the village of Corinth. Johnston was there with his army of 41,000 men, all the time between March 17th—when Grant took command of the Union army—and April 6th, when Johnston and his Confederates routed the Federals out of their beds in one of the most remarkable surprise attacks in the history of modern war.

Grant knew, of course, where the Confederate army was, and he should have had a fairly accurate notion of its numerical strength. It was equal to his own, and, at the time of the battle, a little superior in numbers. Then, knowing himself to be in the presence of the enemy, why did he not entrench himself and make some adequate preparation to resist an attack? He did nothing of the kind . . . his army stayed on the ground in an open camp day after day, without entrenchments, and even without having their batteries properly posted.

Grant's only explanation is that he thought his troops were more in need of drilling and maneuvers than of work with picks and spades.

And why did he leave Lew Wallace's 5,000 men at Crump's Landing, where they might be pounced upon and defeated before the main army could possibly come to their assistance? He never attempted to answer this question.

In various places in this book I have stated my opinion that Grant was a general of genuine and great ability. Any one who considers the Civil War as a whole, and studies Grant's part in it, must come, I think, to the same conclusion. How, then, may one explain his down-at-the-heel carelessness in the weeks that preceded Shiloh, and his amateurish conduct during the battle?

The reason, I think, is that he was in one of his slack periods. These seasons of almost foolish ineptitude occur to all men. Shiloh simply shows Grant at his worst. If that battle had constituted his whole military history we would know him now only as a general of small ability who appeared for a moment in the Civil War. But his career is so large that Shiloh is only an incident . . . and if we are to have a clear perspective of Grant we must look at it in that light.

It should have been apparent to any one who had his eyes open that something out of the ordinary was happening late in the afternoon of Saturday, April 5th, in the thick screen of woods in front of the Union position. Hundreds of rabbits, startled and running as fast as they could, came dashing into the Union lines; and with them ran some timid deer that paused and looked at the soldiers before turning away.

Johnston's army of forty thousand men had left Corinth and was moving into position less than two miles from Grant's outlying pickets—and this multitude of men remained there all night without anybody in authority in the Union army being aware of its presence.

Before sundown one of the Union outposts had a sharp fight with a small body of the enemy, and some prisoners were brought in. A wounded Confederate said that the whole of Johnston's army had come up. All this was reported to Sherman, as Grant had gone for the day, but Sherman made light of the matter, and expressed his opinion that there would be no attack in force.

That same evening Grant telegraphed to Halleck, "I have scarcely the faintest idea of an attack being made upon us, but will be prepared should such a thing take place."

That night the Confederate generals held a council of war. They all knew that Buell was approaching with reënforcements for Grant as fast as the legs of his men could carry them— and it was the right moment, if ever, to attack Grant—but nevertheless some of the generals counseled delay. Beauregard said the Union army was certain to be strongly entrenched. (As a matter of fact, it was not entrenched at all.) Johnston was the commander and he had to decide. "We shall attack at daylight to-morrow," he declared, as he brought his hand down on his knee with a resounding smack. "I would fight them if they were a million."

So spoke a man who was about to die, for the morrow was to be Johnston's last day on earth.

§ 4

The Southern spring had come, and the birds sang in the soft rose-gray dawn. Here and there about the Union camp a few men stirred, still heavy with sleep. The sentinels stood lazily at their posts as the pale stars faded from the sky.

Then, like the bursting of a dam, a torrent of gray-coated soldiers poured from the woods. In an instant the air was foggy with smoke, and the crackling gunfire silenced every other sound. There was no time to form companies or regiments. The divisions in the front part of the camp were swept back pell-mell, in complete disorder, and they went rushing toward the river landing like a mob dashing through a street.

The divisions encamped farthest from the attack managed to get together, and it was they who held back the rushing onslaught that threatened to sweep the Union army out of existence at a blow. They stood firm as the broken regiments passed through their lines . . . broken regiments, units hopelessly disorganized and mixed, men without arms and officers who had lost track of their commands.

But even the organized regiments had to yield. They were not strong enough—there were not enough of them—to withstand the impact of the whole of Johnston's army.

Soon the artillery began to sound, and the throbbing of the guns melted into a long, steady roll of thunder which rattled the windows of the house in which Grant had his headquarters at Savannah.

Grant was eating his breakfast when he heard the rolling thunder of the distant battle. He left the table, uneasy and downcast, and hobbled to the door. His horse had fallen on him a few days before, and his ankle was painfully swollen. "Very heavy firing, isn't it?" he remarked to the members of his staff. "I think it must be at Pittsburg Landing. Get the boat ready at once and let's be moving."

Buell had reached Savannah the evening before with a part of his army, but Grant had not seen him, although he knew of his arrival. He had sent word to Buell on the 5th that "there will be no fight at Pittsburg Landing; we will have to go to Corinth, where the rebels are fortified."

Now he was filled with misgiving, and on his limping way

to the steamboat he had sent another message to Buell, urging him to hurry to Pittsburg Landing, with all the men he had. The little steamer was soon churning upstream, Grant and his staff standing in the bow and listening to the deepening roar. The boat's nose was held against the wharf at Crump's Landing for a moment while Grant instructed Lew Wallace to start toward the scene of action. But Wallace got lost in the woods, or took a wrong road—he says that it was the road he was ordered to take—and did not join the struggling army until sundown, after the day's fighting was over.

When Grant arrived on the battlefield in the middle of the forenoon the plight of the Union army was critical, indeed. The Union left flank had been pushed back to the river, and Johnston's assault still showed no signs of abating.

About one o'clock Buell came on the field with the head of his column, but most of his reënforcements did not get on the ground until after the first day's fighting was over. Buell says:

> The face of the bluff was crowded with stragglers from the battle. The number there at different hours had been estimated at from five thousand in the morning to fifteen thousand in the evening. The number at nightfall would not have fallen short of fifteen thousand. . . . At the top of the bluff all was confusion. Men mounted and on foot, and wagons with their teams and excited drivers, all struggling to force their way closer to the river, were mixed up in apparently inextricable confusion with a battery of artillery which was standing in park without men or horses to man or move it.

He found Grant resting and nursing his swollen ankle in one of the cabins of a steamer at the landing. During the morning he had been out along his confused lines, but his presence had not made any change in the situation. The military critics, John C. Ropes among others—and Ropes knew more about war than most generals—say that Grant counted for little or nothing in the conduct of the battle.

Buell and Grant held a sort of desultory conference in the steamer's cabin. In his story of the battle Buell gives the impression that Grant seemed to be somewhat dazed by the condition of affairs. "He appeared to realize that he was beset by a pressing danger, and manifested by manner more than in words that he was relieved by my arrival. . . . Certainly there was none of that masterly confidence which has since been assumed with reference to the occasion." (*Battles and Leaders of the Civil War*, Vol. I, p. 493.)

This last sentence concerns a story that has appeared in almost all the biographies of Grant. The story is that Buell, dismayed by the outlook, asked Grant, "What preparations have you made for retreating?" To which Grant is said to have replied, "I have not yet despaired of whipping them, general."

"Of course! But if you should be whipped," Buell is supposed to have said, "how will you get your men across the river? These transports will not take more than ten thousand troops."

"If I have to retreat," Grant answered, according to the story, "ten thousand will be as many as I shall need transports for."

Buell calls this tale "ridiculous and absurd." He says that no such conversation took place, and that the contingency of a retreat was not mentioned by either of them. Notwithstanding such explicit denial, this myth has continued to exist, and probably has a good, long hearty life still ahead of it.

By sunset the Union army was on the edge of a total collapse, and it seemed to many officers of judgment who were on the spot that Grant and his entire army would be captured, or driven into the river. But Grant says that "there was, in fact, no hour during the day when I doubted the eventual defeat of the enemy."

Late in the day stragglers and prisoners brought to the Union army a rumor that General Albert Sidney Johnston had been killed. This report was soon followed by a cessation of the Confederate offensive.

The rumor was true. General Johnston had been struck in the thigh by a bullet while he was riding along his advancing lines. He bled to death from a severed artery in a few minutes while his staff, kneeling about him, searched at random for his wound. The simplest kind of first-aid surgery would have saved his life. A few moments before he was shot he had sent his staff surgeon, who was riding at his side, back to the rear to look after some wounded Union prisoners. As the unskilled young men of the staff tried in vain to staunch the flow of blood, Johnston's face became pale with the shadow of death. He clasped his brother-in-law's hand, smiled faintly, and expired.

The Confederate leadership—on Johnston's passing—fell upon Beauregard, who was a sort of Southern McClellan—a splendid organizer and planner, but lacking in the highly daring qualities that make a general a great leader in battle.

At the moment of victory Beauregard drew back, ordered the attack to cease, and ended the day. The loss of Johnston was a catastrophe of incalculable and far-reaching momentum. If Grant was at his worst at Shiloh, it is equally true that Johnston was at his best. Had he lived there is no doubt that he would have pushed his attack on to its utmost possibilities.

The night of the 6th was an utter blackness, with the rain pouring down in torrents. The disorganized Union army, without any kind of shelter, wandered like a discontented rabble about the river bank. The Confederates slept in the tents of the captured camp. But Wallace's fresh troops had come up, and all night long Buell's army streamed into the Union position.

Grant sat under a tree in the rain, trying to keep his cigar lighted. The log-house near the landing had been turned into a temporary hospital, and Grant took refuge in it for a little while, but he soon went back to his place under the tree, for he says that he could not stand the sight of the wounded, or look at the surgeons at work. I wonder why he did not go aboard one of the steamers, where there were dry cabins? Very probably he was thinking of the newspapers, and what they would say. He knew that he was in for hot criticism on the results of the day, in any event, and he did not want to see himself pictured as sleeping on a steamer while his army lay all night in the rain.

Did Grant consider a retreat while he communed with himself? I don't think he did; I do not believe that the idea of going back across the river ever occurred to him as a possible recourse. His character was extremely obstinate, and there was his superstition against turning back. I do not believe he would have retreated even if Buell and Wallace had not arrived with their reënforcements.

Deep in his nature there was a strain of fatalism. It was covered up by his stolid manner, and by the mildness of his speech, but one who studies him a long time catches glimpses of it now and then . . . a hundredth of a second's flash of a dark pool of desperation at the bottom of his character. He was a profound believer in luck—both good and bad—and after Donelson he appears to have had an abiding faith in his own lucky star. He seems to have said to himself at times, "Now I have done all I can do; let the Fates do their worst."

So he hung on, hugging the river bank, and at dawn he was sending his staff out with instructions to his generals for an immediate advance. The 25,000 fresh troops of Buell and Wallace formed the core of his attack on the Confederate position, and by the side of them he sent in his disorganized masses, hurriedly formed into impromptu companies and regiments.

The Confederates had no reënforcements, and they were worn out from their impetuous fighting of the previous day.

Slowly they were driven back all day of the 7th, and by nightfall they were in full retreat toward Corinth.

§ 5

Shiloh was the greatest battle that had ever been fought on the American continent, up to that time. Though its results were not decisive in any sense, it was unquestionably a Union victory, despite Grant's shortcomings. For a few days the Northern press was aflame with exultation—then, as the details and gossip came in, comment, analysis, criticism and vituperation began.

All the discussion revolved around Grant, and his popularity declined day by day. On April 9th the first news of the battle appeared in the New York *Tribune*. Glorious victory . . . Grant, the superb general, wins again. Hats off to Grant.

The *Tribune* of April 10th rhapsodizes eloquently. Grant's bravery commended. Marvelously courageous man. Silent man, too. Smokes lots of cigars and seldom speaks; but when he does speak his words are meaty with wisdom.

On April 11th the eulogies are rather flattened out. The Union army was surprised, says the *Tribune*. So that's the way it was. Surprised while the troops were still asleep. Grant was nine miles away. There was confusion everywhere, and cowardice. The soldiers hiding on the river bank refused to fight. The gunboats in the river saved the army from complete disaster.

By April 16th the *Tribune* had begun to thunder in earnest. Grant had no idea of the enemy's approach, yet the Union generals had been warned again and again. "An investigation should be made of the utter inefficiency and incompetency, if not the downright treachery, of the generals."

Next day there was a blazing editorial—"let us have the facts." The army was shamefully surprised. "Why does not General Grant tell the truth?"

On May 3rd the *Tribune* said: "There was no more preparation by General Grant for an attack than if he had been on a Fourth of July frolic."

The editor of the *Ohio State Journal* was at Pittsburg Landing. The *Tribune* reproduced a dispatch from him. He said that he heard much about Grant among the soldiers and little to his credit. "No respect is felt for him, and no confidence is felt in him; and his conduct was the one topic of discussion around campfires."

At that time there was a common saying among the enlisted men that "if you hit Rawlins on the head, you'll knock out Grant's brains." Grant was never very popular with the soldiers of his army. They hardly ever saw him. He remained aloof and silent, and whenever he did appear he looked like a dusty farmer wearing an unbuttoned uniform.

A. K. McClure, of Philadelphia, a nationally prominent Republican, and a strong supporter of the Lincoln administration, went down to Washington for the purpose of urging the President to remove Grant from command. McClure said that Lincoln listened to him quietly for a long time, and when he had finished sat in silent reflection. Then he shook his head and said, "No, I can't do it. I can't lose this man. He fights."

Old Jesse Root Grant, living quietly at Covington, with nothing to do but read the news of the day, fumed and raged when he saw his soldier son riddled by criticism. He could not keep out of an argument, or his hands away from pen and ink, so we find him writing letters to the newspapers, far and wide, defending his son's reputation and belittling that of other generals. These well-meant paternal activities evoked a letter from Grant to his father, in which the general showed his annoyance.

> I would write you many particulars, but you are so imprudent that I dare not trust you with them; and while on this subject let me say a word. I have not an enemy in the world who has done me so much injury as you in

your efforts in my defense. I require no defenders and for my sake let me alone. . . . You are constantly denouncing other general officers, and the inference with people naturally is that you get your impressions from me. Do nothing to correct what you have already done, but for the future keep quiet on this subject.

In the meantime the scholarly Halleck had arrived at Pittsburg Landing to take charge of things. He made Grant a kind of assistant to himself—at least, that was the understanding. Grant was called "second in command." He says in his *Memoirs* that he had become merely a spectator, and that his position was most embarrassing.

Halleck began to approach the Confederate position at Corinth at a rate of speed resembling that of a tortoise which has nothing in particular to do. The army would march two or three miles in the direction of the Confederates, throw up huge entrenchments and remain behind them for a week, while reconnoitering parties were sent out, spies came in, and information was sifted and tabulated. Swarms of fresh troops had come to Halleck's army. By the middle of May he had 120,000 men—a force about three to one larger than Beauregard's army. He could have marched straight against his opponents and smashed them without half trying.

In six weeks, after occupying successive positions, he had progressed fifteen miles, and stood at last in sight of Corinth, the flaunting stronghold of the foe—otherwise a placid little Mississippi village with some earthworks around it.

The Union army was set to work with pick and spade entrenching itself. Next morning some citizens of Corinth came out and said that there was not a Confederate soldier in the place. Beauregard had left, and his leaving had been so leisurely done that he took away not only all his men, but also every scrap of his supplies.

Of course this was funny. It made Halleck, with all his learning, look ridiculous, and the administration at Washington began to feel that something would have to be done about him.

While these elaborate maneuvers were in progress, Grant was tagging along with the army, without anything to do. He was a moody person—then as always—and such strained situations are intolerable to moody people. Yet, despite his sour discontent, he discovered a source of amusement and laughter. It was about Rawlins' horse. An army mule, tied near Rawlins' horse one night, had nibbled away the flowing tail of the handsome charger. Rawlins did not know what had happened. He thought some mischievous soldiers had shaved his horse's tail until Grant—from his profound knowledge of mules and horses—explained the occurrence. When Grant and his staff rode out every day Grant cackled with laughter at Rawlins on his shave-tail mare.

But even that comical incident was not sufficiently entertaining to relieve Grant's irritation at his neglected situation. He applied for permission to leave the department, and the permission was granted by Halleck, rather gladly, one may presume.

His things were packed, and his orderlies were taking down the tents, when Sherman came by. "Why, what's this?" Sherman asked, in astonishment.

"I'm going to leave," Grant replied. Sherman says:

> I then begged him to stay, illustrating his case by my own. Before the battle of Shiloh I had been cast down by a mere newspaper assertion of "crazy," but that single battle had given me new life. . . . I argued with him that if he went away, events would go right along, and he would be left out, whereas if he remained, some happy accident might restore him to favor and to his true place.

Grant decided to remain after his conversation with Sherman. The happy accident soon occurred. Halleck was courteously kicked upstairs. On July 10, 1862, Lincoln sent for him to come to Washington and be the general-in-chief of all the armies. Halleck had written books on strategy; he was generally supposed to have the most profound mind in the army. When such a highly esteemed man makes a mess of his job the only thing to do, according to human custom, is to promote him—so Halleck was promoted.

Halleck departed, and his departure left Grant in command.

§ 6

Grant now moved in an ever-widening circle of experiences. New events and strange men stood before him every day. His individual importance had become an accepted fact. People no longer asked who General Grant was, for even the most ill-informed had heard of him.

But these fresh contacts with men, these triumphs and discouragements, sharp and vivid as they were, had little or no influence on his personality or his methods. His character was formed before the war began, and it was not sufficiently plastic to change, or develop, after he appeared on the sky-line of history. He was never a part of his experiences; they merely flowed by him without leaving any substantial deposit, except in memory. The only discernible effect of his rise in the world was to give him more confidence in himself.

Whenever he met the enemy his plan, described in Lincoln's salty speech, was to "hold on with a bulldog grip and chew and choke as much as possible." His strategy was a synthesis of concentration, swift moves and attacks that paralyzed and smashed the enemy through their energy and relentlessness.

There is no eagerness in such men as Grant, but only quiet resolves and a kind of stolid desperation. He said that he never sat up at nights wondering what the enemy was going to do. "I try to make the enemy wonder what I am going to do," he declared.

Beneath this leaden opacity there was another Grant that few men ever knew . . . a shy and sensitive soul that clung to friendships with an attachment that was almost childish in its ingenuousness. Grant's confidence in the people he liked had a primitive, tribal quality about it. His friends could never do any wrong, nor make a mistake; while those outside his tribe never could do anything that was wholly right.

The first member of the Grant clan was Rawlins, and the next was Sherman. The Grant and Sherman mutual admiration society began at the time of Fort Donelson. These two men did not resemble one another in the least, except that both were stubborn fighters.

Sherman was a restless person. He was the reverse of reticent, and would express himself on any conceivable subject, whether he knew anything about it or not. He had the hot imagination of a high-school boy. "To secure the safety of the navigation of the Mississippi River," he declared, "I would slay millions,"—and he advised the bombardment of helpless towns on the Mississippi and its tributaries on the supposition that they might conceal a few men capable of bearing arms.

One of his fixed notions was a dislike of newspapers and newspaper men. "I never see my name in print," he declared, "without a feeling of contamination, and I will undertake to forego half of my salary if the newspapers will ignore my name." When the army was before Vicksburg somebody told him that three newspaper correspondents had been killed by a bursting shell. "Good!" Sherman exclaimed. "Now we'll have news from hell before breakfast."

Sherman was the only one of the leading generals on either side who could write interestingly. His *Memoirs* are simply his volubility poured into print, and they are fascinating, vivid and sometimes amusing, though they are very inaccurate. After the publication of the two volumes one of Sherman's friends pointed out some of the more glaring errors. "Oh, never mind," Sherman answered without discomposure. "I may be wrong, but that's the way I remembered it. They are my memoirs, not the memoirs of anybody else."

Besides Rawlins and Sherman, the Grant-Sherman circle eventually included Sheridan, McPherson, Badeau, Bowers, Horace Porter, etc. . . . and many more etceteras and lesser lights.

Grant's admiration for Sheridan ran beyond all bounds. The phraseology of his praise is so extravagant that it defeats itself. Ten years after the war he told Senator George F. Hoar that he believed Sheridan to have "no superior as a general, either living or dead, and perhaps not an equal," and he continued in this eulogistic strain for some time, making it clear that, compared with Sheridan, such distinguished military gentlemen as Julius Cæsar, Frederick the Great, Robert E. Lee and Napoleon were only second-raters.

As a matter of fact, Sheridan was nothing more than an intrepid cavalry leader, dashing and very theatrical. His experience was limited, for he had an independent command in only three or four engagements, and in every case his force greatly outnumbered that of the Confederates.

On the battlefield Sheridan's maner was that of a hysterical youth at a dog fight. He would ride up and down, shouting, screaming, waving his hat, begging, threatening and applauding.

Grant's unstinted praise of this cavalryman caused him to be promoted over the heads of really great soldiers, such as Meade and Thomas.

§ 8

With Grant's rise to fame rumors and anecdotes of his drinking habits were in everybody's mouth. Most of them were highly exaggerated yarns. Late in 1863 a wondrous story about Lincoln, Grant and liquor began to appear in the newspapers. The tale, as it runs to-day in the current version, is that a party of clergymen called on the President to protest against Grant being put in high command. Their objection to him was that he drank whisky, wine and beer, and was consequently an unsafe person. Lincoln is said to have replied, with the twinkle in his eye that distinguished folks are always supposed to have when they make a point of humor: "Well, I wish some of you would tell me the brand of whisky that Grant drinks. I would like to send a barrel of it to every one of my other generals."

It is a good story; its only defect is that it contains no vestige of truth. Lincoln himself denied its authenticity, not only once but many times. This piece of fiction was made up by Charles G. Halpine, a newspaper man and correspondent of the New York *Herald*, and it appeared first in that newspaper on November 26, 1863.

In disclaiming the story, Lincoln remarked that it was over a hundred years old, anyway. He said that it had originated with George I. Somebody had complained to George about General Wolfe . . . asserted that he was mad. Thereupon that red-faced, outspoken monarch fell into a royal mood and said, "If General Wolfe is mad I hope he bites some of my other generals."

CHAPTER XIX

THE NORTH AT WAR

§ 1

THERE was consternation in New Orleans on the morning of April 28, 1862. That noble and leisurely city, the largest and wealthiest in the Confederate States, stood facing an impromptu Judgment Day. A swarm of Federal war vessels, under command of Admiral Farragut, had passed the forts and were coming up the river.

The fleet advanced slowly, feeling the water for torpedoes. From the city levees the masts of the ships could be seen, over the tops of the trees, across the snaky curves of the river, moving majestically. For a time an indomitable Confederate gunboat, the last survivor of the defeated Southern flotilla, limped after them at a distance, swimming far behind and firing a shot now and then, like a fierce and wounded terrier following a pack of hostile bulldogs.

The silent city lay under a cloud of smoke. Farragut and his officers thought the whole of New Orleans was burning, but it was only some thousands of cotton bales on the wharves, which the Confederate authorities had set afire to keep them from falling into the enemy's hands.

The sun hung like a blood-red disk in the darkened sky. The streets were filled with the litter of hurriedly emptied warehouses, with wagons and drays taking the goods of merchants to safety in the country, with pale-faced and bareheaded men moving ledgers and bags of money to secret hiding places.

The capture of New Orleans was not the only Confederate catastrophe that reverberated from the Mississippi basin in the spring and summer of 1862.

The taking of Corinth was another blow. The village of Corinth was of no consequence, but it was on the Memphis and Charleston railroad, the most important line of communication between the Southern states west of the Mississippi and the Atlantic seaboard. When it fell into Union hands Arkansas, western Louisiana and Texas were virtually isolated. There was still another gateway open, through Vicksburg, though the railway that ran from Vicksburg to the east was erratic in its junctions and wanderings, and could not be expected to carry the traffic that had passed over the Memphis and Charleston road.

With Corinth gone, there was no hope for Memphis. A fleet of Union gunboats was in the river above it, ready to descend, and Halleck's army stood at Corinth in its rear. Under these conditions it was certain that Memphis would be lost to the Confederacy in a few weeks.

The navy reached Memphis before Halleck got there. It was taken by the Union naval forces on June 6, 1862, in a dramatic river battle between the Union and Confederate vessels. The fight took place in front of the city and thousands of spectators stood on the high bluffs and watched the destruction of the Confederate fleet.

The emaciated Southern newspapers, printed in muddy ink on coarse gray paper, ridiculed and minimized these misfortunes. The great mass of Southern people, poorly informed and half-illiterate, took the word of the newspapers as gospel truth.

§ 2

The army of 120,000 men that Halleck had gathered at Corinth was gradually diminished by the supposed necessity of action in other fields. If it could have been kept together, under Grant's command, after Halleck had left, there is reason to believe that Grant could have marched it straight through Mississippi and Alabama to Mobile. That is what he wanted to do.

Such a cross-country campaign would have upset all the Confederate military plans, would have disorganized the entire Confederate system of supply and transportation, and might have brought the war to an end before 1865.

As the general commanding in the occupied territory, Grant found himself an administrator as well as a soldier.

In his capacity as military governor he was besieged by a buzzing crowd of people who wanted permission to do this and that . . . business men who had come down from the North to make money out of the war—some of them his own relatives . . . cotton speculators . . . people who wanted passes to go outside his lines on some pretext or other . . . lawyers who represented Southern clients . . . peddlers who were trying to take contraband goods into Confederate territory. He had to make municipal regulations, oversee the police, look after the currency, help people get back their stolen cows, and put a lot of suspicious characters into jail.

He was not fitted for these duties, either by experience or temperament, and sometimes he showed almost incredible streaks of bad judgment. Witness, for example, his General Order No. 11, which was conceived by him for the purpose of expelling all the Jews from his military district. There was a great deal of under-cover, illicit trading in cotton around Memphis, for Northern cotton mills were in need of raw material, and the huge profits to be made in buying cotton from Southern farms and reselling it to Massachusetts factory owners brought a horde of speculators into Grant's territory. Some of these illicit traders were Jews, though most of them were Yankees and dyed-in-the-wool Protestants.

However, Grant's General Order No. 11, which was intended to prevent trading with the enemy, mentioned only the Jews. It reads:

The Jews as a class violating every regulation of trade established by the Treasury Department, and also department orders, are hereby expelled from the department within 24 hours from the receipt of this order.

Post commanders will see to it that all of this class of people be furnished passes and required to leave, and any one returning after such notification will be arrested and held in confinement until an opportunity occurs of sending them out as prisoners unless furnished with permit from headquarters.

No passes will be given these people to visit headquarters for the purpose of making personal application for trade permits.

Despite the positive tone of this tactless and ill-advised order, Grant was not destined to play the part of an Egyptian Pharaoh. The order was revoked immediately by the War Department over his head, and it was never actually put into effect except for a few days.

With the single exception of General Order No. 11 I have not found anything else in Grant's words or actions to prove that he was an anti-Semite. I do not believe that he ever thought of the subject at all. There were extensive portions of his mentality which appear to have been dormant all his life. In attempting to expel the illicit traders he simply put them down as Jews—according to my opinion—because the people around headquarters continually spoke of them as Jews.

Grant's own family was represented among the cotton traders. In 1863 one of his kinsmen appeared in the Mississippi region and bought cotton right and left. Some people thought that he was under General Grant's protection, and others said that the general was a partner in these money-making operations. Neither of these assertions was true. Grant never made any money out of the war—except his salary.

When Grant's money-making relative tried to ship some of his cotton to the North, Rawlins—on his own initiative—wrote out an order expelling him from the military district. Thereupon Grant went to Rawlins and asked him to recall or suspend the order. James H. Wilson, Rawlins' friend and biographer, says:

> Rawlins broke into a flood of violent language, conclud-
> ing with the declaration that if he were a general com-
> manding an army of a hundred thousand men and a rela-
> tion of his violated one of his important standing orders
> he would march him out and hang him to a tree. . . .
> Grant was naturally amazed at this outburst . . . but
> made no reply . . . whereupon Rawlins retired to his
> office pale with rage.

In a few moments Rawlins went to Grant and apologized, winding up his apology with this quaint remark: "I thought I had mastered both my tongue and my temper, for when I made the acquaintance of the ladies here, I resolved to quit cursing and flattered myself that I had succeeded."

Grant said quietly that it was all right, that he was not offended. Then he suggested that Rawlins might destroy the order and "tell the gentleman to whom it refers that his health requires him to take the first steamer back to Cairo."

§ 3

The Civil War was an epoch of astounding business activity at the North. After the first panicky shock, following the firing on Fort Sumter, almost every branch of trade and industry reveled in prosperity until the war came to an end. In 1862 the Northern states, after producing enough wheat to supply their own people with bread, actually exported sixty million bushels to Europe. This was unprecedented. Never before had more than twenty million bushels been sent abroad in any one year.

It so happened that there was a disastrous failure of food-stuff crops in England in 1861 and '62, and the British people depended largely on the American food supply. This condition of affairs—perhaps more than any other single factor—was effective in preventing recognition of the Confederate States by Great Britain. Wheat, instead of cotton, was king. The debates in Parliament on the question of Southern recognition brought out this fact very clearly. To recognize the Confederate States as an independent nation would have probably led England into the war. There is no doubt that the stream of American wheat would have been stopped immediately, and the leaders in Parliament were keenly aware of this contingency.

If American wheat was king across the seas, oil and wool and railroads and lumber and mining made up an imposing royal family at home.

Oil had been found in Pennsylvania in 1859; and in the early days of the war the discovery of oil wells, the making of new fortunes, the blaze and stir of an unsuspected Eldorado, sometimes crowded the war news off the front pages of the newspapers.

Woolen factories worked day and night, and the consumption of wool increased two and a half times. The dividends of woolen mills rose, in some instances, to forty per cent. The Northern cotton mills, too, were exceptionally prosperous, despite the difficulty of obtaining raw material. At the beginning of the war most of them had a considerable supply of cotton on hand. As its price rose from twelve cents to one dollar a pound, the manufacturers raised in a corresponding measure the selling price of cotton cloth.

Great fortunes were made in railroads, in manufacturing, and in speculation, but the largest crop of newly rich millionaires consisted of government contractors. Supplies for the army were bought, in prodigious quantities, without adequate supervision. Fraud ceased to be a fine art, and became merely a rough handicraft. There was no need of finesse; any one who could not make money out of the government was looked upon with contempt by the horde of dishonest and slippery-minded dealers in food and military equipment.

Rifles manufactured at government arsenals cost only nine dollars apiece, but the same type of weapon, sold by contractors to the army, cost the government twenty dollars. Tin canteens, which could be bought by anybody for thirty-six cents each, were sold to the government for sixty cents; and inferior shoes, their soles lined with paper, were paid for at high-quality prices by the War Department.

A despicable form of swindling developed in the manufacture of uniforms for the soldiers. In many cases where the specifications called for woolen cloth a kind of fabric known as "shoddy" was furnished instead. This substitute was made by beating woolen rags of all varieties into a pulp and pressing the pulp between hot rollers to form a fabric, somewhat like the process used in the manufacture of newsprint paper. The resulting product was really a flimsy felt; it would go to pieces in the first heavy rain, but clothes made of it were accepted by unscrupulous government agents who had a financial understanding with the manufacturers. In time the matter of worthless uniforms became so scandalous that the word "shoddy" passed into popular speech, and was used to denote both things and people of a low grade.

Another species of dishonesty appeared in the sale of ships to the government. Half-drowned tubs of vessels that had been lying at wharves for years were resurrected, puttered over, charmed into life, and sold for enormous sums.

The ship *Suwanee*, worth not over ten thousand dollars, was chartered to the government for four months for sixty thousand dollars. The *Salvor*, a captured blockade-runner, sold by the government at auction, was purchased by Clyde, of Philadelphia, for twelve thousand dollars. Thereupon, the government turned around and leased the ship from Clyde for twelve thousand dollars a month. Marshall O. Roberts sold two ships to the nation for one hundred thousand dollars each.

They were in such bad condition that one of them was con-
demned as unseaworthy in a few days and the other was lost at
sea.

At the court-martial of Major McKinstry, an army quartermaster, it was shown that he had bought a thousand horses and
mules at one hundred and nineteen dollars apiece, when they
could have been obtained in the open market at eighty dollars
each.

On another occasion McKinstry had been ordered to purchase a lot of soldiers' blouses. It was proved that instead of
advertising for bids from concerns in the clothing business, Mc-
Kinstry gave the order to a hardware store . . . three thousand soldiers' blouses at three dollars apiece. His friends in
the hardware trade then went around the corner and bought
the blouses at a price of two dollars each from a clothing
merchant.

Grant was a nightmare to the dishonest army contractors
in his department. His long experience as quartermaster had
taught him how to estimate the prices of things, and he was an
excellent judge of values. These qualifications, coupled with
Grant's absolute honesty, served to make the tricky army contract a losing venture at Cairo in 1861, and in western Tennessee the following year. He wrote to E. B. Washburne in
1862:

> I learned from undoubted authority that there was a
> combination of wealthy and influential citizens formed,
> at the beginning of this war, for the purpose of monopo-
> lizing the army contracts. One of their boasts was that
> they had sufficient influence to remove any general who
> did not please them.
>
> The *modus operandi* for getting contracts at a high
> rate, I suppose, was for a member of this association to
> put in bids commencing at as low rates as the articles
> could be furnished for, and after they were opened all
> would retire up to the highest one who was below any out-

side person, and let him take it. In many instances probably they could buy off this one for a low figure by
assuring him that he could not possibly get the contract,
for if he did not retire it would be held by the party below.

But everybody did not attempt to get rich quick. The
shoddy merchants and grasping contractors amounted to only
a small part of the population. Over the heads of these trick-
sters one sees the martyrs and the heroes. Thousands of men
—better say tens of thousands—gave up their profitable busi-
nesses and professions, and entered the army. And the Northern soldiers, like those of the South, fought bravely for four
years, stoically enduring privations, disease and disaster.

Yet, notwithstanding the nobility of all this sacrifice and
altruism, the total effect of the war was to lower the moral
stamina of the Northern people. The greedy emotions of the
shrewd and dishonest percolated slowly, like a deadly virus,
through the nation's soul. Men who were slick enough to de-
spoil the government became the type and symbol of intellectual
prowess. In the end the whole country stood gaping with
open-mouthed admiration at the shoddy aristocracy, at the
Goulds and Barnums, at the quack medicine millionaires, at the
generals who stole Confederate cotton, at the glittering short-
changers of high finance. The ancient ethical landmarks were
washed away by the incoming tide of a new and far-flung capitalism which was motivated by profit instead of productivity.

One of the sinister figures of the time was General Benjamin
F. Butler, a Massachusetts lawyer and politician. He was a
Democrat who possessed some sort of underground influence
with his party, and with leading men generally, which was all
out of proportion to his apparent ability or achievements.
Even Lincoln was paralyzed by him, and was afraid to remove
him from his command—until after the presidential campaign
of 1864, and Lincoln's reëlection, when he was dismissed
abruptly.

Butler managed to get himself appointed a major-general at the beginning of the war, although he had neither military experience nor the fighting instinct which must be the foundation of success as a soldier. He was crafty, scheming, greedy—and plausibly dishonest. Upon the occupation of New Orleans by the Union forces Butler became military governor of that city. His brother soon appeared on the scene and engaged in illicit trade with the Confederates on a large scale. Supplies, some of which were contraband of war, were sold by Butler's brother to the Confederates, and cotton and sugar taken in exchange. Cotton was worth five times as much in New York as it was in New Orleans. On the other hand, flour—which sold at $6.00 a barrel in New York—was worth $24.00 a barrel in New Orleans. There were fabulous profits in this trade.

Senator Hoar wrote in his *Recollections* (Vol. I, p. 343) that during Butler's occupation of New Orleans he made a requisition of $80,000 in gold on a New Orleans bank. After the war the bank sued Butler for the return of the money. Butler declared that the money had been turned over to the government. "In that case," the bank's attorney said, "your receipt from the government will constitute a good defense." He added: "Your neighbors in Lowell will not think very well of you when they see you riding in your carriage, and know that it was purchased with money taken from this bank." Before the trial Butler reluctantly paid back the $80,000. "Well, you've beaten me in this," he said to the bank's representative, "but you've made one mistake. You said the people of Lowell would not think very highly of me when they saw me riding through the streets in my carriage and knew it was paid for by the money of this bank. On the contrary, the people would think me a fool for not having taken twice as much."

§ 4

The actual cash outlay of the national government for war expenses, during the four years of the war, was approximately three billion dollars. Such a sum was wholly beyond the capacity of the government to raise by taxation, and some other means had to be devised. Early in 1862 Congress authorized the issue of $150,000,000 of "greenback" paper money and made it a legal tender for all debts, public and private, except customs duties, which were to be paid in coin. The gold received from the customs was held in reserve to pay interest on the government's gold bonds. This flood of legal tender paper money, without any gold reserve behind it, and without an accompanying promise of redemption at a specified time in the future, constituted a startling innovation in American government finance. The greenback paper dollar was merely a piece of paper, adorned with scroll work, a patriotic picture, and the words "One Dollar." It was essentially different from the paper dollar of to-day, which is exchangeable at any time for gold. The Legal Tender Act was passed only after considerable debate; the administration urged its passage as an absolute necessity. After that there were other emissions of paper money, until January, 1864, when the outstanding total was about $450,000,000.

One of the first results of the Legal Tender Act was to put a premium on gold. Consequently gold became a commodity and its price ran up and down in terms of paper money. A Gold Room in the New York Stock Exchange was opened for speculation in the precious metal. When the greenbacks first appeared their value in gold was about 97 cents to the dollar, but before a year had passed the paper dollars had dropped to 75 cents. In the middle of 1863 they were down to 58 cents, but even this value was not stable. The price of gold in relation to paper fluctuated widely in response to news from the war. In July, 1864, the paper dollar touched its lowest market value, when it declined to 35 cents. In other words, a man who possessed a gold dollar at that time could buy nearly three paper dollars with it.

The Legal Tender Act was like a gorgeous Christmas gift to debtors, to people who owed money on promissory notes, to farmers whose lands were under mortgage. All such obligations could be, and many of them were, settled in depreciated paper.

But it was not beneficial in the least to the working people and factory hands of the big towns. Their wages rose a little, but not much, while the cost of living went to the sky. The cities were full of discontented and suffering people.

These issues of greenbacks relieved temporarily the acute financial distress of the government, but if enough legal tender money to meet the total expenditure on account of the war had been set afloat it would have wrecked the economic system of the Northern states, just as a similar expedient, carried out in wholesale fashion, destroyed the finances of the Confederacy.

The chief fiscal reliance of the Lincoln administration was on bond issues, and in the sale of the bonds to the people another innovation appeared. Until the Civil War the average working citizen of the Republic knew nothing about bonds. He thought of them—if at all—as sacrosanct documents in the vaults of banks. The Treasury called to its aid the house of Jay Cooke & Company, of Philadephia, a concern that had made a reputation in the successful flotation of railroad bonds.

Cooke was the originator of the modern "drive" method of bond selling. He appointed agents all over the country—men who addressed public meetings and stood on street corners urging the ordinary public to buy government securities. There were flaring advertisements in the newspapers, and—as a contemporary writer remarked—"every device that had been successful in patent medicine selling was used." The campaign was a phenomenal success. The sales soon rose to twelve million dollars a week. Men who were experienced in financial affairs were astonished to learn that the country contained so much ready money.

There was a tremendous profit to be made at the expense of the government in purchasing these war bonds. The principal and interest of the six per cent bonds was payable in gold, but the bonds could be bought with paper money. Let us consider a typical transaction made, let us say, when gold was selling at 150. A man with a thousand dollars in gold could turn it into fifteen hundred dollars in paper money. Then with this fifteen hundred dollars he could buy an equivalent amount of six per cent gold bonds. The fifteen hundred dollars in bonds would bring him ninety dollars a year in interest, or nine per cent on his original investment. But the nine per cent was not all. The government would eventually redeem the bonds at par—that is, it would buy back his bonds for fifteen hundred dollars in gold. He would thus make an additional fifty per cent on his thousand dollars. No wonder the bonds sold well. The government paid from ten to fifteen per cent for the money it borrowed.

§ 5

There is not even an echo of any of this in Grant's war career. He never mentions bonds, or finance, or business in any of his letters that have come to light. We must conclude that he was a single-minded soldier, completely absorbed in the duties that lay near at hand.

§ 6

Along with the growth of tawdry ideals, the tolerance of moral evasions, and the worship of material success, there arose the contempt for law and order which is an inevitable outcome of all wars. This sense of lawlessness among the people was nourished by the course of the Lincoln administration.

The President and other executive heads of the government paid small attention to the constitutional limitations of their authority—and their example was contagious. Free speech was virtually abolished; newspaper offices were raided by squads of soldiers; newspapers were suppressed without warning and without opportunity for defense or explanation; all the telegraph offices were invaded and stacks of miscellaneous telegrams were seized; the writ of *habeas corpus* was suspended; and thousands of men were imprisoned because of their opinions. During the course of the war not less than 36,000 Northern citizens were put in jail for speaking or writing against the administration, on the ground that they were giving "aid and comfort to the enemy."

In some respects Congress became an innocuous debating society, and the Supreme Court's rulings—when they interfered with the administration's course—were disregarded, as one disregards the chatter of children. William H. Seward, the Secretary of State, boasted to Lord Lyons, the British envoy, that he possessed more power than the sovereign of the British Empire. "I can send any man to prison," he declared, "with or without cause, and keep him there." Wendell Phillips, himself an abolitionist, attacked Lincoln, and declared him "a more unlimited despot than the world knows this side of China."

How did all this come about? How did it happen that Lincoln, the most thorough-going believer in popular government, in democracy, in the right of free speech and opinion, who has ever occupied the White House, felt impelled to turn himself into an American Czar?

The explanation is that he had one fixed idea during the Civil War . . . he wanted to save the Union. That is the clue to all his actions. "Of what use is it to preserve the Constitution," he said, in effect, over and over, "if by preserving it we lose the Union? In that case, what would the Constitution be worth?"

He understood clearly that he was breaking down constitutional barriers, and setting aside basic human rights that are as old as the Anglo-Saxon people, but he hoped—when the rebellion had been suppressed—to make amends, and to put the ancient legal forms back in their rightful place.

Like all truly great men, Lincoln had several personalities, and these diverse sides of his character were often in direct conflict with one another. The real Lincoln will probably never be known, for his picture is now so completely encrusted with a patina of stained glass fictions and apocryphal rubbish that nobody knows where truth ends and myth begins.

His canonization as an American saint and hero took place after his death. While he was alive nobody of importance whom I have been able to discover, except James Russell Lowell and a few abolitionists, considered him a really great man. The intellectual classes looked upon him as an unfortunate choice that had to be endured. Yet he was a great man, and in the truest sense, but the country had to grow up to his stature.

Stanton, Secretary of War, held the most important wartime post in the cabinet. He was overbearing, insolent, cringing and—if we may believe Welles, and others—a physical coward. It is amusing to read in Welles' *Diary* of Stanton's frightened antics when it was believed in Washington that the Confederate iron-clad *Merrimac* was coming up the Potomac river.

But he was honest and industrious. He would not take bribes, or receive favors—nor would he give them. He pursued crooked army contractors with relentless energy, though his own lavish and extravagant purchases—made with the best of motives—probably cost the government more in waste than all the looting that was done by the sellers of shoddy goods.

He was extremely outspoken in his comments on people. There is an interesting illustration of this trait in Chittenden's *Recollections*. Stanton was talking with an army officer when a well-known official passed by. "That man," Stanton remarked, "is a pretender, a humbug and a fraud. Did you ever in all your life see the head of a human being which so closely resembled that of a codfish?"

"He is not responsible for his head or his face," the officer remarked.

"A man of fifty *is responsible* for his face," Stanton declared emphatically.

§ 7

Lincoln read to his cabinet in July, 1862, the first draft of his Emancipation Proclamation. This Proclamation was considered only a war measure and was to be effective only in the states that were in rebellion. Even as a military procedure its constitutionality was doubtful. Slavery was not abolished in the border states, nor in any of the territory under Union control.

Lincoln issued the Emancipation Proclamation with great reluctance. The plan that he had favored at first was one based on compensation to the owners of slaves at the rate of four hundred dollars for each slave in their possession. Congress was finally brought around to the President's views as to compensation, and a resolution embodying his ideas was passed by both houses in April, 1862. Under the terms of this resolution any state that decided to abolish slavery was entitled to payment for the slaves owned by its citizens. The purpose of the resolution was to cause disaffection in the Confederate States, and some of Lincoln's advisers thought it might bring two or three of the seceded states back into the Union.

Its effect on secession was negligible. All of the Southern states looked upon the offer with scorn, if one may judge by the opinions that appeared in print. Southern people generally considered it insincere, and nothing more than a piece of deception to get them to lay down their arms. But they did not know Lincoln. His offer was perfectly straightforward.

There is not a shadow of doubt that the whole Confederacy could have come back into the Union in 1862 on these terms.

The Emancipation Proclamation was a more drastic measure. It was not referred to Congress for action, as it was issued by Lincoln in his capacity as head of the army, and was defined, therefore, as a military order.

Conscription at the North began in 1863. For the first two years of the war the government had relied on volunteers. Volunteering fell off most decidedly about the beginning of 1862; and, thereafter, it was encouraged in most of the states by a system of bounties. In time, as men became harder to get, these bounties—paid by the county, state, and nation—grew very large. Early in 1863, before national conscription went into effect, a volunteer enlisting in New York City could obtain a total bounty of $677—and, if he was a veteran, $100 in addition.

This system of bounties was thoroughly vicious. It brought into the armies a class of thieves and rascals who enlisted solely for the bounty money, and who deserted at the first opportunity. These hair-trigger deserters were called "bounty-jumpers." They would often cross over into the next county and enlist again under another name.

The bounty-purchased soldiers made poor fighting material. Officers writing from the front frequently declared that whole companies and battalions of the bounty men surrendered to the Confederates without resistance, preferring a Southern war prison to service under fire.

The employment of negroes as soldiers began in 1863, and colored troops were used first, in an experimental way, at the siege of Vicksburg. Before the end of the war there were about one hundred thousand negroes in the Union army. Most of the officers of high rank were not favorably impressed by the negro troops. Sherman considered them a joke, and Grant usually kept them in the rear, guarding his wagon trains.

In the spring of 1863 Congress passed the first national

conscription act. No distinction as to age was made under the act; it made all "able-bodied citizens" subject to the draft, but there were numerous special exemptions. Substitutes were allowed, and there was a commutation feature which provided that any drafted man might obtain an exemption on the payment of three hundred dollars. This arrangement for evading service by the payment of money to the government was heartily resented by workingmen and others to whom three hundred dollars was a large or impossible sum. It was, in truth, a barefaced device for enabling the well-to-do to escape the war altogether . . . more brazen in its unfairness than the "twenty-nigger" law in the South.

The profiteers stayed out of the war by the simple expedient of writing a check for three hundred dollars, or by hiring substitutes to take their places. These draft-evaders became targets of public derision, but they thought that was better than being targets for Confederate marksmen.

One of the stories that survives is of a Mrs. Malaprop of the day.

"Has your husband gone to the war?" some one asked her.

"Oh, no; he couldn't go," she replied, "but he sent a *prostitute*."

The first drawing of names under the Conscription Act took place in New York City on July 11, 1863—just one week after the battle of Gettysburg—and it led to the most formidable and bloody riot that has ever occurred in American history.

The draft in New York might have gone on peaceably if the situation had not been complicated by the rancor of an acute labor dispute. Some weeks previously the longshoremen on the New York piers had struck for higher wages and their places had been taken by negroes. These negro strike-breakers were protected by armed guards. Now, the strikers, pinched to the bone by the poverty of unemployment, were called from their dismal homes to be drafted into the army. That meant they were to face Southern bullets to give freedom to the negro race, in spite of the fact that their jobs had been taken by negro strike-breakers. It was too much for human nature to bear—at any rate, it was too much for the nature of husky stevedores to bear.

On Monday morning before ten o'clock bullets were whistling down Third Avenue and the conscription office at the corner of Forty-sixth Street had been smashed and gutted. Buildings were burned, negroes were hanged on lamp-posts, stores were despoiled of their contents, and drunken men and women reeled here and there. Dead and wounded men lay in the streets. The number of people who were actually killed or wounded has never been determined, but it has been estimated at one thousand. Many men and women were burned to death in a building at Second Avenue and Twenty-second Street.

By Tuesday the rioters controlled the city. The police and the small body of militia were swept aside. Colonel O'Brien, commanding the Eleventh Regiment, was caught by the rioters and beaten to death on Second Avenue. For hours his body lay in the street and was mutilated by the savage, gin-soaked mob.

On Wednesday the Common Council met in the agony and sweat of a disintegrating city, and voted to appropriate $2,500,000 as a fund on which any poor man could draw three hundred dollars to purchase his exemption. Before adjourning the Council passed resolutions denouncing the draft.

CHAPTER XX

THE VICKSBURG ADVENTURE

§ 1

WE left Grant in Mississippi, where he spent the last six months of 1862 in holding on to the territory that the Union forces occupied after the battle of Shiloh. While he was establishing himself in northern Mississippi and western Tennessee he was contemplating an attack on Vicksburg, the last remaining Confederate foothold on the great river. In the fall of 1862 he moved down from Memphis through the state of Mississippi toward the Confederate river fortress. This was his first attempt at Vicksburg. It was brought to an end by the Confederates breaking his communications by the destruction of the Memphis railroad in his rear, and by their raid on his great supply depot at Holly Springs, Mississippi.

Mrs. Grant was at Holly Springs at that time, on her way to spend Christmas with her husband. She was accompanied by her slave maid Julia and her son Jesse—then a child of four. Jesse Grant says that his earliest recollection of the war "is the escape of mother and myself from Holly Springs, Mississippi. . . . I remember now, as though it were yesterday, the young officer coming to tell us that the enemy was close upon the town, and the confusion of our hurried departure, at night, in a box car. I can see the dim, shadowy interior of the empty box car, with mother sitting quietly upon a chair, while I huddled fearfully upon a hastily improvised bed upon the floor. . . ."

Grant considered himself in a very serious situation. His

army was without anything to eat, and the Confederates had demolished the only railroad over which he could obtain fresh supplies from the North. It went against his grain to turn back, but he did; and as he retreated he began to live on the country. The northern counties of Mississippi were rich in food, and the Union foragers took nearly everything that could be eaten in a belt of farming country about thirty miles wide. The army lived better than it had when it depended on government rations.

Grant said later that if he had known how easy it was to support an army in a food-growing country he would have disregarded the destruction of his supplies and continued on his way toward the south.

Before the disaster at Holly Springs there had appeared on the scene a general who did not belong to the Grant and Sherman group, or even to the clan of West Point. He had a letter from Lincoln in his pocket, a talkative tongue in his mouth, and some military ability in his head, mingled with a highly developed egotistical outlook on things. John A. McClernand was his name, Illinois was his home, and his intention was to capture Vicksburg with an army of his own.

Before the war McClernand had served in Congress and was popular with his fellow-citizens. When the war broke out he entered the army, and was soon made a major-general. His military elevation was not due wholly to political reasons. He had shown courage and considerable resourcefulness as a commander of troops at Belmont, Fort Donelson and Shiloh.

McClernand went to Washington in October, 1862, and conferred with the President. He was a fellow-townsman of Lincoln, and knew him well. He told the President that if he were given a free hand he felt sure he could take Vicksburg, and that he would personally raise an army in the Middle West for that purpose.

Lincoln gave him a free hand, so McClernand thought, but there was a little unobtrusive string tied to his authority. He was instructed, in a formal order, to proceed to Illinois, Indiana and Iowa, for the purpose of raising an army of volunteers, "to the end that, when a sufficient force not required by the operations of General Grant's command shall be raised, an expedition may be organized, under General McClernand's command, against Vicksburg. . . ."

McClernand's instructions were secret, and were to be shown only to the governors of the three states mentioned. Although his contemplated operations against Vicksburg fell within Grant's military district, no copy of the order was sent to Grant. This is perhaps indicative of the lack of confidence that was beginning to be felt in Grant in the lofty councils of Washington.

When McClernand left Lincoln he carried away the impression that he had been designated by the higher powers to besiege and capture Vicksburg. But the words—"a sufficient force not required by the operations of General Grant's command"—inserted in his instructions like a piece of careless verbiage, vitiated the entire import of the document.

The appointment of McClernand had been opposed by Halleck, who was then acting as general-in-chief at Washington. Through some internal evolution of his own mentality Halleck had become friendly to Grant. He may have seen that Grant was the coming man.

In some way Grant, far down on the Mississippi, heard of the projected McClernand expedition. The news had an ominous sound. It looked as if Grant was about to be laid on the shelf of dusty generals. If he had seen McClernand's instructions from the War Department he would not have been alarmed, for in that case he would have ended the episode by needing all the troops McClernand could raise. But he was not sure what the administration intended, so he turned over his command to Sherman and took a steamer to Cairo to visit Admiral Porter and try to find out what had happened.

Porter told Grant that he had been to Washington, and had

heard Lincoln say: "I have a greater general now than either Grant or Sherman. I have commissioned McClernand to raise an army and capture Vicksburg by way of the Mississippi." And Porter added that he did not like McClernand, even if Lincoln did.

Grant reflected a moment. If he could get to Vicksburg ahead of McClernand, would not that give him a sort of right of way, so to speak? Of course it would, but he would have to move fast. He would need the help of the navy, and there was Porter, willing to coöperate in anything.

"How soon can you start down the river with your gunboats?" Grant asked, and Porter replied: "To-morrow morning." Grant then said that he intended to leave at once, having been in Cairo about an hour, and that as soon as he got back to Memphis he would send Sherman and as many troops as he could spare to the vicinity of Vicksburg.

"Well, I'll be there with the gunboats," Porter assured him.

McClernand's fate was settled. It would have been better for him if he had never seen Lincoln, for Lincoln's letter in his pocket, coupled with his pretensions and self-assurance, served to write his name in large letters on the black list of Grant and his friends. He stood next to Grant in rank, and was obviously hoping to step into Grant's shoes. The Grant-Sherman combination considered him a formidable menace. We shall now turn our attention to Vicksburg and come back to McClernand later.

§ 2

The town of Vicksburg stands on a bluff two hundred feet high on the east bank of the Mississippi. Before the town the huge river bends in a hairpin curve. From the edge of the bluff the view is magnificent. The western bank—and the land within the hairpin—is so low that any one standing on Vicksburg hill can see across land and water to a far, dim-blue horizon. The smooth yellow Mississippi comes out of the West, sweeps in mighty grandeur before the town, and flows toward the West again. Batteries placed on this elevation commanded the river for miles in each direction when the Confederates had finished their fortifications in the spring of 1863.

The place was impregnable to any attack that could be made by way of the river. Iron-clad steamers might possibly run past the batteries, but they could do little or no damage to the Confederate works, on account of their inability to elevate their guns sufficiently.

The northern approach to Vicksburg by land was equally difficult, but in a different fashion. A few miles north of the town the Yazoo river, coming from the east, empties itself into the Mississippi. Its miles of swamps and shallow creeks—a wilderness of mud and fallen trees—formed a natural and impassable line of defense, except in one or two places, which the Confederates had fortified with batteries and rifle-pits.

From the east Vicksburg was approachable over a map full of ravines and broken hills, but it was not practicable for an armed force to advance from that direction without coming down through the center of the state of Mississippi, and through Jackson—the capital of the state—which lies about forty miles east of Vicksburg. This detour was necessary to avoid the Yazoo creeks and mud.

Grant's first attempt was made along this line. Sherman was sent up the Yazoo with 32,000 men, while Grant himself marched southward into Mississippi. Sherman landed at Chickasaw Bluffs, a few miles above Vicksburg. This is one of the places where an army might emerge from the Yazoo morass. The plan was that Sherman, landing at Chickasaw Bluffs, would keep the Confederate garrison occupied while Grant approached from the east. It was a thoroughly unsound piece of strategy. In the first place, the two coöperating columns were too far apart to be of assistance to one another;

and in the next place, there was no means of communication between them; and, finally, they were both sure to encounter natural obstacles which would render their mutual effectiveness a highly speculative question.

The whole scheme was thrown into complete disorder by the raid of the Confederate general Van Dorn in Grant's rear, with the destruction of the Union supply base at Holly Springs. Grant retreated, but Sherman did not know it, so he attacked the strong Confederate position on the bluffs and was badly beaten, losing about two thousand men.

It was at this time—around New Year's day of 1863—that McClernand arrived at Sherman's camp. He took command and Sherman became his subordinate. But the persistent Halleck was still nagging away on the McClernand matter in Washington, and he contrived to get an order through, with the approval of the higher powers, that McClernand was to command the Vicksburg expedition only if Grant were not present. Thereupon Grant resolved to be present as soon as possible, and he did appear in person in the early part of January, 1863.

He says that it was made evident to him "that both the army and navy were so distrustful of McClernand's fitness to command that, while they would do all they could to insure success, this distrust was an element of weakness. It would have been criminal to send troops under these circumstances into such danger."

He adds that he felt great embarrassment in the matter, as McClernand was next in rank to himself, and "It would not do, with his rank and ambition, to assign a junior over him. Nothing was left, therefore, but to assume the command myself."

Grant was on the ground, and all the military problems revolved around him. The main question was how to get in fighting reach of Vicksburg. It was easy enough to bring an army within ten miles of the town. That could be done by putting the troops on board a fleet of steamers at Memphis and landing them on the west side of the river—at the beginning of the hairpin curve. The houses of Vicksburg would then be visible on the sky-line, across the river, but the place could not be reached, and the army would be as useless as if it were a hundred miles away.

Perhaps I have not yet made clear the nature of the country. The river contains the dripping rain of half a continent. One can hardly call it a river; it is one of the wonders of the world; it is to rivers what Pike's Peak is to a pleasant little hill. In that amphibious land one meets creeks and bayous everywhere. Roads end suddenly in a waste of swirling water flowing in the midst of a tangled forest. The river is higher than the land, and levees of earth and stones strive to keep it in its course. But it escapes. Creeks flow from it, running strangely backward and upstream. In these drowned and stricken forests one loses the sense of direction. The world becomes a wilderness of yellow water, trees and trailing vines . . . but not altogether; there stands Vicksburg, on its tall hill, a solid vision in a melting cosmos.

For months Grant endeavored to get to Vicksburg. His tenacity had the persistence of a hungry animal scratching at a door. The campaign was not one of maneuver, but of transportation.

His army turned itself into an army of canal-diggers and wood-choppers. They built bridges; they stood up to their waists in mud; they made jokes among themselves about growing tails like beavers. There was not another general in the Union army—probably not one alive in any army—as well qualified as Grant for a military operation of this kind. As we watch him in this terribly arduous Vicksburg campaign we see behind him the shadows of his early years . . . the teamster boy of an Ohio settlement, bringing in the heavy logs from the woodcutters' camp . . . the young plowman, with calloused hands, driving his plow through the tough black soil . . . the conqueror of horses . . . the sweating quartermaster, with his

GENERAL WILLIAM TECUMSEH SHERMAN

From a photograph made after the Civil War when General
Sherman was about sixty years old.

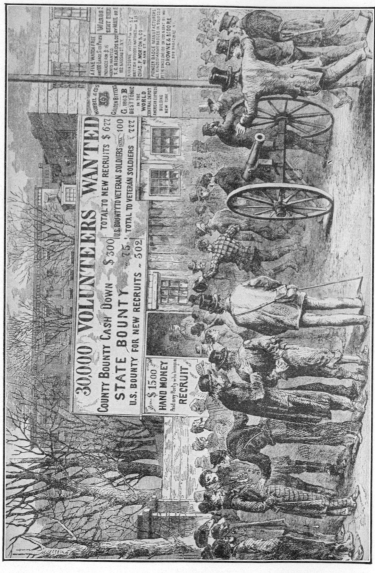

Recruiting Office in City Hall Park, New York

wagon train of cantankerous mules on the hot plains of Mexico. If Destiny ever brought the man and the hour together it was when Grant stood before Vicksburg.

§ 3

About a hundred miles north of Vicksburg a tributary of the Yazoo runs close to the Mississippi. In former times the two rivers were connected by a waterway called Yazoo Pass, but the pass had been closed by a levee, as the great river, in the spring floods, ran into the Yazoo in such volume that it drowned out the low-lying plantations.

Grant conceived the idea of cutting away the restraining levee, and providing thus a channel from the Mississippi to the Yazoo. He thought that he would then be able to put his army on steamers, and the expedition, preceded by the gunboats, might approach Vicksburg by the back door.

The experiment was tried, the channel was cut, and the Mississippi rushed into the smaller river. The gunboats went in and swam like black insects on this swollen flood. About half-way to Vicksburg they were confronted by a Confederate fort—called Fort Pemberton—which was ingeniously placed on a bit of high ground. The fort was strongly armed and its target practice was good. The gunboats barked at it for half a day, and had their sides dented, their hulls smashed, and their smokestacks knocked off in return. They came slowly back against the swishing current. The plan was a failure.

Grant tried this and that. Desperate, hare-brained schemes, most of them. On one occasion Porter's vessels got tangled up in a bayou that was too narrow for them to turn around in, and then Porter found that the Confederates had cut down trees so that they would fall across the stream and stop his progress. While he was considering this state of affairs a Confederate regiment appeared in the swamp and after that it was as much as a man's life was worth to be seen on the decks

of the vessels. Porter began to back his gunboats slowly down-
stream, but he soon discovered, to his chagrin, that the enemy
had felled trees in his rear, too. It seemed to be all over with
the navy. Porter was about to blow up his boats and try to
escape when Sherman's troops arrived unexpectedly on the
squashy banks of the creek. They drove off the Confederates,
but it took three days to raise the trees from the stream so the
gunboats could gingerly back out.

The attempts along the line of the Yazoo were abandoned
after that experience and Grant turned his attention to the
west bank of the Mississippi. If it were only possible to get
below Vicksburg and come up from the south—on the east
bank—the great problem of getting there would be solved.
From the south the place was readily accessible, over fairly
good roads.

To reach the region south of Vicksburg the army would
either have to run past the batteries on steamers, or march
overland on the west bank and cross over the river to the east
bank below the town.

The difficulty about the first alternative was that, while
ironclad gunboats might possibly run by the batteries, it would
certainly be hazardous in the extreme for transport steamers
loaded with troops to attempt such a passage. The sinking of
a single steamer might mean the drowning of a thousand men—
and who could be sure that the loss might not run into appalling
figures?

The second alternative was equally doubtful. The army
was on the west bank of the river, and it was certain that,
with the laying of a few bridges, and the repair of muddy
roads, it could be marched to some point on the river below
Vicksburg. But what then? It would still be on the west
bank, with nearly a mile of rolling river to cross. The transport steamers—or some of them—were absolutely essential to
get the troops over the river. They were needed as ferry
boats.

Then it occurred to Grant to dig a canal across the hairpin curve. The army engineers thought that if a small channel was dug the Mississippi would do the necessary widening. So the work was started . . . first to cut a canal of moderate size, turn the river into it, and then take the whole expedition, gunboats, steamers and all, through this cut-off.

It sounded well, but it did not work. The canal was nearly finished when the Mississippi rose in one of its huge, overpowering freshets. It burst the retaining dam at the head of the canal, and the toiling, mud-stained soldiers had to run for their lives. If the onrushing water on the hairpin curve had been deep enough to carry the steamers the unexpected flood would have solved Grant's problem . . . but it was not deep enough. The project was abandoned.

The plight of the army was deplorable. It was beset on every side by trouble and threatened disaster. The camps were swept away by the Mississippi floods, and for a time the troops were huddled on the levee—a strip of land from ten to fifty feet wide, with the yellow water of the freshet racing along on each side. Smallpox broke out, and the daily death list was terrifying. Under these circumstances almost any other general than Grant would have called the expedition a failure.

Grant did not call it a failure, but many other people did, newspaper correspondents especially . . . a failure, with such adjectives as *stupid, miserable, disgraceful* and *egregious* prefixed to the word. Grant said nothing, but Sherman fumed and swore. He declared that the Northern newspapers had been bought up by Jefferson Davis, and he wanted to treat the newspaper correspondents as spies. He could not turn around, he said, without "some little whippersnapper of the press" dogging his footsteps, and lying about him in a newspaper. "I have ordered the arrest of one," he wrote, "shall try him, and if possible execute him as a spy." And he adds, "I will never again command an army in America if we must carry along paid spies."

Some of the criticisms of Grant were extremely venomous. Murat Halstead, editor of the Cincinnati *Gazette* and a personal friend of Salmon P. Chase, Secretary of the Treasury, was one of the hostile critics.

Here is a sample of his bad humor, contained in a letter written by him to Secretary Chase on February 19, 1863:

> I write you this morning to send you a copy of a private letter I have from our army in front of Vicksburg. It is from a close observer who endeavors to tell the truth: "There never was a more thoroughly disgusted, disheartened, demoralized army than this is, and all because it is under such men as Grant and Sherman . . . while hundreds of poor fellows are dying of smallpox and every other conceivable malady, the medical department is afflicted with delirium tremens. . . . How is it that Grant, who was behind at Fort Henry, drunk at Donelson, surprised and whipped at Shiloh, and driven back from Oxford, Miss., is still in command?"
>
> Governor Chase, these things are true. Our noble army of the Mississippi is being wasted by the foolish, drunken, stupid Grant. He can't organize or control or fight an army. I have no personal feeling about it; but I know he is an ass. There is not among the whole list of retired major-generals a man who is not Grant's superior.

General McClernand contributed to the running fire of criticism; that is, he was as critical as a military officer can be of his superior without getting into trouble for insubordination. He talked injudiciously, and declared that he was "tired of furnishing brains for Grant."

All this criticism must have had its effect on the administration, for we find Lincoln appointing Charles A. Dana assistant Secretary of War and sending him to Vicksburg to stay with Grant's army. Dana went as an observer; he was the eyes of the President and Secretary Stanton.

The coming of Dana probably saved Grant's career. His

letters to Washington were, from first to last, full of confidence in Grant. He became a personal friend of everybody at Grant's headquarters, and as we read over his reports we see the anti-McClernand note beginning to appear shortly after he arrived.

Grant learned—though, probably, he already knew—that troubles come in crowds. In the midst of all this worry he lost his false teeth. He left them in a wash-bowl full of water when he went to bed one night aboard one of the steamers, and a careless servant emptied the wash-bowl into the river next morning.

So there it was: The army perched on a narrow levee and in danger of being drowned; men dying of smallpox; Vicksburg inaccessible; and Grant without his teeth.

There was a hurry-up call to S. L. Hamlen, his dentist in the North, and Hamlen came down the river as soon as he could. His work must have been satisfactory, for a few months later Grant authorized "S. L. Hamlen, dentist, to practice his profession anywhere within this military command."

§ 4

The officers of the staff discussed the idea of running past the batteries. Several gunboats had already gone by without much damage. General James H. Wilson says he suggested to Rawlins the plan of sending the gunboats and enough steamers to use as ferry boats past the batteries—the army to march down the river on land—and he says that Rawlins became enthusiastic over the suggestion, and told Grant about it. However, Grant himself says (*Memoirs*, Vol. I, p. 460) that he had such a movement in contemplation the whole winter.

At any rate, the idea was adopted, and it turned out to be successful. Porter thought his gunboats could make it, but he was in doubt about the river steamers. These were selected by him, and their thin decks were protected by bales of cotton and hay. Barges were lashed on each side of them as a further protection. The steamers did not carry any troops, but only volunteer crews.

The passage was made on April 16th, a moonless night. The Confederates burned houses on the shore for illumination, and the river was almost as light as it is at noon. The vessels were under fire for two hours and all of them were struck many times. One of the steamers was set afire by burning cotton and destroyed, but the crew escaped. Otherwise there was hardly any damage done, strange to say.

The army met the fleet below Vicksburg. The shell-battered steamers nosed themselves up to the bank, and the troops were carried across, a regiment at a time. At last the Union army stood on the Vicksburg side, on high ground, with an open road before it. But it came across without supplies, except three days' cooked rations, which the men carried. Even the tents and officers' horses were left behind on account of the limited means of transportation. Until some new line of communication was opened Grant and his troops would have to live on the country. They began to do it at once. Squads of foragers went out catching horses as soon as the army found itself on dry land. Brierfield, the nearby plantation of Jefferson Davis, was raided, and a splendid riding horse from the Davis stables was brought to Grant. He named the horse "Jeff Davis" and it became his favorite mount.

Why did not the Confederates attack Grant as he crossed the river, or while he was still organizing his command after landing on the eastern bank? Their army was larger than his, and the chances were certainly in their favor.

The only answer to this question is to be found in the astonishing incompetency of General John C. Pemberton, the Confederate commander at Vicksburg.

Pemberton was one of the favorites of Jefferson Davis. He was a feeble, vacillating person—nervous and timid, with dead black eyes in a sallow face. He shut himself up in Vicksburg and buried his army behind its mud and sand. This ostrich-like style of defense was all he knew or could comprehend.

When Grant crossed the Mississippi Pemberton had about 42,000 men. With this force he should have been able to beat Grant, who brought at first only 30,000 men across the river. Grant was on the eastern bank more than a week before his force equaled that of the Confederates opposing him.

From his landing place Grant marched northward toward Vicksburg. In the meantime, General Joseph E. Johnston, who had been sent by the Confederate government to take charge of all the military operations in that district, arrived at Jackson, forty miles east of Vicksburg, with about 12,000 men.

Johnston arrived too late to join forces with Pemberton; Grant had already thrust his army between Jackson and Vicksburg. But he had not come too late to give Pemberton advice and orders . . . all of which were very sound, and might have helped if Pemberton had followed their directions.

"Don't allow yourself to be shut up in Vicksburg under any circumstances," was the import of Johnston's counsel. "Come out and strike Grant; it will be absolutely fatal to remain in your works."

The ostrich, with his head buried in the sand, was finally prodded into action. Pemberton sallied forth with a part of his army and encountered Grant. He was overpowered and beaten. He should not have come out without his entire command at his back. But Pemberton was possessed by the incurable vice of doing things by halves.

As Grant drew his army into the region between Jackson and Vicksburg he had an enemy on both flanks—Johnston on his right and Pemberton on his left. His expedition was in danger of being entirely surrounded.

He took the initiative instantly. His blows were so quick and so vigorous that the Confederates were not able to stand on their feet long enough to carry out any definite plan.

Grant's movements at this time were dazzling in their

celerity, in their energy, in their effectiveness. He fought Pemberton with his left hand and defeated him, while with his right hand he struck at Johnston and drove him out of the state capital. Then he turned to face Pemberton again, but the Confederate commander had retired behind the defenses of Vicksburg.

In studying Grant's campaigns one is puzzled by the uneven character of his ability. At Shiloh his course was that of a dullard who sits down and waits for fate to show her hand. He was at his worst at Shiloh, and at his best at Vicksburg— and the astonishing thing is the wide gap between his best and his worst.

As we contemplate his operations before Vicksburg we cease for a time to think of him as a soldier of talent and energy. Such words are too pale. We think of genius, for if there ever was genius displayed in warfare, it was in Grant's Vicksburg campaign. One asks, why there and not at Shiloh?

I think the answer to this question is that the conditions at Shiloh were wholly different from those at Vicksburg. He arrived on the battlefield at Shiloh when his army was disorganized and panicky. The thing to do was to inspire his men, get the army reformed and into the battle again. This was beyond his capacity. It required a talent that Grant did not possess. He was not an inspirer of men—and he was also a poor battle tactician.

At Vicksburg he faced a problem of transportation. The campaign had passed its critical period when he finally got his army across the river. Time and the limp inefficiency of Pemberton did the rest.

In nineteen days after the crossing of the river Grant marched one hundred and eighty miles, fought and won five battles and captured 6,000 prisoners and nearly a hundred pieces of artillery . . . and during this time he was in a hostile country, without a base of supplies or a line of communications. For ten days the War Department did not hear from him at all.

By May 20th the doomed Pemberton was penned behind his trenches, and on May 22nd Grant endeavored to carry the whole line of the enemy's works by storm. The attack was a disastrous failure. The blue-coated boys struggled over the entanglements and climbed the Confederate works, only to be shot down. As the attacking line sagged back Grant got a message from McClernand, whose corps was on the extreme left of the Union line, saying that he had managed to capture and hold one of the enemy's outlying works, but he put his message in grandiloquent language. "The Union flag is flying over the fortress of Vicksburg," he wrote. He asked Grant to continue the assault, and said that with the support of the other two corps of the army, he thought he could push on further. Grant says: "I occupied a position from which I believed I could see as well as he what took place in his front, and I did not see the success he reported." Nevertheless, Grant decided to order another general assault, anyway, which was again repulsed with further loss.

Sherman and McPherson came to Grant's headquarters to discuss McClernand's failings. Dana heard it all, and his reports to Lincoln show that he partook of the prevailing mood. McClernand's wife, with her servants and baggage, had come to visit her husband, and at a time when every possible ounce of transportation was needed for military supplies. Not only that, but McClernand's men lacked discipline; and furthermore, McClernand's rifle-pits and trenches were pitiable little affairs that would make any West-Pointer ashamed. All that was said, and more.

McClernand was walking a tight-rope, and men on tight-ropes should not commit indiscretions. But McClernand did. At the bottom he was a vainglorious, boastful person, though he had considerable military ability. He was indiscreet enough to issue a congratulatory order to his troops in which he said that they had distinguished themselves in the assault, and that if they had been properly supported they would have taken and held a section of the enemy's works.

At that time there was a rule in effect that no order issued by a corps commander should be published in a newspaper until a copy of it had been sent to army headquarters. McClernand forgot all about this rule, and the correspondents wired his address to their newspapers.

Sherman came dashing up to Grant with a St. Louis newspaper in his hand. "Just look at that!" Grant looked, and read, with horror. Then it was passed to Rawlins and he read with horror. He declared that dismissal from command was not punishment enough; he thought McClernand ought to be put under arrest. McPherson was horror-stricken, too, when he saw McClernand's address printed in full, although no copy of it had been deposited with the headquarters staff.

Grant took his pen in hand. It was late at night. He wrote an order relieving McClernand from command for having allowed one of his orders to get to the newspapers before a copy of it had been sent to headquarters. He gave the order to Wilson, his aide, to deliver the first thing in the morning. Wilson says naïvely, in his recollection of the occurrence, that he decided to deliver the order that night—as late as it was—because he and the rest of the staff thought the Confederates might make a sortie before dawn, and that "McClernand would make a gallant resistance. His troops were veterans and, although somewhat loose in discipline, had never been beaten. They were justly regarded as among the best in the army. . . . It was also regarded as certain that McClernand would be in the thick of the fight; in which case Grant would probably overlook his past offenses and withhold the order." The safe thing, it seemed, was to deliver the dismissal to McClernand before he had a chance to distinguish himself. Wilson got to McClernand's headquarters at one o'clock in the morning, delivered the order, and the army was saved.

As a person with a grievance McClernand went about Washington for awhile, but nothing came of it. Grant had captured Vicksburg by that time—and that was the answer to every complaint.

§ 5

After the failure of the general assault Grant sat down patiently to reduce Vicksburg by a regular siege, and the soldiers and citizens in the town sat down just as patiently to a diet of mule meat and corn-bread.

The siege was uneventful, wearisome and dull; and the weather was almost unbearably hot. Grant started drinking again, as he always did under such conditions. Dana mentions one intemperate episode. On this occasion Dana was invited to accompany Grant on a trip of inspection up the Yazoo river to a place called Satartia. They went in a small steamboat. As soon as Grant appeared on board he "fell ill," to use Dana's refined language. He was so ill that he tumbled into a berth and lay there like a dead man. As they came near Satartia a Federal gunboat met them, and Dana learned that if they went any further they would be in danger of capture.

Dana awakened Grant and told him the situation but he says Grant was too ill to decide, so Dana ordered the boat turned around. The next morning Grant appeared at breakfast, freshly shaved and in a clean shirt and collar. "Well, Mr. Dana," he said, "I suppose we are at Satartia now."

"No, general," Dana said, "we are back at Haines' Bluff."

That was on June 6th. At one o'clock the next morning Rawlins began his solemn rites as Grant's personal conscience. At that hour he wrote a letter to Grant in which he discussed the entire question of temperance in its relation to Grant and the national welfare. Among other things Rawlins said:

> You have full control over your appetite, and can let drinking alone. Had you not pledged me the sincerity of your honor early last March, that you would drink no more during the war, and kept that pledge during your

recent campaign, you would not to-day have stood first in the world's history as a successful military leader. Your only solution depends upon your strict adherence to that pledge. . . .

Rawlins' admonitions were effective; we hear no more of liquor drinking for awhile.

On July 1, 1863, Pemberton decided to surrender. His army and the people of the town were starving. There was a truce on July 3rd while the terms of surrender were discussed. As the limp white flags rose in the hot summer air the Northern and Southern troops fraternized, and the Northern soldier boys divided their day's rations with the hungry Confederates.

Grant and Pemberton sat under a tree between the lines talking for an hour, while their officers and aides stood at a distance, watching them. Grant smoked a cigar, while Pemberton pulled moodily at blades of grass.

The formal capitulation of the fortress took place on July 4th. At noon the guns of Grant's army began to thunder the national salute from their ring of hills. Mingled with the roar of artillery the strains of "The Star Spangled Banner" floated through the streets of the stricken town.

The terms of surrender were extremely generous. All of Pemberton's officers and men were paroled and allowed to go to their homes until properly exchanged. The number of prisoners was 31,600, and the war material turned over to Grant included one hundred and seventy-two cannon, and sixty thousand muskets.

The capture of Vicksburg was the greatest victory ever gained by an American army from the founding of the Republic up to the year 1863. It put an end to the criticisms that had been hurled at Grant for two years. Even the most insistent fault-finding collapsed before such a stupendous accomplishment.

The President wrote Grant a personal letter of thanks, and made him a major-general of the regular army. (Until then he had been a major-general of volunteers.) As soon as Vicksburg was occupied the town was thronged with visitors from the North—Congressmen and their wives and daughters, the families of generals, and numerous committees for the inspection of one thing or another. The place took on a holiday air. There were vistas of broadcloth suits, bright dresses, parasols, fans and satin slippers. The ex-rebels who remained in the town started flourishing business enterprises and took in bushels of United States money.

Soon after the surrender Grant went down to New Orleans on a visit, and was handsomely entertained there by his army friends. He seems to have "fallen ill" on several occasions. While he was returning from a review given in his honor his horse ran away with him, dashed against a carriage and fell with his whole weight on Grant's leg. He was carried in a litter to the St. Charles Hotel, and there he lay in bed for two weeks.

On his return to Vicksburg he found Mrs. Grant and his four children. With them he spent a couple of months pleasantly in a quiet shady residence high on the bluff, facing the river.

The administration had come to look upon Grant as the best-fitted of all the Northern generals to pull an army out of a desperate situation.

The state of affairs at Chattanooga was desperate, indeed, and Grant was summoned by wire on October 10, 1863, to meet the Secretary of War at Indianapolis, and receive instructions from him. The President wanted Grant to go to Chattanooga and take command there. His new military district included all territory west of the Alleghenies, with the exception of Louisiana.

As the train bearing Grant and his staff stood in the smoky railroad station at Indianapolis black-bearded, be-spectacled Secretary of War Stanton came in. He had come from Washington to meet Grant. He grasped the hand of Dr. Kittoe, the staff surgeon, impulsively, and exclaimed: "How are you, General Grant? I knew you at sight from your pictures."

CHAPTER XXI

GRANT IS MADE GENERAL-IN-CHIEF

§ 1

THE Federal army, under the command of General W. S. Rosecrans, was penned up in Chattanooga; and the Confederates, under General Braxton Bragg, sat on the encircling hills waiting for the Federals to starve down to the level of mule meat, hard tack and white flags.

All the railroads that entered Chattanooga were held by Bragg. The Tennessee river is navigable up to the town, but a Confederate battery, and a swarm of sharp-shooters, posted near the foot of Lookout Mountain, prevented any steamboats with food or reënforcements from coming up.

The only line of supply still open was over a wagon road sixty miles long that ran across desperately steep hills to Bridgeport, Alabama. But this route was hopelessly impracticable as a means of supplying the 40,000 soldiers of Rosecrans' army. The horses sank in the semi-liquid mud up to their bellies; the loads had to be light; and sometimes it took a wagon train four days to make the trip from Bridgeport. Besides these natural obstacles the wagon trains were raided frequently by Confederate cavalry.

Rosecrans was a competent general who had become mentally paralyzed by defeat. On September 19 and 20, 1863, he had been badly beaten at the battle of Chickamauga and driven into his works around Chattanooga. Thereafter he seems to have lost every trace of initiative, and settled down quietly to await starvation.

The Union army was pinched by famine. Charles A. Dana wrote that when he reached Chattanooga, after a ride

302

from Bridgeport, his supper consisted of one square of fried hard-tack with a tiny piece of salted pork and a cup of coffee without sugar or milk. Guards were posted daily at feeding time over the horse troughs to keep the soldiers from stealing the horses' corn.

Now, Grant—with the aura of victory around him—arrived. He was still on crutches, and had to be helped off his horse. He and his staff rode over from Bridgeport in a drizzling rain, along a trail of wretchedness that was marked by the bodies of more than ten thousand dead horses and mules. This was on October 22, 1863.

Before leaving Louisville he had relieved Rosecrans from command by a telegram, and had put Major-General George H. Thomas, the next officer in rank, in his place. Of course, Grant intended to take full command himself as soon as he reached Chattanooga.

The food supply was the most pressing problem—but it was one that was already in the course of solution when Grant arrived. A few days before Rosecrans had been relieved from command both he and General Thomas had approved a plan which seemed likely to open the navigation of the river, and when Grant reached Thomas' headquarters the plan was about to be carried out.

This incident is a striking illustration of the vagaries of luck. Rosecrans was deposed because his army was starving on its feet. But if he had been left in command for ten days longer a continuous stream of food, clothing and ammunition would have been pouring into Chattanooga.

As it was, Grant got the credit with the public—and even with the rank and file of the army—for having opened up a line of supply as soon as he reached his new post. But the fact is that if he had remained on the Mississippi the army in Chattanooga would have been supplied with food just the same. He had nothing to do with it, except that he let the relief plan work out as it had been already conceived.

The author of the plan was Brigadier-General W. F. Smith, chief of engineers of the Army of the Cumberland, and the procedure was as simple as the alphabet. Smith made a reconnaissance down the river and he saw that a single Confederate battery was the key to the situation. If this battery could be taken, and the position held, then steamers would be able to come up the Tennessee either to Brown's Ferry, about three miles (by land) below Chattanooga, or to Kelly's Ferry, some miles further down the river. From these points supplies might be safely brought in wagons over a fairly good road.

On the night of October 26th, four days after Grant's arrival, fifty-two pontoons loaded with men, drifted silently down the river from Chattanooga. Just at daybreak this expeditionary force landed on the Confederate side at Brown's Ferry and took the battery and its infantry supports by surprise.

Before the position was fairly taken Union engineers were turning the fifty-two pontoons into a bridge. Later in the day several regiments and a battery of artillery that had marched overland from Chattanooga came across the bridge and entrenched. The Confederates made an effort to drive out the invaders and destroy the pontoon bridge, but without success.

Thus the siege was raised. Bragg's army remained on its hill-tops overlooking the town—at a distance—but it was no longer a siege. Large bodies of troops, Sherman's army among them, as well as food and supplies, came in.

§ 2

The siege of Chattanooga was over, but the armies still faced each other. The Confederate position was very strong. Missionary Ridge, which the main body of Bragg's army occupied, stands about four hundred feet above the Chattanooga plain. This Ridge constituted the right of Bragg's position. His left rested on Lookout Mountain, and between the ridge and the mountain there is a valley. At the southern end of this valley a line of breastworks connected the two wings of his position. Imagine, if you will, the disposition of the Confederate army in the shape of a horse-shoe. The two tips of the horse-shoe are Missionary Ridge and Lookout Mountain. The town of Chattanooga is almost between the tips.

Grant resolved to strike Bragg in his stronghold. Standing in the valley, and looking up at these towering hills, one cannot help being astonished at the audacity of Grant's idea. Lookout Mountain is simply unscalable by troops. Its sides are like a steep roof, with a single narrow road winding in snaky curves about them. At the top of the mountain there is a perpendicular parapet—a cliff rising stonily from the slope.

Missionary Ridge, on the other side of the horse-shoe, is not quite so steep; but, even so, one climbs it with considerable effort. Without a gun on my shoulder, I was very tired when I reached the crest where the Confederate batteries had been.

The battle of Missionary Ridge was the most dramatic spectacle of the war. It was the only engagement of the first importance in which every movement could be seen by a spectator standing in one spot. It had the theatrical quality of a vast stage play in the open air. The blue swarms of men climbing the slopes looked, in the distance, like animated dolls; and the bursting shells resembled puffy balls of white smoke tinged with fire.

On November 25, 1863, Grant's army assembled in the valley, in full view of the Confederate position. Bragg's officers, secure in their supposedly impregnable works, looked down on the Union army and thought that Grant intended merely to review a few brigades. More and more troops poured into the valley, and the blue lines kept extending themselves. The Confederate staff officers at Bragg's headquarters said to one another: "Now we shall see a real Yankee dress parade."

All at once the long line of bayonets moved toward Missionary Ridge and began to ascend the steep slope. It still seemed to be a review, but a review that had suddenly gone crazy.

Bragg's arrangements were peculiar, and were probably the chief contributing cause of his defeat. His troops were not kept compactly on the summit of the Ridge, but were distributed along its sides as well as on the top. At the base of the elevation, on a level with the plain, he had a line of rifle-pits; and half way up the slope there was another line.

When the Confederate riflemen were driven out of the first line they began to climb to the summit and were an effective shield for the Federal troops behind them. As the second line of rifle-pits was carried the number of Confederates moving in front of the attack was increased. Union soldiers and Confederates came over the crest of the Ridge in a mingled mass of blue and gray.

Grant's original intention was to carry only the first line of Bragg's defense, but when the men had driven the Confederates out of the rifle-pits at the foot of the Ridge they pushed on without orders. Grant, watching the attack from a knoll in the valley, turned to General Thomas and said angrily: "Who ordered those men up the heights?"

"No one," Thomas replied. "They're doing it of their own accord."

"It's all right if it succeeds," Grant remarked. "If it doesn't, some one will suffer."

The attack ran out of the frame of its original plan, and the summit of Missionary Ridge was taken by the rank and file on its own initiative. One of the inexplicable panics that sweep through crowds pervaded the Confederate army. Thousands of Bragg's men threw away their arms and fled like frightened children in spite of all efforts of their officers to check their rout. Bragg himself was almost taken prisoner.

On the other side of the valley the Confederates abandoned Lookout Mountain without much of a defense. Although their position on its crest was unassailable they were afraid that the entire mountain might be surrounded. To disguise their retreat they kept up a spirited fire of small arms and artillery. At the time there was a heavy fog around the mountain's top, and nothing could be seen. It is these innocuous fireworks that have been celebrated in poetry and painting as "The Battle Above the Clouds."

Grant's victory was complete. The Confederates were decisively beaten, and lost more than six thousand prisoners. There was no other Union success of the war—not even Gettysburg or Vicksburg—that caused so much rejoicing.

If we analyze this achievement we find that Grant did not have much to do with it. The question of feeding the garrison and raising the siege was solved by W. F. Smith before Grant arrived; and the battle of Missionary Ridge was won by the soldiers of the army who, by common impulse, went beyond anything that had been planned.

§ 3

There is no longer any question about Grant. The mystery of good fortune enfolds him like a gleaming cloud. Critical eyes are blinded by its radiance. He stands on the lofty plateau of fame, so close to the sun that he is seen only as a silhouetted phantasm, and the subject of a hundred uncertain myths. He is credited with the work of silent, efficient men of whom the public never hears; and when he falls into lapses and blunders—as every mortal does—the resultant disasters are laid at the doors of other people.

It is hard to see how he escaped being nominated for President in 1864, while his accomplishments were ringing in the air. He was approached by both the Democrats and Republicans, though it does not appear that either party, or anybody, made the slightest effort to ascertain if he had the knowledge, judgment and statesmanship to make a good President.

Lincoln was worried; he wanted a second term for himself.

He sent for a Galena man named Jones, who was a personal friend of both himself and Grant; and, through Jones' cautious soundings, Lincoln learned that the famous general did not want to be President, or have anything to do with politics.

To newspaper men who made inquiries as to his intentions, Grant said that he could do only one thing at a time, and for the time being he was busy with the Civil War. But what did he want after the war? Ah, as to that, his ambition was modest, indeed. He said that he would like to be mayor of Galena long enough to have a decent sidewalk built down to the railroad station. A drolly humorous reply . . . so it was considered. Laughter all around; notebooks on the correspondents' knees; hastily scratched telegrams—and the news went winging its way over the country that General Grant's only demand of his country was to have a sidewalk repaired.

Lincoln was undoubtedly relieved by Grant's announcement, so when Congress created the grade of lieutenant-general, Lincoln immediately raised Grant to that rank, and put him at the head of all the armies. He was instructed to report to the President at Washington.

§ 4

Grant entered the city of Washington for the first time in his life on March 8, 1864. In appearance he seemed older than his forty-two years. None of the men in the bustling lobby of Willard's hotel recognized him as he came in with his son Frederick, then a lad of fourteen.

The clerk at the desk was astonished when he read the name that this rather dingy looking guest had written on the register. The hotel had often entertained generals of high rank, but their coming had been preceded by a flock of aides who inspected the rooms and ordered the furniture changed around. Then, when all was ready, the general in full dress uniform would sweep in and disappear upstairs, surrounded by his escort. There was none of this swankiness in Grant's behavior. In a few hours he was mingling with the miscellaneous crowd in the lobby.

Richard Henry Dana, author of *Two Years Before the Mast*, happened to be at the hotel. He records his impressions:

> A short, round-shouldered man, in a very tarnished major-general's uniform, came up. . . . He had no gait, no station, no manner, rough, light-brown whiskers, a blue eye and rather a scrubby look withal. A crowd formed around him; men looked, stared at him, as if they were taking his likeness, and two generals were introduced. . . .
>
> I joined the starers. I saw that the ordinary, scrubby-looking man, with a slightly seedy look, as if he was out of office and on half-pay and nothing to do but hang around the entry of Willard's, cigar in mouth, had a clear blue eye, and a look of resolution, as if he could not be trifled with, and an entire indifference to the crowd about him. Straight nose, too. Still, to see him talking and smoking in the lower entry of Willard's, in that crowd, in such times—the generalissimo of our armies, on whom the destiny of the empire seemed to hang! . . .
>
> He gets over the ground queerly. He does not march, nor quite walk, but pitches along as if the next step would bring him on his nose.

On the day following his arrival Grant was given his commission as lieutenant-general commanding all the Union armies, by President Lincoln in the presence of the cabinet. Lincoln spoke a few sentences, handed Grant his commission, and the new general-in-chief read a little prepared speech. He was nervous and his hands shook. Gideon Welles, Secretary of the Navy, says in his *Diary*, "General Grant was somewhat embarrassed."

§ 5

Grant came to chief command at the right moment for the good of his own career. The nation had been educated in

war for three years, and was finally prepared to face its harsh
realities without a quiver.   If he had been raised to high
command in the East in 1862 instead of in 1864 it seems probable that he would not have lasted a month, for at that time the
people of the North could not have endured the long and
grim roll of casualties that measured his progress through
Virginia.

But since 1862 the country had seen the war drag on
through the changing seasons.   It had long since ceased to be
a military holiday; the winged spirit of adventure was no longer
in the air.   Nothing remained but blood and bayonets, muddy
trenches and the drudgery of camps . . . and from the national
treasury money poured in a torrent.

Public opinion, which is always made by the upper classes—
by the financial and intellectual nobility—had crystallized into
an angry desire to beat the South at all costs—to smash it
flat—without regard to methods, or to losses.   The curious,
spectral being called the intelligent public had become tired of
arguments, and wanted to hear nothing but the brass bands of
a victorious army.

Lincoln, with his ear to the ground, sensed the combativeness of the nation.   He realized—and, I think, with infinite
sadness—that the people expected nothing of him but to win
the war, and that they cared but little for his ideas on any
other subject.

Yet, at this very moment when the leaders of the country,
its newspapers, and its aristocracy of money and brains, were
most firmly resolved to win the war at all costs, the resistance
to the draft, and to war taxation, was greater than it had ever
been before.   The war did not have many friends among the
great mass of people who had to do the actual fighting.   But
this opposition was turgid, blank and inarticulate.   The brilliant spokesmen were all on the other side.

The extraordinary strength of this silent revolt was shown
by the popular vote in the presidential election of 1864.

McClellan was nominated by the Democrats on a platform which meant that every vote for him was a vote against the war. McClellan received 1,800,000 votes against Lincoln's 2,200,000, and it seems probable that he would have got an actual majority if the full force of the administration's political machinery had not been used against him. The soldiers at the front were allowed to vote, and there was a great deal of electioneering in the army. But officers who made speeches in favor of McClellan found themselves suddenly and unaccountably mustered out of the service. Republican campaign documents were distributed, in many cases, by the regimental adjutants to the men drawn up in line, while the Democratic leaflets were not allowed in the camps at all.

§ 6

The predecessors of Grant in Virginia had made a discouraging string of failures.

McClellan had begun his campaign in 1862 with the bright rainbow of ardent hopes resting on his head. His popularity with his soldiers, with the press and the public, was enormous.

But McClellan was a brittle person. He had the fatal defect of going to pieces easily, of letting his courage leak away. His "On to Richmond" trip began with the accumulation of armament in unprecedented quantities, with the massing of the largest army that had ever been seen in America—and it ended in the Chickahominy swamps, where McClellan sat under the dripping trees and wrote ill-tempered letters of reproach to Lincoln, in which he declared that he had been deserted by the administration.

His invasion of Virginia eventually came to an end without even the comfort of having met a great disaster.

Then came the boastful Pope, whose career was short. He wrote bombastic addresses to his army from "Headquarters in the Saddle," and announced that he was about to ferret out "the rebel Jackson," whom he intended to destroy forthwith. But while he was getting ready to run Jackson to earth the latter made one of his famous swift marches and appeared suddenly between Pope's army and the city of Washington. Before Pope could change front to meet this unexpected state of affairs Jackson fell upon him and defeated him decisively at the second battle of Manassas. So Pope passed from his high position in the saddle to the region of pen and ink, with which he labored to explain, justify, incriminate and condemn.

McClellan was tried again. The army received him with cheers and huzzas. The soldiers, "tears in their eyes," surrounded him and clung to his horse's mane.

The time was critical. The muscular Southern army, clanging with victory, had crossed the Potomac and was in Maryland. Washington and Baltimore were about to drop into the Confederate pocket. But McClellan saved them. He defeated Lee at Antietam, and drove him from Maryland. With a little more aggressiveness he could have destroyed the Confederate army before it had time to get across the Potomac. But he did not follow Lee at all. Instead of pursuing the defeated enemy he sat down to nurse his army and talk about his victory.

Lincoln relieved him from command—this was in November, 1862—and turned over the army to General Burnside. Upon taking command Burnside "wept like a child," and said that he was not fit for the job. That was his assertion, and he proved the soundness of his own estimate of himself a few weeks later when, on an icy December day of 1862, he hurled the Union army against a stone wall at Fredericksburg. Lee's men stood safely behind the stone wall, and shot down the Northern troops with the ease of men at target practice. The Union dead, wounded and missing amounted to 12,300 against a Confederate loss of 4,500. The Northern people were aghast at the horror of the thing—though they became accustomed later on to these gigantic slaughters—and

Burnside's official head was vigorously demanded by the press and the public. Lincoln put Hooker in his place, and Burnside passed into the silences for a while.

Hooker was undoubtedly the worst commander the Army of the Potomac ever had. He was boastful, dissolute and lazy; and he had the personal habits of a weary night-club proprietor. Lincoln made a mistake in selecting him, of course, but all men in complicated positions make mistakes now and then. Upon taking command Hooker said: "My plans are perfect, and when I start to carry them out may God have mercy on General Lee, for I will have none."

He encountered Lee in one battle, that of Chancellorsville, on May 1 to 3, 1863, and was utterly beaten under circumstances which made his further retention in command nothing less than a national disgrace.

The greatest defeat that has ever fallen upon an army under the American flag occurred at Chancellorsville. Hooker had 97,000 men opposed to Lee's 57,000. Only the coming of darkness saved Hooker's army from an abject, pell-mell rout, but as it was he lost 16,000 men during the three days' fighting.

Hooker's successor was General George Gordon Meade, a soldier of ability and large experience. Meade was a man of culture, of wide intellectual horizons. He loved ideas and books, and could talk interestingly on many subjects. His associates were people of taste and feeling. Meade was undoubtedly out of place—fundamentally misplaced, I mean—in the atavistic, primitive business of warfare, yet he applied himself so diligently to his profession that he was a first-rate general. His chief personal defect was irascibility. During a campaign in the field he was usually so ill-tempered that the officers of his staff were afraid to speak to him.

He was put in chief command three days before the battle of Gettysburg, while the marching army was strung along the roads for fifty miles. Although he checked the Confederate invasion of the North on the field of Gettysburg his victory was not as complete as it should have been. This was hardly Meade's fault; he had not had time to become thoroughly acquainted with the disposition of his own forces.

When Grant took command of all the armies, East and West, he announced that he intended to accompany the Army of the Potomac. A curious arrangement this was, for it seems obvious that his proper place as general-in-chief was in Washington, close to the radiating lines of telegraph. But such a situation would have been intolerable to him; he detested offices and office-work, and could not manage anything at a distance. So, after establishing a general plan of campaign, he left Halleck in Washington, as a national chief of staff, to receive reports and transmit orders.

Grant's presence at the front with the army in Virginia put Meade in an anomalous and uncomfortable position. Meade offered to resign . . . but let Grant tell it in his own words. He says (*Memoirs*, Vol. II, p. 116):

> I had known General Meade slightly in the Mexican war, but had not met him since until this visit. . . . Meade evidently thought that I might want to make still one more change not yet ordered. He said that I might want an officer who had served with me in the West, mentioning Sherman specially, to take his place. If so, he begged me not to hesitate about making the change. He urged that the work before us was of such vast importance to the whole nation that the feeling or wishes of no one person should stand in the way of selecting the right men for all positions. For himself, he would serve to the best of his ability wherever placed. I assured him that I had no thought of substituting any one for him. As to Sherman, he could not be spared from the West.

Grant added that the incident "gave me a more favorable opinion of Meade," and that he "tried to make General Meade's position as nearly as possible what it would have been if I had been in Washington or any other place away from his command."

He did not succeed very well in this effort. With Grant present, and on the field, authority naturally centered in him. In a certain sense Meade became merely a transmitting intelligence, receiving orders from Grant and passing them along. But in another sense he was responsible for the conduct of the battles, for Grant never became a tactician, even with all his experience.

Before the campaign was over Meade made his own position even more uncomfortable through a row with the newspaper correspondents. One of the newspaper men, after the battle of the Wilderness, wired his newspaper that Meade had wanted to retreat, and that only the verdict of Grant had kept the army from withdrawing. There was no truth in this report; it was merely camp gossip. When the article appeared in print, and Meade saw it, he lost his easily losable temper and had the correspondent drummed out of camp, carrying on his breast a placard bearing the word "Liar" in large letters. Thereupon the newspaper correspondents with the army unanimously resolved not to mention Meade's name again. The newspaper readers of the day almost forgot that Meade was alive, for he was surrounded by a silence like that of the tomb.

That was a deplorable error on the part of Meade. It made his effacement by Grant complete.

Colonel Lyman, of Meade's staff, wrote bitterly in his *Diary* that he was "boiling and fuming over the personal neglect of General Meade and the totally undeserved prominence given to Sheridan."

From this the reader may infer that Meade did not belong to the tribe of Grant, Sherman and Sheridan, and the inference will be entirely correct. But Grant did speak highly of Meade on various occasions, and on May 13, 1864, he wrote to Stanton that "General Meade has more than met my most sanguine expectations." When, however, it came to the distribution of the greater honors, Meade was left out.

After the end of the war, when Sheridan was made a lieutenant-general, instead of Meade, on Grant's recommendation, we find this passage in Meade's letters to his wife: "My own sweet love, you can imagine the force of the blow, but . . . we must find consolation in the consciousness . . . that it is the cruelest and meanest act of injustice, and the hope, if there is any sense of wrong or justice in the country, that the man who perpetrated it will some day be made to feel so."

§ 7

In the spring of 1864 the Southern Confederacy was only a hollow shell, with all its strength on its outer edges. Three years of warfare had destroyed many thousands of its best men, and the morale of its people had been weakened by deprivations.

But, despite the poverty of the people and the terrific losses that the Southern armies had sustained, there were still 480,000 men on the Confederate muster rolls on January 1, 1864. Probably fifty per cent of these men were actually under arms and in ranks—and most of those in service were veterans of many battles.

Grant saw clearly the nature of the problem that stood before him. He realized that the Southern armies would have to be beaten and depleted of men . . . in other words, they would have to be fought to a standstill. An essential feature of his plan of campaign was, as he said himself, "to hammer continuously against the armed force of the enemy and his resources until by mere attrition, if in no other way," the South should be conquered.

To accomplish this he had at his service a total of 533,000 men, under arms and present for duty, when he took command, though there were 860,000 men on the rolls.

Now begins the great strategy of the war, but to Grant it was not strategy—for he did not know the meaning of the word —but only common sense.

The first feature of his plan was a concentration of military strength into two or three areas. The second feature was a simultaneous movement along the whole line with the Confederate armies as an objective; and the third feature was the penetration of the Confederacy's hollow shell, with a consequent destruction of the enemy's railroads and resources.

To carry out these ideas Grant planned three major operations, with a number of smaller or secondary movements—all contributing, however, to a common result.

The business of the Army of the Potomac, as he conceived it, was to crush Lee's army and destroy it. His method of doing this was to invade Virginia from Washington and encounter Lee on his own ground.

At the mouth of the river James was another Union army, with its headquarters at Fortress Monroe. It was called the Army of the James, and was unfortunately under the command of General Benjamin F. Butler, whom we have already met in his rôle as the profiteering hero of New Orleans.

Grant's plan included the coöperation of the Army of the James. Butler was instructed to move up the James river as Grant began his overland march toward Richmond from the north. The function of the Army of the James was to get as close to Richmond as possible, and to threaten that city and its lines of communication with the South. In the meantime Grant would encounter Lee in battle.

The basic features of this scheme were excellent; they rested on the soundest military conceptions. Lee had the advantage of interior lines, it is true, but this advantage was nullified by Grant's immense superiority in numbers. Lee was so closely held, and had to fight so hard, that he could not detach even a regiment to meet the Army of the James.

At the beginning of the campaign the Army of the Potomac

contained nearly two men for every man that Lee was able to bring to the field. Meade commanded 118,000 troops against Lee's 62,000.

Grant's plans went to pieces through the incompetency of General Butler. Butler's advance up the James threw Petersburg and Richmond into a wild state of alarm. These places had been stripped of troops to furnish reënforcements for Lee. Old men, boys, department clerks and convalescents had muskets thrust into their hands and were hurried down the river to do what they could to stop Butler's coming. These nondescripts made a feeble defense, which Butler mistakenly estimated as the work of a large and highly organized army. He had Richmond within his grasp, but he was so impressed by the battalions recruited from the high schools and the Homes for the Aged that he retreated into a sort of pocket of the James—a peninsula in the shape of a bottle—and fortified himself there. He was thoroughly "bottled up" in this Bermuda Hundred peninsula, to use Grant's phrase, and remained bottled and useless until Grant fought his way down from the north and rescued him.

One pauses here to wonder why Grant did not relieve Butler from command, and put some fighting member of the Grant clique—Sheridan, let us say—at the head of the Army of the James. The answer is that he was afraid to depose this brazen Massachusetts politician for reasons which remain, on the whole, obscure and mysterious even to this day.

The failure of Butler's part of the program made it necessary for the Army of the Potomac to do virtually all the fighting. If Butler had played his part Lee would have had to fall back on Richmond with his entire army—or, if not, he would have had to detach a large force for the defense of that city.

The third operation of major importance—according to Grant's plan—was the invasion of Georgia by Sherman. When the campaign began Sherman was at Chattanooga, and opposed to him was the Confederate general, Joseph E. Johnston.

Sherman's army, like that of Grant, was much superior in numbers to its opponent. Under Sherman's command, as an invading force, there were 98,000 men. Johnston had only 43,000, but his disadvantage in numbers was offset—partially, if not wholly—by the fact that he was on the defensive in a country full of hills and ravines that could be easily fortified. He was in a position to resist Sherman's advance at every step.

Besides these major projects, which formed the frame of Grant's campaign, there were a number of secondary expeditions—such as the invasion of the Shenandoah Valley—but none of these was expected to be decisive.

All these operations were to be simultaneous; they were all to begin on the first of May, 1864.

CHAPTER XXII

GRANT AND LEE

§ 1

GENERAL GRANT wore white cotton gloves on the first day of the battle of the Wilderness. His staff had never seen him wear gloves before, and the officers wondered. White cotton gloves. He was visibly nervous for the first time during the war. Horace Porter says Grant smoked twenty cigars before nightfall, and whittled sticks all day.

He kept his coat buttoned, too. Gloves and buttoned coat, and shoes shined. Probably he felt that his first day's appearance on the brilliant stage of Virginia required some sprucing up.

On the second day he discarded his cotton gloves, and before a week had passed he looked the same as he had at the siege of Vicksburg—like an Illinois wheat farmer who has come into the village bank to cash a check.

The short campaign of the Wilderness stands as the bloodiest military enterprise in American history. It began on May 5, 1864, when the Army of the Potomac crossed the Rapidan and encountered Lee; it ended, properly speaking, six weeks later, when Grant moved his army to the south side of the James and appeared before the entrenchments around Petersburg.

At the beginning of this overland movement Grant had 118,-000 men. By June 14th the losses in the Union army amounted to a total of 54,926 in killed, wounded and missing—or almost as many men as there were in the whole of Lee's army when the campaign began. Yet reënforcements poured in so steadily

WARTIME PHOTOGRAPHS OF GENERAL GRANT

General Robert E. Lee

that, despite his heavy losses, Grant had as many men at the end of the campaign as he had at the beginning. The North, even as determined as it was at that time on the conquest of the South, was aghast at this enormous destruction of life.

Considered from a military standpoint the campaign was a great success for the Union cause. Grant wore Lee's army down to the bone. He held on to it so tightly, and fought so fiercely, that it could hardly breathe. As Grant's army was depleted by losses new men came from the North. But Lee's reënforcements came in little batches, or not at all. In six weeks Grant had pushed Lee, by main strength, across the northern part of Virginia, and finally stood almost in sight of Richmond.

§ 2

Let us glance at the essential features of the campaign.

Grant crossed the Rapidan on May 4, 1864, and turned south. The road, on the south side, leading from the crossing place, runs through a peculiar region called the Wilderness. It is a tract about twelve miles square. At the time of the Civil War the Wilderness consisted of deserted farms—abandoned because of the poor soil—thick and tangled woods, tall weeds, gullies and ravines—a country without vistas. On such a terrain it is impossible to employ either artillery or cavalry effectively.

Grant thought that if he was not opposed at Germanna Ford on the Rapidan he would not have to fight at all in the Wilderness, but he was mistaken as to Lee's intentions. The Confederate commander purposely allowed him to cross the Rapidan without hindrance. Lee's plan was to fight Grant in the Wilderness, where the Confederate officers knew the ground, and where Grant's superiority in numbers would be offset by the nature of the battlefield.

Lee's eager army struck Grant's long column, and all day

long the Wilderness was filled with smoke and a pandemonium of sound. The dry leaves under foot caught fire, and when darkness came the sky was glowing with the reflected light of forest fires. Many of the wounded were burned to death where they fell.

At the close of the day the situation of Grant's army seemed appalling. Rawlins said (according to James H. Wilson) that Grant met it "outwardly with calmness and self-possession, but after he had asked such questions and given such orders as the emergency seemed to call for, he withdrew to his tent and, throwing himself face downward on his cot, instead of going to sleep, gave vent to his feelings in a way which left no room to doubt that he was deeply moved."

What does that mean? Does it mean that he wept? I think it does. He did weep at times. When he heard that McPherson had been killed before Atlanta he went into his tent and sobbed for half an hour. At the bottom he was emotional in an epoch when emotion was considered weakness, so he usually concealed his feelings under a mask of wooden-Indian stolidity.

Most of the officers of the Army of the Potomac expected to receive orders to retreat across the Rapidan; but the orders, when they came instructed the army to prepare to move on Lee's army at daybreak. The Confederates, too, were up at dawn. Lee had decided to attack Grant as soon as it was light enough to see. So they came together again, head-on, in the second day's fight at the Wilderness . . . and the second day was even more bloody than the first. It was really a drawn battle, with Lee having a shade the better of it.

During the night word came fluttering through the somber woods that preparations were to be made at once for abandoning the position. So Grant had decided, after all, to go back across the Rapidan? Men looked at each other with this question on their lips. To retreat—as all his predecessors had done—after his enormous losses . . . lives wasted . . . men left dead on the field and nothing accomplished.

These depressing thoughts were in the soldiers' minds as they moved about the uncertain camp fires and got their things together to make a night march. Before day the great army, with all its artillery and trains, rumbled down the broken roads—not toward the Rapidan, but southward, toward Richmond. Tired men reeling in moonlight.

As Grant himself rode along the marching column a little before daybreak a wave of cheers greeted him. The army realized that here was a man who did not intend to turn back. He had gone around Lee's right and was moving on Spottsylvania—a step nearer the heart of the Confederacy.

But Lee had anticipated him. His shattered army was up and moving, too. As Grant's columns approached Spottsylvania the advance guard reported that the Confederate army was in front of them. Lee had taken a shorter route. Before long the Federal advance was again brought to a stop, and the drumming guns began to sound on the horizon.

At Spottsylvania there was a series of battles, all characterized by the same motif . . . a head-on attack of Union troops, launched against the Confederate works, while Grant felt cautiously around his opponent's right flank.

On May 11th he wrote to Halleck: "We have now ended the sixth day of very hard fighting. . . . I propose to fight it out on this line if it takes all summer."

We have observed that Grant had an instinct for slogans and catchy phrases. "I propose to fight it out on this line if it takes all summer" became as popular as "I propose to move immediately upon your works."

When the ghastly tale of casualties spread through the North the public took heart from Grant's confidence. Something was being accomplished, at any rate, even if the achievement cost an appalling number of lives.

It was a matter of common observation at headquarters that Grant and Rawlins were drifting apart. Rawlins was bitterly opposed to Grant's policy of hurling the army against heavily

entrenched positions, and he said so. He called it a "murderous
policy of military incompetents." He thought that Grant
was influenced in adopting this form of attack by Colonel
C. B. Comstock of the staff. Comstock was an engineer—a
West-Pointer—whose constant refrain was "Smash 'em up!
Smash 'em up!"

I think Rawlins was mistaken, and that Comstock's views
and Grant's merely happened to coincide. The whole of Grant's
military history shows that the smashing, head-on attack was
his style of warfare.

After Spottsylvania there was another flank turning, and
another advance toward the Confederate capital. The soldiers
of Grant's army saw the nature of this simple strategy, and
they called it, "sidling toward Richmond."

Lee was ahead of him again, and was again pushed back.
The fighting went on steadily, day after day. The opposing
armies rolled over each other in the mud and dirt, like two
determined wrestlers. At the end of each bout the Confederates had been thrown back a few inches, or a few feet, or a
few miles. It was warfare in the rough, without art or
strategy.

On June 2nd the Union army had got within six miles of the
exterior fortifications of Richmond. Grant was on the ground
that McClellan had fought over two years before. There
could be no more "sidling" movements; Richmond lay straight
ahead, toward the southwest; and Lee's army stood squarely
across the road, behind a line of formidable breastworks.

Grant decided on an assault with his entire army, and it
took place at four-thirty on the morning of June 3, 1864. This
engagement is known in history as the battle of Cold Harbor.
It was the shortest important battle in the Civil War. The
main attack on the Confederate works was over in an hour,
though intermittent firing was kept up until noon. During
that time Grant had lost seven thousand men, while the Confederate casualties were less than a thousand. Grant may not

have known that the attack was hopeless before it began, but the soldiers of his army knew it. Thousands of them, expecting to be killed, pinned to their coats little strips of paper bearing their names and addresses, so their bodies might be identified.

The uncommunicative Grant was more than ordinarily reticent about the Cold Harbor disaster. In his final official report of the army's operations he gives only two sentences to this catastrophe: "On the 3rd of June we again assaulted the enemy's works in the hope of driving him from this position. In this attempt our loss was heavy, while that of the enemy I have reason to believe comparatively light." In his *Memoirs* he says: "I have always regretted that the last assault at Cold Harbor was ever made . . . no advantage whatever was gained to compensate for the heavy loss we sustained."

The effect of the Wilderness campaign on the public mind was to lower Grant's prestige. The peace party, which included most of the Democrats and some Republicans, called him "Grant, the Butcher," and the reverberating gloom and depression shook the nation's confidence in the final outcome of the war.

Even before the slaughter at Cold Harbor the Army of the Potomac had begun to lose its morale. The rank and file was profoundly affected, and the officers, as well as the soldiers, were at times on the verge of mutiny. General Warren, one of Grant's corps commanders, said to Captain Lyman at Cold Harbor, "For thirty-six days now it has been one funeral procession past me."

But look at the other side. Lee's army was dwindling away, and the long shadows of sunset were falling on the Southern Confederacy. Though Lee's losses were smaller than Grant's, they were much larger than he could stand. A steady stream of desertions flowed from his army, while recruits came slowly.

Lee could not risk a battle in the open; he was to remain behind his entrenchments until the end. He defeated Grant disastrously at Cold Harbor, yet Grant did not budge an inch. The omens of ill fortune are written large on Lee's sky, and he sees them. There is an undertone of despondency in his letters to his family. In these slow-paced, fatherly epistles we find him relying on Providence, the last refuge of discouraged generals.

§ 3

The roots of Robert E. Lee's character were deeply implanted in the past. He was the last representative of the age of chivalry, and he saw the modern world as the Chevalier Bayard would have seen it. In another sense he reaches back to Oliver Cromwell. Like that impetuous Puritan, Lee combined the fighting spirit of a young warrior with the moral impulses of an elderly bishop.

The sentimentalists have long since taken the image of General Lee to their museum of heroes, where the light of stained glass windows falls over it like a colored veil. In the pallid glow of the shrine one tiptoes about, whispers, and admires. The new generations which pass through this quiet sanctuary emerge blinking into the sunshine with the idea that Lee was merely a nice, gray, God-bless-you gentleman who patted little children on the head and was kind to everybody. A general who wept over wounded soldiers and talked like a father to his men.

None of this portrays him the least bit. Lee was a man's man, a fighter by instinct, and a soldier through his love of the profession of arms. A red-faced fighting man who became excited at times and shook his fist at the enemy. His chief military trait was headlong combativeness.

He was much more of a fighting man than Grant, who detested war. Lee, on the contrary, loved war as one loves a favorite game. At Fredericksburg he said, while he overlooked the battle on the plain below him, "It is well that this is terrible, or else we might grow fond of it."

He was a devout Christian, a praying soldier who believed that God puts His hand into human affairs and manages all things for the best. Certainly no man can be a Christian and a soldier at the same time, for the two ideas are wholly incompatible, but Lee—like millions of other men—managed, in some occult way, to reconcile them.

He lived up to the high ideals of his race. He had the feeling of *noblesse oblige*—the sense that great authority implies great responsibilities and great humility. At his headquarters table during the Civil War meat was served only twice a week, and the regular diet was boiled cabbage, sweet potatoes, and corn bread. When his staff officers grumbled at this plebeian diet Lee explained that he did not think it right to live in any better style while the men in his army had so little to eat.

His personality was sharply defined, and marvelously self-contained. He had the true patrician contempt for the riff-raff of public opinion; he went his own way, had his own methods, and was ready to stand or fall by them. There was a feeling of personal grandeur in his life. He lived and thought on a plane of loftiness.

"In all essential respects," Mr. Rhodes says, "Lee resembled Washington." He did, indeed, yet the likeness is not wholly satisfying. There was something in Lee that Washington did not have. After much reflection I have come to the conclusion that Lee was Washington, as Washington would have been with a Puritan conscience. Washington liked fun, but Lee never had any fun, and did not want any. He was so remote from the joy of life that he turned away from the simplest pleasures. On his campaigns he often slept on the bare ground when there was a house and a bed near at hand. General Richard Taylor, who knew him well, says that "General Lee was never so uncomfortable as when he was comfortable."

And there is another difference between Washington and Lee. The Father of our Country was keenly interested in politics, but Lee had no taste for politics or statecraft. His intellectual range was, in fact, very limited, and his excellence as a soldier filled his whole personality to the brim. It was suggested, in 1864, that if the Confederacy should win its independence, Lee ought to follow Davis as President; but Lee, when he heard of this, declared that he did not possess the requisite training to be President, and would not accept the office under any circumstances.

Such modesty is both commendable and unusual, but as a policy it has its weak points. Lee was so thoroughly convinced of his own subserviency to civil authority that he sat silent while Davis proceeded to carry out his own half-baked military schemes. Lee wanted to abandon Richmond in 1864 and concentrate the Southern armies at some point farther south. But Davis would not listen to any such plan, and Lee quietly acquiesced. Lee was entirely right; the abandonment of Richmond would have been a great stroke of strategy; it would have enabled Lee to take his army to Georgia and beat Sherman and then return and fight Grant.

With all his nostalgia for the past, for the dignity and urbanity of the vanished eighteenth century, Lee was nevertheless a mid-Victorian in thought and action. He believed that life has a purpose, which was the prevailing obsession of the Victorian era. But life has no special purpose—none that is demonstrable. There is nothing to life but the living of it. This state of mind was quite incomprehensible to General Lee.

Such men, oppressed by a sense of duty, are admirable but not charming. Lee was singularly lacking in charm. He was almost as uncharming as Grant—and that is saying a good deal, yet he and Grant were utterly different in character. Lee was too cold, too serious, and too indirect in speech, to spread the warm glow of good-fellowship around him. He considered duty "the sublimest word in the English language"; and his insistence on personal rectitude was rather overwhelming in a world of poor, weak mortals. One begins to think that General Lee was not a person, but a force, like God or electricity.

His lack of modernism is astonishing. His ideas about everything but warfare were antiquated, but in that branch of knowledge he was thoroughly up to date. He heard that his daughters were reading novels, and he wrote to them from the army that novel-reading was a waste of time. They ought to pay strict attention to more serious works of the intellect. They ought to spend their time on history, and philosophy, and he recommended a perusal of the ancient classics.

Was Lee a greater general than Grant? This is a natural question, but one that it is impossible to answer. Both Lee and Grant were generals of great ability. Every one whose opinion is worth having agrees as to this. But it is hardly possible to compare their respective merits, as one compares two ears of corn, for the conditions surrounding them were so different.

There is no doubt, I think, that Lee was a better tactician than Grant; he was worth much more than Grant when it came to moving troops on a battlefield. But Grant had more tenacity, or stubbornness. I do not believe that Grant would have retreated from the field at Gettysburg.

The ultimate test of a general's ability is not success—for even Napoleon was beaten—but the capacity to use whatever resources he has to the best advantage. Judged by this standard Lee must certainly be considered a captain of the first rank.

§ 4

After the slaughter of June 3rd even the stubborn Grant concluded that Lee's position at Cold Harbor was impregnable. There could be no sense in having the army destroyed in hopeless assaults, especially in view of the fact that the army tacitly declined to be destroyed. In those hot, uncertain days of early June it was commonly understood by all the officers that if another attack against the Confederate works was ordered the men would refuse to obey.

But Grant could not stand still. To remain where he was would be simply playing into the enemy's hands. Lee would have liked nothing better than to have kept the Union army in a state of inert catalepsy before his Cold Harbor trenches for an indefinite period. The Confederates needed time to recuperate and reorganize.

Grant decided to move his army to the south side of the James. He would then stand between Richmond and the states to the south. It would be Lee, instead of Grant, who would have to defend his line of supplies, for Grant could bring supplies and reënforcements by steamer up the James river, while Lee would have to depend on the two railroads that ran southward from Richmond. In time, Grant thought, the Union lines might be extended further and further toward the left, so that eventually he would have both the railroads that entered Richmond from the south in his possession. When that was once accomplished Lee would be forced to abandon Richmond immediately, or surrender both the city and his army.

The move to the south side of the James was decided upon, and the Army of the Potomac began to cross the river on June 14th. Lee was completely deceived. He thought that Grant intended to move to the north of Richmond, and he persisted so long in his belief that he was on the verge of an irretrievable catastrophe before he discovered what Grant was actually doing.

Twenty miles to the south of Richmond is the town of Petersburg. It was garrisoned at the time by a small force under General Beauregard. Petersburg was the military gateway to Richmond. The Weldon railroad ran through Petersburg. With the town in Union hands there would be only one other railway line—that running up from Danville—over which Lee could obtain men and supplies from the south.

Grant knew the importance of Petersburg. His instructions

were that the head of the column should move against it with the least possible delay after crossing the river. The Union forces might have gone ahead like a steam-roller and smashed Beauregard, but they didn't. The generals on the spot organized skirmish lines, made reconnaissances, wrote down their observations, and did everything they could think of except attack Beauregard in force.

The fact is that the Army of the Potomac was so unnerved after Cold Harbor that it had lost its dash. For months there was a pronounced reluctance on the part of the rank and file to go up against Confederate entrenchments. This state of affairs does not appear in the official records, but it makes a rather glaring appearance in the diaries and letters of officers.

Beauregard sent frantic hourly telegrams to Lee, who was still fifty miles away on the other side of Richmond, facing Grant's almost deserted trenches. Meanwhile the blue-clad soldiers continued to pour across the river. By the sixteenth Grant had 48,000 men on the south side, while the Confederates in Petersburg numbered about 14,000. Grant himself arrived on the sixteenth, but even he was unable to get an attack under way.

Beauregard's telegrams had ceased; he was sending staff officers instead . . . gloomy men who sat in Lee's tent at two o'clock in the morning and told him that the horizon in front of Petersburg was blue and silver with men and bayonets, and that at night the sky glowed with the reflection of the Union campfires. But Lee continued to believe that the movement was merely a ruse.

The little town of Petersburg was excited as it had never been before. Beauregard had taken every white man who knew how to load a gun. An attack in force might have been made on the Confederate works late in the afternoon of the sixteenth, but it was found, when everything else was ready to move, that the chief of artillery had sent all the horses to water and they could not be brought back before night. That hour's delay probably saved Petersburg for the Confederates for nine months.

Lee was at last awake to his danger, and he moved with speed. He became convinced at three o'clock in the morning that Grant's army was before Petersburg, and by four his troops were on the way. Next afternoon, when the long deferred Union assault in force was about to begin, Grant's officers—listening—heard the hum and stir of an army moving into position. Lee had arrived.

CHAPTER XXIII

THE SUNSET OF THE CONFEDERACY

§ 1

THE siege of Petersburg was long and dreary. It lasted from the middle of June, 1864, until the first of April, 1865. The network of trenches, forts and redans that constituted the Confederate defense was too strong to be taken by assault. Grant hammered at them with his artillery and gradually extended his lines to the left. As he had more than twice as many men as Lee it was only a question of time before the Southern lines would become too thin to hold. They could not be stretched indefinitely to parallel Grant's extension.

Grant's plan was to "sidle" far enough to the left to obtain possession of both the railroads which entered Richmond from the South. In the meantime his cavalry, under Sheridan, circled in far-ranging raids and tore up miles of the railroads again and again.

There were no more headlong assaults on the Confederate works. A change had come over Grant's spirit. He, too, like everybody else, was appalled at the losses at Cold Harbor—or so I think, though he never said so—and for the last six months of 1864 his men burrowed in trenches and dug their way slowly toward the Confederate position.

A Pennsylvania colonel who knew all about coal mining suggested that a mine might be run under one of the key positions of the Confederates, and Grant told him to go ahead and try it. The mine was an enormous affair. The Pennsylvanians worked for a month at it, and then crammed it full of powder in barrels.

Lee knew the mine was being dug, and his officers made

desperate efforts to locate it by countermining, but without
success. It was exploded on July 30th. A huge crater was
made, and about two hundred Confederate soldiers went up in
the air. Then the Union troops were piled into the crater . . .
far too many of them. They were so many that they became
a packed mob, floundering in the loose earth. The Confederates quickly recovered and lined the edge of the crater.
Within an hour they had artillery playing on the squirming
mass of helpless men. The mine episode was a complete fiasco.
Grant lost 4,000 men in killed, wounded and missing.

Although transportation from the south became uncertain,
and finally almost impossible, the Confederate authorities were
able, during the first months of the siege, to obtain an abundance of food supplies from the Shenandoah Valley, to the west
of Richmond. But in the early fall Grant sent General Hunter
—and, after him, General Sheridan—to raid the Shenandoah
granary. They made a thoroughly heartless job of it, burning
everything in sight, homes of non-combatants, bridges, mills,
schoolhouses, churches, as well as barns full of corn and wheat.

In an attempt to draw off part of Grant's army from its
position in front of Richmond Lee detached General Jubal A.
Early and sent him on a raid into Maryland. Early came
within a hair's breadth of capturing the city of Washington.
On July 11th he appeared in the suburbs of the capital. If
he had known how feebly Washington was defended he would
have gone in, no doubt, and taken possession of it. But he
did not know that Grant had denuded the defenses of the
troops; so, after a little desultory firing, he went away. On
this raid Early burned Chambersburg, Pennsylvania, in retalia-
tion for the devastation in the Shenandoah Valley.

§ 2

While Grant's army was crossing the Rapidan, around the
first of May, 1864, Sherman, in far-off Tennessee, began his

march toward Atlanta. Johnston retired slowly through northern Georgia, like a man walking backward over rough ground. Walking backward, stumbling, and holding on to positions as long as he could. His defense was probably the best that could be made, considering the great superiority of Sherman in men and artillery. He said that he intended to make a final stand before Atlanta, but he never got a chance, for President Davis relieved him from command when Sherman had driven him into the heart of Georgia. In his place Davis appointed General John B. Hood, an impetuous dare-devil fighter, who was so combative by nature that he was totally unfitted to be in command of an army on the defensive.

Hood played into Sherman's hands. Sherman wanted him to come out of his works and fight, and that is exactly what Hood did. His army was almost destroyed in the July battles among the Atlanta hills. Then Hood crept back into his works and sat down, awaiting the end. But the end did not come for several weeks—not before September—when Hood abandoned Atlanta in order to save his army from being captured.

As soon as Sherman got possession of Atlanta, he expelled the entire civilian population of the city; all except negroes. He kept the negroes and fed them army rations. But all the white people—old, young, men, women, children, the lame, the blind, and the sick—were turned out of their homes and sent adrift on the country roads. The protest of the mayor and a citizen's committee was met by Sherman's curt statement that he intended to burn the city anyway.

But Sherman, although he was in some respects a barbarian, had a curious set of proprieties of his own. On one occasion during his march through Georgia he made his headquarters in the house of a lady whose daughter was at the point of death. Sherman's occupation of a room in this house added greatly to the woman's sorrow. She wept continually at the thought of a Yankee general living in her home. Sherman moved, and even took his troops away from the neighborhood. "The poor woman is distracted and cannot rest," he wrote. "She will soon be as prostrate as her dying daughter. Either the army must move or she."

Sherman's march to the sea was not a part of the preconceived plan which he and Grant had in mind when Sherman set out from Chattanooga. His objective was Atlanta, and his further progress through Georgia was the result of circumstances. He expected that Hood, after Atlanta was evacuated, would remain continually in front of him, and try to keep him from going any further. But Sherman did not take Jefferson Davis into consideration. Davis believed himself to be a strategist, and Napoleonic fancies unfolded in his mind.

Well, what would Napoleon do in this case? Davis asked the question and answered it. He imagined that Napoleon would swing around behind Sherman, cut his communications with the North and invade Tennessee. Then Sherman would have to run back home.

Davis meditated on these strategic possibilities and ordered Hood to Tennessee. This idea fitted in precisely with Hood's hare-brained temerity, and he obeyed eagerly enough.

The trouble with this plan is that it was conceived without any regard for the essential facts of the situation. Governor Brown of Georgia was threatening to secede from the Confederacy because the Richmond administration had not furnished enough troops to defend the state. Yet, while this threat was vibrating in the air, Davis sent the only Confederate army in Georgia out of the state and into Tennessee. There were thousands of able-bodied men who might have joined Hood if he had remained; but after Hood had departed Governor Brown was so disgusted that he disbanded the state militia and sent the men home to harvest the crops. "This," Grant dryly remarked, "served a most excellent purpose in gathering in supplies of food and forage for the use of our army in its subsequent march."

I know that all of this sounds like a sort of grown-up Alice in Wonderland, but it is true—and there is even more. President Davis came to Georgia before Hood had started northward, and while he was there he made a number of encouraging public speeches. In all of them he outlined his plans and told what Hood was going to do. Sherman read all about it in the Confederate newspapers. The element of secrecy, which makes military strategy effective, was overlooked altogether. Sherman sent General Thomas back to Tennessee to fight Hood, which he did—at the battles of Nashville and Franklin—and defeated him so disastrously that Hood's army disappeared thereafter from the Confederate calculations.

Sherman had been in Atlanta for weeks, wondering what to do next, when Davis and Hood made up his mind for him. Why not march down through the state to Savannah and connect there with the Union blockading fleet? He would have to abandon his communications with the North, but what difference would that make? He could live on the country.

The march to Savannah was really an extended military picnic. Sherman had only one hundred and three men killed in this jaunt. There was almost no fighting on the way. He went with a torch through a defenseless state. His horde of thieves stole whatever they could take away and destroyed the rest. He wrote, in his official report, "One hundred million dollars of damage has been done to Georgia; twenty million inured to our benefit, the remainder simply waste and destruction."

Sherman's path was marked by ruin and homeless women and children; nevertheless, he wrote: "War at best is barbarism, but to involve all—children, women, old and helpless—is more than can be justified." But he says in his *Memoirs* that he did not restrain the army "lest its vigor and energy be impaired."

Savannah was taken just before the Christmas of 1864, and early in the new year Sherman began his march northward through the Carolinas.

It was about this time that he wrote to Halleck: "The truth is, the whole army is burning with an insatiable desire to wreak vengeance upon South Carolina."

And he added tearfully: "I almost tremble at her fate, but feel that she deserves all that seems in store for her."

Halleck, a flabby general sitting in an armchair in a Washington office, had degenerated until he was nothing more than Grant's clerk, but his ferocity was unbounded. He wrote fiercely to Sherman: "Should you capture Charleston, I hope that by *some accident* the place may be destroyed, and, if a little salt should be sown upon its site, it may prevent the growth of future crops of nullification and secession."

Charleston was not burned, though Columbia was. The burning of Columbia was probably accidental. Sherman attempted to have the fire extinguished, but without success, as his soldiers were both drunk and indifferent.

In his official report Sherman lays the burning of Columbia on General Wade Hampton, the Confederate commander who had just evacuated the city. But in his *Memoirs* (Vol. II, p. 287) he confesses that this accusation was a lie. He says: "In my official report of the conflagration of Columbia I distinctly charged it to General Wade Hampton, and now I confess I did it pointedly to shake the faith of his people in him."

What a contrast all this is to Lee's conduct when the Southern army invaded Pennsylvania! Lee issued orders that non-combatants were not to be molested, that no houses were to be burned, and that when food was taken it should be paid for. Lee himself happened to run across one of his men in the act of stealing. He had the man tried, and, upon being found guilty, he was shot.

Sherman's technique of destruction improved in artistic expression during the campaign. It was undeniably crude at first. In those early days his raiders would burst into a house like a herd of schoolboys, all mouth and legs, scrambling and yelling. Without saying "how-de-do" or taking off their hats to the lady of the house, they would run through the rooms, grabbing indiscriminately everything they could carry away, even such unwieldy articles as rocking chairs. Then they would raid the barns and poultry yards, lead off the horses and cattle and set fire to the house.

In time a more effective course of procedure developed. Before Sherman entered South Carolina arson had dropped into disfavor. It seemed better to ruin houses and leave them standing, on the principle of the medieval torturer that a man with all his limbs broken and his eyes burned out makes a more interesting picture than a dead man.

In the exercise of the perfected art a squad would appear at the master's house on a plantation, and its leader—selected for his suavity—would enter and inform the shrinking women that they were not to be harmed and the house would not be burned. While the courtesies went on part of the squad was engaged in prodding the ground around the house—particularly in the vegetable garden—with bayonets, in search for buried silverware and other valuables. Another detail was busy at the stables, taking away the horses and cattle.

All the food on the place—chickens, hams, corn, eggs and potatoes—occupied the attention of another detachment. Two or three men, detailed for the purpose, occupied themselves with the subject of liquor. These Southern houses often contained valuable stocks of ancient wines and brandies. When the liquor supply on the place was located the raiding party invariably got drunk, but the remainder of the intoxicating loot was carried away to be distributed among the generals of Sherman's army.

The most interesting proceedings occurred in the house. If there were any paintings they were slashed into ribbons, and mirrors were cracked. An ax was generally used on the piano, and sometimes its insides were filled with flour and molasses. The window panes were knocked out by the butts of guns, the crockery in the pantry was broken into fragments, the feather beds were cut open, and the feathers scattered over the house.

Then the library was carefully looked over for volumes that had fine bindings or appeared to possess more than ordinary value. These costly books were carefully wrapped up and carried off, to be sold later through some Northern bookstore. The rest of the library was ruined by ripping the covers off the books and tearing out pages by the handfuls.

The women were made to give up their jewelry if they had not already concealed it. Their wardrobes were broken open, and their lingerie was scattered about the place. This was done for the purpose of selecting dresses, stockings and underwear for the women camp-followers of the army. The remainder of the clothing was either given to the slave women or torn up in jolly games which the raiders played about the yard.

At one house of which I have personal knowledge there were five or six barrels of flour in an out-house. The raiders had no means of moving these barrels, but before they left they emptied them on the floor and mixed kerosene with the flour.

To keep themselves from starving the women of this household went to the place where Sherman's camp had been and picked from the ground the loose grains of corn that had been spilled when his cavalry horses were fed. This corn was ground in a coffee mill. The coarse meal—baked into cakes— was all this family had to eat for more than a week.

The stolen silverware and gold watches, and so on, were called "trophies." Under this euphemistic title even the officers, some of them highly placed, loaded themselves with plunder. Sherman himself did not take any "trophies," though he did not forbid his staff to take them.

Perhaps some of my readers think that Americans could not have stooped to such low-down actions. To those who are in doubt as to my veracity I will say that they may enlighten themselves by going to any large public library. There they will find in print the testimony of countless witnesses. I have merely condensed this evidence, and have left out the worst part—as the worst is always an exception. There was considerable stooping done by Americans during the campaign.

These atrocities were committed by only a part of Sherman's army, by the jail-birds, the tramps and the scum of Northern cities that had been caught in the net of conscription. These men, by some natural process of selection, became his foragers, and were commonly known as "bummers." And, of course, their ravages were approved by Sherman, else he would have put a stop to them.

Most of the soldiers of the invading army were honest, decent youths from Middle Western farms who never thought of stealing, or of treating women badly. And it is a pleasant relief to this tale of savagery to record that, in numerous instances, the better class of Sherman's soldiers protected Southern homes at the risk of their lives; and there are authentic stories of privates and officers who gave their army rations and blankets to families that had nothing left in their desolate houses.

There is no doubt that Sherman's gigantic raid helped materially in bringing the war to a close through demoralization of the South.

On the other hand, it contributed to the South's lack of confidence in the North for many years after the war was over. The activities of Sherman's troops confirmed the worst prejudices of the Southern people. Their secession leaders had told them that the population of the North was composed of blackguards and scoundrels. The people's belief in these assertions was rather half-hearted until Sherman appeared; then they felt convinced that their leaders were right.

A generation had to pass away before the men and women of the Southern states realized fully that the inhabitants of the North were precisely like themselves; that a Yankee was merely a Southerner who lives in a colder climate; and that it was absurd to blame the decent people of the North for the brutalities of a few thousand men in Sherman's army.

In the last year of the war the whole conflict assumed a more savage aspect. Both Lincoln and Grant approved of Sherman's methods. Men who had lived so long under the nervous strain of killing other men while trying to be gentle and chivalrous at the same time finally gave it up as a bad job and laid magnanimity aside until the time for its use would be more propitious.

Grant has lost the kindly manner that he possessed in the early years. Hard, animal-like streaks are beginning to appear in his nature. He has visibly coarsened in fiber. He still thinks war is unnecessary, foolish and brutal—but he does not hate it so profoundly as he once did. Too many honors have come to him through the blood and misery of fighting.

A reflection of Grant's changed attitude is seen in his refusal to exchange prisoners. The Confederates were hard put to it to take care of their prisoners of war. At Andersonville in Georgia they held about 30,000 Northern prisoners who were dying like flies. These men were supplied with the same rations that were issued to the Confederate soldiers, but they were unused to corn bread and the hot climate. The Confederate authorities offered to exchange them, man for man, for Southern soldiers in Northern prisons. Grant flatly refused to exchange on any basis. He said that an exchange would merely prolong the war, as the released Southerners would go back at once into the Confederate armies.

Finally, in the last months of the war, the Confederate authorities notified Washington that they would release their prisoners, even without a corresponding exchange, if the Northern administration would send steamers to Southern ports to take them away. They could not feed them any longer. But the shipping was needed for other purposes—so the War Department declared—and most of the prisoners were not released until the end of the war. In reflecting upon these delays and evasions one cannot avoid the conclusion that the War Department and Grant wanted the prisoners kept in the South—

they had plenty of men, anyway—so that the Confederates would be obliged to feed them.

Immediately after the war Major Henry Wirz, the commandant of Andersonville prison, was tried by a Union court-martial for inhumanity to prisoners and for the murder of some of them. His trial was one of the most extraordinary farces that I have ever come across. There was not a shred of reliable evidence against him, but on the contrary there was a great deal in his favor. The court would not allow his witnesses to be heard. Prisoners who had been at Andersonville wanted to testify in his favor and were not permitted to speak. He was convicted and hanged.

§ 3

As Grant's army settled down to its long siege of Richmond a town of logs and boards grew up around City Point, the steamer landing on the south side of the James.

City Point became the general-in-chief's headquarters and the center of administration for his army of 120,000 men. The houses that clustered about the landing were arranged in regular streets. The community presented an animated appearance with its crowds of officers, orderlies and clerks. There were huge warehouses, hospitals, telegraph offices, guard-houses, headquarters for this and that, cottages for the staff officers and war correspondents and larger houses for the generals.

The modern impulse to turn every human activity into a standardized industry was shown in excellent form at City Point. In the presence of all this system, these letter files, these checked-up invoices, these inky clerks, any one of perception must have felt that the siege of Richmond was no longer an adventure, but a business, or a trade.

Miles to the west of the headquarters village were the trenches and rifle-pits. Their line curved in a great sweep of yellow upturned earth for ten or fifteen miles, but the line grew longer month after month as Grant continued to reach further toward the left. If the town of City Point was the main office of the siege industry the miles of trenches constituted its plant. Here, in these baking hot ditches, the men of the army lay during the long summer.

General Grant, the head of this enterprise, occupied a log and board house of three or four rooms. During the winter Mrs. Grant and the children came down to make a long stay, and more rooms were added to the house. There was a feeling everywhere in the North that the war was drawing to its close, and this belief was strengthened by the substantial appearance of things at City Point.

Not only that. Sherman was in the heart of the Confederacy, scattering fire, hunger and terror. The Southern armies were broken and demoralized. Southern credit was gone, Southern resources were exhausted, and the Southern ports were falling into the hands of Union admirals.

But Lee still held Richmond. The Confederate trenches were a Gibraltar of earth and logs. Now and then Grant made an experimental assault in the attempt to discover a weak spot in Lee's lines, and on these occasions the sullen trenches blazed with rifle fire, and the Union attacks petered out in a chaos of dead and wounded men.

As the end of the war approached crowds of visitors came to City Point . . . Congressmen and their families, gravelooking commissions with authority to investigate one thing or another, war reporters, special writers, politicians, and preachers with a mission. In the cool autumn months bevies of young girls, chaperoned by the wives of generals, fluttered through the cabins. They burst in on Meade, and had him bowing and scraping and asking anxiously for his young men: "Colonel Lyman, where are all my young men?" he demanded, looking at the rows of pretty girls in their lovely frocks. "Go find all my young men, and bring them here."

Grant's father came down and made a long visit. He was interested in hides. If he could only obtain the hides of the cattle slaughtered for the army there would be a fortune in it, so he went peering about the butcher pens, and figuring on scraps of paper. Perhaps he could get them for nothing, as his son was the autocrat of the place, but his hopes turned to ashes.

"No hides for you," said his son, sententiously.

"But I don't want them for nothing; I'll make a bid for them like anybody else."

"Well, father, if you can't see why you shouldn't bid for them, I don't believe I could enlighten you even if I should tell you," was the reply.

President Lincoln was a frequent visitor. Sometimes he came on Grant's invitation, but usually he would appear without invitation or previous announcement. With his black clothes and tall hat he "looked like a boss undertaker," Horace Porter wrote.

He would sit sprawled in a chair at Grant's table and listen by the hour to whatever was going on, hardly ever saying a word. It is a rather curious fact that he never told an obscene story to Grant. He seemed to respect the general's almost maidenly modesty, and reserved his stories for other occasions.

Once he brought Mrs. Lincoln with him, but that one experience was enough. It is generally known, I believe, that Mrs. Lincoln became insane after the war, and she was probably out of her mind during this visit to City Point. She fell into a rage because, on a trip to the front, Mrs. Ord rode on ahead with Mr. Lincoln. She declared that she never allowed her husband to see any woman alone. When General Ord's headquarters were reached Mrs. Lincoln descended from her carriage and abused Mrs. Ord to her face in public. What she called the lady I do not know; those who heard her remarks declared them to be unprintable. Mrs. Ord burst into tears. (Badeau, in his *Grant in Peace*, p. 355, describes this incident in detail.)

It was on this same visit that Mrs. Lincoln said sharply to Mrs. Grant: "How dare you sit down when I am standing?" Then she taunted Mrs. Grant with wanting to supplant her in the White House. Lincoln did not appear to be able to control the situation. As his wife's words rolled on he kept saying, "Mother—now, mother—do be quiet!"

§ 4

Grant made an effort to get rid of Butler, and failed, very much to his chagrin.

On July 1st he wrote to Halleck that he regretted the necessity of asking for a change of commanders, "but General Butler, not being a soldier by education or experience, is in the hands of his subordinates in the execution of all orders military."

Grant wanted W. F. Smith put in command of Butler's Army of the James. We have met Smith before—at Chattanooga. It was he who devised the means of relieving the famine at that place. Smith was now on the James river, acting as Butler's second in command.

The order to relieve Butler came immediately. General Butler, with the paper in his hand, went to City Point, brushed aside the polite hindrances of aides and secretaries, and thrust the order under Grant's nose. "General Grant, did you issue this order?" he demanded. Charles A. Dana, who was sitting with Grant at the time, says that Grant's face flushed and he seemed ill at ease. He read the paper slowly, and replied, "No, not in that form." Dana saw that Grant was embarrassed and the interview would probably be unpleasant, so he took his leave, but he says he felt that Butler had cowed Grant in some inexplicable way.

Butler remained for about an hour with Grant. Then he rode back to his headquarters and remarked to his staff that the order would be revoked. It was revoked at once, and

Smith—instead of Butler—was relieved from command and sent home. Smith wrote to Grant and said: "I want simply . . . to ask you how you can place a man in command of two army corps, who is as helpless as a child on the field of battle and as visionary as an opium-eater in council?"

Grant made no reply to these pertinent questions, and they still remain without an answer. Smith, who certainly got the tarred end of the stick in this transaction, became a bitter enemy of Grant. He wrote that Butler's mysterious hold on the general-in-chief had to do with the liquor supply; that Butler furnished Grant with whisky. This statement seems to me to be rather feeble. Why should it be necessary for anybody to furnish Grant's liquor? He could get all he wanted, openly and above board.

A more plausible explanation puts the episode in the circle of political necessities. Butler was a domineering, tricky and powerful Democratic politician. Lincoln was undoubtedly afraid of him during the presidential campaign of 1864, and very likely Lincoln whispered his state of mind to Grant. Butler, removed from his place in the army, would certainly become a loud-mouthed critic of the administration and of Grant's doings in Virginia.

Grant ignores the whole thing in his *Memoirs;* he does not even mention it. But he does say (Vol. II, p. 152): "General Butler certainly gave his very earnest support to the war; and he gave his own best efforts personally to the suppression of the rebellion."

There was some kind of intrigue beneath these surface events; more than I or any one else has been able to find out. While Grant was President it was an open boast of Butler that he had a hold on the President. Judge E. R. Hoar, who was in Grant's cabinet, repeated Butler's words to Grant, and he says that Grant shut his mouth tightly, and made no comment.

The end of Butler's career in the army came early in January, 1865. Lincoln had been reëlected safely, and Butler was no longer a danger to the administration. He was relieved from command by an order from Washington. In his farewell address to his army, he said: "The wasted blood of my men does not stain my garments." As a matter of fact his troops had not done enough fighting for their blood to stain anybody's garments.

§ 5

In the latter part of March, 1865, the news got about in Richmond that Mrs. Jefferson Davis had sold her carriage horses, and a day or two later some Richmond ladies who had been at the President's receptions and knew Mrs. Davis, recognized some of that lady's belongings in a dry goods store— placed there for sale. Then it came out that Davis' wife and family had departed for the South, and the well-informed who heard these stories knew that the end had come. Davis would never have sent his family away if he had thought Richmond could hold out.

On Sunday, April 2nd, Lee sent a note to Davis; it was so urgent that the message was delivered to him in church. Lee wrote that his line had been broken in three places, and that Richmond must be evacuated immediately. By that night the Confederate army—what was left of it—was on the road to Lynchburg. Richmond was burning, and the public stores were being looted by the riff-raff of the local population.

Lee hoped to reach Lynchburg and, after getting the supplies which he had ordered sent there by rail, to turn toward the south and attempt to effect a junction with Johnston's army in North Carolina. He thought that he and Johnston combined might beat Sherman, and then turn to meet Grant, who would undoubtedly pursue him.

The fleeing column was hard pressed—beset on both flanks and in the rear by Grant and Meade. It had to fight a continuous running battle. For the last three days no rations

were issued—for there were none—to either men or horses,
yet there was plenty of food on the way. When Lee surrendered there were enough rations on cars and on the way to him
to supply 60,000 men for four months. But in spite of many
desertions the morale of those who remained was excellent.
The tired, famished, disorganized men held together and drove
off the Union attacks with an amazing spirit. An hour before
the surrender at Appomattox Fitzhugh Lee came in with two
hundred Union prisoners.

On April 7th Grant sent a letter to Lee under a flag of truce
in which he said, "The results of the last week must convince
you of the hopelessness of further resistance," and he went on
to say that he did not want to be responsible for "any further
effusion of blood." He demanded the surrender of Lee's army.

The Confederate chieftain replied that he did not consider
the situation hopeless, but he would like to hear Grant's terms.
Several other notes passed back and forth, while the two
armies proceeded on their way. The relative positions of the
Union and Confederate armies, as they were at that time, may
be represented by two long strings laid parallel to each other.
Both strings are headed toward the west. The southern one
represents Grant's army; the one to the north the Army of
Northern Virginia. Grant's effort—and it was successful—
was to keep himself between Lee and the South.

Appomattox Court House was reached. It is about ninety-
five miles west of Richmond. There we must lay another string
on the table, vertically in respect to the others. Sheridan's
cavalry stood straight across Lee's path.

Grant says:

> Lee's army was rapidly crumbling. . . . I know that I
> occupied a hotel almost destitute of furniture at Farm-
> ville. . . . The next morning when I came out I found a
> Confederate colonel there, who reported to me and said
> that he was the proprietor of that house, and that he was
> a colonel of a regiment which had been raised in that

neighborhood. He said that when he came along past home, he found that he was the only man of the regiment remaining with Lee's army, so he just dropped out, and now wanted to surrender himself. I told him to stay there and he would not be molested.

Sheridan was ahead; Grant and Meade were south of Lee and behind him. Lee's force had melted away until only 25,000 men were left, and of these only about 8,000 had any arms or ammunition. Hordes of gaunt, ragged men, without guns in their hands, or anything to eat, filled the roads. Yet the army kept its invincible faith in Lee.

On the night of April 8th the shattered army slept on the ground, under the clear stars, in the fields around Appomattox. As the hungry men lay in the army's last bivouac they could hear the muffled sounds of the foe's maneuvers all around them. Now and then from somewhere in the distance came the sharp rattle of gunfire—sudden bursts, over in a minute.

If there ever are ghosts in this world they must have haunted that poor little beaten army on the last night of its existence . . . the ghosts of its superb battle days, and of the years when it had fought so long and so valiantly. The ghosts of Fredericksburg; of Chancellorsville; of the sunlit heights of Gettysburg, where the ardent Southern guns blazed among the Pennsylvania hills; of the fierce, bloody duels in the Wilderness.

Then the daylight came, sifting through the April green of the Virginia woods and filling the valleys with its quiet presence. All around there was the movement of vast hosts, and artillery rumbling into position. But the Army of Northern Virginia did not move. The stricken lion lay dying.

§ 6

"Where's General Lee?" Grant asked of an orderly who stood waiting in the road.

THE McLEAN HOUSE AT APPOMATTOX, VA., WHERE LEE SURRENDERED TO GRANT ON APRIL 9, 1865.

The orderly pointed to a brick house set in a flower garden. "Over there," he said.

Grant turned around to his staff. "Well, let's go over and see him."

Lee, and Colonel Marshall of his staff, had been there for about an hour, chatting pleasantly with Colonel Babcock, one of Grant's aides, while they waited for the general-in-chief to appear.

The Union generals arrive; they fill the little room. Grant shakes hands with Lee, and introduces him around: "General Lee, this is General Sheridan, and General Rawlins, and Colonel Badeau, and Colonel Parker—" Lee bows slightly as each name is pronounced. He looks keenly at Colonel Parker for an instant, and then turns a sharp glance on him again. Parker is a full-blooded Indian; Lee evidently thinks him a negro. "General Grant, and gentlemen," Lee says, "this is Colonel Marshall, of my staff"—and Marshall, standing by the mantel, bows coolly. They all sit down. The Union staff officers whisper among themselves. They are saying to one another how large and impressive Lee is; they thought he was a smaller man.

Grant is dusty, and rather frowzy in appearance. As he glances at Lee's splendid new uniform he apologizes awkwardly for his looks. He did not have time, he says, to change his clothes.

"This is a pretty country," Sheridan remarks, but nobody pays much attention to him, for Grant and Lee are talking about their days in Mexico. A little desultory conversation —strained undoubtedly—and then Lee says, "General, I have come to meet you in accordance with my letter to you this morning, to treat about the surrender of my army, and I think the best way would be for you to put your terms in writing." Grant thinks so, too. There is a pause while Grant writes his terms out with a pencil on a piece of paper.

Remarkably magnanimous terms they are. The men shall

be allowed to depart for their homes after signing a parole not to fight for the Confederacy any more. They are not to be molested as long as they obey the law. Only public property is to be taken by the victors; the officers may carry their side-arms and personal baggage.

Lee reads the paper. "General," he says, "our cavalrymen furnish their own horses; they are not government horses; some of them may be, but of course you will find them out— any property that is public property, you will ascertain that, but it is nearly all private property, and these men will want to plow ground and plant corn."

Grant answers that the United States does not need the horses of small farmers, and that any man who claims to own a horse or mule can take it away with him. "That will have a very happy effect," Lee remarks.

Lee rises to go. He says that his army is in a very bad condition for want of food and forage—the men have been existing on parched corn for three days—and that he would have to ask for rations. Grant inquires if twenty-five thousand rations would be enough, and Lee replies: "Plenty; plenty; an abundance." He and Colonel Marshall bow and ride away.

The army of Northern Virginia is no more.

Next day cheering, boisterous crowds will be surging through the streets of the Northern cities, while the bells ring, the cannons boom, and "The Star-Spangled Banner" will be throbbing and blaring in the air. The name of Grant will be on every man's tongue.

§ 7

The paroles had to be printed on a slow army printing press. It took all of the next day, while the Gray and Blue fraternized.

Meade met Lee riding pensively. "Don't you know me, General Lee?" he said. "I'm George Meade."

"Oh, is that you, Meade?" Lee replied. "How did you happen to get all that gray in your beard?"

"I'm afraid you're the cause of most of it," Meade answered, in the way of the ancient amenities.

CHAPTER XXIV

THE ERA OF ANDREW JOHNSON

§ 1

LINCOLN is dead; slain by a half-crazed actor who was eaten to the bone by a desire to be seen and heard. This assassin lived in a fog of whisky and vanity. He had his little moment when he shot the greatest of Presidents in the back and went limping across the stage of a theater, waving a dagger and bellowing, *"Sic semper tyrannis!"*

It seems strange to us now that at the time of Lincoln's assassination many people of high standing in the North felt a relief at his passing. Among them were nearly all the "Radical" Republican leaders. They were astonishingly outspoken in their opinions; their words made a crude discord in the nation's sorrow.

The Radicals of 1865 constituted the party of inveterate haters of the South. They were called "Radicals" because they insisted on employing radical, or drastic, punitive measures in dealing with the conquered states. Lincoln's plans for magnanimous treatment of the ex-Confederates had already evoked their determined opposition.

The last meeting of the Lincoln cabinet took place on April 14th, a few hours before the President was assassinated. Grant was present at this assembly of the cabinet as an invited guest. At that time the President said:

I think it providential that this great rebellion is crushed just as Congress has adjourned and there are none of the disturbing elements of that body to hinder and embarrass us. If we are wise and discreet we shall reani-

mate the states and get their governments in successful
operation, with order prevailing and the Union re-estab-
lished before Congress comes together in December. . . .
I hope there will be no persecution, no bloody work after
the war is over. No one need expect me to take any part
in hanging or killing those men, even the worst of them.
Frighten them out of the country, open the gates, let down
the bars, scare them off. Enough lives have been sacri-
ficed. We must extinguish our resentments if we expect
harmony and union.

Lincoln was opposed to confiscation, to any sort of dragoon-
ing methods in the conquered states, and to universal negro
suffrage—though he thought that negroes who could read and
write, and those who had served in the army, ought to be allowed to vote. But the states themselves should regulate the
suffrage; he contended that the question did not fall within the
frame of national functions.

Such a course, on Lincoln's part, would have brought him
in head-on collision with the Radicals in Congress, and they
constituted a majority. George W. Julian—an entertaining
writer who was then a member of the House—wrote that he attended a political caucus the day after Lincoln's death and,
"while everybody was shocked at his murder, the feeling was
nearly universal that the accession of Johnson would prove
a Godsend to the country." He added that Mr. Lincoln's
views on reconstruction were "as distasteful as possible to
Radical Republicans." Charles Sumner wondered if his death
"was not a judgment of the Lord."

The Radical politicians were not alone in their belief that
God might have planned the murder. Consider Ralph Waldo
Emerson, a philosopher rapt in the contemplation of ageless
time, and therefore supposed to be remote from politics. He
said at Concord on April 19th: "And what if it should turn
out in the unfolding of the web that he [Lincoln] had reached
the term; that the heroic deliverer could no longer serve us;

that the rebellion had touched its natural conclusions, and what remained to be done required new and uncommitted hands —a new spirit born out of the ashes of war."

Rev. Albert S. Hunt, a Methodist, thought, like Emerson, that the Lord may have been an accomplice of John Wilkes Booth. Mr. Hunt said: "Wherever Lincoln has erred it has been on the side of mercy . . . and there are those who listen to me to-day who think that Providence has permitted this calamity to befall us that a sterner hand might rule in our national affairs."

General Benjamin F. Butler ranged himself on the side of Providence. He declared at a public meeting in New York the day after Lincoln's death:

> Perhaps I may say reverently that this dispensation of God's good providence is sent to teach us that the spirit of the rebellion has not been broken by the surrender of its armies.

These opinions did not represent the feelings of the American people as a whole. The nation was filled with sorrow, and the regret at Lincoln's tragic death was deep and genuine.

Vice-President Andrew Johnson was looked upon by the Radicals as a "Godsend," and as "a man anointed and consecrated to do a great work." He ascended to the presidency amid the quiet exultation of politicians. Senators Wade, Chandler, and othei dyed-in-the-wool Radicals—such as Thaddeus Stevens—called on Johnson, clasped his hand and patted him on the back. "Johnson, we have faith in you," Wade exclaimed. "By the gods, there will be no trouble now in running the government."

President Johnson smiled. "I hold that robbery is a crime," he declared. "Rape is a crime; *treason* is a *crime* and crime must be punished. Treason must be made infamous and traitors must be impoverished."

The Radical Senators went away with pleasant thoughts

buzzing in their heads. Dreams of festivals, sacrifices and flowing blood. How astonished they would have been if they had known that, before three years had gone by, they would be arrayed against Johnson and moving heaven and earth to impeach him!

§ 2

Now the incomprehensible Sherman drives these momentous events out of the attention of the public as incontinently as one drives a flock of crows out of a corn-field.

Although Lee has surrendered, the war is not yet over . . . not wholly. General Joseph E. Johnston still has an army of Confederates in North Carolina, and there are smaller bodies elsewhere in the Southern states. The Confederacy has obviously gone to pieces, and it is clear to Johnston that there is nothing left to do but to talk over the terms of surrender, and he suggests to Sherman—by flag of truce—that talk is in order.

So Sherman and Johnston talked in a farmhouse while the two war-bitten armies sat down and waited.

The remarkable document that was created at this conference can hardly be called a protocol of surrender. It was, in fact, a sort of outline for the rehabilitation of the Southern states. It stepped ponderously on the toes of civil authority; it knocked down all precedents; it wandered afar in the spreading fields of national policy.

Here are some of its provisions. The Confederate armies —not only Johnston's command, but all armed forces wherever they may be—are "to be disbanded and conducted to their several state capitals." They are to carry their arms with them and deposit them in the state arsenals.

The United States—according to Ambassador Sherman—is to recognize the existing state governments, provided the officials and legislators swear allegiance to the Constitution. The

Federal courts are to be reëstablished; and the people of the states lately in rebellion are guaranteed in all their political rights and franchises. As to property—they are guaranteed that, too. But "property" is not defined . . . under the terms of the agreement it may include slaves and thus constitute a legal basis for a demand for compensation on the part of Southern slave-owners.

In addition, there is to be a general amnesty, and the executive authority of the United States is not to disturb anybody who lives in peace and quiet.

What in the world had happened to Sherman, the house-burner and scourge of mankind? Only a few months before he had written that, in his opinion, all the fighting men in the South would have to be killed. Yet, here he is, agreeing to send them home with arms in their hands. His deeper motive was—so I think—a desire to exhibit his power.

He burned the city of Atlanta and expelled its inhabitants, and left ruin and desolation behind him in Georgia and the Carolinas, but his actions were intended to show the Confederate leaders that he was the master of the situation. And when we consider his arrangement with Johnston we find the same motive. It gratified his sense of authority to grant amnesty to all the rebels, to end the strife at once, to play a tremendous rôle. Sherman was not a hater; that is one of the striking facts about his character. There is nowhere, in any of his writings, a line of hate of the Southern people.

The terms of surrender were sent hopefully to Washington for approval, while the Sherman and Johnston truce continued. The terms were rejected, of course . . . instantly rejected by President Johnson and his cabinet. Grant read them before passing them along, and wrote to friend Sherman that he felt satisfied they would not be approved.

The excitable Stanton rushed about Washington with a garbled version of the Sherman-Johnston document in his hand. He declared that the republic was tottering, and that Sherman had sold himself for money to the Confederate leaders. He sent urgent telegrams to Sherman's officers instructing them not to obey their chief. General Grant was ordered to go to North Carolina at once and supersede Sherman in command.

Grant came down from Washington across the ruined and desolate country. His train crept slowly over the uncertain rails, halting now and then while the track was being repaired. While he was at Sherman's headquarters he did not show himself to the troops, out of deference to his friend's feelings, nor did he assume command of the army. General Johnston did not know that Grant had been there until he read his endorsement on the new terms of surrender. The terms, as finally approved, were identical in substance with those that were made with Lee at Appomattox.

Grant's sympathy at that time for the stricken South is revealed clearly in a letter to his wife, written from Raleigh on April 25th. He wrote:

> Dear Julia: We arrived here yesterday. . . . Raleigh is a very beautiful place. The grounds are large and filled with the most beautiful spreading oaks I ever saw. . . . The suffering that must exist in the South the next year, even with the war ending now, will be beyond conception. People who talk of further retaliation and punishment, except of the political leaders, either do not conceive of the suffering endured already or they are heartless and unfeeling and wish to stay at home out of danger while the punishment is being inflicted. Love and kisses for you and the children. Ulys.

§ 3

Andrew Johnson was hand in glove with the Radicals for a few weeks; or, at any rate, they thought he was; and he evidently thought so, too, if one may judge by his utterances. All his opinions were vehement, and the most vehement of them was that the rebel leaders ought to be hanged. Their estates should be confiscated, he declared, "and divided into small farms, and sold to honest, industrious men."

He had placed himself with precise certainty among the lions, yet while the echoes of Sherman's musketry were still in the air he began to behave like a lamb. On May 29th he issued a proclamation of general amnesty in which he pardoned the entire rank and file of the Confederacy, with the exception of a few classes, such as the higher Confederate officials, military officers above the rank of colonel, and men who were worth more than twenty thousand dollars. But even the ex-rebels belonging to the excepted classes could obtain pardons by making individual applications.

Then he began to reconstruct the conquered states through executive action, as Lincoln had evidently intended to do. Instead of sending his iron-heeled cavalry into the South to drag its leading men to jail, Johnson wrote friendly letters. He urged the Southerners to reanimate their state governments, to hold conventions, and set their houses in order. He demanded only three things: That the new state governments recognize the negro as a free man; that the secession ordinances be annulled or repealed; and that the Confederate public debt be repudiated.

His Radical advisers urged him to force negro suffrage on the South by executive order. Johnson refused. He was a strict constructionist; he lived by the letter of the Constitution as conscientiously as the priests in Solomon's temple lived by the Mosaic law; and under the Constitution the granting of the suffrage was a privilege belonging to the states.

Besides, Johnson was not in favor of universal negro suffrage —and when he was not in favor of anything he was always bitterly opposed to it. His life is a record of bitter oppositions, bitter enthusiasms, bitter animosities. He was a bitter person.

He even loved his invalid wife bitterly . . . with a bitter intensity.

Though he was against negro suffrage in general, he thought that some negroes might be wisely granted the right to vote, and he urged the Southern states—by suggestion only—to grant the suffrage to negroes who could read and write, or who had served in the Union army, or who owned two hundred and fifty dollars in real estate. All of the Southern states ignored the suggestion. In taking this attitude they were greatly encouraged by the political condition of the negro in the North. Only six of the Northern states allowed negroes to vote. The question came up in Connecticut and Ohio in 1865—and in both these states negro suffrage was defeated by large majorities.

In short, Johnson's vindictiveness toward the ex-Confederates had melted away. He had become the most magnanimous of Presidents, and this startling change had taken place in a few months.

The feeling of astonishment among the Radical leaders was at first so profound that it did not leave room for any other emotion, but before long amazement evolved into rage. Congress was not in session—it would not convene until December —and in the meantime nothing could be done about Johnson's proceedings. But the vials of wrath were being filled and tightly corked to await the day of their opening.

The outstanding Radicals—Sumner, Chase, Wade and Stevens—did not call at the White House any more. They were the leaders of the Republican party, and Johnson had come into office as a Republican. He had lost the support of his party leaders. "If something is not done," Thaddeus Stevens wrote to Sumner, "the President will be crowned king before Congress meets"; and Sumner anxiously asked if there was not some way to stop Johnson "in his insane course."

Johnson was in opposition to the leaders of his party; he was destined soon to be a President without a party. His first loss of popular prestige, as distinguished from the support of party leaders, occurred in February, 1866, when he delivered a fatuous address at the White House, in which he said intemperately that Charles Sumner, Thaddeus Stevens and Wendell Phillips were attempting to destroy "the fundamental principles of this government," and that some of his enemies desired his removal by assassination. His opponents took great delight in giving this speech a wide circulation. They declared that he had made it while he was drunk.

When Congress met in December both houses refused to seat the Senators and representatives from the reconstructed states. Congress treated the President's measures with contempt and took charge of affairs.

At first sight Johnson's actions appear as chaotic as the disconnected pieces of a picture puzzle. But they fit together when one understands their proper relations. The key to them is to be found in his antecedents and in the suppressed aspects of his character. He was a Southern "poor white," born and raised in a North Carolina community which was dominated by an overriding aristocracy of slave-owners. His parents were illiterate, dog-poor, and looked down upon by their wealthy neighbors. He learned the character of the slave aristocracy through his own personal experience.

As a boy he had been apprenticed to the local tailor, but before he had reached the age of twenty he crossed over the mountains to Tennessee and opened a tailor shop of his own in the village of Greeneville. He was a serious youth, itching for prosperity and renown. His career reminds one of the success stories of great men that appear so frequently in the floridly optimistic magazines. The humble beginning, the honest though poorly paid toil, the shunning of gay companions, the climbing spirit, the meeting with the pure-sweet girl, the ripening love, the early marriage, the little home, the growing bank account, the slowly spreading acres—all these, and more of the same kind, are in Andrew Johnson's life. His wife taught him to write after he had married; he had already taught himself to read.

He entered politics as a fierce Democrat. At that period most of the men of property and culture in the Southern states were Whigs. Johnson called them "a scrub aristocracy." But the Whig party disappeared eventually, and the South became solidly Democratic . . . so Johnson found himself on the same side of the political fence as the slave-aristocrats. He was with them, but not of them. When he reached the United States Senate he was snubbed by the Senators from the South because he did not belong to their class in society, and because he boasted of having worked with his hands. His political thinking was inextricably mixed with his personal feelings and prejudices.

A Union man of outspoken views was in danger of losing his life while secession was coming to a head in the turbulent state of Tennessee and Johnson was an intense Unionist. But he was not afraid; his courage, moral and physical, was high. The Union troops overran Tennessee and Lincoln made Andrew Johnson military governor of the state. In the meantime he had become a Republican in name, though he was always a Democrat in thought and principle.

The Republican national convention of 1864 contemplated this sturdy Southerner who had always stood up for the Union and came to the conclusion that he ought to have some kind of substantial recognition. So he was elected Vice-President.

I think Johnson has been generally misunderstood. He has been called a turncoat, a hypocrite, and even a traitor. The Radicals called him a turncoat, because he did not follow the Republican party—but he was always true to himself. Hypocrisy was certainly no part of his dogmatic personality. Indeed, it would have been better for him if he had been something of a hypocrite. And as for treason, one may say with confidence that, far from being a traitor, Johnson was in fact the great outstanding patriot of his time. His four years in the White House were occupied in a ceaseless battle to preserve the Constitution.

He was accused of being an habitual drunkard, and this reputation has endured persistently through two generations, yet it rests on nothing more substantial than the evidence of a single episode. When he went to the Senate chamber to be inaugurated as Vice-President on March 4, 1865, he was ill with diarrhea. Somebody told him that a stiff glass of brandy would be good for him. While he was waiting he asked for brandy, poured himself a tumbler full, and drank it down at a gulp. He was unused to liquor in such quantities and became maudlin drunk. His speech was a rambling, incoherent babble that might have continued for hours if the secretary of the Senate had not stopped him. If he was drunk on any other occasion there is no evidence of it. Hugh McCulloch, Secretary of the Treasury, who lived with him for several months in 1865, says that he never drank any intoxicating liquor at all.

But his high temper and extravagant language, devoid of grace and charm, led many people to the conclusion that he was a drunkard. The Radical leaders nourished the myth of his drunkenness and passed it on to posterity.

At the close of the Civil War he still had a mental picture of the South in terms of slavery. This, I think, was the basic reason for his program of confiscation and trials for treason. But his vindictiveness faded away when he realized that the slave-aristocracy was already destroyed. It was worse than useless, he felt, to attempt to punish the members of the former ruling class in the conquered states. They were already ruined; anything else in the way of reprisal would serve only to make them martyrs and heroes. At the bottom he was all generosity . . . a generosity that was buried under the débris of many harsh conflicts.

Johnson's motives did not appeal to Congress, nor did Congress understand them. Before the session was two months old, the Congressional thumbs were turned down on gladiator

Johnson and the speeches in Congress glittered with the shine of verbal daggers.

§ 4

Imagine a land in which almost every corporation, every business enterprise, and every individual, is bankrupt, and you will have a picture of the South in the six months after the Civil War. The banks held nothing but Confederate money and some impossible mortgages and promissory notes.

Most of the stores were closed, with scraps of board nailed across their broken windows. There was no use for them to keep open; they had nothing to sell. The few that continued in business would part with their goods only in exchange for farm products, so that before long dry goods stores became grocery establishments through a natural process of evolution.

Confederate bills blew about the streets. Nobody took the trouble to pick them up; they were far too plentiful to be kept as curios. Gold and silver had disappeared, the banks were closed, the shops were deserted, the houses were falling down . . . but the land remained.

The fertile soil warms its back in the Southern sunshine while plow-horses that have heard the roar of battle pick their way through its furrows. The Confederate soldiers are behind the plow. It is they who will make a new South. Great pyramids of stored-up cotton, grown during the war, stand in the farm-yards. It is worth three hundred dollars a bale, in gold —or five times as much as a bale of cotton was worth before the war. In a few months buyers will be coming from the Northern mills. The cotton will be taken away, and money will begin to pass from one man to another.

Many of the great plantations are lying fallow, their fields overrun by weeds; it is impossible for their owners to hire field-hands. These plantations depend on negro labor, and the freed negroes are trooping through the country in droves.

They have nowhere to go, but they have a notion that they must go somewhere to prove their freedom.

The negro was a free man but not a citizen. The Thirteenth Amendment had abolished slavery, but it said nothing about the black man's status in the new social order. Certainly it could not be the intention of the conquerors to give the negro the right to vote, the Southerners reasoned, for hardly one negro in fifty had the faintest notion of what voting meant. The whole race was not only ignorant . . . it was more than ignorant. The most illiterate among the whites had a sort of semi-inherited idea of the structure of society, and of the basic legal relations of one man to another. But the freedmen did not possess even this rudimentary sense. Under the shell of obedience that slavery had put about the black man the African mind still moved in its primitive circle.

Deep in the negro's heart there is a murmur of ancient memories. He cherishes an inarticulate concept of another order of things. This is not his land, nor his day in history, and he knows it. If it were his country he would refashion it in his own way.

He wanders in our maze of mechanism, shrewdness, order and energy like a lost child in a tangled wood. An overwhelming sense of the immediate colors his perceptions. It is a mystery to him that the white man is so obsessed by an imperative need of action while the flesh pots are so near and so beguiling and the sun is shining so gorgeously

Plucking at the sleeves of white men, he asks what this means and that means. He wants to find his way, and his searching is pathetic.

Our ideas appear to him to be gaunt and angular, for his own logic is rounded, smooth, and highly charged with an emotional content.

Yet he is ready to forgive our painful logic if we will only be kind to him. He is lovable as a good-natured child, with a child's craving for affection, but his easy temper is deceptive.

It is merely the pliability of surrender, the purring of a wild creature that has been caught and tamed.

§ 5

Grant did not bother himself with political questions in these early months of peace. In later years he floundered in politics like a poor swimmer in rough water, but not in 1865. That year, so noisy with political dissension, was the most carefree, and probably the happiest, of his life.

He thought that something ought to be done about Mexico —and this appears to express the sum total of his political ideas in the year after the war. He believed, as did many other Americans, that the French attempt to force the Archduke Maximilian upon Mexico was an affront to the United States . . . and it was, of course, an insolent defiance of the Monroe Doctrine. It occurred to Grant that the North and South might be united in a campaign to expel Maximilian and the French. The Blue and Gray fighting side by side. General Longstreet in command of Union troops; General Sheridan at the head of an army of Confederate veterans.

If this idea had been carried out it might conceivably have united the North and South as nothing else could have done at that time. But Seward, Secretary of State, maintained that the French could be forced out through diplomacy—and they were, after awhile.

Grant's pay as general commanding the army was more than he needed for his modest scale of living. He had at last attained the financial security that he had longed for all his life. He had authority, adulation, whisky, cigars, fast horses, and a few intimate friends. These constituted the circle of his felicity.

In June he went to Chicago to attend an enormous fair for the benefit of disabled soldiers and their families. Julia went with him. Mrs. Sherman, who was one of the managing ladies of the fair, asked him to contribute something, and he turned over "Old Jack"—his cream-colored horse that he had ridden at Fort Donelson—to the committee, to be sold at a raffle. Upon arriving at Chicago he mounted Jack and rode him to the fair grounds in a rousing procession of flowers, cheers, flags and brass bands. There the governor of Illinois met him in the roaring tumult and led him to the edge of the speaker's stand, where he faced a lake of upturned faces.

Silently he stood before the crowd, while the cheering went on. He was expected to speak, and that to him was the worst of all human ordeals—except dancing. But Governor Yates had to get in his own say first. He did not mind speaking. As soon as it was quiet enough for a fog-horn to be heard, Governor Yates raised his hand.

"See that hand," he declaimed in a fog-horn manner. "That very hand signed the commission of Ulysses S. Grant as a colonel, and it was the best day's work it ever did."

The crowd looked fretfully at the governor's hand for a moment, then it yelled again for Grant. But the great general bashfully declined to speak, and mumbled that Governor Yates would talk for him; and the governor did.

A few weeks later he went to Galena, Illinois. The first thing that Grant saw as he alighted from the train was a flower-decked arch, which bore an inscription in gigantic letters: *General, the Sidewalk Is Built*. Then the procession passed under the arch.

The genius of the place ran to arches. There were several of them, with the names of battles on them—and a huge one, inscribed: *Hail to the Chief Who in Triumph Advances*.

After the ceremony of the arches came the festival of meats. Barbecue sandwiches and coffee were supplied freely to the thousands of country visitors, and as the people munched their food they gazed at their famous fellow citizen.

The closing event was the presentation of a sixteen-thousand-dollar house to the victor of Appomattox. The money had been raised in Galena by popular subscription. The committee of presentation, in tall black hats and frock coats, stood smiling while Grant went through the rooms and looked at the plush furniture, the heavy chairs, the gilt clock, the photograph of Lincoln, the ornate Bible on the marble-topped parlor table, the steel engraving of a Stag at Bay, the "Big Acorn" cooking stove in the kitchen, the vast double beds, the what-nots in the corner, already filled with sea-shells and mice carved in wood, and at the calf-bound sets of Washington Irving and Fenimore Cooper. It was a well-furnished house. Grant stood in the center of the parlor and murmured a few words of thanks.

Galena was outdone by Philadelphia in the matter of housegiving. The Philadelphians gave him a residence that cost considerably more than sixteen thousand dollars. The citizens of New York City gave him one hundred thousand dollars in cash, and Boston's gift was a library which cost five thousand dollars.

Behind one of his fourteen horses—most of them had been presented by admirers—he would drive to his office every morning. He became a familiar sight on the streets of Washington . . . usually sitting in a light buggy, a cigar between his teeth, the reins wrapped tightly around his hands, and a swiftly runnning horse before him.

In July, 1866, Congress raised Lieutenant-General Grant to the exalted position of full general. He was the first officer to attain this rank since George Washington.

Grant's associates in Washington at first were mostly army officers, but it was not long before the politicians began to pay him a great deal of attention. It seemed almost certain that he would be the next President, and the Radicals moved skillfully and quietly to convert him to their way of thinking.

Accompanied by Mrs. Grant, he attended the Sunday services of the Methodist church occasionally, though he never became a member of the church. His religion, such as it was, appears to have been a kind of ethical paganism. Like Washington, Lincoln, Franklin and Thomas Paine, Grant believed in God, but Grant's God was not the God of the Christians. He conceived the Deity as a dark, inscrutable Providence with mysterious ways and a tendency to interfere arbitrarily now and then in human affairs . . . a Providence that seems to be pretty nearly synonymous with Luck.

According to M. J. Cramer, a preacher who married one of the General's sisters, Grant believed that "all evil must be punished in some form at some time." He went on—still according to Cramer—to say that "as nations have no organized existence hereafter, they must be punished here for their national sins"—hence he looked upon the Civil War as a divine punishment for the sin of slavery.

Cramer tried, apparently, to convert Grant and to induce him to become a member of the church, for he talked continually about religion with his famous brother-in-law. At one time he declared to Grant that he did not believe there was really an out-and-out atheist in the world, because religion— no matter what its form may be—is an innate, or an intuitive, element of man's soul, and all religions presuppose a deity, or deities, of some kind or other. To this Grant replied: "Why, Mr. Cramer, I think your views are about right." This is as near as he ever got to making a confession of religious faith.

One of Grant's public statements leads one to the conviction that he considered God a pacifist and an internationalist, but a little slow in action. He said:

> I believe that our Great Maker is preparing this world in His own good time to become one nation, speaking one language, and when armies and navies will no longer be required.

CHAPTER XXV

THE TURMOIL OF RECONSTRUCTION

§ 1

THE Southern legislatures, existing by the grace of Andrew Johnson, applied themselves to a practical solution of the negro problem. A number of laws came from these deliberations, laws that varied slightly according to the prevailing conditions in the various states, but all intended to settle the status of the ex-slaves. A typical code was that of Mississippi, which provided that any negro, over eighteen years of age, who should be found without employment would be subject to fine or imprisonment, or to being hired out, at the discretion of the court. Freedmen were not allowed to own or lease lands except in incorporated towns, and there was a provision for apprenticing negro children whose parents would not, or could not, support them. Masters of such apprentices were given the power to use "moderate corporal chastisement," in the way of correction. Negroes were not allowed to testify in cases involving white men.

The ideas of the overthrown slave régime peep through these codes. The motive of their framers was unquestionably to keep the negro in a sort of perpetual peonage while preserving all the outward forms of his freedom. This was frankly admitted by many leading Southerners. The legislation was all on the side of the white man. It put the negro in jail if he was found without a job, but it did not touch the question of wages. How much should he get for his work? The codes are silent on that point.

371

The "Black Codes" made an extremely unfavorable impression in the North. The Chicago *Tribune* said: "We tell the men of Mississippi that the men of the North will convert the state of Mississippi into a frog-pond before they will allow any such laws to disgrace one foot of soil in which the bones of our soldiers sleep and over which the flag of freedom waves."

The Union generals in command of the garrison troops in the Southern states did not share in these opinions. Almost to a man they were on the side of the Southerner. General Schofield wrote: "They [the negroes] do not even know the meaning of the freedom that has been given them, and are much astonished when they are informed that it does not mean that they are to live in idleness and be fed by the government."

He continued: "I have yet to see a single one among the many Union men in North Carolina who would willingly submit for a moment to the immediate elevation of the negro to political equality with the white man."

General Sheridan, commanding in New Orleans, thought that Congress should legislate as little as possible in reference to the colored man. "His social status," Sheridan said, "will be worked out by the necessity for his labor."

The American negroes are the only people in the history of the world, so far as I know, that ever became free without any effort of their own. In the story of the negro race there is no epic of Spartacus and the gladiators, nor of Magna Charta, nor of the Salle de Paume, nor of a black Lenin or Trotzky. The war that freed them was a war against their masters; their freedom came as an incident of that conflict.

So they had no mission to rehabilitate society. It was not their business. They had not started the war nor ended it. They twanged banjos around the railroad stations, sang melodious spirituals, and believed that some Yankee would soon come along and give each of them forty acres of land and a mule.

In the summer of 1865 the President sent Carl Schurz on an extended tour throughout the South to observe conditions. Before he went Johnson got an impression that Schurz was favorable to the presidential policy of reconstruction.

Schurz stayed three months in the sun-baked Southern towns. When he returned he presented a long report which was far from what Johnson expected. Schurz declared that there was "no loyalty among leaders or masses," and that through new legislation, "the South is establishing a form of slavery like the old chattel slavery."

The President was disturbed. He knew that Schurz's document had to go before Congress, and he sought some means of counteracting it, so he made up his mind to send Grant on a tour of inspection, with the idea that Grant would bring back a different set of opinions.

Grant left Washington in the latter part of November, 1865, and was back within ten days. Very short trip. He visited Raleigh, Charleston, Augusta, Savannah and Atlanta. Some of the old inhabitants of Augusta have told me that they remember him as he sat in the Planters' Hotel and listened to those who came to talk to him. They say that he had a peculiar gesture in conversation; that when he had anything to say he would raise his hand, with his fingers bent at a right angle to his palm, and chop the air with it; he would make his points with this vigorous, downward chopping motion. They also declare that he said, "immejetly" instead of "immediately," that his manner was pleasant, and that he had a pocket that seemed to be inexhaustible in the way of cigars.

His report was wholly favorable to Johnson's policy. He wrote:

> I am satisfied that the mass of thinking men of the South accept the present situation of affairs in good faith. . . .
> My observations lead me to the conclusion that the citizens of the Southern states are anxious to return to

self-government within the Union as soon as possible; that while reconstructing they want and require protection from the government; and that they are in earnest in wishing to do what is required by the government, not humiliating to them as citizens, and that if such a course was pointed out they would pursue it in good faith.

At this time the Radicals had not captured Grant, though they were already laying siege to him. Eventually they won him to their side, and Grant adopted most of the current Radical ideas; but this did not happen until Rawlins had convinced him that, in sticking to Johnson, he was clinging to a sinking ship.

§ 2

Congress becomes a cave of the winds. Ideas sail through the murky air on gusts of talk, and Congressmen sit hunched up over the knotty problems of political metaphysics like a group of medieval scholastics trying to decide how many angels can stand on the point of a needle.

The subject of debate is just exactly what relation the states lately in rebellion bear to the rest of the Union. The arguments are fine-spun and wrapped in interminable yards of legal verbiage. Charles Sumner, who declares that he has studied everything on the nature of republics from Plato to John Marshall, contends that the seceded states have committed suicide. That seems incredible, for obviously the Southern people still exist and have elected complete state governments. But that means nothing to Sumner. So he talks of wholesale suicide, and one gets an unpleasant impression that there are dead bodies lying around the house. Mr. Sumner, who leads the Radicals in the Senate, is ready to turn himself into a coroner.

He thinks that, as the states which entered the Confederacy are no longer existent—having died by their own hands—

the whole domain of secession is a territory under the authority of Congress. Military or territorial governors should be appointed, and universal suffrage given to the negro, while white men who have taken part in the rebellion should be denied the right to vote. After awhile the conquered territories should be permitted to enter the Union as states, but Mr. Sumner declares that their admission ought not to take place for a long time.

Sumner's views were implacable and statuesque. When he once adopted an idea he never let it go. In the face of opposition he would support his theories with formidable citations from history, law, economics, belles-lettres, anthropology, chemistry and religion. He would quote Spinoza and the Boston Cooking School in the same breath. But he rarely, if ever, cited common sense. It is rather interesting to observe that, although he contended that the negro ought to be given the ballot as an inherent human right, he detested negroes . . . personally. He did not want them around him, and would not shake hands with them.

The Radical leader on the floor of the House was Thaddeus Stevens, of Pennsylvania. He was, without doubt, the most powerful personality in Congress. Stevens maintained that the ex-Confederate states stood in the position of "conquered provinces"; that they had voluntarily abandoned the protection of the Constitution when they renounced their allegiance to the Union, and had therefore no rights which the conqueror was bound to respect. They were, in effect, he declared, a foreign nation that had been overthrown by the Union armies.

His proposals were drastic, to say the least. The first thing to do, he thought, was to confiscate the land, or—as he called it—"strip the proud nobility of their bloated estates." He wanted to reduce the Southern landowners, so he said, "to a level with plain republicans; send them forth to labor, and teach their children to enter the workshops or handle the plow, and you will thus humble the proud traitor." Of course, the leaders of the Confederacy should be tried and hanged, according to Mr. Stevens; and almost everybody else who had taken any part in secession was to be disfranchised.

Stevens' policy consisted simply of a set of hates strung together in a definite pattern. The core of his reconstruction theory was vengeance, yet his intellect was so vigorous, penetrating and brilliant that one is surprised at his failure to rise to a higher level of statesmanship. His nature was tinged by some dark motivation of which he was, perhaps, unconscious. He belonged to that grim and saturnine breed,

"Dont le rêve obscur salit tout ce qu'il touche."

Here and there flowers of generosity grew in the malevolence that encrusted his soul. He was charitable to the poor people of his neighborhood, and he set aside a fund to be used in growing "roses and other cheerful flowers" around his mother's grave. His affection for negroes was probably genuine and profound, although Gideon Welles thought him insincere, and wrote, "Almost all which this vicious old man does is premeditated, dramatic and for effect."

He was entirely right in his assertion that the Southern states had renounced the protection of the Constitution when they seceded. But that had nothing to do with the case—as it stood in 1865. Secession was defeated, slavery was legally abolished, and the South was no longer in rebellion. The states, both Union and Confederate, had to live together under the same roof, no matter whether they liked the arrangement or not. It was absolutely necessary to be reconciled all around unless the country was to continue indefinitely in a state of turbulence.

There was another motive, besides love of the negro, in these maneuvers. The Republican party was in danger of losing its majority in Congress. To understand the situation we must go back again to the Constitution. Before the war each slave, in accordance with Article I of the Constitution, was counted as three-fifths of a person when the periodical enumerations were made for the purpose of determining how many representatives a state was entitled to in Congress. But now the negroes were free, although they were not allowed to vote, and each negro had to be counted as a whole person.

The result would be an increased representation from all the Southern states . . . in short, the South would be stronger in Congress than it had been before the war. That would not do at all—looking at the matter from the Republican standpoint, and considering the probability that the Southern delegations would be solidly Democratic. The Southern Democrats, combined with those of the North and a few liberal Republicans, might upset all the Radical calculations and—as one of the Radicals put it—"nullify the results of the war."

The leaders of the Republican party came to the conclusion that the Southern states must be excluded from Congress until they had been "reconstructed"—which meant that they were to be kept out until negro domination had been forced upon them. Most of the important Radicals were quite outspoken about this; they came right out and said that reconstruction was a synonym for a Republican South, so far as they were concerned, and that they expected to obtain that desirable result through giving the ballot to the freedmen.

The chief difficulty in carrying out this program lay in the fact that Congress, under its constitutional limitations, could not make any laws concerning the qualifications of voters. The business of regulating the suffrage—and deciding who should vote—was left entirely to the states by the framers of the Constitution . . . each state to determine the matter for itself. To make negro suffrage compulsory in the Southern states a constitutional amendment was required . . . and here came another hitch. A constitutional amendment—to be effective—must be ratified by three-fourths of the states. At that time there were thirty-six states in the union—eleven of them ex-Confederate. To ratify a constitutional amendment the affirmative votes of twenty-seven state legislatures would be required, and it was virtually certain that the ex-Confederate states would reject any amendment which made the negro a voter.

The intellectual limitations of those in authority at that time are painfully obvious. In reality the negro question was not a political, but an economic, problem; yet it was treated as a political issue. The entire discussion stepped off on the wrong foot. It became involved with the alien rancors of the dead, with incredible prejudices on both sides, and with an ignorance that was both wide and profound.

What the negro really needed was some practicable method of establishing himself in the world, but Stevens' plan of confiscating the lands of the former slave-owners and dividing them among the negroes was the worst of all possible measures. Suppose it had been carried out. Then we would have had, on one hand, a dispossessed race—and a fighting one—embittered, and destined to be perpetually at war with the order of things. Another Ireland.

On the other hand, the negro would have made a first-class mess of his ownership. He had never worked except under direction. He did not know how to lay out crops, how to get the most out of the land, how to calculate, how to buy or sell. One may be sure that the best of the Southern lands would have been before long in the hands of Northern syndicates of optimistic capitalization; and the negro would have gone back into a position of semi-slavery, but by a different route.

The Freedmen's Bureau was the most promising of all the efforts to put the black man on his own feet economically, but it came to an end, unfortunately, in eclipse and shame.

This Bureau, organized under Lincoln's direction, was a welfare organization with considerable legal authority. It grew into a sort of government employment agency with wide powers of supervision. At first its work was carried on by army officers, but in a year or two they were superseded by another set of officials—ex-preachers, most of them, who told the negroes that a black man was "God's image in ebony."

The Freedmen's Bureau supervised the contracts between the freed slaves and their former masters. In some localities it opened schools for negroes, and everywhere—at first—the organization encouraged the negroes to work and endeavored to obtain fair wages for them. It was not long before the organization gained the confidence of the planters, but it would have been much more successful if a few Southern men and some intelligent negroes had been employed in its general management.

Its tendency was in the other direction. The Bureau degenerated. The revivalists and politicians who got control of it turned it into a branch of the Republican party. Its corps of agents in the South gradually evolved into a legion of stump speakers with a wishing eye on land that might be picked up at a low price.

The clique that controlled the Freedmen's Bureau organized a Freedmen's Savings Bank. Headquarters in Washington, with hindquarters in every Southern state. An impressive list of organizers. The idea was to teach the ex-slaves the value of thrift. Deposits from one dollar up were thankfully received, all earning interest, little by little, and working while you sleep.

The local agents of the Bureau mingled finance, religion and the Republican party in their exhortations to the colored people. They prayed for the salvation of the negro race, raised hallelujahs on their freedom from bondage, and took their dimes and dollars. Deposits poured in, all for small sums, but the total amounted to millions.

Then the bank failed. The pitiable savings of the negroes had disappeared in a rosy cloud of theft and large salaries. The bookkeeping was so muddled that the most expert accountants could not make head or tail of it. The depositors got only a few cents on the dollar and it took thirty years to give them even that trifling dribble. This outcome was very unfortunate, for the basic idea of the Bureau was a sensible one. It was a genuine attempt—at the beginning—to solve the negro problem by economic means.

So the negro fell back into the morass of politics. Yet, in spite of the inept plans for his salvation and the prejudices that have surrounded him, he has succeeded in doing something for himself. And he must thank himself for whatever he has done, for most of the so-called aid that has been given him has been pretty thoroughly misguided.

§ 3

On Christmas Eve of the year 1865, six young men were killing time in a law office in Pulaski, Tennessee. One of them suggested that they get up a secret society. Good idea. A secret society for amusement, with pass-words and ear-wriggling signs. Before they parted at midnight they had organized the *Ku-Klux Klan*. They decided to wear sheets over their heads as a disguise—long, flowing sheets, with holes cut for the eyes. Next evening they put on their sheets, mounted their horses, and called on some girls. They were the life of the party.

The idea spread, and before long there were Klans in most of the Southern states. Then the notion that the Ku-Klux might serve a useful purpose occurred to some of its leaders, and it was quickly passed along. "Let us reorganize the South according to Southern ideas," they said; and as the affirmative opinion seemed to be unanimous, they set out to do it. The Klans were tied together in a general organization, called The Invisible Empire.

(I may as well say here that the Ku-Klux Klan of that day had no connection with the so-called Ku-Klux that arose in the second decade of the twentieth century. This later Klan took the name of the earlier one, but its only purpose seems to have been to make money for its organizers.)

The Ku-Klux Klan—as it existed in the late sixties—was the most formidable secret society in the history of the American people. It was singularly bare of ideas; it was not a debating society; it had hardly anything to do with theories, except the broad theory that the South belonged to the Southern white man. Its point of contact was on individuals, and it used terrorizing methods to accomplish its purposes.

The first thing to do was to make the negroes go to work. A cavalcade of white and ghostly figures would appear before a negro cabin on a moonlit night.

"Come out here!"

The negroes would come out. "What are you doing to earn your living?" one of the ghostly horsemen would say.

"Who you?"

"We're the ghosts of the Confederate dead," would be the sepulchral answer, and all the sheeted horsemen would groan dismally. "Are you working at anything?"

"No, sah," the shivering negro would reply. "I'se not wukking now."

"Don't you know that everybody around here wants field-hands?"

"No, sah; I didn't know dat."

"Well, we're telling you. You'd better have a job by tomorrow night or the Confederate dead will come to see you again. And if you are still hanging around, doing nothing but steal chickens, the Confederate dead will lay you under ground."

It was soon learned that they meant exactly what they said. The Ku-Klux had no hesitation at whipping or killing idle or disorderly negroes, nor did they show much more consideration for white men whom they considered undesirable.

§ 4

At the end of the war Northern political adventurers poured into the Southern states. They were known as "carpet-baggers," as they usually brought all their possessions in a lean carpet bag. They were unprincipled scamps in the main, the riff-raff of the North. Within a year they managed to get themselves into practically all the Federal offices in the South, as most of the leading men in every community were disfranchised, and incapable of holding office, on account of having taken part in the rebellion. Most of these adventurers had no intention of settling permanently in the South; they meant to remain only long enough to acquire a fortune, and—once in office—they applied themselves diligently to ingenious schemes for the stealing of public funds.

All the carpet-baggers were not rascals. Among them were men of excellent motives who came to the South under the delusion that the poor, beaten Southerners needed the guidance and personal aid of the more enlightened citizens of the North. These men attempted to stop the brazen thefts and misuse of authority, but their efforts were unsuccessful. Some of them became disillusioned pessimists and went back home in a short time. Others passed through a spiritual conversion which made Southerners of them. They remained in the South and got to be rabidly anti-Northern. Numbers of them joined the Ku-Klux Klan.

The term "scalawag" was applied to the Southern equivalent of a carpet-bagger. A scalawag was any Southerner who became a Republican, and accepted a Federal office, or who advocated votes for negroes.

The carpet-baggers did not get control of the state governments until the negroes were given the suffrage, so their opportunities were limited for a year or two, while they held only the Federal offices. But they did very well for themselves, even in that restricted sphere, especially in the matter of cotton which had belonged, or was supposed to have belonged, to the Confederate government.

This cotton was scattered throughout the Southern states, on plantations. The Confederate government had sold bonds to its citizens for cotton, and in most cases the cotton was marked and left with its former owner. Upon the dissolution of the Confederacy, the cotton so marked became the property of the Federal government, and a swarm of officials was appointed to locate it.

The search for Confederate cotton was a sort of carpet-baggers' festival. In theory the cotton agents were supposed to seize only the bales which bore the distinguishing marks of Confederate government ownership, but in practice they took nearly all they could lay their hands on.

The statistics relating to this blatant robbery are guess-work, but it is a certain fact that most of the cotton agents went back to the North bulging with money; and it is entirely probable that not more than half the seized cotton ever reached the Federal government.

§ 5

The Ku-Klux Klan took a long breath, rolled up its sleeves, and started in to exercise its peculiar talents on the carpet-bagger situation. Its activities widened into a species of guerrilla warfare, with the carpet-baggers on one side, and the Ku-Klux and Southern sentiment in opposition.

Lawless and irresponsible, yet bound by its own standards and traditions, the Ku-Klux movement of the sixties was essentially a kind of Fascism—but a Fascism adapted to the American scene. It constituted a government within a government. In some parts of the South this shadowy empire was much stronger than the governments set up by the military and the carpet-baggers. Besides keeping the negroes at work, the activities of the Klan consisted principally of the elimination of undesirable white men.

The matter of elimination was usually accomplished by means of threats. Warning letters. Skulls and crossbones. Fierce invectives. Gloomy forebodings. All these solemn portents on a sheet of paper thrust under the door of the unwelcome resident. Sometimes the threats did not work, and the next step was a brutal whipping by unknown parties clad in white sheets. The whipping generally drove its recipient out of the county, or the state. If threats and whipping failed, the process of elimination was brought to a close by a quiet murder—also by unknown parties.

Most of the army officers shared with the Southerners an active dislike for the politicians and carpet-baggers. It was a curious situation. The garrisons spent money in the Southern towns and, without exception, I think, treated the inhabitants as friends and neighbors. The people, as a rule, liked the troops, and some of the officers and men married Southern women. The carpet-bagger was the pariah of the community.

The letters of warning sent by the Ku-Klux were always written in a peculiar, lugubrious style. They were flatly pessimistic pieces of literature. Instead of the ordinary "Dear Sir" at the beginning of a letter the Ku-Klux usually started theirs with "God damn your soul." After this cheerless salutation the letter would run along in this fashion:

> Take heed, for the pale horse is coming. His step is terrible; lightning is in his nostrils. He looks for a rider. Now this is to warn you, William Gober, that carpet-baggers and scalawags cannot live in this country. If you are not gone in ten days we shall come to you and the pale horse shall have its rider.

The terror inspired by the Ku-Klux lasted for many years after the Klan had passed away. I remember that in the little South Carolina town in which I was brought up there lived an ex-carpet-bagger named John Woolley. He had settled down in the community, had joined the Methodist church, and paid his bills, but the people of the place still treated him with a cold, snappish courtesy. This was in the middle eighties. The Ku-Klux organization had been dissolved so many years back that only middle-aged men could speak of it with personal knowledge. I heard them talk, and resolved to do a little Ku-Kluxing myself. I was at that time a boy of ten.

In great secrecy I fashioned a tiny wooden coffin with a jack-knife. Then I cut out a little spade and put it in the coffin. Next, I took a piece of paper and drew a skull in red ink at the top of the sheet. On the paper I wrote in a childish scrawl: "John Woolley. God damn your soul," and continued with this rhyme:

> Here's your coffin and spade;
> In your grave you'll soon be laid.

I signed the epistle, "K. K. K." The whole concoction, wrapped in black paper, was cautiously laid by me on Mr. Woolley's doorstep one dark night. Next morning he appeared on our peaceful little streets with a double-barreled shotgun. "I'm ready for 'em," he announced. "I've got their warning, but they can't scare me." Despite this confident statement, I must say that he looked very scared, indeed. I remember clearly that he sat before the village drug store with his shotgun on his knees and wiped the cold sweat from his brow.

The Federal courts, in their efforts to ferret out the leaders of the Klan, ran up against a blank wall of reticence. Nearly every witness who came before the courts had heard vaguely of the Klan, but it was in the next county; there had never been any Ku-Klux activities in their neighborhood—and in the next county the Federal officers heard the same story.

The Ku-Klux Klan did a little good and a great deal of harm. Like all other militant secret societies, it put people on trial without giving them a hearing. It turned prejudice into an established system of conduct; and the glamor of its actions fastened a spirit of lawlessness on the Southern people. Any gang of ruffians could put on sheets and call themselves

Ku-Klux, and many of them did. Long after the Klan was disbanded, so-called Ku-Klux outrages continued. Highway bandits who were caught red-handed often called themselves Ku-Klux, and credited their activities to a high and mysterious mission.

CHAPTER XXVI

GRANT BECOMES PRESIDENT

§ 1

THE war between the President and Congress began in a splutter of speeches and threats. If Johnson had shown any desire to meet the moderates half-way, he might have voted down the Radicals and obtained control of legislation. But he did nothing of the kind; his attitude was one of obstinacy and challenge; in the end he drove the moderate faction of the Republican party over to the Radical side. The first phase of the struggle was a battle of vetoes. The President vetoed one bill after another. As soon as they came back to Congress they were passed with feverish enthusiasm, over the presidential disapproval.

In June, 1866, Congress passed the Fourteenth Amendment to the Constitution and submitted it to the states for ratification.

The first section of the amendment declared that all persons born or naturalized in the United States are citizens of the United States and of the states in which they reside. The next section gave the states the option of enfranchising all adult male citizens or suffering a reduction of their representation in Congress. The third section was intended to exclude ex-Confederates from Congress and, indeed, from all Federal offices. "But," this section continues, "Congress may, by a vote of two-thirds of each House, remove such disability."

It may be noted that the amendment does not confer the right of suffrage on the negro; it only penalizes the states which refuse to allow him to vote by reducing their representation in Congress.

It would have been better for the Southern states if their legislatures had promptly ratified the Fourteenth Amendment, but they were not wise enough to do it, and all of them, except Tennessee, rejected it. For two years it dangled idly in the political air, lacking the requisite three-fourths of the states necessary for its ratification.

We shall let it dangle for a few pages while we turn to some other aspects of the situation.

§ 2

President Johnson's manner was unfortunate. He was to learn, before his term was over, that men are judged more by their manner than by their virtues. One of his failings was that he frequently lost his temper and dignity, and he would wrangle loudly with any one who differed from his opinions.

In the summer of 1866 he undertook a speechmaking tour through some of the Northern states. He wanted to make friends and gain popular support for his measures. As companions on this tour, which he called a "swing around the circle," he took General Grant and Admiral Farragut with him. Grant said later that he went because he considered the President's invitation as a military order. Johnson's purpose in taking Grant and Farragut with him was undoubtedly to make his own appearance before the public more impressive.

The tour was a melancholy failure. In Cleveland he had a noisy dispute with his audience, and when somebody called out that he ought to be more dignified he shouted that he cared nothing for dignity. At Indianapolis his speech, interrupted every instant by rowdies, descended to the level of a barroom brawl. Grant attempted to quiet the audience by coming to the edge of the platform and saying: "Gentlemen, I am ashamed of you. Go home and be ashamed of yourselves." This admonition had no effect; the audience still remained, entirely unashamed. "It was a most painful spectacle," wrote a newspaper man with the presidential party, "to see the President of the United States standing on a platform, facing a laughing and indifferent crowd, his face flushed with passion, his hands clenching and waving in mad gesticulation."

The President's opponents were quick to take advantage of his decline in popular favor. When Congress met in December, 1866, Thaddeus Stevens introduced a bill providing for military government in all the Southern states, except Tennessee. The unrepressed activities of the Ku-Klux was one of the arguments behind this measure, and another was the rejection of the Fourteenth Amendment by the Southern legislatures.

This bill, known as the Reconstruction Act, swept away the state governments which Johnson had created, and divided the Southern territory into five military departments, each to be commanded by an officer to be named by the general commanding the army. While the Reconstruction Act was being discussed in the Senate Grant let it be known that he would rather leave the designation of the military commanders to the President. The bill became a law over the President's veto on March 2, 1867.

On the same day Congress passed a bill which forbade the President to issue any orders to the army except through the general in command—that is, through General Grant. The Radicals had begun to feel sure of Grant, for they had taken his measure and had learned that he had no emphatic ideas of his own, but was insensibly influenced on political questions by the men around him.

The second day of March is a memorable date. After the Reconstruction Act was passed on that day the members of Congress, without leaving their seats, put through another far-reaching anti-presidential measure called the Tenure of Office Act. This bill provided that "every person holding any civil office to which he had been appointed by and with the advice and consent of the Senate," should be entitled to hold such office until a successor had been appointed in the same way; that is to say, with the approval of the Senate. The purpose of the law was to prevent Johnson from dismissing the Radicals from office and putting his own supporters in their places. However, he might, under the law, suspend officials when the Senate was not in session, but these suspensions were only temporary, and required the consent of the Senate to turn them into permanent dismissals.

The Secretary of War, Edwin M. Stanton, held views on almost all subjects directly contrary to those of the President. Stanton was bitterly opposed to Johnson's policies, and Johnson considered him a sort of Radical spy in the midst of his official family.

Johnson decided to remove Stanton after the latter had refused to resign on request. He was removed—or suspended—in 1867, immediately after Congress adjourned, and General Grant was appointed Secretary of War *ad interim*. Johnson, at that time, still thought that Grant was on his side in the controversy with Congress.

Gideon Welles, who was Johnson's Secretary of the Navy, had a long talk with Grant on August 22, 1867, and wrote it all out in his *Diary* the same day. Mr. Welles was greatly depressed over the General's limitations. He wrote:

> It pained me to see how little he understood of the fundamental principles and structure of our government, and of the Constitution itself. On the subject of differences between the President and Congress, and the attempt to subject the people to military rule, there were, he said, in Congress, fifty at least of the first lawyers of the country who had voted for the Reconstruction law, and were not, he asked, the combined wisdom and talent of these fifty to have more weight than Mr. Johnson, who was only one to fifty? Congress had enacted this law . . . and was not Congress superior to the President?
>
> "Would you," said he, "allow the rebels to vote and

take the government of their states into their own hands?"

I replied that I knew not who were to take the government of those states in hand but the intelligent people of the states respectively to whom it rightfully belonged. . . . A majority of the voters—and they decide for themselves who shall be voters—is the basis of free government. This is our system. . . .

Grant said he was not prepared to admit this doctrine; it was something of the old states-right doctrine, and he did not go to the full extent of that doctrine. He looked upon Georgia and the other states south as territories. They had rebelled, been conquered, and were to be reconstructed and admitted into the Union when we felt that we could trust them. It was for Congress to say who should vote, and who should not vote, in the seceding states as well as in a territory, and to direct when and how these states should again be admitted.

That, I told him, was not only a virtual dissolution of the Union, but an abandonment of our republican federal system. It was establishing a central power, which could control and destroy—a power above and beyond the Constitution. . . .

I have quoted this interview at length because it embodies the best exposition of Grant's political notions of that time. It reveals also how far he had gone over to the Radical side. Welles adds, in his *Diary:*

General Grant has become severely afflicted with the Presidential disease, and it warps his judgment, which is not very intelligent or enlightened at best. He is less sound on great and fundamental principles, vastly less informed, than I had supposed possible for a man of his opportunities.

In the meantime the military government of the South under the Reconstruction Act was taking shape. The governing generals, under the act, were directed to call state conventions for the purpose of forming new state constitutions; and, after that, state governments were to be established. All male citizens over twenty-one years of age, irrespective of color—except those who had been disfranchised for taking part in the rebellion—were to be allowed to vote for delegates to the constitutional conventions.

It was also provided in the act that the new state governments, created in this manner, might bring their states back into the Union and seat their representatives in Congress, by ratifying the Fourteenth Amendment.

As a point of history, it is interesting to observe that this procedure allowed the negro to vote on the question of his own right to vote.

New state constitutions were formed; the Republican ticket, from governor down, was elected in all the Southern states; the "Black Codes" went into the legal trash pile; carpet-baggers filled most of the offices; the Fourteenth Amendment was ratified by all the Southern states through their legislatures of negroes and carpet-baggers; and reconstruction began according to the plans of the Radical Congress.

§ 3

As soon as Congress met the Radicals in control of the Senate passed a resolution which disapproved and set aside the President's action in suspending Secretary Stanton.

When the news of the Senate's procedure reached Grant he abandoned instantly his place as Secretary of War. I mean that he simply walked out of the office and Stanton walked in. Grant was still the commanding general of the army, and he returned to his office at army headquarters.

His prompt abandonment of the job as Secretary of War brought on a disagreeable altercation with President Johnson in which Grant's veracity was questioned. Johnson had always contended that the Tenure of Office Act was unconstitutional, and he wanted to create an opportunity to bring it before the Supreme Court. It was his purpose to test the matter in the case of Stanton and Grant. He said that this situation had been explained to General Grant, and that Grant had agreed to hold on to the secretaryship despite the action of the Senate—which Johnson anticipated—or, at least, to give Johnson sufficient time to appoint some other man in his place if he decided not to hold it himself. That would have forced Stanton to go to the courts to have himself reinstated.

In an angry letter Johnson accused Grant of not keeping his word. Grant replied that he had never given the President any reason to believe that he would disobey the law, and that he considered Congress the final authority. He continued in the same letter:

> And now, Mr. President, when my honor as a soldier and integrity as a man have been so violently assailed, pardon me for saying that I can but regard this whole matter from beginning to end as an attempt to involve me in a resistance of law for which you hesitated to assume the responsibility, and thus destroy my character before the country.

One cannot help feeling that Grant's letter was rather childish in its general tone, and specifically in accusing the President of attempting to "destroy my character before the country." He does not show up very well in this episode.

On January 14, 1868, Grant attended a meeting of the cabinet and tried to explain his action to the President. He told Johnson that he had intended to resign the office and give the President a chance to put some one else in his place, but his time had been so occupied with various duties that he did not get around to it. The members of the cabinet thought his manner shuffling and evasive. Gideon Welles believed that Grant had become a catspaw of the Radicals, and wrote,

"There is no doubt that Grant has been in secret intrigue in this business, acting in concert with and under the direction of the chief conspirators." A few days later Welles wrote in his *Diary* that the episode "is throughout highly discreditable to Grant's integrity, honor, ability and truth. . . . He has vulgar cunning, is deceptive and unreliable."

Grant did not deserve these harsh epithets, unless my conception of his character is utterly at fault. I am convinced that he was simply bewildered. He never understood intricate political moves; he was a lost child in the wilderness of politics. I think he came to the conclusion that the best thing he could do, for everybody's sake, was to walk away from the office and let it go at that.

The lack of frankness that he exhibited in this and other episodes was not the insincerity of hypocrisy, but another kind of insincerity that comes from confusion of mind.

Both the Democrats and the Republicans had claimed Grant since the close of the Civil War, and either party would have nominated him for President in 1868. The effect of the Johnson episode was to align him definitely with the Republican party and opposed to Johnson and all his works.

§ 4

Johnson was still full of fight. He dismissed Stanton again and appointed General Lorenzo Thomas in his place. In doing this he disregarded the Tenure of Office Act altogether. Stanton refused to be dismissed and General Thomas attempted to take possession of the office by force. He succeeded only in getting himself arrested.

Such a strained situation could not endure very long, and the Radicals resolved to bring it to an end by impeaching the President, but they discovered that it was rather difficult to find adequate grounds. The article of the Constitution which deals with the subject of impeachment says that it shall be done only for "treason, bribery, or other high crimes and misdemeanors." Obviously the President had not committed anything that could be legally called treason or bribery. But how about high crimes and misdemeanors? Would not his total disregard of the Tenure of Office Act come under that head?

Before the articles of impeachment were adopted by the House they were given prolonged consideration. Everything was put in them that the Radicals could think of; they were a kind of rag bag of legal odds and ends . . . but the only serious charges were those growing out of violations of the Tenure of Office Act.

In his reply Johnson said that he considered the Tenure of Office Act unconstitutional. He argued that as the chief executive he was legally responsible for the actions of the Secretary of War and that made it necessary for him to hold the power of appointment and removal.

His trial before the Senate began on March 30, 1868. It was the first time in our history that a President had been brought before the bar of the Senate on charges of impeachment, and the nation almost held its breath in the thrill of suspense.

Grant was not a good hater. His nature was too indolent and easy-going to cherish long resentments, but he did hate some people, and Johnson, who had publicly called him a liar, was one of them. Probably he felt a little ashamed of his own behavior in the Johnson-Stanton crisis; and with certain types of men a sense of shame turns readily into hate. His anxiety over the impeachment was almost as great as if he had been on trial himself. He wanted to see Johnson convicted, and he went to the trouble of calling on various Senators at their homes for the purpose of persuading them to vote for impeachment.

After six weeks of testimony and argument the Senate voted on May 16th. Thirty-five Republicans voted against Johnson; twelve Democrats and seven Republicans voted for him. An impeachment can be carried only by a two-thirds vote, so Johnson won. His margin was narrow; one vote on the other side would have impeached him.

But the Radicals took comfort in the thought that Johnson's time was nearly over. They expected to elect General Grant and then they would have things their own way.

There was no opposition in the Republican convention that met in Chicago on May 20th. Grant was nominated unanimously, and Schuyler Colfax, Speaker of the House of Representatives, was selected as the nominee for Vice-President.

The platform on which the Grant campaign was made was about as hazy and meaningless as political platforms usually are. There was something about equal suffrage for "all loyal men"; all attempts to repudiate the public debt were denounced; and then there was a section calling for the reduction of taxation. Two paragraphs were devoted to Andrew Johnson; he was declared to be a thorough rascal.

In his letter of acceptance Grant said: "If elected to the office of President of the United States it will be my endeavor to administer all the laws in good faith, with economy, and with the view of giving peace, quiet and protection everywhere. . . .

"Peace and universal prosperity—its sequence—with economy of administration, will lighten the burden of taxation, while it constantly reduces the national debt. Let us have peace."

It was thought at the time that the critical issue of the campaign would be the question of the payment of the public debt. The interest-bearing obligations of the government amounted to more than two billions of dollars, and consisted chiefly of the bond issues of the Civil War. These bonds, it will be recalled, were sold to the people in exchange for depreciated paper money, though it was specified that the interest on them was to be paid in gold. It was provided, however, that the principal was payable in "dollars." As paper money—or greenbacks—were legal currency the Democrats argued that the payment in "dollars" be made in paper.

By 1868 most of these bonds had got into the hands of wealthy people who had purchased them at prices which expressed various degrees of depreciation. The Democrats contended that it would be unfair to the taxpayers and a discrimination in favor of the rich to redeem the bonds in gold. They had been purchased with paper money; so why not pay them off in the same medium? "The same currency for the bond-holder and the plough-holder" was a political slogan in the agrarian West.

The Democratic platform declared that there should be "one currency for the government and people, the laborer and the office-holder, the pensioner and the soldier, the producer and the bond-holder." The Democrats also maintained that government bonds ought to be taxed, and that the Reconstruction Acts of Congress were usurpatious, "and unconstitutional, revolutionary and void." On this platform stood the Democratic nominees: Horatio Seymour, of New York, for President; and Frank Blair, of Missouri, for Vice-President.

Somehow the financial issue got lost, or minimized, during the campaign, and the battle was fought over the condition of affairs in the South. Grant was elected on his popularity as a war hero, as the victor at Appomattox. During the campaign he remained at his home in Galena, made no speeches and seldom appeared in public. His majority of the popular vote was only 309,000 . . . a result which was disappointing to the Republican managers. Coolidge says:

> If it had not been for the negro vote in the South, which was still unsuppressed and which prevented that section from being solidly Democratic, as it afterwards became, Seymour would have been elected.

No President since Washington, and Lincoln (for his second term), had gone into office so favorably regarded by men of both parties. The Democratic campaign had not been directed against Grant, but against the Republican platform. But there was one jarring note. On his inauguration day, March 4, 1869, he declined to ride in the same carriage with Andrew Johnson, so the retiring President did not attend the inaugural ceremonies. Among the well-balanced men of the time this fit of childish petulance on Grant's part was considered a poor beginning for an administration that was to be based on the formula of "Let us have peace."

§ 5

Next morning the General sat at his great shining desk in the White House and pondered on the problems of state. He was then forty-seven years old.

His elevation to the office of President was the greatest disaster of his life, but he never had the faintest inkling of that fact. He considered it a huge triumph. He was elected for two terms; he remained in his exalted post for eight years, and at the end he knew hardly any more about life and affairs than he knew at the beginning. His administration ended in disrepute, but he was never quite aware of it, for he thought all the criticisms came from disgruntled people who envied him.

He appeared to think that the presidential office was not a responsibility but a prize. It was simply a reward for his services, or so he thought. And why should he have thought anything else? He had been elected because he had won the war, and deserved the appreciation of the American people. That is what he was told by his admirers; and it was the truth. His fitness to handle the affairs of the government had never been brought in question; certainly the matter had never been generally discussed . . . that is, before his election. It was discussed afterwards, at length and rather acrimoniously.

The selections for his cabinet astonished everybody, including most of the men who were selected. Consider Adolph E.

Borie, of Philadelphia, who was made Secretary of the Navy. He was in Washington just before Grant's inauguration, and he passed an hour or two in the company of the President-elect. Nothing was said to him about a cabinet position then. A few days later, while reading a newspaper on a train, he was amazed to find himself put down as Secretary of the Navy. Mr. Borie was a gentleman of wealth—he had made a fortune in profiteering operations during the Civil War—but he was so little known that when his name came before the Senate for confirmation both the Pennsylvania Senators said they had never heard of him. He retired from office as soon as he decently could, for his range of interests was so limited that he knew less about the navy than the average man knows of astronomy.

The whole business of the cabinet appointments was wrapped in mystery until after the inauguration. This secrecy deeply offended the leaders of the Republican party—men like Sumner—not only because none of them was given a place in the cabinet, but also because not one of them had been consulted.

When the cabinet surprise package was opened immediately after the inauguration Elihu B. Washburne stood at the top of the list as the new Secretary of State. Our old friend Washburne, of Galena, who had tied himself to the Grant kite years before. The members of Congress, all of whom knew Washburne, considered this selection as something in the nature of a comedy. Mr. Washburne was half-illiterate, ill-mannered and incredibly undiplomatic. He held the job only a week. It appears that he was really listed as Minister to France, and he wanted to go to Paris with the prestige of having been the American Secretary of State, so Grant accommodated him.

For Secretary of the Treasury the President named Alexander T. Stewart, an enormously wealthy dry goods merchant of New York. Mr. Stewart was overjoyed. He rushed down to Washington, engaged a string of rooms at a hotel and leased a house. But some member of Congress unearthed a forgotten law, enacted in George Washington's time, which says that no man engaged in a mercantile business shall be at the head of the nation's financial system.

The millionaire merchant was so eager to get the office that he offered to transfer his business to trustees who would apply the entire profits to charity during his term of office—but that failed to move the Senate. It was said at the time by those who did not like Grant that Stewart's costly gifts to Mrs. Grant of articles from his mercantile establishment had inspired the President to appoint him. I do not believe these expensive presents had anything to do with it. He said that he gave the Treasury portfolio to Mr. Stewart because that gentleman had made a great success of his own financial affairs, and he thought he would do as much for the government. The real reason, in my opinion, was that he liked Stewart personally.

It was confidently expected by nearly everybody that the Treasury portfolio would go to Jay Cooke, of Philadelphia. Mr. Cooke was not only as successful as Mr. Stewart, but in addition he had a large experience in government finance. It was he who had made such a tremendous reputation in selling bonds during the Civil War.

Mr. Cooke and his friends were disappointed when Grant failed to select him for the Treasury; and they were even more chagrined when, after it had been settled that Stewart could not serve, a Massachusetts man named George S. Boutwell was given the place. Mr. Boutwell was a man of honesty and virtue, but without any special aptitude for financial affairs. Another Massachusetts man, E. Rockwood Hoar, was selected as Attorney-General. He was a lawyer of distinction and his office was ably conducted.

John Bigelow wrote, soon after Grant's inauguration:

> He [Grant] seems to have no comprehension of the nature of political forces. His Cabinet are merely staff officers, selected apparently out of motives of gratitude

or for pecuniary favors received from them. His relatives
and other friends were among the first provided for. . . .
No President before was ever got in the family way so
soon after inauguration.

Washburne departed for France, and Hamilton Fish, of New
York, was appointed Secretary of State. Mr. Fish was re-
luctant to take the place, but he did take it, and his appointment was a great success. He was a suave, diplomatic person
of culture and understanding, and he managed to keep the
United States out of foreign complications which might have
led the country into war if there had been a smaller man in
his place.

John A. Rawlins was made Secretary of War. He was no
longer in Grant's confidence; beneath their friendliness there
was an unspoken attitude of strain, and Grant's appointment
of his old friend to a place in the cabinet seems to have been
made after considerable hesitation. Rawlins was a mere
shadow as a war secretary. When his appointment came he
was far gone with tuberculosis, and died during the year of his
appointment.

The Secretary of the Interior, Jacob D. Cox, of Ohio,
was a fortunate choice. He had a rich background of knowledge and a vigorous intellect.

In spite of Grant's personal preferences as a basis for selection, the cabinet was a pretty good one. Mr. Bigelow's observation that its members were nothing more than staff officers seems hardly justified, though that remark expressed
the trend of contemporary criticism. Certainly Fish, Cox and
Hoar were men who stood on their own feet.

Most of the able men in the cabinet left it before Grant's
first term was over, and their places were taken by shallow
politicians and money-seekers. Hamilton Fish was the only one
of the President's official advisers who remained for the entire
eight years of Grant's administration.

In all, twenty-four men occupied the seven places in the

cabinet for various periods of time. The changes were so rapid that the public could not keep up with them. It seems to have been difficult to work with Grant. Some of the members resigned because they said they did not know what was going on; that the President never asked their views on any subject; and that unsatisfactory appointments were made over their heads. Others were almost literally kicked out. Marshall Jewell, one of the Postmasters-General, met the President accidentally one day. Before Jewell had time to utter "Good-morning" Grant said: "Mr. Jewell, I want your resignation." He got Jewell's resignation at once, and left that ex-official wondering what it was all about.

§ 6

Grant appointed a few of his relatives to minor offices, and was charged with nepotism. It was said that he intended to let loose a swarm of Grants and Dents on the country; to rule the land with his cousins; to establish a royal family that would fatten on the public purse. Some of the opposition newspapers compared the Dents and the Grants to Egypt's plague of locusts.

I have run down this accusation, and it shrinks as one gets close to it. All told, he appointed only twelve of his relatives to places under the government during the eight years of his two presidential terms, and there was not a single important office in the lot.

The chief functionary at the White House was Frederick Dent, his brother-in-law. He seems to have been a sort of glorified usher who received callers and made appointments. Another brother-in-law was a customs official at San Francisco; a second cousin was the Receiver of Public Moneys in Oregon.

Another Dent—Mrs. Grant's brother—held the position of government Indian trader in New Mexico; and there was the collector of the port of New Orleans—James F. Casey, a relative of Grant by marriage. This Casey made himself notorious in Louisiana through his political activities. His brother Peter got himself appointed postmaster at Vicksburg, Mississippi.

Old Jesse Root Grant held the job of postmaster at Covington, Kentucky, but he had been given the place by Andrew Johnson.

The President's father-in-law—Colonel Frederick Dent, the elder—was a sort of professional Southerner. He lived at the White House for weeks and months at a time, reading newspapers, smoking cigars and mixing mint juleps. Grant's friends found the Colonel's discourses on damned Yankees and upstart "niggahs" rather amusing.

It is interesting to observe that Grant's father never became friendly with Colonel Dent. When old Jesse visited Washington he used to stay at a hotel. The White House, he declared, was full of the tribe of Dents, and he did not like them.

Grant frequently invited his mother to visit him at the White House, but she never came; in fact, she was not in Washington at any time while her son was President.

CHAPTER XXVII

ADVENTURES IN HIGH FINANCE

§ 1

THE atmosphere was heavy with problems that required the most adroit and experienced statesmanship for their solution; and the honest soldier in the White House was not a statesman.

It was Grant's misfortune that he was put at the head of the government at this time. The job really needed a man who combined the best qualities of Thomas Jefferson, Abraham Lincoln and Lord Beaconsfield—with perhaps a dash of Alexander Hamilton added to the mixture.

The moral standards of the nation had touched low water mark. All the great altruists had been quietly lifted over the backyard fence of public affairs and sent home, but their sentiments—hammered out in the shape of crisp slogans—were still carefully cherished. Phrases took the place of honesty. The spiritual decay of the time ate its way through the tissue of events. It was an epoch of rusty souls.

Money had become the measure of human values, and most of the men who possessed money in large quantities did not possess anything else. War profiteers, contractors in shoddy goods, manipulators of the stock market, vendors of quack medicines, brazen promoters of fake enterprises . . . it was people of this type who filled the public eye. Millionaires without taste, suavity or ordinary common decency. Money was a raw force, untempered by taste or elegance..

In the councils of the nation finance clamored for a leading place—not because it represented wisdom, service or productivity, but simply because it owned and controlled. And why not?—said the stalwart, red-faced thimble-riggers of the stock market. You may talk all you please, but everything comes back to money in the end. We've got money; and money talks. It speaks louder than all your highfaluting ethical views and social standards. "The public be damned!" said Commodore Vanderbilt.

Almost every well-known man in political life represented a financial interest and everybody had an ax, to grind.

§ 2

A large job of ax-grinding was going on when Grant became President, but it was being done so quietly in back-rooms amid whispers that he did not know anything about it until it was over. It appears in history as the Credit Mobilier scandal, and it concerned the building of the Union Pacific Railroad.

During the Civil War there was much discussion in the North about the need of a railroad across the continent to connect California with the east, and before the war was over a company was formed for the purpose of building such a road. It was generally conceded that the railroad could not be built without government aid, so Congress put the national treasury behind the undertaking.

Twelve million acres of government land along the road's right of way were given outright to the Union Pacific Company. Besides, the government agreed to lend the company twenty-seven million dollars in United States bonds. These bonds were turned over to the promoters in various lots from time to time, according to the mileage that had been completed. But the loan of approximately twenty-seven million dollars was not made a first lien on the property. The organizers of the enterprise persuaded Congress to permit the road to issue twenty-seven million dollars of first mortgage bonds, and this obligation took precedence of the loan from the government.

Their plan had gone through Congress so smoothly that they were inspired by its success to attempt an even more ambitious operation. Why turn all this wealth of land and money over to the company? Why not secure it for themselves by contracting to build the road?

They looked around for ways and means to accomplish this desirable end, and before long they acquired the ownership of a small Pennsylvania corporation called the Credit Mobilier. This strangely named concern was engaged in financial enterprises, but under its liberal charter it was empowered to do practically anything and to take anything that it could get.

The promoters then made a contract with themselves, as owners of the Credit Mobilier, to build the railroad. The price per mile that was agreed upon gave the Credit Mobilier more than three times the actual cost of the work. But even before they entered into the contract with the construction company the promoters had mortgaged the road—which was nonexistent at that time—for $27,000,000, and the land grants for $10,000,000. Most of the proceeds of these mortgages was turned over to the Credit Mobilier, through some financial hocus-pocus. The Union Pacific began its existence flat broke, or virtually so, with all its actual assets in the hands of the little Pennsylvania corporation, and the government holding a worthless second mortgage.

These financial jugglers felt that, to be on the safe side, they would have to pass a little sugar to the leading members of Congress, for at any time somebody might rise in that august assembly and want to know exactly what had become of the government's contribution. Oakes Ames, a member of the House of Representatives, was one of the directors of the Credit Mobilier. He was put in charge of the Congressional sugar-bowl.

Mr. Ames' plan was sleek and subtle. He did not offer anybody a bribe. No; his method was a much better one. He sold stock in the Credit Mobilier to his fellow-members . . .

to a carefully selected list of them . . . at par. In selling the stock he explained that he was simply letting them in on a good thing which had come his way. Most of those whom he approached bought the stock. A few hesitated; they were too poor to make an investment and would have to decline his offer. Ames whispered a little secret to them. He was on the inside of the Credit Mobilier, he said, and he knew for a certainty that the concern would soon declare one or more dividends large enough to pay for the stock. They could buy the shares he offered them without making any investment at all. He would simply turn the stock over to them on memorandum. Then, when the dividends came they could pay him out of the proceeds.

Very attractive, indeed. A chance to make money without any risk at all.

Some of the members refused to take the stock on any terms, but not one of those who declined thought of mentioning the matter on the floor of the House.

During the year 1868, when these intimate transactions took place, the Credit Mobilier paid dividends on this gorgeous scale:

Jan. 4. 80 per cent in first mortgage bonds of the Union Pacific Railroad; 100 per cent in Union Pacific Railroad stock.

June 17. 60 per cent in cash; 40 per cent in Union Pacific Railroad stock.

July 3. 75 per cent in first mortgage bonds of the Union Pacific Railroad; 75 per cent in Union Pacific Railroad stock.

Sept. 3. 75 per cent in first mortgage bonds of the Union Pacific Railroad; 100 per cent in Union Pacific Railroad stock.

Dec. 19. 200 per cent in Union Pacific Railroad stock.

Exposure of Mr. Ames' methods came about as an incident of a family row in the small circle of insiders, which led to the publication of some of his letters in the New York *Sun*. This occurred in 1872, during the third year of Grant's administration. In the meantime the road had been completed, the Credit Mobilier had wound up its affairs, and the entire matter had passed into the secret history of the time.

The public pretended to be grievously shocked at these disclosures, but it was not, really. The American nation is never shocked, and seldom surprised, by the venality of its official servants. The public is merely interested, and looks upon a stroke of thievery, and its exposure, investigation and prosecution, as a sort of game. To the average American a Congressional investigation is nothing more than a political prize-fight, before which the whole nation may sit as spectators.

The news about the Credit Mobilier caused a tremendous stir. It was the Teapot Dome of the day. Several high-class reputations were hopelessly wrecked, including that of Schuyler Colfax, Vice-President of the United States. Before the investigating committee Mr. Colfax testified that he had never accepted any stock, nor had he received any dividends. Upon being confronted by a twelve-hundred-dollar canceled check, made out to his order by Oakes Ames, he attempted to face down the evidence by declaring that somebody else must have received the check and cashed it. Then the records of his own bank were brought in and it was proved that he had deposited the sum of twelve hundred dollars to his credit on the same day that the Ames check was paid. After that the plight of the Vice-President became rather pitiable and he melted into a succession of incoherent stammers.

The President was not convinced, however. He wrote to Colfax:

Allow me to say that I sympathize with you in the recent Congressional investigations; that I have watched them closely; and that I am satisfied now (as I have ever been) of your integrity, patriotism, and freedom from the charges imputed, as if I knew of my own knowledge your innocence.

This letter is signed: "Affectionately yours, U. S. Grant."

If Grant had ever made any money himself, even in the most legitimate way, it would be extremely difficult to defend his reputation successfully, for he had an instinctive liking for wealthy financial mountebanks—and, indeed, for almost any one who possessed wealth without the burden of culture. The making of money was always a deep mystery to him, and his respect for money-getters was like that of the ancient Greeks for the Delphic oracle.

But the proof of his own personal honesty is absolutely convincing. He was a poor man all his life, yet as President he could have made money in ways which would have stood any amount of investigation. I think one of the strangest things about him is that he did not accumulate a fortune, for surely many closely veiled bribes in the form of sound and profitable investments must have been offered to him.

Ames tried to justify himself by declaring that his actions were intended as a public service, and that they were in keeping with the habit of the time. He remarked rather naïvely to the investigating committee that it was the same thing "as going into a business community and interesting the leading business men by giving them shares."

The House committee of investigation recommended that Ames and James Brooks, another member of the clique, be expelled from the House. After much talk the House resolved that, as the offenses had been committed some years previously, there were "grave doubts" as to the power of the existing House to expel members for actions which had taken place before it came into being. So Ames was not expelled, but he died soon afterwards, "of a broken heart," according to his friends.

The report of the committee revealed the fact that the Credit Mobilier, its stockholders and friends, had obtained, apparently, a profit of about $23,000,000 on an initial investment of less than a million.

The government made an effort, through the courts, to recover some of its misused appropriation. When the case got up to the Supreme Court that tribunal decided that the government had no valid cause for complaint. The money and land had been given to help build the railroad. Well, the road was built, wasn't it? The purpose for which the appropriation was designed had been accomplished, so that was all there was to it.

Grant had nothing to do with this affair, and its outcome does not reflect either credit or discredit on him. The appropriation had been made, and the money distributed, before he became President, though the scandal occurred during his administration. My purpose in telling about it here is merely to show the state of public morality when he went into office.

He was as much surprised as any man in the street over the exposure, although he had been President for more than three years when it occurred.

§ 3

In discussing the events of Grant's administration I shall not follow their chronological order, but bring various topics together as they appear to fall in the same category. The financial scandals of his time click like beads on a string. They were so close together that the fingers of history touch several of them at the same time. I shall not have the space to mention all of them, but those I describe are typical. His administration was a vast smoky confusion, with here and there a gleam of light. Grant did not have much to do with these shady episodes. They occurred in his presence, yet at times one feels as if he was not there at all.

§ 4

Jay Gould and James Fisk, Jr., shrewd money-makers and complete rascals, planned a speculative campaign to obtain a corner on gold in the summer of 1869. There was not much gold in the country outside the national treasury, but the treasury held about one hundred million dollars in coin. The Gould and Fisk campaign was simple enough. All they had to do was to buy contracts for the delivery of gold, and keep on buying until they had in their hands more gold, in the shape of contracts, than there was in existence outside the national treasury. With buying the price would rise. At that time gold was traded in on the Stock Exchange as a speculative commodity. Although it had been practically demonetized and driven out of general circulation by the "greenback" paper money, it was still urgently needed by the business community for the purpose of paying certain obligations, and for transactions that were made in other countries. An importer who had to meet a bill in Europe would instruct his broker to buy gold for him and he would send the actual coin abroad. Usually he had to pay a premium of about thirty-five or forty cents on the dollar.

Gould's plan was to corner the gold supply by accumulating contracts for the metal; then, when the price had gone high enough to suit him, he and Fisk would call for delivery. The sellers would be unable to deliver, and at the crest of the high prices Gould and Fisk would quietly sell their contracts and fade out of the scene.

Clever scheme; but a weak spot in it was the United States Treasury, which made a practice of selling some two millions of dollars' worth of gold each month, in order to keep it in circulation. In case the price should rise to fantastic heights the national Treasury might release an enormous amount of gold all at once, and the Gould and Fisk bull campaign would burst like a toy balloon.

They came to the conclusion that they would have to get the President on their side.

Now one of Grant's brothers-in-law, A. R. Corbin, appears before the footlights of this drama. He is a slippery, uneasy man of sixty-seven, with his eye on the fleshpots of high finance. Gould and Fisk honor Corbin with their confidence, and he is eager to be the jackal for this pair of lions.

Grant came to New York, and Gould met him at Corbin's house. It was merely a little formal talk in a parlor; nothing special was said. But Grant was going to a Peace Jubilee in Boston in June—this was in 1869—and Corbin managed things so the President made the trip on the Fall River steamboat line, which Fisk owned, or controlled.

Fisk called himself an admiral . . . a title of his own. He liked pomp and uniforms, and as admiral of the Fall River Line he wore a gaudy outfit. A florid, vulgar person was Fisk —a country peddler of low instincts who had become, through financial sleight of hand, a power in Wall Street. His reputation in New York was so low that it can be expressed only in words that are not fit to print.

The steamboat was decorated like a circus parade. The whistle blew, the horns snorted and the drums rattled and boomed. Fisk, dressed in his uniform, stood at the gangway. He was waiting for the President of the United States. Jay Gould was waiting, too, in one of the luxurious staterooms . . . a fragile, dark man whose sole purpose in life was to lay his hands on money.

That evening, as the boat floated gently through Long Island Sound, Gould and Fisk entertained the President at dinner . . . champagne, cigars, French brandy, and a high-toned discussion of world affairs. Well-read men, philosophers and humanitarians, talking with a statesman. Men of poise and balance who have laid aside their business preoccupations to survey humanity in the abstract. The farmer . . . Gould has a tender spot in his heart for the farmer. Everything depends on the farmer; he feeds us all; he is the backbone of the nation, the salt of human worth. Grant says "That's so," and a box of fine Havanas passes around.

The farmer's prosperity, Gould thinks, depends on maintaining the price of gold at a high level. With gold at a large premium the farmer can ship his wheat to Europe, and keep a stream of Europe's money flowing to us, thus vitalizing the veins of commerce. Balance of trade. You know, Mr. President, what an important thing the balance of trade is? Of course . . . of course . . . the balance of trade is . . . is . . . is . . . uh . . . absolutely necessary.

Gould's possessiveness, exuding from him, flowed through the brightly lighted room, and enveloped Grant like a spider's web.

The only trouble about holding up the price of gold is the absurd selling of the metal by the national treasury. So Mr. Gould thought. Good Lord, the Treasury of the United States ought never to sell gold; it ought to be taking it in, instead of giving it out. You just leave business alone and it will get all the gold it needs from Europe. If the Treasury would not sell gold, but let it find its own level, the farmer would simply purr with prosperity.

Grant was not so sure about that. He remarked, diffidently, that he thought there was a good deal of inflation in the country, that the current prosperity was somewhat artificial. Gould and Fisk expressed great respect for the President's views, but they could not help feeling that he was wrong, in a measure. They were close, you see, to the great industrial heart of the nation. Yes, the President realized that . . . he realized that he was in the presence of men of power and achievement, but he thought, nevertheless, that the government ought to sell gold now and then. It encourages people to have gold circulating around.

Gould and Fisk came back from Boston with the President, and on their return to New York they took the Presidential party to the opera, where Grant, Mrs. Grant and their daughter sat in a box with Gould, Fisk and Corbin. Gould's purpose in doing that was undoubtedly to show the public how friendly he was with the President.

The speculation appeared hazardous and uncertain, and Gould and Fisk would have dropped it; but Corbin assured them that he had the President fixed, so they wavered between their desire to make money and their suspicion that Corbin was a liar. In August there was another steamboat trip to Newport, and this time the President was not so emphatic in his opinion that the bubble of inflation ought to be pricked.

But Corbin did not have him fixed. What had really happened was that Grant had been moved by Gould's arguments. Early in August he wrote to Secretary Boutwell, of the Treasury, to go slowly in selling gold, as he did not want to put down the price of crops, and he repeated some of Gould's clever sophistries as his own.

The Gould and Fisk speculative campaign began about the first of September, when the price of gold stood at 132. Their operations were carried on so quietly that even their own brokers did not know what they were trying to do, and by the middle of September they held contracts for at least twice the available supply of gold.

Of course Corbin had to be taken care of, and a million dollars' worth of contracts was bought for him, and carried by Gould. And there were "other parties," Corbin whispered, in the background, who must have a share. He hinted that one of the "other parties" was Mrs. Grant and that Horace Porter— the President's secretary—was another. Neither Mrs. Grant nor Porter knew anything of these transactions, but as the price of gold rose Corbin told Gould that Mrs. Grant wanted twenty-five thousand dollars on account. Gould gave him a check for that amount. It never reached Mrs. Grant. The fact came out later that Corbin had used it to pay off a loan of his own at a bank.

Gold passed into the 140's and was going higher. The commotion in the Gold Room reached the front page of the newspapers, and the conservative business interests of the country were sending urgent telegrams to the Treasury wanting to know why the government had stopped the sale of gold.

Gould was involved for at least fifty millions, and anxiety sat on his dark brow. He urged Corbin to write a letter to the President arguing against the sale of any gold by the government. Corbin wrote such a letter—mild in tone—and sent it by a special messenger to the little village in Pennsylvania where the President and Mrs. Grant were spending a holiday. This place was not a railroad station and had no telegraph facilities. Horace Porter received the missive from the dusty, tired and breathless messenger and told him that it was "All right"—meaning that the letter had been received in good order. The messenger dashed to the nearest telegraph station —he had been instructed to wire the reply—and telegraphed to Gould that the answer was "All right."

With that assurance in their hands, the clique felt encouraged and proceeded to put the price up still higher. In the meantime Grant had read his brother-in-law's letter, and he asked Mrs. Grant to write to Mrs. Corbin that the President was "much distressed" by her husband's speculations. Corbin showed this letter to Gould, who saw instantly that Corbin had deceived him all along. His prophetic instinct told him that within twenty-four hours gold would be pouring from the Treasury in torrents. He went to Wall Street and gave instructions to a new and thoroughly secretive set of brokers to sell all the gold they could. But he acted outwardly like the most optimistic of bulls, and publicly bought a little gold. He left Fisk in the lurch. To the very end Fisk thought that Gould was on his side.

The public was now in the market, following these leaders on the bull side. On the Friday which is now known as Black Friday—September 24, 1869—the price of gold went to 162, and the Gold Room was a madhouse. Fisk himself was on the floor, taking contracts by the million, and boasting that he would send the price to 200. At times the buying and selling was so confused that while gold was being bought by Fisk's brokers at 155 it was selling on the other side of the room at 140.

Then word came from Washington that the government had begun to sell, and that Grant had instructed the Secretary of the Treasury to put four million dollars of gold on the market immediately.

In half an hour the price went down from 162 to 135, but the receding of the tide left a herd of ruined speculators on the littered beach of finance. Later in the afternoon a disheveled crowd roamed through the narrow streets looking for Gould and Fisk with the intention of lynching them, but they had escaped.

Gould's prompt selling had saved his fortune—he made several million dollars from the adventure—but Fisk was temporarily ruined. When he learned how Gould had betrayed him he did not resort either to a shotgun or a manner of proud disdain. The pair became greater friends than ever. Fisk was the kind of man who admires anybody clever enough to swindle him.

Grant emerged from this episode with a slightly tarnished reputation. The public knew nothing of the inside facts, but everybody knew that Grant had associated on friendly terms with Gould and the unspeakable Fisk. The natural supposition was that he had countenanced their schemes.

§ 5

Here is another bead on the string of confusions:

A harmless-looking piece of paper was handed down from the high tribunal of the Supreme Court in February, 1870.

This document, so casually sent out in the American world,

was the Supreme Court's decision in the case of Hepburn *vs*. Griswold. It contained more explosive material than a half dozen Gold Conspiracies.

The court ruled that the Legal Tender Act of 1862 was unconstitutional so far as it concerned debts contracted before the passage of the act. There was consternation in financial circles. The act had been in force for eight years, and countless promissory notes, mortgages and other obligations made prior to the act had been paid in legal tender currency. All these payments would have to be made over again, in gold, according to the clear import of the decision.

The most astonishing feature of the Hepburn-Griswold case is that Chief Justice Chase, who wrote the decision, had been Secretary of the Treasury in 1862, and he had acted as midwife at the birth of legal tender money. At that time he had declared the issue of legal tender money "indispensably necessary." His endorsement of the bill was read in Congress and it was the deciding factor in getting the act passed.

Eight years later Mr. Chase, as Chief Justice of the United States, held a different opinion. He now argued that the act impaired the obligation of contracts by forcing persons to accept dollars of less value than they had agreed to take.

At that time there were two vacancies on the Supreme Court bench, and of the seven justices sitting, three were opposed to the opinion of the Chief Justice. On the same day the decision was handed down President Grant appointed two new justices to fill the vacancies. Another legal tender case was quickly brought up, the new justices took sides against Chief Justice Chase, and the court reversed itself by a vote of five to four . . . so cheap legal tender money was safe for awhile, at any rate.

It was said by the political opponents of the President that he had "packed the court," but this charge was without any foundation. It has since been clearly shown that Grant had decided on naming Messrs. Strong and Bradley as Associate

Justices some time before the Legal Tender decision appeared.

As a matter of fact Grant was on the other side of the argument and was strongly in favor of doing away with the legal tender currency altogether. He must be classed as a gold standard man. Before his administration was over, he approved the Specie Resumption Act, which reëstablished gold, and made the legal tender money redeemable in coin.

§ 6

There was a pervading itch for money. The Credit Mobilier scandal had hardly passed into history before Congress became involved in another financial affair called the Back Pay Grab. This particular grab was different from the other grabs of the epoch in that it was open and above board. On the last day of the session Congress passed a bill which raised salaries all around: The President from $25,000 to $50,000 a year; and senators and representatives from $5,000 to $7,500. No objection to that; but Congress spoiled it all, in its enthusiasm, by making the measure retroactive, so that its beneficiaries might draw the increased pay for the past two years.

Grant would have vetoed the bill, but it was tacked on to the general appropriation bill as a rider, and he could not veto the salary clause without vetoing the entire act. That would have made an extra session of Congress necessary in order to provide appropriations for carrying on the government.

The Back Pay Grab, which would have cost the nation only a few hundred thousand dollars, caused almost as loud an uproar as the Union Pacific swindle. The spectators of the Congressional prize-fight yelled themselves hoarse. Many senators and representatives were so frightened by the clamor that they returned their extra back pay to the Treasury—and one of the first acts of the new Congress, which met in December, 1873, was to repeal the law except as it applied to the President and the members of the Supreme Court. The issue that it raised was a live one in the Congressional campaign of 1874, and was largely responsible for the general defeat of the Republicans in the elections of that year.

And there were the Sanborn contracts.

This scandal developed, in some inexplicable way, from General B. F. Butler's influence with the administration. I have already said that Butler's hold on Grant was a mystery, from the time that Grant tried ineffectually to get Butler dismissed from the army until the end of Grant's administration.

In 1873 Grant made Butler's fellow-townsman, William A. Richardson, the head of the Treasury department. Soon after he became Secretary of the Treasury Richardson appointed John D. Sanborn—who was a friend of Butler—as a special agent for the collection of delinquent taxes. The contract provided that Sanborn was to receive, as his compensation, one-half of the money that he managed to collect. For a while his activities were confined to delinquents in the internal revenue division. Then, obviously with the consent of the Treasury department, he began to collect all sorts of taxes, even in cases where there was no delinquency. His income grew and he lived easily while the money rolled in. These promising prospects were cut short by a pestiferous Congressional committee, and Mr. Sanborn was pried loose from the fatness of the land.

The House committee that looked into the matter thought that Secretary of the Treasury Richardson ought to be dismissed from the cabinet. Nothing came of it, for Grant sent for individual members of the committee and pleaded with them to withhold the resolution. He said that he would get Richardson to resign. The report was killed quietly. Richardson left the cabinet and was made immediately a justice of the Court of Claims. In his place as Secretary of the Treasury the President appointed Benjamin H. Bristow, a Kentucky lawyer of standing and ability. This was in June, 1874.

Mr. Bristow came into office fully resolved to make a record for himself. He was conscientious, shrewd and persistent.

His ambition was to be the best watch dog the Treasury ever had, and he applied himself to activities that are generally known as "ferreting." He turned out to be a first-class ferret, but just at that time ferrets were considered particularly undesirable by the coterie of short-change artists and political quacks that surrounded President Grant.

For some time before Mr. Bristow entered upon his duties there had been vague talk of a "Whisky Ring" composed of distillers who were evading the internal revenue tax on distilled spirits. The method of collecting this impost was to license each distillery and have on the spot a Treasury agent who was supposed to check up the shipments from the distillery, to certify to the quantity of whisky produced, and to affix a government stamp on each barrel. The idea of giving these hirelings a gratuity to let untaxed liquor go out occurred apparently to a number of distillers at the same time. There was an exchange of views among them, and the so-called "Whisky Ring" came into being.

Mr. Bristow ran across some authoritative statistics showing the amount of liquor shipped from St. Louis, the principal distillery center. These figures had been issued by the Merchants' Exchange of St. Louis with the honest motive of glorifying the importance of that town, but they got the St. Louis makers of fire-water into a peck of trouble. The new Secretary of the Treasury compared the volume of shipments with the collected tax, and he learned that only about one-third of the total amount of whisky had paid any taxes at all. The Whisky Ring had so many Treasury clerks in its pay that all the early attempts to get at the bottom of the frauds were unavailing; the distillers learned, through underground intelligence, when their plants and books were to be inspected and were invariably prepared before the inspectors arrived.

After a few months of these futilities Bristow secretly employed a corps of private detectives. They got into the plants and secured all the necessary evidence. The trails ran from the distilleries towards Washington . . . dim, wavering paths hard to follow, but Bristow and his assistants did follow them . . . and they came to an end in the President's office. Or, so it seemed.

At that time Grant's principal secretary was General Orville E. Babcock, a pleasant and obliging officer whom we have met once before, at Appomattox, where he sat conversing with General Lee before Grant arrived.

Bristow learned that Babcock had been in correspondence with the leaders of the Whisky Ring, that he had collected money from the distillers, that he had taken valuable presents from them, and had used their money to finance Grant's campaign of 1872.

When this information came to the President's attention he said that he did not believe it, and added that "If Babcock is guilty there is no man who wants him so much proven guilty as I do, for it is the greatest piece of traitorism to me that a man could possibly practice."

With his evidence in hand Bristow decided to raid the distilleries. On May 10, 1875, sixteen of them in St. Louis, Milwaukee and Chicago were visited without warning, and their records seized. It was a sensational affair, though it petered out to almost nothing in the end. Grant wrote, "Let no guilty man escape," but nearly all the guilty men did escape. There were two hundred and fifty-three indictments and about sixty distillers and government agents pleaded guilty and were fined small amounts. Three men were sent to prison.

Babcock was indicted with the rest. The President said he wanted to testify in Babcock's behalf, and his deposition was taken at the White House. He declared that Babcock had never tried to influence him in an improper way, and that he did not know any campaign funds had been raised among the distillers. Then he declared that he believed Babcock to be guiltless in thought or deed.

Such unqualified testimony, coming voluntarily from the

President of the United States, settled the matter. No jury would convict Babcock after the President had spoken so handsomely of him.

So Babcock was acquitted. When he appeared at the White House, obviously ill at ease, to resume his duties Grant called him into the President's room, where he remained a long time. What was said at this conference has never been revealed. All we know is that Babcock came out of the President's room, grumpily emptied the drawers of his desk, put on his hat and went away. He never had any duties at the White House again, although Grant seems to have remained on friendly terms with him.

Secretary Bristow was destined soon to suffer the sad fate of zealous reformers who poke their fingers into the machinery of political corruption. Indignant politicians and beneficiaries of the Whisky Ring called on the President, and in the friendly atmosphere of cigar smoke they proceeded to enlighten the General as to Bristow's real motives. Why, the man wants to be President himself, that's all. Plain as a door-knob. You think so? I don't think so; I know it; we all know it. He's a snake in the grass, Mr. President. His big idea was to drag the White House into the affair so as to discredit the administration. Watch dog of the Treasury? Yes, he's a watch dog, all right . . . watch dog of his own shrewd little game to be in your place.

You see how he harped on that twenty-four-hundred dollar diamond ring that McDonald, the whisky man, gave as a present to Babcock? Tried to make a big play on that, but it was nothing in the world but a gift of one friend to another.

Oh, I know that; I know Babcock's sound as any man.

Of course he is . . . and then Bristow got the newspapers raving about that carriage and pair of horses that McDonald gave you, Mr. President. Was afraid to mention it himself, but he started the newspapers on the trail.

Yes, yes . . . but as for the horses and carriage there

wasn't any need of following a trail. It was all open and above board. Thousands of people knew about it.

Surely it was, but the great reformer Bristow doesn't want to see it in that light.

After Grant had listened for several weeks to talk of this kind the Presidential air, when Bristow approached, was like a breeze from an iceberg. He saw that he was no longer wanted in the cabinet, so he handed in his resignation and disappears from our narrative.

§ 7

The Whisky Ring scandal still hung in the sky like a waning moon when there began to be talk of another exposure. This time it centered on W. W. Belknap, the Secretary of War, who had succeeded Rawlins on the latter's death. The *dramatis personæ* of the Belknap Case are:

General Belknap—
  Secretary of War—a cabinet officer without any financial means except his salary. He is a pleasant, popular person, with a desire to oblige everyone—particularly his handsome wife.

Mrs. Belknap—
  Wife of the Secretary of War. Very fashionable, and socially ambitious. Wears expensive French clothes, drives about Washington in a splendid carriage, and is known as the last word in elegance. Everyone wonders where she obtains the money to do it.

Caleb P. Marsh—
  An astute person, who takes money wherever and whenever he can get it, without troubling himself about its origin.

John S. Evans—
  A nondescript, with an uneasy countenance. He is licensed by the War Department as the official post

trader at Fort Sill in the Indian Territory—a very lucrative position.

H. Clymer—
Member of the House of Representatives and Chairman of the House Committee on Expenditures of the War Department. A ferret, in a small way, with honesty wrapped around him like a snow-white cloak.

Mrs. Belknap, sometime in 1870, was a guest of Mr. and Mrs. Marsh. In a conversation about the War Department and its affairs she told Marsh that post-traderships in the Indian Territory were very profitable. The traders had a monopoly as merchants around the military posts. They charged high prices for goods and had no competition.

She suggested that Marsh might get a trader's post if he wanted it. He replied that he would like to have such a place, if there was as much money to be made as she thought there was. Yes, there would be a lot of money in it, but she would have to get a share of the profits for her services in persuading her husband to give Marsh the place. Then she added: "If I can prevail upon the Secretary of War to award you a post you must be careful to say nothing to him about presents, for a man once offered him ten thousand dollars for a tradership of this kind, and he told him that if he did not leave the office he would kick him downstairs."

(I have condensed this conversation from the evidence printed in the *Congressional Record*, 44th Congress, 1st Session, Vol. IV., Feb. 10th to March 28, 1876.)

Marsh made application to the Secretary for the post at Fort Sill, which was already held by a man named Evans. Belknap looked over Marsh's application and said that he thought it would be all right, but what about Evans? Marsh did not know anything about that part of it. Well, Evans was at that time in Washington, Belknap remarked, and perhaps

Marsh had better look him up. They might get together in some partnership arrangement.

When Marsh saw Evans the latter was much disturbed over the matter. He had made quite an investment of money at Fort Sill; he did not want to lose it, and so on. Then there was some going back and forth. Marsh called on Mrs. Belknap and talked with her. From these conferences the idea emerged that Evans might keep the post if he would pay Marsh twelve thousand dollars a year. Evans hemmed and hawed, and went to see the Secretary. He learned from Belknap that Marsh was going to get the appointment if he wanted it—so he went back to Marsh and signed an agreement whereby he was to pay Marsh twelve thousand dollars a year, in consideration of being allowed to continue in the position.

Half of the money was turned over by Marsh to Mrs. Belknap until her death, which occurred not long after this transaction was concluded. Thereafter Marsh, who did nothing at all for his share of the proceeds, continued to send the remittances to Secretary Belknap himself. If Belknap happened to be in New York, where Marsh lived, at the time of the quarterly payment he received it in person, usually in cash.

Mr. Clymer, investigating the expenditures of the War Department, heard rumors of the post trader at Fort Sill paying somebody in New York a bribe to keep his place. Clymer had Evans brought before him, and with that clue he unraveled the entire transaction. He learned that Evans had paid Marsh more than forty-two thousand dollars; and then he summoned Marsh and made him tell about Belknap.

At eleven o'clock on the morning of March 2, 1876, Clymer rose on the floor of the House and charged Belknap with malfeasance in office, and demanded that he be impeached. Some kind friend of Belknap who was on Clymer's committee had taken the news to the War Department early that morning. There was a good deal of rushing around right after breakfast. Belknap rushed over to the White House with his resignation in his hand, the ink still wet on it. They can't impeach a man who has already resigned, can they?

Grant accepted the resignation immediately, and Belknap was out of the War Department forty minutes before Clymer charged him with malfeasance in office. In accepting Belknap's resignation the President wrote: "Your tender of resignation as Secretary of War, with the request to have it accepted immediately, is received and the same is hereby accepted with great regret." Grant said emphatically he did not believe Belknap to be guilty, although at that time he knew nothing whatever about the nature or validity of the evidence.

Belknap had got out of office by the skin of his teeth, but the Senate tried him, anyway. He pleaded ignorance as his defence. The money that came from Marsh was income from his late wife's investments, or so he thought. But Marsh testified that Belknap had never spoken of investments, nor had he ever made any inquiry as to the source of the money that he received.

The proceedings dragged on through hundreds of pages of small type. Conviction failed for lack of a two-thirds majority. Most of the Senators who voted against conviction declared themselves convinced of Belknap's guilt, but as he had already resigned, they were in doubt as to the Senate's jurisdiction.

CHAPTER XXVIII

THE RECONSTRUCTED SOUTH

§ 1

UNDER the supervision of the military governors the Southern states were reconstructed. In all of them the Republican ticket was elected with large majorities; and the legislatures, made up principally of carpet-baggers and negroes, settled down to the grinding duties of statesmanship. The highly placed Radical Republicans at Washington—contemplating their own work—felt like the spirit of destiny. They were convinced that a good job had been done; and that one problem, at least, was permanently settled.

Grant shared this opinion, or adopted it. The plan of reconstruction must be a wise one, he thought. It had been conceived in Congress, which included not less than fifty lawyers.

The South Carolina legislature consisted of ninety-four negroes and thirty white men. Of the white men seven were carpet-baggers. The remaining twenty-three white members—natives of the state and Democrats—sat grim and silent. They were hopelessly outnumbered, and all they were able to do was to record their unavailing votes against the spoliation of the state.

The Speaker is black, the clerk is black, the doorkeepers are black, the little pages are black, the chairman of the Ways and Means is black, and the chaplain is coal-black. At some of the desks sit colored men whose types it would be hard to find outside of Congo; whose costumes, visages,

427

attitudes and expressions, only befit the forecastle of a buccaneer.

This quotation is from *The Prostrate State*, by James S. Pike, a Maine newspaper man who went down to South Carolina in 1873—after the state had been reconstructed five years— to see for himself what was going on.

There was a mysterious crackling sound in the legislative chamber, in the intervals between the speeches. Mr. Pike wondered what it was, and leaned over the railing of the visitors' gallery to look and listen. Then he saw that all the negro members were cracking peanuts, eating them and throwing the shells on the floor.

§ 2

A bill to aid the building of the Blue Ridge Railroad was put through the South Carolina legislature. This railroad never existed; it was a sort of chartered ghost owned by leading Radicals and carpet-baggers.

The backers of the scheme lacked the delicate suavity of Oakes Ames and the clever business-like capacity of the Credit Mobilier, but such roundabout methods were unnecessary. The negro legislature went at the state treasury like a man smashing the window of a jewelry store with an ax. The bill provided that $1,800,000 in state scrip—a kind of bond that circulated as money—was to be loaned to the management of the non-existent railroad.

The measure was passed with enthusiasm. Then the state treasurer, who had a generous heart, proceeded secretly to give the railroad company $5,000,000 instead of $1,800,000 in scrip. And, after all, the road was never built. Nobody ever really expected it to be. Later on the state courts declared the whole thing illegal from start to finish, but by that time the state scrip was circulating among the people.

Before the war the state of South Carolina had been in the banking business. It owned the Bank of South Carolina, which issued banknotes. With the fall of the Confederacy the bank failed, leaving $1,250,000 of its banknote money outstanding. Most of the bank's bills had been lost or destroyed; people considered them worthless.

But to the carpet-bag mind nothing was worthless if it could be twisted into a profit. The defunct Bank of South Carolina was full of juicy possibilities. The notes of the bank should be redeemed by all means, declared the Northern adventurers in control of things. The credit and honor of the state are behind these sacred obligations, and shall we allow the good name of South Carolina to be tarnished? No! Never! Never! A thousand times No!

Before this staunch sense of civic honor had boiled over into a thousand Nos and Nevers the Radical politicians had quietly bought up, for a few cents on the dollar, all the bank-notes they could find. They had come to the conclusion that there were only a half million dollars of them in existence, but they got the legislature to appropriate $1,250,000 for their redemption. The notes were to be redeemed by exchanging them for state bonds.

Then the redemption began. The banknotes were taken in at par. The act provided that, as they were received, they should be destroyed. Instead of being destroyed, however, they were handed back at once, and next day would appear for redemption again. This fiscal operation was a great success all around.

It was a fine game, but there has to be a serpent in every Eden. The negro members of the legislature became inquisitive, and then insistent and greedy. They got tired of voting for this and that, and never getting anything but their pay. After a couple of handsomely profitable measures had been defeated by negro members they were given now and then a very small slice of melon. But the negro statesmen did not fare so badly, after all. There was a free barroom in the State House, where the members of the legislature were allowed to drink all they pleased; and there was a committee on legislative expenses which distributed its largess with a prodigal hand. In the list of supplies furnished gratis to members we observe such items as Westphalia hams, plush chairs, suspenders, a metallic coffin, ladies' chemises, gold watches, feather beds and perfumes.

The votes of negro legislators were bought and sold in all the Southern states. Zebulon B. Vance, of North Carolina, tells an amusing story of an elderly negro member of the legislature of his state who was found late at night in his room counting a pile of money, and laughing to himself. "Why, what amuses you so, Uncle Cuffy?" he was asked.

"Well, boss," was his reply, "I's been sold in my life 'leven times an' fo' de Lord dis is de fust time I eber got de money."

The carpet-baggers of South Carolina reflected moodily on the condition of the negro . . . not on his little rebellion in the legislature, for that was easily subdued by passing out a few hundred dollars in bills of the lower denominations. No; the minds of the statesmen were fixed on the distant horizon, on the ultimate future of the negro race.

As they contemplated it they realized that they were facing a vast sociological problem. Listen . . . we've freed the negro, haven't we? We have shed our blood on a hundred battlefields that he might breathe the pure air of freedom, and what have we done for him since? Nothing.

Think of our heroic dead, and the cause for which they died. *In the beauty of the lilies Christ was born across the sea, with a glory in his bosom that transfigures you and me; as he died to make men holy, let us die to make men free, while God is marching on.*

Well, there's no use dying over it now; the negro is free already; let's do something practical. Now you're talking; we are practical men. We'll set the negro up as a landowner; that's what we'll do. How can you expect him to be a self-respecting citizen, a man of honor and probity, if he hasn't a foot of land? *God's image in ebony.* Precisely.

It's our duty; we owe something to this poor, down-trodden race. The state will buy the land and . . . say, do you know that you can get land at fifty cents an acre in this state?

Not much good, is it?

Of course not, but we didn't make the land. . . .

The white fingers of the Radical leaders went over the county maps, picking out swamps and desolate sandy tracts. Mysterious men appeared at the doors of landowners and purchased these worthless sections . . . from twenty-five to fifty cents an acre.

The laudable purpose of the Northern gentlemen was explained to the African legislature, and $802,000 was appropriated. Now the mysterious men showed up at the Land Commission and resold their fifty-cent land at an average price of five dollars and twenty cents an acre.

As a piece of thievery this land deal was excellent, for it had the fine quality of being absolutely law-proof. The commission bought the land in exact accordance with the terms of the act, and put the negroes on it. If they couldn't earn their bread on the farms that the state had given them, was it the Commission's fault?

The total amount paid for printing by the state of South Carolina in the seventy-eight years from 1790 to 1868 was $609,000. In the eight years under carpet-bag and negro rule, from 1868 to 1876, printing cost the state the imposing sum of $1,326,000. The most expensive year was 1873, when the official printing account ran up to $450,000. The Radical governor of the state confessed later that he had been paid $15,000 to approve this bill.

Mr. Pike, of Maine, was shocked and astonished at what he saw. He was disappointed, too, for he had expected to find a very different order of things. He wrote that "the rule of South Carolina should not be dignified by the name of government. It is the installation of a huge system of brigandage." The men in control, he concluded, "are in no sense different from, or better than, the men who fill the prisons and penitentiaries of the world. They are, in fact, precisely of that class, only more daring and audacious."

§ 3

Railroads and carpet-baggers seemed to fit together with the neat compatibility of spoon and dish. One of the railroad dishes in Florida was very capacious and the spoon of unusual size. The state decided to help the Jacksonville, Pensacola and Mobile Railroad Company build its line. The Republican legislature willingly voted $2,800,000 in state bonds, and these were sold in London at a price which brought the state a net sum of approximately $1,400,000. The money was turned over to the imaginary railroad—and that was the last of it. Three years later only nineteen miles of the road had been constructed, and the money was all gone. For years the hopeful and trusting bondholders in London continued to pester the state about the money they had furnished; but Florida, like most of the Southern states, had refused to recognize the validity of bonds issued by its carpet-bag government.

In Georgia the railroad drama was played differently, for there the railroad was already in existence. It had been in operation for twenty years and was highly prosperous. The state of Georgia owned the Western & Atlantic Railroad . . . a state property, built with the state's money before the war. It had an earning capacity of about fifty thousand dollars a month. The Radical state government pondered over this situation. The railroad could be robbed by making extravagant purchases of material in its name, and forcing the sellers to divide their profits. That was one way of going about it— but such an arrangement might come to an end at any time. Who could tell how long the Radicals would remain in power?

A better plan would be to lease the road to some private concern. Excellent idea. Twenty-year lease. Why should the state be in the railroad business, anyway?

The Western & Atlantic road was leased to a corporation formed for the purpose, at a rental of twenty-five thousand dollars a month for twenty years. Behind the leasing corporation, composed principally of Northern financiers, one sees the dim shapes of Georgia carpet-baggers and scalawags.

Henry C. Warmoth, the unscrupulous leader of the Louisiana carpet-baggers, went over to the side of the conservative Republicans in 1872, after he had accumulated a fortune during his four years as Radical governor of the state. During his term of office the state debt had risen from $7,000,000 to $50,000,000, and there was nothing to show for it. Warmouth saw the end of Radical Republican rule approaching, and he wanted to be safe when the house began to fall.

During the whole of the Reconstruction period a sort of intermittent civil war went on in Louisiana . . . bloody riots in New Orleans . . . the slaughter of a whole community of negroes at the village of Colfax by white men . . . and numerous murders in every part of the state. In the last few weeks of the campaign of 1868 more than two thousand persons were killed, wounded or assaulted.

Both the conservatives and the Radical Republicans claimed the election of 1872, and Grant sent troops to the state to enforce order. He decided that Kellogg, the Radical candidate for governor, had won. This was obviously an offhand decision, for the conduct of both sides was so fraudulent that there was no telling what the actual results were. But despite this rather overwhelming doubt the Kellogg faction was installed under the protection of Federal troops.

The Georgia legislature eventually found itself with a Democratic majority. Flushed with triumph, the legislature expelled twenty-four negro Republican members. Thereupon the Washington authorities ordered the negroes reinstated. This was done by Federal soldiers, who entered the legislative chamber and dragged the white men out. Negroes took their seats while soldiers stood guard over them.

§ 4

During these feverish years the Southern white men carried on a campaign of intimidation. They frightened negroes away from the polls by strange and comical devices. In one county they rode about the polling places with coils of rope on their saddles and asked one another when the hanging was going to begin. "As soon as the polls open," was the reply. "Then we'll start the hanging in about fifteen minutes, I guess." The negroes went back home without voting.

On another occasion the Ku-Klux scattered pigs' blood and scraps of negro clothing along the roads for a mile in every direction from the voting place. Negroes going to the village to vote saw these portents of disaster and turned around in their tracks.

One wonders why the Southern whites did not succeed in aligning the negro voters on the Democratic side, instead of trying to keep them from voting. They did make many attemps to turn the negroes into Democrats, but these efforts were frustrated by the Radical leaders, who told the freedmen that a Democratic victory would send them all back to slavery.

To meet the situation Congress passed in May, 1870, an Enforcement Act, which was designed to make the Fourteenth and Fifteenth Amendment effective. Later on another section of the Enforcement Act came into being. As it applied directly to the Ku-Klux outrages it was commonly known as "the Ku-Klux law." Under the acts the President was empowered to set aside the writ of *habeas corpus* and put states or counties under military law. In October, 1871, Grant declared nine counties of South Carolina to be in a state of rebellion and put them under martial rule. During the next two years more than a thousand people in the South as a whole were tried and convicted under the Ku-Klux Act. Ten years later the Supreme Court declared it to be unconstitutional.

Grant was bewildered by these complications and unavailing measures, yet his bewilderment did not appear to disturb his peace of mind. The laws had been passed by Congress, and his plain duty—it seemed to him—was to enforce them. He remarked, in a conversation when some one told him that the whole procedure was a mistake, that "the best way to treat a bad law was to execute it." This was the extent of his political philosophy in relation to the South.

Many causes contributed to bring an end to Radical rule in the Southern states. After a few years people of sense and standing in the North grew sick of the whole adventure. It interfered with business. The Southern communities were in chaos; taxes were outrageously high; the bonds of all the ex-Confederate states were at a low level; Southern merchants could not pay their bills. These facts percolated through the Northern mind, and gradually changed its attitude.

Even the old-time abolitionists—some of them, at any rate—experienced a change of heart. James Russell Lowell wrote:

"The whole condition of things at the South is shameful, and I am ready for a movement now to emancipate the whites. No doubt the government is bound to protect the misintelligence of the blacks, but surely not at the expense of the intelligence of men of our own blood."

There is a reflection of these views in Grant's telegram from his summer home at Long Branch in 1875 to Attorney-General Pierrepont in reference to a call by the Radical governor of Mississippi for the assistance of Federal troops. The President said:

> The whole public are tired out with these annual autumnal outbreaks in the South, and the great majority are ready now to condemn any interference on the part of the government.

The Reconstruction program fell into disfavor in the North, but its complete failure was due to the resistance of the Southern people. In states where the whites were in the majority the Radicals were simply voted out; in other states, with black majorities—South Carolina, Mississippi and Louisiana—the negroes were intimidated, and kept from voting.

It was the misfortune of the Reconstruction policy to fall into the hands of mean and unprincipled people. Under their treatment it languished and finally committed suicide. Its net result was a solidly Democratic South that will probably remain solidly Democratic for a long time, and the elimination of the negro as a political force. The tragedy of Reconstruction and its negro legislatures is still a living memory in the minds of Southern white men. It retarded the negro incalculably in his development.

§ 5

Life at the White House went on placidly through these hectic years. Grant passed into the autumn of his life, and became fat and puffy. He had given up riding, though he drove a pair of swift horses down Washington's long avenues every afternoon. Occasionally he appeared at Mrs. Grant's receptions and chatted with the guests.

The General insisted on bringing to the White House one of his favorite quartermaster sergeants and making him the chief steward. The sergeant's idea of a dinner was plain fare and a lot of it. For a while the family and its guests sat down before enormous dishes of roast beef and roast turkeys. When Mrs. Grant remarked to him that the dinners were not sufficiently elegant, the sturdy sergeant provided even larger turkeys—the largest that could be found in the market. Finally the General had to part company with the sergeant. He was given a job as a doorkeeper, or something, in one of the departments, and a brisk Italian chef took his place.

Miss Nellie, who was an awkward little girl when the Grants came to the White House, soon grew up amazingly. She became a beautiful young woman, with delicate features and eyes that were melting in their loveliness. Her charm shed a spiritual radiance. She was probably the most attractive of all the young women who have ever lived in the White House.

Mr. and Mrs. Borie went to Europe for a few months, and Nellie accompanied them. On her way back a young Mr. Algernon Sartoris made her acquaintance on the steamer, and during his stay in America he spent most of his time in Washington, calling on the President's daughter. They were clearly in love with each other.

This young man was an Englishman, a nephew of Fanny Kemble, the famous actress. Mr. Sartoris is described as handsome, pleasant-mannered and a "good singer." He married Nellie Grant at the White House on May 21, 1874.

The bridesmaids were the daughters of Grant's friends— the Misses Fish, Drexel, Dent, Porter, Barnes, Frelinghuysen, Conkling and Sherman. The society columns of the day run into frothy billows of description of the event. We read that the bride "wore a white satin dress elaborately trimmed with point lace. Her veil was tulle and her hair was adorned with orange blossoms." The bridegroom wore a morning costume and a high-bred English manner. There was a Methodist wedding ceremony, and music by the Marine band.

The account continues with half a column about the wedding presents . . . dinner sets, lace fans, diamond rings and toilet articles. The most expensive gift appears to be a dessert set given by A. J. Drexel, of Philadelphia. The newspapers said it cost $4,500. General Grant gave his daughter a ten-thousand dollar check.

The marriage did not turn out well. Nellie, who went to England with her husband, found it impossible, after a few years, to live with the handsome singer. The Sartoris family took sides with Nellie. After she had left her husband they provided her with a large income, and continued among her intimate friends.

§ 6

The doings of the Grant administration estranged many Republicans of liberal tendencies. They were opposed to the Radical Southern policy of the President, to his high-tariff notions, and particularly to his urgent desire to annex the negro republic of San Domingo (which I shall discuss in the next chapter). In time this simmering discontent boiled down into a "Liberal-Republican" party. The center of the revolt was in Missouri, and among its leaders were Carl Schurz and B. Gratz Brown—both of that state. Outside of Missouri the party included such men of national prominence as David A. Wells, the economist; Samuel Bowles, editor of the Springfield *Republican;* Horace Greeley of the New York *Tribune;* William Cullen Bryant; Charles Francis Adams; and Jacob D. Cox, formerly Grant's Secretary of the Interior. One may fairly say that it was a rebellion of intellectuals and reformers against the moneyed interests and anti-Southern Radicals who seemed to hold Grant's exclusive attention.

A Liberal-Republican convention met at Cincinnati in May, 1872, and nominated Horace Greeley for President. The vice-presidential nominee was B. Gratz Brown.

The nomination of Greeley was a gigantic mistake. He had long passed his prime, and had become a queer, crotchety man who held a mass of contradictory opinions that were continually at war with each other in his mind. He believed in a high tariff, and was so insistent about it that this low-tariff convention had to leave all mention of the tariff out of its platform, except to declare in a weak clause that it was a matter to be decided by Congress. Then, to make matters worse, the Democrats met and endorsed the Liberal-Republican candidates without making any nomination themselves. The result was a hybrid mixture of incompatible political elements—all of them essentially weak.

Grant was nominated for a second term by the unanimous vote of the regular Republican Convention, which was held in Philadelphia. As candidate for Vice-President the Republicans selected Henry Wilson of Massachusetts.

The canvass was conducted with venom on both sides. Greeley especially was held up to contempt, ridicule and vituperation. He said, after it was over, that at times he did not know whether he was running for President or for the penitentiary.

Greeley did not carry a single Northern state, and only six states in the South. He was the worst beaten man who had ever run for the Presidential office.

Within a month after the election he lost his mind and died of some affection of the brain. Instantly his opponents forgot the ridicule they had heaped upon him in his last days, or perhaps they were a little ashamed of it. President Grant and some of the members of the cabinet attended his funeral.

It appears probable that with a more powerful candidate

than Greeley the Liberal-Republicans would have won. There was a strong undercurrent of dissatisfaction with Grant and his ways around the close of his first term, but Greeley was not able to consolidate or direct the forces of revolt.

Now the General is in the White House for four years more. If he ever had any doubt of himself, his stunning victory over the infirm and eccentric Greeley thoroughly removed it.

CHAPTER XXIX

DIPLOMATIC EPISODES

§ 1

GRANT was immensely impressed by things of monumental size. He understood quantity better than he understood quality. From the beginning of his administration he had the territorial expansion of the United States in mind. He had convinced himself, through some process of esoteric reasoning, that a large and powerful country, with bulldog tendencies, ought to be happier than a smaller one. He thought of far-flung possessions, and of the American drum-beat being heard around the world.

At first glance it may seem difficult to reconcile this policy with his spirit of pacifism, but both ideas really fit into the same pattern. He expected to expand our territory by treaty or purchase, and not by conquest; and he thought that the taking over of the smaller peoples would keep them out of trouble and promote the cause of universal peace.

It never occurred to him, apparently, that the addition to our system of alien races would increase the complexity of our own problems. And one would naturally think that the anarchy existing in the Southern states was enough to keep any President very busy, without looking for other anarchies to conquer.

One of his first moves, after he became President, was an attempt to annex the Caribbean republic of San Domingo. He failed to accomplish it, and his failure is astonishing when one considers his immense popularity at that time. We can ascribe it only to his awkward ineptitude in handling the matter.

The state of affairs in San Domingo was almost as bad as the state of affairs in Louisiana. The Dominicans, like the Louisianians, had two rival governments, each claiming to express the will of the people. The fighting between the two factions in San Domingo was not as fierce and bloody as it was in Louisiana, but it went on for a longer time.

At one of the cabinet meetings soon after Grant became President he remarked that the navy department wanted Samana Bay, on the east coast of San Domingo, as a coaling station, and that he intended to send Colonel Babcock down to San Domingo to examine the harbor and sound the government of San Domingo on the question of its acquisition. (This was the same Colonel Babcock who became involved later in the Whisky Ring scandal.) I think that Grant had the idea of acquiring the whole of San Domingo in his mind at that time, but he said nothing about it at the cabinet meeting.

Babcock went, saw, and came back. Soon after his return the cabinet gathered one day and found the table loaded heavily with specimens of Dominican ores, hardwoods, coffee berries and other tropical products. Babcock had brought them there and arranged them on the table as an exhibit. The President was ready to tell the cabinet about his plan of annexation, and he wanted to bring out his idea impressively.

While Babcock was in San Domingo he had met General Baez, an intelligent quadroon, who claimed to be president of the Dominican republic. His assertion was flatly denied, however, by another quadroon named Cabral, who declared that he was president and that he was going to have Baez shot as soon as he could catch him. Baez treated this threat with contempt. According to him Cabral was merely a low-down, no-account disturber of the peace, without any following. Baez stated further that as soon as he could get hold of Cabral he intended to put him up against a wall and shoot him. At the time of Babcock's visit neither of them had caught the other.

Babcock, either on his own initiative, or following President Grant's instructions—I do not know which—drew up a treaty with Baez for the annexation of the whole of San Domingo by the United States.

As soon as the cabinet met the President smiled at his associates and said, "Babcock has returned, as you see, and has brought a treaty of annexation." He picked up a document which was lying on the table. "I suppose it is not formal, as he had no diplomatic powers; but we can easily cure that. We can send back the treaty and have Perry, the consular agent, sign it; and as he is an officer of the State Department it would make it all right."

The members of the cabinet were amazed. All turned toward Hamilton Fish, Secretary of State, with inquiry in their eyes; but Mr. Fish had not seen the treaty; he had heard of its existence only the day before. At last Mr. Cox, looking at the President over the intervening products of San Domingo, broke the embarrassing silence. "But, Mr. President," he asked, "has it been settled then, that we want to annex San Domingo?" Grant's face flushed; he remained silent. Nobody asked to see the treaty. After a moment of hesitation the President called for the next order of business, and San Domingo was never mentioned in a cabinet meeting again.

But that did not end the matter. Grant's obstinacy was well able to stand rebuffs, and he made up his mind to put the treaty through regardless of the cabinet's attitude.

Hamilton Fish went to the White House the next day and offered to resign, for the reason that a treaty had been negotiated without his knowledge. But the President persuaded him to stay in the cabinet. "I need you," he said, "and Mrs. Grant needs your wife." He was thinking, no doubt, of Mrs. Grant's social inexperience. Mrs. Fish was an old lady with steel-colored curls. She wore black jet ornaments and carried the whole of the Social Register in her memory.

Before Fish left the White House Grant had induced him to advocate the plan of annexation. Rhodes remarks that thereafter Fish was a "loyal though not an ardent supporter" of the annexation policy.

But how about Charles Sumner, chairman of the Foreign Relations Committee of the Senate? That intense egoist had been ignored entirely . . . the deadliest insult he could imagine. He whetted the Senatorial bowie knife and concealed his feelings behind a dark silence, like a Sicilian bandit behind a wall. He would just love to have that treaty appear in the Senate. It would be murdered in cold blood, if it were the last act of his official life.

Grant sent Babcock to San Domingo again to have the treaty put in good diplomatic form. When it came back—Babcock with it—in November, it looked impressive with its seals and ribbons. It had been signed by Baez and the American consular agent in San Domingo. Now nothing remained to do but to rush it through the Senate.

The provisions of the treaty were very simple. The United States was to take over the republic of San Domingo and hold it as American territory. Baez and his friends were to get $1,500,000 of American money for the avowed purpose of paying off the Dominican public debt. But something had to be done to hold up the head of the sinking Baez government while the treaty was being discussed, so Grant ordered naval vessels to the island. They patrolled the coast and landed marines now and then.

Grant was not nearly as adroit as his twentieth century successors. The puttering over the treaty was really unnecessary. He might have ordered the Navy Department to occupy San Domingo without saying anything to Congress about it. It could have been done while Congress was not in session. Then, when the affair eventually burst into argument, what could be simpler or more plausible than for him to declare the occupation a necessary proceeding—that he had landed marines and taken charge of things for the purpose of keeping order and upholding civilization? He never realized what a potent word Civilization is.

In attempting to get the treaty ratified Grant shed the dignity that surrounds a President. He called on senators at their homes and pleaded with them to vote for the annexation program. San Domingo was a sun that filled his whole sky for a time. He had an exaggerated idea of its importance, of the wealth of its natural resources. One of his arguments was that the island would furnish a colonizing ground for American negroes.

One evening in January, 1870, he called on Sumner and asked him to support the treaty in the Senate. Sumner remarked that he had not seen the treaty and Grant promised to send the document to him by Babcock, who would explain its features. Although Sumner's injured feelings were soothed a little by this action he was greatly annoyed during the interview by Grant's apparent ignorance of his position in the Senate. The President referred to him four times as the Chairman of the Judiciary Committee. But he accompanied his caller to the door, shook hands and said: "Mr. President, I am an administration man, and whatever you do will always find in me the most careful and candid consideration."

Grant concluded from this statement that Sumner meant to give his support to the treaty, but he really meant nothing more than he said, which was that he would consider it carefully and candidly.

When the treaty got to the Committee on Foreign Relations Sumner came out in an opposition to it that was bitter and unyielding. He carried a majority of the committee with him, and the measure appeared before the Senate with the committee's disapproval. On June 30, 1870, the treaty failed of ratification in the Senate, and was relegated to the trash pile of imperialism.

Despite this rather contemptuous rejection Grant still clung to the annexation scheme. He attempted to revive it in December, 1870, and six years later—in his last regular message to Congress—he dragged in the subject again. In this message he said, both naïvely and significantly, that if his plan of annexation had been adopted the soil of San Domingo "would soon have fallen into the hands of the United States capitalists."

There we have at last, in Grant's own words, the milk in this cocoanut.

§ 2

He allowed the San Domingo matter to occupy far more of his attention than it deserved. He lacked the sense of scale in political affairs. It was a minor question, but the rejection of the treaty by the Senate affected him profoundly. He conceived a violent hatred for Sumner, which was returned in full measure. During the fall and winter of 1870 all Washington was amused by what each of them said of the other. Grant's detestation of the Massachusetts senator overcame his reticence, and he got in a blow whenever he could, even at dinner parties where there were many strangers. One of the stories about this feud shows what Grant thought of Sumner's estimate of his own importance. Some one remarked that Mr. Sumner did not believe in the Bible. "Oh, no; he wouldn't," said the President, "he didn't write it."

Sumner discoursed to all who were within hearing on Grant's ignorance and incapacity. Then he would go on to other related and collateral topics, such as the crowd of military officers that hung around the White House and ran errands for the President; the appointment of Grant's relatives to official positions; his adoration of moneyed people, and his habits of accepting presents from them. Most of these acidulous observations were promptly repeated in the President's ear.

George F. Hoar wrote that he was taking a walk with Grant one day on Pennsylvania Avenue. The President, he said, talked in a quiet and friendly manner until they turned the corner near Sumner's house in Lafayette Square. Grant shook his closed fist at the house and said, "That man who lives up there has abused me in a way which I never suffered from any other man living."

Grant wanted Sumner removed from his place as Chairman of the Foreign Relations Committee, and he spoke to a number of senators about it, unofficially. The Senate stood ready to support the administration in most measures of public policy, but it was not quite ready to allow the President to name the chairmen of its committees, so nothing was done about the suggestion from the White House.

However, there were other ways of showing Sumner his proper place. He had friends in official positions, and the President could remove them. One of Sumner's close friends was John Lothrop Motley, the American Minister to England. The day after the San Domingo treaty was rejected by the Senate Grant directed Fish to recall Motley at once. A few days later Grant asked if Motley had been recalled, and Fish replied that he had written him to that effect. That wouldn't do, the President declared. He wanted Fish to send Motley a cablegram, telling him to get out of the embassy forthwith. Fish said that such a procedure would not be dignified, but Grant wanted it done, anyway. It was not done; Fish finally persuaded him to let Motley receive his dismissal through the formality of a state document.

Motley got his recall from the postman, but he refused to be dismissed. The Tenure of Office act was still in full bloom— it had not yet been repealed—and Motley sat back under its kindly shelter and defied Grant to do his worst. He insisted that as his appointment had been made by the advice and consent of the Senate, he could be dismissed only with the Senate's approval. The Senate was not then in session.

Grant had the State department notify the British government to pay no attention to Motley and to consider the first

secretary of the embassy as a *chargé d'affaires*.   For six
months Motley went about London, furnishing the melancholy
spectacle of an American Minister who was not in the confidence of his government.   He spent most of his time in telling
his troubles to English officials and their wives.

When the Senate met in December Motley was recalled and
Grant appointed Robert C. Schenck, of Ohio, in his place.
Mr. Schenck's sole claim to distinction rests on his authorship
of one of the best treatises on poker-playing that has ever appeared in print.

Schenck made a great hit in London at first.   He taught
the art and science of poker to the English aristocracy.   They
found it a ripping game, and poker parties became fashionable.
But, after such a bright beginning his popularity declined
rapidly.   He was interested in an enterprise called the Emma
gold mine, and he used his official position to sell mining stock
to the English people.   The mine appeared to be a fizzle as a
money-maker, and the English press, in its decorous way,
treated the affair as a scandal.   Schenck resigned and came
home.   Later on the Emma mine turned out to be a very
profitable investment, but most of Schenck's poker pupils had
already sold their stock for anything it would bring.

§ 3

It is pleasant to turn from these confused gyrations of
the Grant administration and record its few notable successes,
such as the establishment of the principle of international
arbitration through the Treaty of Washington; the peaceful
and successful adjudication of the Alabama claims; and the
upholding of American dignity in controversies with other
nations.   Under Grant the financial affairs of the national
government were put on a sound basis.   Taxes were reduced;
money was stabilized, and a law for the resumption of specie
payments was passed.   He instituted a humane policy toward

GENERAL GRANT AS PRESIDENT

Photograph taken during his first term as President.

NELLIE GRANT

The only daughter of General and Mrs. Ulysses S. Grant.
Photograph from the Meserve Collection.

the Indians. He attempted civil service reform, but the spoils system had lasted too long to be displaced in a few years.

§ 4

During the War several Confederate cruisers had been built in English shipyards, or purchased from British subjects. Their crews had consisted chiefly of English sailors. Three of these vessels—the *Alabama*, *Florida* and *Shenandoah*—had done great damage to American commerce.

For some time after the war the American claim against the British for reparations was given small consideration by Her Majesty's government. The easy nonchalance of our ministers to England had created an impression in English official circles that the *Alabama* claims, as the collective losses to American commerce were called, would not be pressed.

But it was a live question in America, although it had been temporarily thrust into the background by other and more urgent problems. For awhile the controversy, from the American side, was directed by Charles Sumner, who—as Chairman of the Foreign Relations Committee of the Senate—assumed arbitrarily the functions of the State Department. Grant thought that Mr. Motley took his instructions from Sumner instead of from the Secretary of State, and this was certainly true, in part. Mr. Sumner had fantastic notions of how much the British ought to pay to square accounts with us.

Let us consider his arithmetic.

He estimated that the rebellion had been suppressed at a cost of four billion dollars. The British, he contended, through their aid and comfort to the rebels had prolonged the war at least two years. With these assumptions as a premise he argued that the British government owed the American nation half the cost of the war, or two billion dollars. Besides, the *Alabama* and other English-built Confederate cruisers had destroyed fifteen million dollars' worth of American commerce, but to that sum should be added the commerce not destroyed but "driven from the ocean," which he figured at a hundred and ten million dollars. Total charge against the British Empire . . . $2,125,000,000.

This is the reasoning of a man who has lost all sense of proportion, who has gone mad in the contemplation of his own ideas. He realized that the British nation could not, or would not, pay any such sum, and he was ready to propose another expedient. If the English would give us the whole of the dominion of Canada we would be willing to cancel our claim. These preposterous notions were circulated by Mr. Sumner and brought to the attention of the British ministry. The Queen's ministers saw clearly that, with such ideas in the minds of the American representatives, it would be useless to hold a conference on the subject of reparations.

Grant saw the absurdity of these proposals and put the negotiations in the hands of Hamilton Fish, where they belonged. Through Mr. Fish's diplomacy a Joint High Commission—five Americans and five Englishmen—met at Washington in the spring of 1871 to discuss various matters in dispute between the two nations. Among these questions—and the most important of all—was that of the *Alabama* claims. Mr. Sumner was not included among the five Americans who sat at the Commission's round table. Through Grant's continual nagging he had been deposed as Chairman of the Foreign Relations Committee by the Republican caucus which met at the assembling of Congress on March 4, 1871. Rhodes says, "Grant's insistence on the deposition of Sumner must go down in history unjustified. If it was done, as I believe, out of pure vindictiveness, it was a revenge unworthy of so great a general in the President's chair."

Whatever may have been Grant's motives, it seems clear that Sumner would have been a hindrance, instead of a help, in the negotiations that were going on during that spring in Washington.

Early in May the Joint High Commission completed its work; the Treaty of Washington was laid before the Senate and promptly ratified. In the first article of the Treaty Her Majesty's Government expressed regret for the depredation committed by the *Alabama* and other vessels.

The treaty provided that the *Alabama* claims should be referred to a Tribunal of Arbitration, consisting of five members, one of whom was to be appointed by the President of the United States, and another by Her Britannic Majesty. The other three arbitrators were to be chosen by the Emperor of Brazil, the King of Italy and the President of Switzerland.

Grant selected Charles Francis Adams—former Minister to England—as the American arbitrator, and as counsel to present our case he appointed William M. Evarts, Caleb Cushing and Morrison R. Waite. The Tribunal met in December, 1871, at Geneva, and carried on its deliberations until September 14, 1872. The United States was awarded $15,500,000 in gold as reparation for the loss sustained by the Confederate cruisers.

The Geneva arbitration made a resounding impression on European governments. Out of it has grown, indirectly, the whole of the arbitration movement of the past fifty years.

While the *Alabama* matter was being settled beside a Swiss lake, Charles Sumner remained in the sight of the Potomac and nursed his wrongs. His enemy Grant was about to be nominated for a second term, and Sumner resolved to do whatever he could to prevent it. On May 31, 1872—five days before the Republican National Convention met—Sumner delivered, on the floor of the Senate, a violent attack on the President. It was generally known for several days that Sumner intended to expose Grant's incapacity, duplicity and general unfitness, and on the morning of May 31st the galleries of the Senate were jammed with spectators.

His attack could hardly be called a speech in the ordinary sense. It might be described more accurately as a diatribe.

Its devastating comments were so exaggerated, and came so palpably from personal spite, that they went far over the mark, like a projectile fired with too great an elevation. The most striking impression that was left upon Sumner's audience was that Mr. Sumner did not like General Grant in any manner, shape or form; and that whatever Grant did was wrong, even if it seemed right.

He declared that the President continually exalted the military over the civil power; that he was surrounded by army officers; that any one who brought gifts to Grant's door was sure of obtaining his favors; that he appointed his relatives —and the relatives and friends of his relatives—to office regardless of their fitness; that this favoritism could only be described as "a dropsical nepotism swollen to elephantiasis." He went over the San Domingo affair in detail; then he made a discourse on the cabinet appointments and the unsavory financial episodes. He ridiculed Grant's friend Washburne, who held the office of Secretary of State five days "as a compliment." Compliment, indeed! "Whoever heard before of a man being nominated Secretary of State merely as a compliment?"

Mr. Sumner's attack had no effect whatever on anybody or anything. Five days later Grant was nominated unanimously for a second term by the Republican Convention.

§ 5

The prosperous era in the North that followed the Civil War grew by degrees into a financial and industrial boom, which collapsed in the late summer of 1873. All of a sudden banking concerns began to fail, among them the famous house of Jay Cooke & Co., which had been looked upon as an invincible fortress of finance. There was too much commercial paper afloat; there were too many undigested securities, too many new enterprises. The country could not stand it, and the result was the disastrous panic of 1873.

Everyone looked to Washington for relief. The administration was the target of a thousand dynamic importunities. Why not ease up the currency situation by issuing more greenbacks? The business community, or a large part of it, thought that the national treasury could quickly bring relief to the country by increasing the supply of paper money. Under this pressure Grant was undecided at first, it seems, on the subject of inflation, but in his message to Congress in December he said:

> Undue inflation . . . while it might give temporary relief, would only lead to inflation of prices, the impossibility of competing in our own markets for the products of home skill and labor, and repeated renewals of present experiences. . . . The exact medium is specie, the recognized medium of exchange the world over.

The ultimate soundness of this argument is open to question, but as a working basis under the circumstances that prevailed in 1873 it was sound enough.

The disturbed conditions of the country influenced Congress to pass what is generally known as the Inflation Bill in April, 1874. The bill provided that only eighteen million dollars in greenbacks was to be added to the paper currency already in existence, but the opponents of the measure claimed—and probably with reason—that the bill was only an entering wedge. If it became a law, they contended, there would be other issues of paper currency, and Congress would have to manufacture money on a large scale every time there were a few business failures.

Grant did not know what to do about the matter, and pondered over the bill for several days. To veto the measure might be the sensible thing to do, but it would cut straight across the current of public opinion. He wrote a message approving moderate inflation, and was about to sign the bill, when he decided to read his message over again. He said that his own arguments sounded unconvincing. "What is the good of all this?" he said to himself, according to his statement to John Russell Young. "You do not believe it. You know it is not true." He threw away his message of approval, and sent the Inflation Bill back to Congress with his veto on it.

Rhodes declares that Grant's veto in this case was the most praiseworthy act of his second term, "and like the Treaty of Washington and the Geneva arbitration, atones for a multitude of errors."

The country managed to get through without any more greenbacks, and none have been issued since. Whether it was a good thing or not, Grant had more to do with establishing the American nation on a gold basis than any other President.

A year later we find him advocating a resumption of specie payments in his annual message—and his arguments have virility and power.

John Sherman, Chairman of the Committee on Finance, formulated a bill for the redemption of greenbacks in coin, and to make the resumption of specie payments possible the bill authorized the Secretary of the Treasury to sell bonds for the purpose of accumulating gold. In order to give the business world time to adjust itself to the new order of things, it was further provided that the resumption of specie payments should not begin until January 1, 1879. The Specie Resumption act was signed by the President and became a law on January 14, 1875. The country had passed through its greenback crisis, and took its place among the nations that are definitely committed to the gold standard.

§ 6

In his last annual message—that of December, 1876—Grant admits that he had made "errors of judgment," and defends himself on the ground of inexperience. This is the only occasion in his political life where he made this admission. He said:

> It was my fortune, or misfortune, to be called to the office of Chief Executive without any previous political training. . . . Under such circumstances it is but reasonable to suppose that errors of judgment must have occurred. Even had they not, differences of opinion between the Executive, bound by an oath to the strict performance of his duties, and writers and debaters, must have arisen. . . . Mistakes have been made, as all can see, and I admit, but it seems to me oftener in the selections made in the assistants appointed to aid in carrying out the various duties of administering the government— and in nearly every case selected without a personal acquaintance with the appointee, but upon recommendation of the representatives chosen directly by the people. . . . Failures have been errors of judgment, not of intent.

This statement is interesting, and a little pathetic. But in writing it did he forget that Babcock and Belknap were his personal friends?

§ 7

Energy and Perseverance were outstanding qualities in Grant's personality. His energy was slow, turgid and powerful, like the energy of water pressing against a dam.

He was without the wings that lift men to the sky. The horizon stood close about him; he lacked the capacity to feel and understand at a distance. Anything but the job directly under his hand was incomprehensible to him, and meaningless. He was amazingly lacking in political foresight, in range of ideas, in the knack of understanding men and their motives. His intelligence was the kind that perceives the outside but not the inside of men and events.

There was hardly any fluid quality to his mind. When he set out to do anything he kept on, regardless of the flux of circumstances. It was this aspect of his character which led him to make such a hopeless fiasco of Southern reconstruction. He was not able to adapt his policy to the changing conditions in the South.

National heroes are day-dreams of the human race. They are the symbols of the common aspiration, of the common desire. No man is great enough to live up to the reputation of a national hero—and we must consider men like Grant as chips floating on the current of dynamic social forces, riding the wave instead of directing it.

Despite his dominating obstinacy he was greatly influenced by other men—by men who knew how to approach him subtly, and especially by men of wealth. His reverence for success amounted to a religion.

He made strange friendships and had curious, unaccountable dislikes; and, with a touch of pride, he claimed that he never deserted a friend. If he had deserted some of the slick rascals who surrounded him it would have made the story of his administration more pleasant to read.

Of equal value with his energy and persistency was his honest, good intention. He was in no sense a fraud or a trickster. At times he was not wholly frank in his speech, but he thought such occasions justified by the circumstances. At the bottom of his heart he was always sincere, always generous, always meaning to do the best.

CHAPTER XXX

THE TRIP AROUND THE WORLD

§ 1

AT the end of his second term Grant was disgusted and bored with America. For eight years he had hardly done a thing that came out the way he thought it would. He had conceived the presidential office as a glorified opportunity for magnanimous self-expression, but he had been disillusioned as he became involved in the curious technique of expediency. He had found that his simplest decisions carried vast implications; and that stinging criticism was often the reward of what he considered praiseworthy actions. Any man in public life needs a thick shell of indifference to what others say. Grant was never able to acquire this stolidity—though he looked stolid enough—and his sensitiveness to newspaper criticism made him unhappy.

The job of being President required something more than good intentions, and he had never been able to learn what that Something was.

I think he hated politics and politicians more than anything else in the world in the spring of 1877. And he disliked his friends almost as much as he disliked his enemies. Many of them had deceived him, some of them had turned out to be unscrupulous rogues. At the sight of them he was reminded of the unfortunate episodes into which they had led him.

He wanted to get out of the country, away from the American people and their problems. He started for Europe almost without a plan, except the general idea of a long tour abroad. On his first morning at sea he said that "he felt better than

457

he had for sixteen years, from the fact that he had no letters to read, and no telegraphic dispatches to attend to."

There was a big hurrah in Philadelphia on the day he sailed, which was May 17, 1877. The passenger steamer *Indiana*, fluttering with the gayety of flags, lay in the river. The newspapers purred their good-by editorials that morning. Even the opposition sheets, venomous as they had been in the past, waved their inky good-will, on the principle of *de mortuis nihil nisi bonum*. Grant attended a huge round-table breakfast and drank champagne with the governor of Pennsylvania, General Sherman, Hamilton Fish, George W. Childs and Senator Cameron.

The whistles blow, handkerchiefs wave, flags snap in the wind, the crowd cheers, and everything is ready to move. But there is a hitch. Bill Barnes is aboard.

I have neglected to tell you about Bill Barnes. He was a very black, agreeable negro who had attached himself to General Grant during the siege of Vicksburg. Grant had found him quietly working about the headquarter tents. He became the General's valet. His job made him a person of great distinction among the other negroes.

Everybody has his own curse, and the curse of Bill Barnes was liquor. General Grant had no use for drunkards, so Bill was discharged, but the General got him another job. Before long he appeared again at Grant's headquarters and soberly went to work, somewhat abashed and chastened in spirit. This experience was repeated several times. Then Grant discharged him emphatically, and told him never to come again; but he did come again, and was finally considered an unescapable feature of the Grant family life.

The *Indiana* was getting ready to start when Grant went down to his stateroom and found Bill Barnes unpacking his shirts. Now the General climbs to the deck and seeks the captain of the ship. "There is a colored man down in my cabin, Captain. His name is Bill Barnes. If Bill Barnes is to sail on this boat I shall leave with the pilot. It depends on you, Captain; either you arrange for the departure of Bill Barnes, or I go, but Mrs. Grant must not know until Bill is safely ashore."

Bill was disembarked, so to speak, and the ship began its voyage. The Grant party at that time consisted of General and Mrs. Grant and their son Jesse, a young man of nineteen. Later, a number of others joined the party, and at times there were nine or ten people.

At first, the General intended to visit only the principal cities of Europe . . . to go, as he expressed it, "as long as his money would last." But his investments were unexpectedly profitable. Money came in, and the trip grew longer. Eventually it became a voyage around the world. He arrived at San Francisco on September 20, 1879—two years and four months after his departure from Philadelphia.

§ 2

Liverpool—city of cotton—unlike other English towns, gazes across the Atlantic. Its wealth comes from America. Any intelligent citizen of Liverpool can tell you all about Alabama and Texas. Walking encyclopedias on American affairs, especially in respect to the cotton crop and its probable value. Liverpool people liked Americans.

The city spread its hospitality before the distinguished American general. The mayor came down, in his stately way, the gold chain of office around his neck; and after him tripped the aldermen in their robes, which resemble elaborate dressing gowns. Grant was the sensation of the day in England. The welcoming crowds, the waving flags and the cheering set a record that has never been surpassed.

The English working people made the General a popular hero. His career fired their imagination. A British factory hand, existing on twelve shillings a week, without a chance

of ever being elected to any office, or of rising above the grade
of sergeant in the army, could hardly fail to be stirred by the
sight of a plow-boy who had become the greatest general in
the world and had been twice elected President of the United
States.

Though there had never been anything in Grant's actions or
utterances to indicate that he was a close friend of the laboring
man, the British working classes somehow got a notion that he
was. Perhaps this idea arose because of the part he had taken
in freeing the slaves.

The plain fact is that he had no real sympathy for working people. At the very time when crowds of English laboring
men were hurrahing outside his windows he was writing to his
brother-in-law Corbin that the railroad strike then going on
in America should have been put down by force. "My judgment," he wrote, "is that it should have been put down with a
strong hand and so summarily as to prevent a like occurrence
for a generation."

When he arrived at Newcastle the factories closed down,
and eighty thousand British mechanics assembled on a moor
to welcome him. Their cheering could be heard for miles. The
local newspaper gave twenty columns to the event.

Newcastle was not alone in the wildly enthusiastic quality
of its welcome. There were similar gatherings at Sheffield,
Birmingham, Leamington, and other manufacturing towns. At
Manchester the Grant party was lodged regally in the distinguished visitor's apartments in the new City Hall, as guests
of the municipality.

Of course the General had to make speeches, however much
it went against his inclination. They were strained little talks,
devoid of color or humor, and rather stereotyped in substance.
To gatherings of laboring men he said that "labor is highly
respectable." In America, he declared, "We recognize that
labor dishonors no man; and no matter what a man's occupation is, he is eligible to fill any post in the gift of the people."

To mayors and official delegations he discoursed on the subject of hands-across-the-sea and the responsibilities of the Anglo-Saxon race in its relation to the lesser breeds of men.

The British government decided, before Grant arrived in England, that he was to be treated as a distinguished private citizen. This meant that he was to be welcomed with music and speeches, and be given the "freedom" of London and other English cities. He was to meet the Queen and the Prince of Wales, of course, but according to the established etiquette he would rank below royalty and the dukes, the cabinet ministers and the envoys of foreign powers.

This arrangement was not at all pleasing to Mr. Edwards Pierrepont, the American minister; nor to Mr. Badeau, the consul-general of the United States. Their idea was that he should be treated as an ex-sovereign; but the English court officials said: "The Americans give their ex-Presidents no rank; why should we?"

There was much stirring about, and considerable emotion. The American embassy felt that the crisis was profound. Mr. Pierrepont, who had been one of Grant's attorneys-general, called on Lord Derby, the Secretary of State for Foreign Affairs. The genial lord could not at first see the matter eye to eye with Mr. Pierrepont, but finally he did agree that General Grant ought to rank as an ex-sovereign; he was to make the first visit to the royal family, but every other Englishman was to yield him precedence.

How about the ambassadors? Lord Derby pointed out that they represented their sovereigns, and would not give precedence to anybody. According to Badeau, the Secretary of State for Foreign Affairs said that if General Grant should go in to dinner ahead of the envoys the affront to foreign powers would be so great that "there would be a war," but I cannot imagine him saying anything so silly. General Grant knew nothing of this palaver; he did not hear of it until afterward.

The General arrived in London, and the Prince of Wales invited him and Mrs. Grant to dinner to "meet their Imperial Majesties, the Emperor and Empress of Brazil."

Badeau, who was an obstreperous, spread-eagle sort of person, considered the Prince of Wales dinner a ghastly failure. He attended it in company with the Grants. When they arrived they passed first into a large ante-chamber where the Prince of Wales was playing with his two boys—one of whom is now King George V. The other guests had not come. The Prince came forward, shook hands with the General, met Mrs. Grant and spoke a word or two to Badeau. Then the Prince went out, and soon after an equerry came in. The guests were ushered into a long waiting room, where they remained for half an hour.

> After awhile a gentleman-in-waiting appeared and said the Princess desired the ladies to range themselves on one side of the room and the gentlemen on the other. . . . After apparently ten minutes of further waiting in this position, all standing, for no one had been seated or asked to sit since we entered, the great doors at the top of the line on the right were thrown open and the Empress of Brazil came in on the arm of the Prince of Wales. Next came the Princess with the Emperor. They passed directly between the two lines to the dining room.

The Empress of Brazil, who had met Mrs. Grant before, stopped and spoke to her, but the other royal personages swept on without speaking to anybody, much to the disgust of Mr. Badeau. Then a number of dukes and lesser nobles were told off to their partners and followed the Empress and the Prince. "After every noble person present was thus assigned," Badeau says, "General Grant was requested to go in with Mrs. Pierrepont, and Mrs. Grant with the Brazilian minister, whom the Emperor of Brazil looked upon as his servant."

This made Badeau hate the British Empire, and he says it was perfectly plain to him that the royal family did not intend to follow the arrangement which had been agreed upon by the Foreign Office.

After dinner there was music in one of the drawing rooms. There the royalties sat and conversed, while the rest of the company amused themselves outside. Neither Grant nor Mrs. Grant was invited to join this select company. When it got rather late the Prince and Princess came out and courteously bade the Grants good-night.

Badeau said the General's feelings were hurt, but it appears that he spoke without authority, for Grant's own comment does not bear him out. The General said to John Russell Young:

> I received nothing but the utmost kindness from every Englishman from the head of the nation down. Next to my own country, there is none I love so much as England.
>
> Some of the newspapers at home invented a story to the effect that the Prince of Wales had been rude to me. It was a pure invention. I cannot conceive the Prince of Wales being rude to any man.

The Grants visited the Crystal Palace one night as guests of honor. The sky was a shiver of red and green lines of fire. Grant's head, traced in wiggling pyrotechnics, flared gigantically over the palace dome; and when it faded out, the Capitol at Washington took its place. Then a multitude of white London faces, half-drowned in night, passed before the lofty portico and stared respectfully at the great American.

He met Robert Browning, Matthew Arnold, Anthony Trollope and Thomas H. Huxley at the home of George W. Smalley, then the London correspondent of the New York *Tribune*. It was a dinner attended only by literary men. Grant had never read any of the books written by these gentlemen, and was not verbose, anyway, in the company of strangers, so one may infer that the affair dragged a little. But that did not matter; it was the customary tribute that culture pays to action, and the shining lights of the literary world got a chance to see the Civil War hero plain, as Browning once saw Shelley . . . which was probably all they expected.

§ 3

Now comes another desperate hand-to-hand struggle with royal etiquette, and in this battle the visiting team won.

Queen Victoria, through her Lord Steward, invited General and Mrs. Grant to dinner at Windsor Castle on June 26th, and to remain until the following day. The American minister and Mrs. Pierrepont were also included. Young Jesse was left out of the royal invitation.

Thereupon Badeau sent a telegram to Sir John Cowell, Master of the Queen's Household, whom he had known for some time, in which he said:

> Personal and confidential to yourself. I would not, of course, make such a suggestion unauthorized, but if it could be proposed to invite General Grant's son, Mr. Jesse Grant, a young man of nineteen or twenty, it would be a great gratification to General and Mrs. Grant. If this is contrary to etiquette, please consider this telegram not sent.

Next morning Jesse received an invitation, and on the afternoon of the twenty-sixth the party set out for Windsor Castle. The Queen's carriages were waiting at the station, but the Queen herself was not there. According to the Court custom she met royalty only in person. When they reached the Castle they were shown into handsome apartments and informed that Her Majesty was out driving in Windsor Park and would not be visible until dinner time.

Soon after their arrival Sir John Cowell appeared and explained that Jesse and General Badeau were not to dine at Her Majesty's table, but in another room with the Household. Immediately after dinner they would be taken in and presented to the Queen.

Jesse declared that he would not eat with the servants. He had been invited by the Queen, and if he could not sit at her table . . . good-night . . . he would return at once to London. Sir John Cowell was extremely apologetic. Large dinners made the Queen giddy, he said. That is why she tried to keep them as small as possible—so would Mr. Jesse be good enough . . . and so on.

But Mr. Jesse was not good enough to agree to any such arrangement, so he and Badeau went down to the General's rooms to tell him how they felt about it. There they found the Duchess of Roxburgh, one of the ladies-in-waiting, talking with Mrs. Grant. She assured Jesse that the Household consisted of persons of some consequence . . . the ladies- and gentlemen-in-waiting. She belonged to the Household herself. Jesse said he considered them servants anyway, in a sense. The Duchess kept her temper and continued to smile. A well-bred person, evidently, as the temptation to throw something at his head must have been hard to resist.

The young man declared that he had spoken his last word on the subject; that he would pack his grip and walk back to the station. No use to bother about a carriage for him. He would walk. Perhaps he could buy a light supper in some little eating house near the railroad depot.

Sir John Cowell, agitated almost to hysterics, begged him to remain until the Queen returned, when the matter would be brought to Her Majesty's attention. The General remarked that if he were in Jesse's place he would act the same way . . . what was the use of inviting the boy if he were to be packed off into some other dining room?

The Grant party dressed for dinner and sat around waiting for whatever might happen. The Queen returned, and Sir John Cowell came back to the Grants' rooms, greatly relieved, to announce that Her Majesty would be pleased to have Mr. Jesse Grant at her table.

The conversation at the dinner was not very lively. Her

Majesty conversed in a low tone with her son, Prince Leopold, and the Princess Beatrice. She remarked to Mrs. Grant that her duties were arduous, and Mrs. Grant replied: "Yes, I can imagine them; I, too, have been the wife of a great ruler."

After dinner the Queen soon retired, but the Grants stayed up late, playing whist with the lords and ladies.

Jesse says that when he returned to his own apartments, which were shared with Badeau, he found Sir John Cowell there, in a dressing gown, with a bottle of Scotch whisky before him. Sir John amused them with stories of his difficulties with the old lady—the Queen. It appears, from his account, that she did not want to dine with anybody at all except a few snips of royalty, and that when distinguished commoners were invited, Her Majesty often pleaded a sick headache.

As the level of the Scotch in the bottle went down Sir John became more and more communicative. Finally he went off to bed, an admirer of America, a stalwart Republican and ready to vote at our next election, if we would only let him.

§ 4

It is a well-known custom among the families of wealthy or distinguished Americans to trace their lineage back to noble and royal houses. The Grants have this interesting habit. Not General Grant—but his descendants. They have—or had—a Grant Family Association which discussed genealogy at much length, and on many occasions. Ulysses S. Grant, Jr. (known as "Buck"), was the first president of this association. He opened one of the meetings of the society with• a singularly inept speech, which dealt in a confused way with the origin and early history of the Grants. It was printed in the *Grant Family Magazine*—and there I perused it.

"Buck" said that the name Grant may be traced to the Latin Magnus, or in French Le Grand. By an easy transition Le Grand becomes Grand or Grant. There was a Magnus at Senlac, an officer in William the Conqueror's army. That was in 1066, the year of the Norman Conquest of England.

"I think," "Buck" continued, "this Grant in the army at Senlac was a Saxon, and that the family has its origin in that strong and valiant race. There are numerous items to lead to this conclusion. That they were Normans it is easy to believe, as there are several kings of Norway and Sweden at that period bearing the name of Magnus or Grant."

He did not seem to grasp the fact that Magnus was not a name but an adjective or title. Charlemagne was a Magnus . . . or Charles the Great.

"It is related of the Grants that they were the last to yield in the wars of the Conqueror," he continued. "This is a very striking characteristic of the family, and the old Grant motto of 'Craig-e-Lochie'—'Stand fast, stand firm, stand sure'— seems as fitting to ancient heroes of the name as to Ulysses with his proposition to fight it out on this line if it takes all summer."

The prevailing tradition among the descendants of General Grant is that their family came from the Grant clan of Scotland. This connection is mythical . . . I mean that it rests on evidence that is too flimsy to be considered valid. As far as available knowledge goes the ancestors of Ulysses were English Puritans.

But the Scotch myth was in fine working order when the General and his party visited Scotland. He was invited by the Earl of Seafield, head of the Grant clan, to visit Castle Grant. At Granttown, "home of the Grants," he was received like a distinguished son, with smoky Scotch whisky and other honors.

I have traced the General's world tour in red ink on a map. It makes a most complicated zigzag over the face of Europe. He had no definite plan; he wandered about wherever he pleased.

From England he went to Belgium. King Leopold surprised him by calling at his hotel informally. They had a long talk about things in general. Next day he met the King in state, in the midst of his court, and they were introduced as if they had never seen each other before.

The Grants liked Leopold . . . a plain, democratic monarch, they considered him.

After Belgium came Alsace and Switzerland. The General was back in England soon—this time without being bothered by royal dinners. In October, 1877, he went to Paris, where he met Gambetta, whom he thought one of the four greatest men in the world. But he did not have a good time in Paris. The French believed that he had sympathized with the Prussians in the Franco-Prussian war, and they were only coldly polite.

Then to the south of France.

The navy department had put the warship *Vandalia* at his disposal, and the party journeyed in this vessel to Naples, to Sicily, to Egypt and the Holy Land. While the *Vandalia* was sailing through the Mediterranean Grant sat in a deck chair and read *Innocents Abroad*.

The General loitered for a time about Pompeii, which he declared was the only thing he saw in Europe that came up to his expectations. This was a mere form of speech, for he saw a number of sights that were evidently all he expected them to be. The beggars of Naples exceeded his expectations. He was astounded at them. On one of their drives the Grant carriages—glittering harness, sleek horses and shining panels— passed a baker's shop in a poor neighborhood. The Grants caught a glimpse of the baker inside his shop waiting on his customers. But the baker, upon seeing the rich turn-out, threw down his bread, ran out of his shop, left his customers, and pursued the carriages for some distance, beating his breast, weeping, and declaring his poverty. A few silver pieces were flung in the dust. He picked them up and returned to his bakery.

In Egypt the party went up the Nile, with the celebrated Egyptologist, Emil Brugsch, as their guide. The Khedive of Egypt had assigned him to this duty. Mr. Brugsch was interesting but long-winded. In describing a ruin he had a way of going back to 4000 B.C. and giving the history of civilization in all its branches before he got to the ruins that stood before the tired little group.

The General wanted to enter Jerusalem unostentatiously, humbly, but the American consul had a different plan. He passed through the gates of the city to the sound of shawms and trumpets, and amid the trampling of many feet and the noise of many throats.

Now the Holy Land is accomplished; he has seen the Mount of Olives, and the desolate hillside of the Crucifixion. Our red ink line runs back to Constantinople and Greece. The Parthenon was illuminated in his honor. Sultan Abdul Hamid gave him four Arabian horses, and he drank the thick and sticky liquid that is called coffee among the Turks.

Italy again. His Holiness the Pope. Gracious, smooth and silky secretaries of the Vatican. They knew all about America; they told Grant things that he did not know himself. He came away with a conviction that, whatever the Catholic Church might be, one could not accuse it of ignorance.

In Florence he was bored by the Uffizi Gallery and the Pitti Palace. Too many paintings. A good photograph, after all, is the best kind of art. He gazed over Florence from the Boboli Gardens, where the lovely marble flesh of statues peeps from the summer-green of the trees, but the view did not impress him.

The dream of Venice rose out of the blue Adriatic. A city of silence and revery, long dead but living still, as a ghost lives. Grant looked at the curving perspective of marble palaces, the water lapping at their bronze doors; the lordly Square of St. Mark, and the clean shaft of the Campanile soaring into the soft Italian sky, and he remarked: "Venice would be a fine place if it were drained."

France again—straight across northern Italy, from Venice.

France, Holland and Berlin. Our red line on the map is all sharp angles. I wonder what he thought of Amsterdam; of the buttoned-up stolidity of the placid Dutch houses; of the sluggish rivers and the blond boatmen. But whatever he thought or said has not come down to us. The Boswell of the expedition—John Russell Young of the New York *Herald*, who joined the party in Europe—was so preoccupied in recording his own impressions that he quite forgot to set down the General's comments.

After Holland came Berlin, where he met Bismarck, had a long talk with him, and added him to his gallery of great men. The Germans managed to get him to attend, in full uniform, a review of part of their army, though he told them that he did not like soldiering and wanted to be excused.

The next stop was at Copenhagen, where he was the guest of Michael J. Cramer, his brother-in-law, at that time the American minister to Denmark. The Danes detested Cramer. He was a German by birth, and he occupied a good deal of time telling the Danes how much inferior they were to the Germans. He spent his spare hours, when he was not discoursing on German superiority or praying—for he was a preacher by profession—in drinking beer at the Tivoli Gardens, a popular resort frequented by the lower orders. The Danish government would have asked for his recall if he had not been the General's brother-in-law.

The King gave a dinner in honor of the Grants, and the Queen requested him to inscribe his name in her album, which contained the autographs of emperors and kings. While he wrote his name he "was watched by the court," Cramer says. Afterwards the commander of the King's steam yacht said to Cramer: "The manner in which General Grant inscribed his name in the album stamps him as a great man."

Next, the party visited Norway, Sweden and Russia. Grant did not meet the Czar, nor was he shown any particular attention in St. Petersburg or Moscow. Then he crossed Europe, by way of Vienna, and went straight through France to Spain. At Madrid he was received by the young Spanish King. James Russell Lowell, who was our minister to Spain, wrote that Grant liked to go off alone and wander through the streets. "After being here two days, I think he knew Madrid better than I," Mr. Lowell declared.

From Spain and Portugal he went back to England for the third time. He wandered like a man who is in search of something, and who does not know what he is looking for. In July, 1878, he was in Ireland; and then we see him crossing France again to Marseilles, where he embarked, on January 24, 1879, on a French passenger steamer for the Orient.

In India he was the guest of the British government, and was entertained by Lord Lytton, the Viceroy, who still lives in the literary hall of fame as the author of *Lucille*—a vast, stale Victorian piece of poetry. The General did not remain in India long—it was too hot—but soon went on to Siam and China.

Li Hung Chang, then the head of things in the Celestial Empire, seemed to Grant to be just about right in conduct and opinions. He said, after his tour was over, that he had met only four really great men; namely, Lord Beaconsfield, Bismarck, Gambetta and Li Hung Chang. In China and Japan the exotic pleasures of Oriental food were thrust upon the General, whose preferences were limited to the simple fare of the Middle West, notwithstanding his long experience in the higher gastronomic life.

At Canton he attended a state banquet given by the Viceroy in his honor. They started off with sweetmeats, fruit-rolls, apricot kernels and melon seeds. Then came ham with bamboo sprouts, smoked duck and cucumbers, pickled chicken and beans, red shrimps with leeks, spiced sausage with celery, fried fish with flour sauce, chops with vegetables, and fish with fir-tree cones and sweet pickle.

Everybody sat back with a sigh of satisfaction . . . pretty

good dinner, though rather filling . . . but the Chinese announced that the dinner had not started yet. What they had eaten were only the slight and fragile appetizers.

Then they had fresh fruits, fruits dried in honey, chestnuts, oranges and honey gold-cake.

Then they had birds-nest soup and roast duck, mushrooms and pigeons' eggs, sharks' fins and sea crabs.

Then they had steamed cakes, ham pie, vermicelli, baked white pigeons, stewed chicken, lotus seeds, pea soup, ham in honey, radish cakes, date-cakes and a suckling pig served whole.

Then they had a fat duck, ham, perch, and meat pies, confectionery, the bellies of fat fish, roast mutton, pears in honey, the soles of pigeons' feet, wild ducks, thorn-apple jelly and egg-balls.

Then they had . . . but why continue? The dinner consisted of seventy courses, and ended with crystal-cakes, prune juice and almonds with bean curd.

The Chinese are an ancient and respectable people, but they seem to have mixed gastronomy with astronomy, for their eating has a celestial reach, and streams off into distant Milky Ways and constellations of food.

In Japan the General met and talked with the Emperor; and there were other ceremonial occasions, where every one sat on mats and ate the saltless, breadless, butterless dinners of the Japanese.

§ 5

In the meantime Grant's friends back home had been laying plans to elect him for a third term. He knew about it, and their arrangements had been made with his tacit consent. His resentment toward political life had become mellowed by time and distance. For the last two years of his voyage all he had heard of America was contained in periodical bundles of friendly letters.

I do not think he cared much for a third term himself, but his wife did. She was eager to return to the White House. When he got back home in September, 1879, and listened to the adulation of some of the leading Republicans, he became as eager as Mrs. Grant.

He returned in a blaze of glory, and received such a welcome as has seldom been given to any returning traveler in this country. But his political managers thought he had come back too soon. The Republican National Convention was not to be held until June of the next year, and it was probable —or possible—that the steaming enthusiasm of the hour would blow itself away into thin air before the conclave of the party assembled.

A few months after his return from his world tour he set out on a trip to Cuba and Mexico. He had, since his early days, had an affection for the Spanish-Americans. In the back of his mind there was a half-formed idea that if he were not nominated by the Republican Convention he would establish some kind of business connection with Mexico, and his trip to that country was made chiefly to lay the foundation for such an enterprise.

His stock of money was getting low, and he wrote of his financial condition to a number of his friends. If he were not elected President he would have to obtain employment in some capacity suitable to his talents. At one time he thought of promoting a company to dig a transoceanic canal across Nicaragua, and a little later he was considering the presidency of a mining company. But these projects had to wait, for there was the Convention coming on . . . and who could tell? While it was true that the American tradition was opposed to a third term, there was no law against it. He told his friends that he realized that he had made mistakes during his eight years in office, but now that he had acquired more experience he thought he would make a better President. He added that he would do absolutely nothing to obtain the nomination, and did not want it unless it came as an untrammeled expression of the Convention's will.

His campaign manager, Roscoe Conkling of New York, was not as disturbed as Grant was about the untrammeled part of it. He resolved to trammel the Convention as much as he could, and he was a shrewd hand at trammeling.

The chief opponent of Grant was James G. Blaine, who had a large and insistent following of his own. Before the Convention met Conkling looked over the list of delegates, and checked them off as they appeared to be on one side or the other. He saw that in most of the larger states Grant had a majority of the delegates . . . and he figured that if the unit rule were adopted by the Convention Grant would be nominated on the first ballot.

The unit rule means that the whole vote of a state goes according to the majority of its delegates. For example, New York had seventy delegates, of whom fifty were known to be for Grant. Under the unit rule Grant would receive the entire lot of seventy votes.

While Conkling meditated on getting the unit rule adopted he was not idle elsewhere. He managed to gather in nearly all the delegates from the ex-Confederate states . . . negroes, most of them, who could not carry their own states, though they would be of considerable help in carrying the nominating Convention.

§ 6

The Convention met. It was an exciting affair. Conkling, the silver-tongued orator of his time, stood under the banner of New York and put Grant's name before the Convention.

> And when asked what state he
>   hails from,
> Our sole reply shall be,
> He hails from Appomattox
> And its famous apple tree.

So said Conkling—and the Convention and the galleries roared and thundered until the building shook.

It looked like an easy victory for Grant, but the inscrutable Fates had decided that the victor of Appomattox had better let another man have a try at the job. In the first place, the Convention voted down the proposition to adopt the unit rule. In the next place Elihu B. Washburne got himself put in nomination—and Grant never forgave him for it. Washburne did not show much strength in the Convention, but all the votes he got came from delegates who would have voted for Grant. And, in third place, John Sherman, of Ohio, was put up as a candidate. He had no chance of winning; most of his votes were taken from the Grant column.

On the first ballot Grant received 304 votes against 284 for Blaine, and 167 were scattered among the candidates of lesser degree. The number necessary for a choice was 378.

On the third ballot one delegate from Pennsylvania voted for James A. Garfield, and he hung on—a sole Garfield delegate—through the long hours and days. On the thirty-fourth ballot sixteen delegates joined the man from Pennsylvania, and on the thirty-sixth 382 delegates went over to the Garfield side. But Grant's Old Guard held out to the last. On the final ballot he had 306 votes.

Grant's mortification was profound. "My friends have not been honest with me," he said. "I can't afford to be defeated. They should not have placed me in nomination unless they felt perfectly sure of my success." He did not send any letter or telegram of congratulation to Garfield, and for awhile it was rumored that he had made up his mind to support Hancock, the Democratic nominee. But he had no such intention; he was merely sulking in a sullen, Jovian manner. Before the summer was over he had called on Garfield and he let the newspapers know that he was for the Republican candidate.

§ 7

Then came the question of what he should do for a living.
He had about one hundred thousand dollars, the income from
which he considered quite insufficient to support himself and
his wife. The sons were looking out for themselves. Frederick
was then a Lieutenant-Colonel in the army; Ulysses, Jr., had
married the daughter of Hon. Jerome B. Chaffee, a wealthy
man, and was in business in Wall Street; and Jesse, having
passed through the Columbia Law School, was getting along
very well.

At this time of his life Grant had a passion for money. It
was a natural urge that often comes to men who have long associated with men of money without ever having much—or any
—themselves. As he grew older his reverence for money increased. He wanted to play a star part in the financial world,
yet he had absolutely no capacity for commercial or financial
operations. But he thought he had—and his delusion was not
as strange as it seems. It is common among men who have
had no experience in business affairs. He could have lived very
well on his five thousand dollars a year in Galena, but he wanted
to live in New York, where five thousand dollars, even at that
time, did not go very far.

But something was being done by his friends. George W.
Jones, proprietor of the New York *Times*, conceived the idea
of a permanent fund for the General and his family. The sum
of two hundred and fifty thousand dollars was raised by popular subscription, and the principal invested under the direction
of trustees. The chief subscribers, in addition to the *Times*,
were Jay Gould, John W. Mackay and William H. Vanderbilt,
who contributed twenty-five thousand dollars each. It seems
strange that Grant would allow Jay Gould to contribute to
his support, but he did. The income from the fund was about
fifteen thousand dollars a year.

Certainly this income should have been sufficient for his needs. It did not seem to be so, however.

In 1881 he made another trip to Mexico, and soon afterward was elected president of the Mexican Southern Railway. The arrangement with this railroad was peculiar. I cannot make out that he received either salary or stock for his services. What was behind it I do not know; perhaps his love for Mexico and the Mexicans.

He settled down in New York and purchased an ugly red brick house at number 3 East Sixty-sixth Street. Every day he drove down to Wall Street, sat for awhile in the offices of the Mexican Southern Railway, smoked many cigars and signed a few papers. His life was that of a complacent bourgeois, fattening into old age and patting the heads of grandchildren.

His peace was soon to be disturbed violently by a man young enough to be his son, and of whom he had never heard until the fall of 1880.

CHAPTER XXXI

THE TRAGEDY OF GRANT & WARD

§ 1

IN the late 1870's a plausible young man circulated among the banks and money changers of lower Manhattan. His name was Ferdinand Ward, and he was a lad of sound upbringing, the son of a minister of the gospel. A brilliant medley of optimistic financial ideas filled his mind. He professed to know how to lend money at a high rate of interest without the hazard of loss; and he had schemes for paying off the national debt, for reducing taxes, for buying cheap and selling dear without detriment to either the buyer or the seller. He was attractive, magnetic and forceful; but behind all this heat lightning of high finance there was a heavy cloudbank of rascality.

Ward got a position as a clerk on the Produce Exchange. He began to speculate in flour contracts and made a success of it. Then he quit his job, bought and sold railroad securities, made more money, and was called "The Young Napoleon of Wall Street." Men who feel that it is their mission to live up to the reputation of an artificial personality seldom have any scruples. In carrying out his Napoleonic rôle Ward lost whatever principles he had ever possessed.

The main fact about him is that he never had, from the beginning, any financial ability, but only an overwhelming desire. His early successes were accidents, and the rest was reputation and wind.

Ward met "Buck" Grant—otherwise Ulysses, Jr.—in Wall Street. "Buck" was about twenty-eight years old, was getting ready to marry a rich man's daughter, and was feeling like a

478

money-maker himself. The two young men organized the banking and brokerage firm of Grant & Ward. General Grant's son was a large asset in the way of reputation; his connection with the firm gave it a good standing, but Ulysses, Jr. never knew anything about the business, although he thought he knew all about it. He was, in fact, nothing more than a slow-witted figurehead. All he knew was that he received about three thousand dollars a month as his share of the profits, therefore he concluded that the business was sound.

General Grant thought so, too. He was looking around for an occupation, and he had an idea that he would like to be connected with this enterprising firm. Young Mr. Ward thought that would be a wonderful arrangement. General Grant's connection would make the business a national institution. Millions of profit. But—cautious inquiry by Mr. Ward —how much actual cash could the General put into the business? It did not occur to the General that his name alone would have been worth a couple of million dollars to any legitimate financial concern. He did not think of that. After some reflection he said that he could raise one hundred thousand dollars.

"Buck" had already invested one hundred thousand—probably his father-in-law's money—and it was decided that the General should put in a hundred thousand more. Ward agreed to take two hundred thousand dollars as his share; he would contribute securities for that amount. He explained that, as he was actively interested in many corporations, all his ready money was tied up, but he would turn over his share in gilt-edged stocks and bonds. So the Grants put up two hundred thousand dollars in cash, and Ward brought in a bundle of doubtful bonds and worthless stock.

Ward spoke of getting government contracts, and of financing concerns that had obtained contracts at Washington. No; the General was flatly opposed to anything that would make money out of the government. He said:

I did not think it was suitable for me to have my name connected with government contracts, and I knew that there was no large profit in them except by dishonest measures. There are some men who get government contracts year in and year out, and whether they manage their affairs dishonestly to make a profit or not, they are sometimes supposed to, and I did not think it was any place for me.

That point having been settled rather emphatically, Mr. Ward went around among the banks and whispered to them that through the General's influence the firm had obtained government contracts that would be enormously profitable, but that secrecy was essential; it would never do to let it be known that the General was . . . you know . . . well, you know. The bankers nodded wisely. They understood that some things had better be left unsaid. They were hypnotized by the shining aura of General Grant. He was the first ex-President of the United States who had become a member of a Wall Street concern. The financial district added several yards to its mantle of dignity.

The General heard some rumors of the firm having government contracts, and he asked Ward if they were true. "Of course not," Ward declared—and he explained that the contracts they were financing had nothing to do with the government. That statement was correct. He told the Grants that the firm was advancing money to certain contractors who were building an extension of the Erie railroad. These men had very profitable contracts to lay down sections of the road, but did not have the capital to finance their operations. Grant & Ward were advancing the necessary funds, and in return would take a large share of the profit. That was true, too. But the total amount of these railroad contracts was not large; the firm never transacted much real business. Most of its operations existed in the imagination.

Ward was an insatiable gambler. The fire of speculation

GENERAL GRANT ABOUT 1881

Photograph taken while Grant was in business in Wall Street.

From the Collection of Frederick H. Meserve

GENERAL GRANT AT MOUNT McGREGOR

The last photograph that was ever made of General Grant. It shows
him as he appeared at Mount McGregor shortly before his death. He
wrote his *Memoirs* in an invalid chair.

ran through his veins. The firm of Grant & Ward existed
solely for the purpose of supplying him with means to break
the back of the Wall Street stock market. I have come to
the conclusion that he never cared much for money. He was
an exhibitionist, an actor, and his proper place in life was the
dramatic stage. He had to show off; he had to live up to the
glamor that surrounds a young Napoleon of Finance; he
dreamed of tearing the stock market to pieces and of emerging
from its debris with ten million dollars clutched in his hand
and the white light of the newspapers beating on his handsome
figure.

If he had not been haunted by his early glittering reputation
he might have made a stunning success of the firm of Grant &
Ward. With General Grant at the head of the concern he
could have built a huge stock and bond business. As it was,
checks from old soldiers and their friends floated in, and the
General was told by the senders, in long-winded letters which
mingled war stories with tales of penury, to invest the money
to the best advantage. These remittances were turned over to
Ward, who promised that all the General's old friends would
be taken care of faithfully.

Ward's chief method of raising money was very simple. It
could have imposed only on a community as ingenuous as Wall
Street. In an ordinary country village he would have had difficulty in borrowing a ten-dollar bill. His plan was to approach
wealthy men with his story about government contracts. The
contracts were immensely profitable, he would explain, but the
firm, with its small capitalization, was unable to finance them.
They had decided to take in a few men of means—close-
mouthed, important people—who would lend the firm money,
and accept a share of the profits. It was a big thing . . .
very big. "Well, let's see the contracts," these men of substance would say. Ward could not do that; the General had
the contracts in his possession. You see, the General is in a
ticklish position in this matter. "But here are a few orders,"

and Ward would produce forged telegrams from Washington, ordering large quantities of this and that at prices considerably above those prevailing in the current market.

These tricks roped in a number of millionaires, and others not so wealthy. In a short time after a loan was made to Grant & Ward the lender would receive a handsome check as a first division of the profits. This dividend was invariably paid out of the principal of the loan. Thereafter, similar checks, accompanied by cheerful letters, came at irregular intervals. In the meantime Ward was looking up new victims. It was a sort of endless chain.

§ 2

Ward's main reliance, however was not on individuals, but on the Marine National Bank. He had become acquainted with James D. Fish, its president, a gray-haired man of about fifty, and they grew into a pair of conspirators.

I think Fish was deceived by Ward at first, and by the time he saw through the deception both he and the bank were so thoroughly involved that he thought there was nothing else to do but to take sides with Ward and become his accomplice. It is certain that, whatever he had been at the start, he was fully as dishonest as Ward before the end.

The bank certified Grant & Ward's checks in the most reckless fashion, and permitted huge overdrafts, which Fish attempted to disguise by bookkeeping tricks. This could not go on without something being done for Fish, so Ward—with the consent of the Grants—admitted him a special partner in the firm. He drew three thousand dollars a month as his share of the firm's profits.

The Marine National Bank was also graciously accommodating in the matter of discounts. All the clerks in the Grant & Ward establishment signed promissory notes for such extravagant sums as fifty or sixty thousand dollars. The bank discounted them, and turned over the proceeds to Ward. The colored messenger of the firm signed a note for eighty thousand dollars, and that, too, was discounted.

Ward was an expert in human avarice. He understood clearly that as long as investors get dividends they have no interest in the source of their prosperity. One of the General's friends came in. He was on his way to Europe. Long talk about the war . . . what Lee might have done, and what Grant did . . . the condition of the country . . . pretty bad, with Confederate generals sitting, unashamed, in Congress. But the crops are good, and there is plenty of money. And, by the way, the friend of wartime days has fifty thousand dollars to invest. Could the General do anything safe and profitable with it? The General did not know; he would ask Mr. Ward. The General taps a bell on his desk; Mr. Ward enters. Why, yes, as it is one of the General's friends, we will take the money and do our best. Of course, it's all uncertain; you understand that? The friend understood it.

On his return from Europe six months later the General's friend appeared again at the offices of Grant & Ward. My fifty thousand dollars. Ward reflected a moment. Oh, yes, I remember something about that . . . but we have so many customers, you know . . . I don't know how it stands, but I'll look and see. . . .

In a few minutes Ward returned with a check for two hundred and fifty thousand dollars. "You've done fairly well," he remarked, as he handed the check to the astonished investor. Grant's wartime friend held the check in his hand and stared at it. A quarter of a million dollars. Why not make more? He gave it back to Ward. "Take it and go on," he said. "Invest it again." Ward said he would; he took the check, and that was the last of that veteran's fifty thousand dollars. This occurred just before the smash.

Fish began to be troubled. He was headed straight for disaster, and he knew it, but the brassy confidence of Ward

sustained him. Through the fog that surrounds their operations one sees here and there a glint of light. Both Fish
and Ward appeared to believe that Ward's speculations would
eventually produce a large fortune. In that happy event, the
bank would get its money back, everybody else would be paid,
and the whole episode would be dropped into the sea of
oblivion with a stone tied around its neck.

In the meantime the Grant family became even more deeply
involved. Ulysses, Jr., induced Senator Chaffee, his father-in-
law, to put five hundred thousand dollars in the concern as a
loan; and the money-making chances looked so promising that
Colonel Frederick Grant, the General's eldest son, resigned
from the army and came into the firm, bringing some of his
wife's fortune.

Ward looked closely after the General. Every morning
he would put twenty-five excellent Havana cigars on the General's desk; and during the day he was always going in and
out of the General's office, watching his callers, listening, and
taking a peep at his mail.

Grant's carelessness was monumental. Apparently he would
sign anything that was put before him. He signed one letter
which rose from the past to vex him after the exposure came.
This letter was addressed to Fish, as president of the Marine
National Bank, and was dated July 6, 1882. It read:

> My dear Mr. Fish: In relation to the matter of dis-
> counts kindly made by you for account of Grant & Ward,
> I would say that I think the investments are safe, and I
> am willing that Mr. Ward should derive what profit he
> can for the firm that the use of my name and influence
> may bring.

Fish declared in court that he was inspired to commit the
bank so heavily because of the statements made in this letter.
That was not the truth; the bank was already involved head
and ears before the letter was written.

Grant said that he did not remember the letter, although he admitted that the signature was genuine. The body of the epistle was in another handwriting. Ward, in his day of confession and remorse, admitted that he wrote the letter to Fish and slipped it in a pile of others awaiting the General's signature. He did not give them to the General until a few minutes before Grant had to leave the office to take the steamer to Long Branch, where he had a summer cottage. He signed the letter without reading it.

When Fish was on trial he said that he had endeavored to talk things over with Grant and had written him: "You and I don't meet; it might be better if we did. We are more conservative than the young men who run the business. I understand these notes which I have just discounted are to raise money for government contracts." All this was nothing more than an attempt to establish an epistolary justification on Fish's part. There could have been no difficulty about seeing General Grant. All that Fish needed to do would have been to walk over to the office of Grant & Ward and have a plain talk with the head of the firm.

There seems to have been an amazing amount of reticence all around. Grant testified, in the court proceedings, that he and Fish had passed a week-end together, but nothing was said about their business relations. The General wanted to talk business, so he declared, and he remarked to Fish that Ward was a clever young man. Fish made no reply, and there the discussion ended.

The swindling operations of Grant & Ward continued for three years. It is almost inconceivable that stealing of such magnificent dimensions could have run on so long without tripping up somewhere; but it did. The balance-sheets of the firm were pieces of fiction. As Ward became more and more entangled he kept adding to the firm's fictional assets, and therefore made a better showing on paper. Just before the end the firm had a higher commercial rating than ever before.

My readers may think that I am assuming Grant's innocence out of charity for him or respect for his memory. Not at all. The evidence proves conclusively that he was entirely ignorant of what was going on. He put all his own money in the concern, then he became so impressed by Ward's business ability that he induced his wife to invest her savings. His sisters sent whatever money they could spare, to be used by the firm. His little niece inherited twelve thousand dollars, and that was turned over to Mr. Ward. Many of his friends and relatives, on his recommendation, put in various sums. These investments were, of course, a total loss.

All he ever got out of the firm in cash was his living expenses. But he thought he was getting rich. On May 1, 1884, he estimated that his share in the firm was worth not less than $2,400,000.

He experienced the self-satisfaction of a man who has desired wealth all his life and has at last obtained it. He drove down to Wall Street in his carriage every day, and was looked upon as one of the leading figures of the financial metropolis.

The editors of the *Century Magazine* tried to persuade him to write two or three articles on his war experiences—five hundred dollars an article—but he said flatly that he was not a writer, and that he wanted to forget the Civil War, anyway.

§ 3

The end came with the explosive suddenness of an earthquake. On Sunday, May 4, 1884, Ward appeared at General Grant's house and told the General and Ulysses, Jr., that the Marine Bank was in difficulties. The City Chamberlain had drawn out three hundred thousand dollars of the city's funds on Saturday; it left the bank short of cash.

Well, that's too bad, said the Grants, father and son, but what has that got to do with us?

Ward explained that as the Marine Bank had six hundred

and sixty thousand dollars of Grant & Ward's money on deposit, it would cripple the firm seriously if the bank were to fail. It's only temporary, you know—Ward continued. The bank is sound enough, but it will need a day or two to realize on its assets. What it needs just now is some ready cash.

Oh, yes; so that's it . . . a little short of cash.

Solemn faces in the Grant parlor. The air was saturated with the gloom of business inexperience, through which Ward's rascality shone like a candle. Well, what shall we do?

Ward said that if the firm could raise three hundred thousand dollars as a loan and deposit it in the Marine Bank, everything would be straightened out. He thought the General might borrow one hundred and fifty thousand dollars somewhere, and Ward himself would try to borrow an equal amount. It was to be a loan for one day only. The firm would return the money to the lenders on Monday or Tuesday.

Half an hour later Grant hobbled into the home of William H. Vanderbilt on Fifth Avenue. He had fallen on ice the day before Christmas and still limped from a strained muscle.

Vanderbilt, colossus of money, whose cynicism was mixed with the boredom of continual success, sat listening silently, his hairy hands folded across his waistcoat of black broadcloth. Mr. Vanderbilt was an intense realist, and was accustomed to speak his mind without reserve. "I don't care anything about the Marine National Bank," he said. "It can fail without disturbing me; and as for Grant & Ward—what I've heard about that firm would not justify me in lending it a dime. But I'll lend you a hundred and fifty thousand dollars personally." He reached for his checkbook. "To you—to General Grant—I'm making this loan, and not to the firm."

"Thank you. It will be only until to-morrow," the General remarked meekly. Vanderbilt grunted his assent.

Grant felt the humiliation of one who borrows money from strangers, but even then no doubt of the substantial quality of his own fortune came into his mind.

When he got back to his house he found Ward there again. Ward had not been able to borrow any money at all, though he had been to Jay Gould and others. Grant turned over the Vanderbilt check to him. It was never deposited to the firm's account. Ward cashed it early next morning and put the money in his pocket.

The Marine National Bank closed its doors on May 7th. It had been unable to meet its obligations at the Clearing House that morning. The news came that the failure had been brought about by overdrafts on the part of Grant & Ward. "But that can't be," said Ulysses, Jr. "We have more than six hundred thousand dollars on deposit."

Mr. Ward did not appear at the office—he never went there again—but the cashier brought the bank book to the Grants and they thumbed its pages. "Well, there's six hundred and sixty thousand dollars in the bank; that's certain," said the General, "and what about Mr. Vanderbilt's check?"

As a matter of fact, Grant & Ward did not have a cent in the bank, and the firm had overdrawn its account, through Fish's complicity, to the extent of two million dollars.

The Grants sat uneasily in the office and waited in a state of suspended interrogation. Mr. Ward would know; why isn't he here? Somebody had better go over to his house in Brooklyn and see him. Somebody did. Ward admitted that the closing of the bank was a blow to the firm, but he declared that Grant & Ward was too strong financially to be vitally affected. "It will be all right," he said. "We've got to raise a little money; that's all." He shook hands, patted them all on the back, and gave them some more vague conversation.

But the catastrophe was too cataclysmic to be charmed away.

The firm failed; Ward had gutted it clean. It was as bare of insides as a planked mackerel. They sent Ward to jail . . . the melancholy resource of the victims of swindlers. Fish was already in jail; when he heard that Ward had arrived he said melodramatically: "Don't let me get at him. I'll kill the scoundrel."

The Grants convened in their red brick home on Sixty-sixth Street. Where do we stand in the way of money? Pocketbooks emptied on the table. Total assets, eighty dollars in cash, and about one hundred dollars besides that Mrs. Grant had somewhere around the house.

The General lay in bed, in the darkness, during the long hours of the night, suffering the torture of those who learn too late. *If I had only known* . . . words which are like vials of bottled death. And as the days of his life rose before him in memory he sighed at the thought of poverty and helplessness in his old age. Even that could be endured, but how could he endure the remembrance of swindled investors, and of the name of Grant being held up to scorn . . . or pity, which is worse than scorn?

When the full story of Ward's duplicity had come out Grant said, in the melancholy tone of a man who has lost all confidence in human nature: "I have made it the rule of my life to trust a man long after other people gave him up; but I don't see how I can trust any human being again."

To his niece, Clara Cramer, whose aunt had lost all her savings in the failure, he wrote:

> Financially the Grant family is ruined for the present, and by the most stupendous frauds ever perpetrated. But your Aunt Jennie must not fret over it. I still have a home and as long as I live she shall enjoy it as a matter of right; at least until she recovers what she has lost. Fred is young, active, honest and intelligent, and will work with a vim to recuperate his losses. Of course his first effort will be to repay his aunts.

But there was the fund of two hundred and fifty thousand dollars which had been subscribed for him on his return from his world tour. It was held by trustees who were empowered to pay him only the interest. Fifteen thousand dollars a year . . . that was a comfort. Then, all of a sudden, the fund ceased to bear interest. It had been invested in railroad stocks, and the railroads had fallen on evil days. The trustees notified him that there was no more money to be had.

Tradesmen's bills for household necessities came pouring in, and the family would not have been able to buy its daily bread if Charles Wood, of Lansingburgh, N. Y., a stranger to all the Grants, had not generously sent a check for one thousand dollars to the General. He begged that this amount be accepted as a loan "on account of my share for services ending in April, 1865." A few days later the Mexican minister at Washington, moved by Grant's long friendship for Mexico, forwarded a thousand dollars which he wanted the family to take as a gift. They finally took it as a loan. It was on these two contributions that the General and Mrs. Grant lived for some time.

Mr. Vanderbilt said nothing about his one hundred and fifty thousand dollars, but the Grants looked around to ascertain some way to give him security. The General turned over to him the Grant farm near St. Louis, his house in Philadelphia, his home on East Sixty-sixth Street—which was Mrs. Grant's property—and all his personal belongings, such as the swords and trophies that had been presented to him. Vanderbilt wanted to return these possessions, but the Grants declined to take them back. Eventually Vanderbilt gave the curios and swords to the United States government, and they are now in the museum at Washington.

§ 4

Many of the newspapers criticized Grant for going into the firm, and others went so far as to declare that he had profited by Ward's swindling operations. Letters by the hundreds came from the depositors of the Marine National Bank and the customers of Grant & Ward; and Fish—put on trial for wrecking the bank—claimed that he had been led on by the fact that General Grant was in the business, and especially by the General's letter, which had assured him that everything was all right.

Fish was tried first, and General Grant was a witness. He was too ill to go to court, so his deposition had to be taken. He stated that he considered himself merely a special partner in the firm of Grant & Ward, and liable only for his own investment. He did not recall having written any letter to Fish, and his memory was poor on almost everything connected with the disaster. Fish was found guilty and sentenced to seven years in the penitentiary.

The expert accountants finally plowed through the labyrinth of Grant & Ward's accounts. They discovered that the firm had two distinct and different sets of books—those in the office, having been kept for show purposes, were false in every particular. The real state of things was revealed in a secret set of books kept by Ward himself.

The liabilities of the firm amounted to the enormous total of \$16,792,640 . . . and its little handful of assets counted up to only \$67,174 . . . yet the official set of books showed assets of over \$27,000,000.

When Ward was brought into court his mind was vague, and he seemed to be too broken and bewildered to give a coherent account of himself. He admitted that the firm had been insolvent for two years, and he declared that he did not know what had become of the money, except that he "had lost" it.

He was convicted of grand larceny, and sent to the state penitentiary for ten years.

CHAPTER XXXII

THE HOUSE OF PAIN

§ 1

THE disaster had the hazy, intangible features of a dream. Grotesque shapes, their faces washed in darkness, moved dimly behind the sharply molded actualities. Events dissolved into the deepening shadows of an inscrutable Fate.

Had it all happened?

Yes; it had happened. Ward and Fish were in jail; and there was the office with the sad-eyed accountants trying to disentangle the records; and the bored deputy sheriffs; and the columns of scandal in the newspapers. That was all real enough . . . and there was the pile of letters on Grant's table . . . pathetic, tearful letters from people who had lost their savings.

The great adventure of Ulysses Grant, with its splendid years . . . the epic of the marching men . . . the triumphs and the adulation . . . all had come to an end in poverty and despair.

And there was the puzzling stab of pain in his throat. At first it had been a minor discomfort. He had felt it for the first time one day when he was eating a peach; a sharp, cutting sensation at the root of his tongue. Not much attention was given to it . . . he had caught a cold, perhaps. But it continued long after a cold should have disappeared.

§ 2

In the dejected silence of the General's reflections came the remembrance of the *Century Magazine's* offer to purchase articles by him on the Civil War. Three articles they wanted, but they said they would take more, at five hundred dollars each. Fifteen hundred dollars for the three; it would help.

The General wrote an article on the battle of Shiloh; it appears to-day in the *Century* war papers—a dry, informative story, in terse English, as devoid of decoration as a bale of hay. The five hundred dollars came, and he wrote on, forgetting the present, and living again in the time of the Civil War.

Samuel L. Clemens, better known as Mark Twain, delivered a lecture at Chickering Hall one night in November, 1884; and as he was leaving the building he met Richard Watson Gilder, the editor of the *Century*, who told him that General Grant had written some war articles for the magazine.

Mr. Clemens was a publisher himself. He was the chief owner of Charles L. Webster & Co., a concern that published Mark Twain's own books and sold them—not through bookstores, but by agents who made canvasses from house to house. He says in his *Autobiography:*

> Gilder went on to describe how eagerly General Grant had entertained the proposition to write when it had last been put to him, and how poor he evidently was. . . .
>
> The thing which astounded me was that, admirable man as Gilder certainly is, and with a heart which is in the right place, it had never seemed to occur to him that to offer General Grant five hundred dollars for a magazine article was not only the monumental injustice of the nineteenth century, but of all centuries. He ought to have known that if he had given General Grant a check for ten thousand dollars, the sum would still have been trivial; that if he had paid him twenty thousand dollars that would still have been inadequate. . . .

The next day Clemens went to 3 East Sixty-sixth Street. He was already well acquainted with the Grant family, and he had been in the habit of dropping in occasionally to smoke a few cigars with the General. Grant told him that he had written some articles, and was about to begin the writing of his *Memoirs*, which he supposed the Century Company would publish as a book.

Well, as a friend—and if it was not a private matter—Clemens said he would like to know what the Century proposed to pay him for the *Memoirs*. Grant was ready to tell all about it. The Century people were going to pay ten per cent royalty on every copy of his book. They thought they might possibly sell as many as twenty-five thousand copies, but they were not willing to guarantee anything.

Clemens says he told the General that "the *Century* offer was simply absurd and should not be considered for an instant." Grant admitted that he did not know anything about the conditions of the publishing business or how much publishers pay authors for their work. What should they pay? The contract was not signed yet; there was time to change it.

Clemens wanted the *Memoirs* for his own publishing concern. He was willing to give a royalty of twenty per cent; and he told Grant that he would certainly sell more than a hundred thousand copies of the book. Moreover he was willing to pay the General $25,000 as advance royalty. If the Century Company can meet these terms, give them the book —Clemens said. But I know they won't do it—he continued— and then, in that case, I'd like to do business with you.

The appearance of the first of the Grant articles in the *Century* had the effect of increasing the circulation of the magazine to the extent of fifty thousand copies. Thereupon, the Century people, out of the goodness of their hearts, sent the General a check for fifteen hundred dollars as additional payment for his articles, but they could not see their way clear to compete with Mr. Clemens for the *Memoirs*. The head of the Century said he would not guarantee a sale of twenty-five thousand copies on any book ever published.

Charles L. Webster & Co. got the contract, and Grant began the dictation of his *Memoirs* on February 21, 1885.

The gnawing pain in his throat had been diagnosed as cancer, and the news appeared in the daily papers. The uncertain physicians, doubtful of their own knowledge, came and went, while the General sat in an armchair in his library and talked huskily to a stenographer. His face was lean and drawn into deep lines of suffering; now and then he would have to stop his dictation because of pain. As the disease progressed he huddled more deeply in his chair under a pile of shawls and blankets.

After a month or two of dictation his voice failed. Thereafter he sat with a writing board on his lap and wrote with a pencil on large sheets of paper. There were days when he could do nothing at all—when his eyes had the dim, earth-forgotten look of a man already in another world.

The writing of the *Memoirs* was a race with death. He hoped that the book would provide something for his wife to live on after he had gone, and he clung desperately to this earth until the manuscript was completed. The last chapter was written about a week before he died. He never saw the book in print.

The fortune that Grant had been so eager to make during most of his life was earned after he was dead. Mark Twain's firm sold three hundred thousand copies of the *Memoirs* and turned over about $450,000 in royalties to the General's widow.

Adam Badeau rose in vehement self-assertion soon after the funeral obsequies, and announced that he, Badeau, friend and assistant of General Grant, had written most of the *Memoirs*. He made a demand on the family for ten thousand dollars as payment for his share in the collaboration, and he intimated that he was letting them off pretty easy at that, as the work was practically all his own. The Grant family resisted his claim, and the evidence in the case does not bear out Badeau's contention. He did assist in the necessary research. He verified dates and names, and helped Colonel Frederick Grant in arranging the manuscript for the printer. But it appears that he had been paid for his services as the work went on. I have not the least doubt that Grant himself wrote the entire book. I have read every word of the two big volumes, and the work reads as if it had been written by a very sick man. The conditions under which it was written make it a heroic literary creation. The dying man, humble in the presence of poverty and death, turned his memory to scenes of long ago, and scribbled words that were to be printed after he had passed away . . . a message that Death sends to Life.

The Grants said they would be willing to give Badeau ten thousand dollars as extra compensation, considering the great sale of the book, if he would stop claiming that he was the author. But Badeau declared that it was a matter of principle as well as money. He sued the Grants and took his case to the public through the newspapers. Charles A. Dana, of the New York *Sun*, offered to pay Badeau ten thousand dollars out of his own pocket if he would shut up—and eventually somebody did pay him, but whoever did it has been kept a close secret. It may have been the Grants.

§ 3

In February, 1885, Grant's physicians began to issue bulletins to the public, and on fine afternoons a crowd of people would stand in front of his house. I do not know why they stood there; the habit of standing in front of houses is a profound mystery that has never been explained. The newspapers said that the General's admirers loitered about his door out of respect for the stricken man, but we may reasonably believe that their real motive was curiosity. Grant, haggard and thin, would go to a window occasionally and smile and bow.

For some time his friends had been trying to help him by

putting through Congress a bill that would restore him to his former rank in the army, with a provision for his retirement immediately on full pay. This measure had been defeated several times by the Congressional fear of establishing a precedent. The physicians said, in their first bulletin: "The action of Congress in refusing to pass the bill restoring him to his honors has been very depressing to him."

The medical men, in the traditional manner of their profession, hid the truth from him; or perhaps they were not sure themselves of the nature of his disease. But he could not eat. His throat would close with a spasm of pain when he tried to swallow solid food. His meals were limited to liquids, such as soups, and he had to gulp the contents of a bowl at a single swallow to get it down before his throat contracted. In weight he was reduced from about two hundred pounds to one hundred and forty-five.

Other doctors were consulted . . . specialists in cancer . . . men who thrust mirrors down his throat . . . men with grave faces who carried test tubes.

In a final spurt of precedent-smashing generosity Congress did restore him to his place in the army. When a telegram came announcing that the bill had passed the sick man received the news without interest; he turned his head away wearily. It came too late to awaken even a flicker of response. He was living in a universe where Pain was God. Pain covered his sky and filled his world. Pain . . . and the book. The book had to be done, and at the thought of it his feeble hands would flutter over the writing board, and the scrawled white sheets would fall around his feet.

At times the doctor's anodynes, given to soothe his intolerable suffering, would send his mind reeling in a fantastic daze. One day he suddenly rose in his chair and his haunted eyes wandered about the room. "The cannon did it," he whispered, and clutched his throat. "The cannon did it," he repeated to his frightened family, as he sank back in his chair.

Brisk people came, and somehow managed to get in the house. Snappy photographers who set up their easels to take a few pictures . . . photographers who tiptoed about the room and spoke in low tones. And a sculptor who deftly modeled a bust while the General looked on without speaking.

On the twenty-seventh of March he was taken for a carriage drive in Central Park. It was a clear, sunny day. The park was full of children, and there was the sheen of serene lakes and of buds bursting into bloom. He felt better, but when he returned the lawyers were at his house to take his deposition in the case of James D. Fish, former president of the Marine National Bank, then on trial for embezzlement. He testified, partly in whispers and partly on written sheets of paper. The lawyers' examination lasted only an hour, but it left him exhausted, and that night the family thought he was about to die.

An astrologer had predicted his death on the last day of March. The members of the family had read the prediction in a newspaper, and when the thirty-first day of March came they wandered about the house in anxiety. But it turned out to be the best day he had had in months. His first month's pay as a retired general arrived. He held the bills in his lap and passed them out in rolls to his wife and children. He said that evening: "I am much better; I think I shall pull through, after all."

In April he seemed to be improving. He swallowed with less pain, and the newspapers reported that he was on the way to recovery. It was a false hope.

§ 4

The family sent for the Rev. J. P. Newman, a fashionable preacher of the day, whose name was constantly in the news-papers. They did not want the General to die without religious consolation, and the General said that he did not care how much praying was done around him, if it made his wife and children feel better. Mark Twain wrote (*Autobiography*, Vol. II, p. 69):

> Some of the speeches put into General Grant's mouth were to the last degree incredible to people who knew the General, since they were such gaudy and flowering misrepresentations of that plain-spoken man's utterances.
>
> About the 14th or 15th of April, Reverend Mr. N——— reported that upon visiting the General in his sick chamber, the General pressed his hand and delivered himself of this astounding remark: "Thrice have I been in the shadow of the Valley of Death and thrice have I come out again."
>
> General Grant never used flowers of speech, and, dead or alive, he never could have uttered anything like that, either as a quotation or otherwise.

Reverend Mr. Newman was a part of the family circle from his arrival in April until Grant died. In his excess of zeal he made something of a fool of himself. While the General was asleep in his chair Mr. Newman sprinkled water over him and announced through the newspapers that Grant had been converted and baptized. But ex-Senator Chaffee, whose daughter married Ulysses, Jr., and who was at the Grant home every day, said: "There has been a good deal of nonsense in the papers about Dr. Newman's visits. General Grant does not believe that Dr. Newman's prayers will save him. He allows the doctor to pray simply because he does not want to hurt his feelings." The *Christian Statesman* declared that, "It is not on record that he spoke at any time of the Savior, or expressed his sense of dependence on His atonement and mediation." When he was asked near the end what had been his best comfort in life he replied, "The comfort of the consciousness that I have lived a good, honorable life." The New York *Independent*, a religious weekly, took up that statement like a challenge and declared: "It is not enough; great men and small must build their hopes on Christ, or they will build in vain."

Grant was never converted to Rev. Mr. Newman's set of beliefs, but nevertheless he had a religion of his own, in which honorable conduct, truth and justice were the chief articles of faith. He was not an atheist. He believed in God and hoped for a future life. In his last letter to his wife he says something about meeting her in another world. He wrote this letter shortly before his death and put it in his pocket. It says, in part:

> Look after our dear children and direct them in the paths of rectitude. It would distress me far more to hear that one of them could depart from an honorable, upright and virtuous life than it would to know that they were prostrated on a bed of sickness from which they were never to arise alive. They have never given us any cause for alarm on this account, and I trust they never will. With these few injunctions and the knowledge I have of your love and affection and the dutiful affection of all our children, I bid you a final farewell, until we meet in another and, I trust, better world. You will find this on my person after my demise.

The scorpions of remorse run through these words. The Grant & Ward fiasco, with all its shame and ignominy, was in his mind as he wrote. Honor, uprightness, fairness—these were Grant's cardinal virtues. He would rather hear of his children prostrated "on a bed of sickness from which they were never to arise alive" than to know that they had departed from an "honorable, upright and virtuous life." He was thinking of himself. He had not left the path of honor and rectitude, but many people thought he had, and it filled his last days with sorrow. And he says, as plainly as the symbolism of words can speak, that he had rather be there in torture than to have to face the world again. There was nothing left for him to do—and for Grant life consisted of doing.

§ 5

As the hot weather came on the physicians decided that he had better be moved to the mountains, and on June 16, 1885, he was taken from New York City to Mount McGregor, near Saratoga, where he and the family occupied a cottage on the top of the mountain.

When the carriage that had brought him from his home arrived at the Grand Central Station the General got out and walked to the train on his son's arm. He was emaciated, pale, and so weak that he looked as if he would fall at every step. The officials of the railroad met him at the train. Some of them gave him a military salute, which he returned, raising his hand waveringly to his hat. Before he entered the train he turned around and took a long last look at the sky-line of New York.

He was asleep until the train neared West Point. Then he aroused himself and asked to be placed at the window so he could see the gray stone buildings of the military academy across the river. There stood West Point, just as it had stood forty-six years before when he had seen it for the first time. His mind was filled with the memory pictures of those early days, and he whispered an anecdote of cadet life.

At Mount McGregor he sat every day—until near the end—in the veranda of the cottage. Crowds of tourists would come by and gaze silently at him from the road. He seemed to like these attentions. They distracted his mind, and proved to him that his popularity was not wholly lost. Now and then some old-time friend would visit the cottage and sit with him for awhile. Among these friends of former days was General Simon B. Buckner, of Kentucky. How strangely Buckner appears, at times, in Grant's life . . . lending him money in New York, when he returned from California, out of the army and destitute . . . surrendering Fort Donelson to him, the first great Union victory of the war . . . and coming to Mount McGregor when the General was dying.

On the evening of July 22nd Grant wrote on his pad that he wanted to lie down in bed. For weeks he had slept in his easy chair. The physicians read the faint scrawl and looked at each other. To them it was a message full of meaning. As the sun set they said quietly to Grant's sons that the General had probably seen his last day on earth.

"Does it seem good to be in bed?" some one asked, leaning over him.

"Yes," he whispered. "So good."

As the evening wore on his hands and feet became icy cold, and his breathing was strained and difficult. He fell asleep limply. The family, curiously still and solemn, sat in the room. Occasionally one of the physicians would feel his pulse. It flickered like a dying fire.

At three o'clock Colonel Grant, hovering over his bedside, said:

"Father, is there anything you want?"

"Water," he whispered.

They tried to give him water to drink, but he could not swallow, so they placed a sponge in his mouth.

The stark night came to an end; the lamps gleamed faintly . . . little ghosts in the white light of daybreak. From the trees around the house came the twittering of birds.

At eight minutes past eight the dying man drew a deep breath, like a sleeper whose moment of awakening has come.

There was no more breathing. One of the physicians gently turned down the bedclothes and laid his head on the General's heart. Then he straightened up and crossed the dead man's wasted hands on his breast.

The members of the family, with handkerchiefs held to their eyes, went sobbing out of the room.

THE END

Bibliography

THE following works have been read in the preparation of this volume:

Adams, Charles Francis, *Studies Military and Diplomatic.* New York, 1911.

Adams, Henry, *The Education of Henry Adams.* Boston, 1918.

Adams, James Truslow, *New England in the Republic.* Boston, 1926.

Allen, Walter, *Governor Chamberlain's Administration in South Carolina.* New York, 1888.

Anderson, Robert, *An Artillery Officer in the Mexican War.* New York, 1911.

Avary, Myrta Lockett, *Dixie After the War.* New York, 1906.

Badeau, Adam, *Grant in Peace, from Appomattox to Mount McGregor.* Hartford, 1887.

Battles and Leaders of the Civil War. 4 vols. New York, 1887.

Beard, Charles A. and Mary R., *The Rise of American Civilization.* 2 vols. New York, 1927.

Blaine, James G., *Twenty Years of Congress.* 2 vols. Norwich, Conn., 1884.

Bradford, Gamaliel, *Confederate Portraits.* Boston, 1912.

—— *Union Portraits.* Boston, 1916.

Brawley, Benjamin, *A Short History of the American Negro.* New York, 1921.

Burgess, John W., *Reconstruction and the Constitution.* New York, 1902.

Butler, Benj. F., *Butler's Book.* Boston, 1892.

Channing, Edward, *A History of the United States.* 6 vols. New York, 1926.

Childs, George W., *Recollections of General Grant.* Philadelphia, 1890.

Clemens, Samuel L., *Mark Twain's Autobiography*, with an Introduction by Albert Bigelow Paine. 2 vols. New York, 1924.

Congressional Record, 44th Congress, 1st Session, Vol. IV. Feb. 10th to March 28, 1876.

Coolidge, Louis A., *The Life of U. S. Grant.* Boston, 1922.

Cramer, M. J., *Ulysses S. Grant: Conversations and Unpublished Letters.* New York, 1897.

Craven, John J., *The Prison Life of Jefferson Davis.* New York, 1866.

Davis, Jefferson, *The Rise and Fall of the Confederate Government.* New York, 1881.

Davis, Susan Lawrence, *Authentic History of the Ku Klux Klan, 1865-1877.* New York, 1924.

Davis, Varina Howell, *Jefferson Davis, A Memoir.* 2 vols. New York, 1890.

DeLeon, T. C., *Four Years in Rebel Capitals.* Mobile, 1890.

Dewitt, David M., *The Impeachment and Trial of Andrew Johnson.* New York, 1903.

Dodd, William E., *Jefferson Davis.* Philadelphia, 1907.

Eckenrode, H. J, *Jefferson Davis, President of the South.* New York, 1923.

Edwards, Franklin Spencer, *U. S. Grant.* Philadelphia, 1915.

Fiske, John, *The Mississippi Valley in the Civil War.* Boston, 1901.

Fite, Emerson D., *Social and Industrial Conditions in the North During the Civil War*. New York, 1910.

Fleming, Walter L., *Documentary History of Reconstruction*. 2 vols. Cleveland, 1907.

Fuess, Claude M., *The Life of Caleb Cushing*. 2 vols. New York, 1923.

Garland, Hamlin, *Ulysses S. Grant: His Life and Character*. New York, 1920.

Grant, Arthur Hastings, *The Grant Family Magazine*. Feb. 1900-Dec. 1901. Montclair, N. J.

Grant, Frederick D., *Reminiscences of General U. S. Grant*. A paper read before the Illinois Loyal Legion on Jan. 27, 1910, and published in Illinois State Historical Society Journal, vol. 7, 1914-15.

—— *With Grant at Vicksburg*, in *The Outlook*, July 2, 1898.

Grant Family Association, *Reports of the Reunions of the Association*, Nos. 1-7 (1899, 1901, 1903, 1905, 1907, 1914, 1922). Montclair, N. J.

Grant, Jesse R., *In the Days of My Father General Grant*. New York, 1925.

Grant, U. S., *Personal Memoirs*. 2 vols. New York, 1885.

—— *General Grant's Letters to a Friend, 1861-1880*. With an Introduction and Notes by James Grant Wilson. New York, 1897.

Greeley, Horace, *Recollections of a Busy Life*. New York, 1868.

Harrison, Mrs. Burton, *Recollections Grave and Gay*. New York, 1911.

Helper, H. R., *The Impending Crisis of the South: How to Meet It*. New York, 1857.

Henderson, G. F. R., *Stonewall Jackson and the American Civil War*. London, 1898.

Herbert, Hilary A., *The Abolition Crusade and Its Consequences*. New York, 1912.

Herndon, W. H., and Weik, J. W., *Life of Abraham Lincoln*. 3 vols. Springfield, Ill. n.d.

Hibben, Paxton, *Henry Ward Beecher: An American Portrait*. New York, 1927.

Hitchcock, Henry, *Marching with Sherman*. Edited by M. A. DeWolfe Howe. New Haven, 1927.

Hollister, O. J., *Life of Schuyler Colfax*. New York, 1886.

House Miscellaneous Documents, 44th Congress, 1st Session, 1876. No. 186.

House Report No. 31 of the Forty-first Congress, Second Session, 1869-70. Vol. 1.

Jones, J. B., *A Rebel War Clerk's Diary*. 2 vols. Philadelphia, 1866.

King, Charles, *The True Ulysses S. Grant*. Philadelphia, 1914.

Kirkland, Edward C., *The Peacemakers of 1864*. New York, 1927.

Lathers, Richard, *Reminiscences*. Edited by Alvan F. Sanborn. New York, 1907.

Lee, Captain Robert E., *Recollections and Letters of General Robert E. Lee*. New York, 1909.

Livermore, T. L., *Numbers and Losses in the Civil War in America, 1861-65*. Boston, 1900.

Longstreet, James, *From Manassas to Appomattox*. Philadelphia, 1896.

Lonn, Ella, *Reconstruction in Louisiana after 1868*. New York, 1918.

Lyman, Theodore, *Meade's Headquarters, 1863-65*. Boston, 1922.

Lynch, Denis Tilden, *"Boss" Tweed*. New York, 1927.

Lynch, John R., *The Facts of Reconstruction*. New York, 1913.

Maurice, Sir Frederick, *An Aide-de-Camp of Lee: The Papers of Colonel Charles Marshall*. Boston, 1927.

McCall, Samuel W., *Thaddeus Stevens*. Boston, 1899.

McClellan Carswell, *The Personal Memoirs and Military History of U. S. Grant versus The Record of the Army of the Potomac*. Boston, 1887.

McClellan, George B., *McClellan's Own Story*. New York, 1887.

McClure, A. K., *Recollections of Half a Century*. Salem, Mass., 1902.

McMaster, John B., *A History of the People of the United States During Lincoln's Administration*. New York, 1927.

McPherson, Edward, *The Political History of the United States of America During the Great Rebellion*. New York, 1864.

—— *The Political History of the United States of America During the Period of Reconstruction, 1865 to 1870*. Washington, 1880.

Moore, Albert Burton, *Conscription and Conflict in the Confederacy*. New York, 1924.

Moore, Frank, *The Rebellion Record: A Diary of American Events*. New York, 1865.

Nevins, Allan, *The Emergence of Modern America, 1865-78*. New York, 1927.

Nichols, George Ward, *The Story of the Great March*. New York, 1865.

Nicolay, J. G., and Hay, John, *Abraham Lincoln: A History*. New York, 1890.

Oberholtzer, E. P., *Jay Cooke, Financier of the Civil War*. 2 vols. Philadelphia, 1907.

Official Proceedings of the National Republican Conventions of 1868, 1872, 1876 and 1880. Minneapolis, 1903.

Official Records of the Rebellion. Washington, D. C.

Page, James M., and Haley, M. J., *The True Story of Andersonville Prison*. New York, 1908.

Phillips, Ulrich B., *The Life of Robert Toombs*. New York, 1913.

—— *American Negro Slavery*. New York, 1927.

Pike, James S., *The Prostrate State: South Carolina under Negro Government*. New York, 1874.

Poore, Ben Perley, *Perley's Reminiscences*. 3 vols. Philadelphia, 1886.

Post, John L. (compiled by): *Reminiscences by Personal Friends of General U. S. Grant and the History of Grant's Log Cabin*. St. Louis, 1904.

Pryor, Mrs. Roger A., *Reminiscences of Peace and War*. New York, 1904.

Regulations of the United States Military Academy for 1839.

Regulations of the Army of the Confederate States. Richmond, 1862.

Report of the Joint Select Committee to Inquire into the Condition of Affairs in the Late Insurrectionary States. Washington: Government Printing Office, 1872.

Report of Select Committee to Inquire into Government Contracts, House Reports, 37th Congress, Third Session, 1862-63; No. 49.

Rhodes, James Ford, *History of the United States*. 8 vols. New York, 1920.

Richardson, Albert D., *A Personal History of Ulysses S. Grant*. Hartford, 1868.

Ringwalt, J. R., *Anecdotes of General Grant*. Philadelphia, 1886.

Rives, George L., *The United States and Mexico*. 2 vols. New York, 1913.

Rourke, Constance Mayfield, *Trumpets of Jubilee*. New York, 1927.

Russell, William Howard, *My Diary North and South*. 2 vols. London, 1863.

Schlesinger, Arthur M., *A Political and Social History of the United States, 1829-1925*.

Schurz, Carl, *Reminiscences*. 3 vols. New York, 1908.

Schwab, John C., *The Confederate States of America*. New York, 1901.

Seitz, Don C., *Horace Greeley*. Indianapolis, 1926.

Shanks, W. F. G., *Personal Reminiscences of General Grant*, in *Harper's Magazine*, vol. 3, 1865.

Sherman, John, *Recollections of Forty Years in the House, Senate and Cabinet*. 2 vols. Chicago, 1895.

Sherman, William T., *Home Letters of General Sherman.* Edited by M. A. DeWolfe Howe. New York, 1909.
——*Memoirs.* 2 vols. New York, 1875.
Shrady, Dr. George F., *General Grant's Last Days.* In *Century Magazine*, vol. 54.
Smith, E. Kirby, *To Mexico with Scott.* Cambridge, 1917.
Spencer, Ambrose, *A Narrative of Andersonville.* New York, 1866.
Taylor, Richard, *Destruction and Reconstruction.* New York, 1879.
Villard, Oswald Garrison, *John Brown, 1800-1859.* Boston, 1911.
Vincent, John H., *Inner Life of U. S. Grant* in *The Chatauquan*, vol. 30— Oct., 1899-March, 1900.
Van Bort, Ph., *General Grant and the Jews.* New York, 1868.
Webb, Richard D., *The Life and Letters of Captain John Brown.* London, 1861.
Wells, Edward L., *Hampton and Reconstruction.* Columbia, S. C., 1907.
Welles, Gideon, *Diary of Gideon Welles.* 3 vols. Boston, 1911.
Wilkin, J. W., *Personal Reminiscences of U. S. Grant.* In Transactions of Illinois State Historical Society for 1907. Springfield, Ill.
Wilson, James H., *The Life of John A. Rawlins.* New York, 1916.
Winston, Robert W., *Andrew Johnson, Plebeian and Patriot.* New York, 1928.
Young, John R., *Around the World with General Grant.* 2 vols. New York, 1879.

Index

Adams, Henry, on Grant, 208
Alabama, case against Britain, 449 *et seq.*
Andersonville, Ga., Confederate prison in, 342
Atlanta, Ga., Sherman in, 335

Babcock, Orville B., and the whisky ring scandal, 421-422
San Dominican affair, 442 *et seq.*
Badeau, Adam, a friend of Grant, 261, 461 *et seq.*, 495
Baez, Buenaventura, and American annexation of San Domingo, 442 *et seq.*
Beauregard, Peter G. T., 175, 246, 257, 330 *et seq.*
Beecher, Henry Ward, 129, 151
Belknap, W. W., financial scandal, 423 *et seq.*
Belmont, battle of, 209 *et seq.*
Bibliography, 503 *et seq.*
Bigelow, John, on Grant's political sense, 400
Blaine, James G., 474
Boggs, Henry, partnership with Grant, 123 *et seq.*
Booth, John Wilkes, 354, 356
Borie, Adolph E., 399
"Boss" Tweed, Lynch, 150
Boutwell, George S., 400
Bragg, Braxton, at Chattanooga, 302
Bristow, Benjamin H., whisky ring investigation, 419 *et seq.*
Brown, B. Gratz, opposition to Grant administration, 438
Brown, John, 154-155, 158-159
Buchanan, James, administration, 162, 164-165
Buckner, Simon B., 44, 121, 218, 501
Buell, Don Carlos, Mississippi campaign, 224-225, 247 *et seq.*
Buena Vista, battle of, 89-90
Bull-fighting, Grant's opinion of, 98
Burnside, Ambrose Everett, 312
Butler, Benjamin F., and the Army of the James, 317-318
hold on Grant, 346-347, 419
on Lincoln's death, 356

Cairo, Ill., Grant at, 190 *et seq.*
Calhoun, John C., 104, 111
California, 98
Grant sent to, 106, 118
Campaign of 1860, 162 *et seq.*
Campaign of 1864, war opposition expressed in, 310
Campaign of 1868, financial issue, 396-397
Campaign of 1872, 439
Campaign of 1880, 473 *et seq.*
Carpet-baggers, 381 *et seq.*
in South Carolina, 428 *et seq.*
Century Magazine, 186, 404
Cerro Gordo, battle of, 93-94
Chancellorsville, battle of, 200, 313
Chandler, Zachariah, 105, 356
Channing, William E., 129
on Garrison and secession, 127
on slavery, 71
Chapultepec, battle of, 95
Chase, Salmon P., 361, 417
China, the Grants in, 471
Civil War, 31, 40, 64, 83, 119, 137
blockade-running, 243
causes, 108, 173 *et seq.*
contrasted ability of soldiers of North and South, 200
deceptions in, 176
Grant on, 76, 493
hardships, 219, 291
Lee's surrender, 351 *et seq.*
Mississippi campaign, 215 *et seq.*
news fictions, 234, 291, 292, 315
Sherman's terms for Johnston's surrender, 357 *et seq.*
substitute system, 231
swindling in North, 269 *et seq.*
Union tactics, 199, 201-202
Clay, Henry, 104, 112
Cold Harbor, battle of, 30, 324
Colfax, Schuyler, Grant's letter to, 408-409
Columbia, burning of, 338
Compromise of 1850, 112 *et seq.*
Confederacy (*see* South)

Congress, United States, Back Pay Grab, 418
impeachment of Johnson, 395-396
physical fights, 133 *et seq.*
restoration of army rank to Grant, 497
slave issue in, 69-70
Conkling, Roscoe, and Grant's third term candidacy, 474-475
Constitution, United States, 153
disregarded by anti-slavery fanatics, 127
Johnson's efforts to preserve, 364
Lincoln and the, 166
states' rights under, 68
Cooke, Jay, and Company, 274
Corbin, A. R., in the Gould-Fisk speculation, 412 *et seq.*
Corpus Christi, abandoned, 80
army of occupation in, 77-78
Cotton gin invented, 63 *et seq.*
Cotton-growing, 64, 168, 242, 266, 382
Cramer, Michael J. (Grant's brother-in-law), 370, 470
Credit Mobilier scandal, 405 *et seq.*

Dana, Charles A., at Chattanooga, 302
at Vicksburg, 292, 297 *et seq.*
offer to Badeau, 496
on Butler, 346
on Grant, 299
on Rawlins, 207
Dana, Richard Henry, on Grant, 309
Davis, Jefferson, 111
appearance, 82-83, 169
fictions about, 176
Harold's letter to, 232-233
hero of Buena Vista, 89
personality, 169-170
Democratic party, campaign of 1860, 162 *et seq.*
campaign of 1868, 397
Johnson's affiliation with, 363
Dent, Colonel Frederick (father-in-law of Grant), 60, 61
aid to Grant, 122, 135
in the White House, 403
opinion of Grant, 187, 213
Dent, Frederick T. (brother-in-law of Grant), 95, 213
Douglas, Stephen A., 162, 163, 164
Dred Scott decision, 152, 153

Emerson, Ralph Waldo, on abolition, 151

on Lincoln's death, 355
England (*see* Great Britain)
Erlanger et Compagnie, Southern loan, 239 *et seq.*

Farragut, David Glasgow, at New Orleans, 263
Fish, Hamilton, 401, 443, 458
Fisk, James, Jr., gold speculation, 411 *et seq.*
Floyd, John B., at Fort Donelson, 217 *et seq.*
Foote, Andrew Hull, consultation with Grant, 219-220
Fort Donelson, 106, 121, 191, 200, 216 *et seq.*
Fort Henry, 191, 215, 216
Fort Sumter, attack on, 173 *et seq.*
Fourteenth Amendment, 387-388
France, Mexican interference, 367
Franklin, battle of, 337
Fredericksburg, battle of, 312
Freedmen's Bureau, 378 *et seq.*
Frémont, John C., Grant's opinion of, 191 *et seq.*
Fugitive slave laws, 113, 126, 129

Galena, Ill., gift to Grant, 368
Grant in, 136
Gambetta, Leon Michel, Grant's opinion of, 468
Garfield, James A., 475
Garrison, William Lloyd, 71, 127, 151
Georgia, legislature disturbance, 434
Gettysburg, battle of, 201
Gould, Jay, gold speculation, 411
Grant, Frederick Dent (son of U. S. Grant), 105, 123, 308, 476, 496
Grant, Hannah Simpson (mother of U. S. Grant, 12, 13, 34, 403
Grant, Jesse Root (father of U. S. Grant), aid to Grant, 136
at the siege of Richmond, 345
business, 15-16, 31
children, 18
defense of Ulysses, 256
on Ulysses' dismissal from the army, 122
Grant, Jesse Root (son of U. S. Grant), 123, 282, 476
Grant, Julia Dent (wife of U. S. Grant), appearance, 60
at Holly Springs, 282
character, 60, 473
courtship, 58 *et seq.*
in the White House, 437

Mrs. Lincoln and, 346
slaves, 125
Grant, Nellie (daughter of U. S. Grant), 123
marriage, 437
Grant, Ulysses S., administrative ability, 265 *et seq.*
adversity, 125, 135, 187, 489-490
appearance, 16, 25, 39, 56, 351, 437
as an actor, 78
as temporary Secretary of War, 390, 392 *et seq.*
at West Point, 38 *et seq.*
aversion to firearms, 28-29
birth, 14
career as a farmer, 122-123
character, 18, 21, 27 *et seq.*, 35, 46, 61, 76, 104, 120, 254, 259, 270, 322, 342, 441, 455, 457, 460, 500
children, 105, 123
Commissions, 55, 189, 233, 258, 300, 308 *et seq.*, 369
contrasted with Lee, 328-329
death, 502
dislike of obscenity and profanity, 23
dismissed from the army, 121
fictions about, 252, 261
friendships, 260
horsemanship, 21-22, 51 *et seq.*
illness, 492, 495 *et seq.*
in real estate, 123 *et seq.*
liquor drinking, 86, 99, 104, 119 *et seq.*, 213, 299
love of animals, 30
marriage, 59-60, 101 *et seq.*
mathematical ability, 50, 56-57
mentality, 22, 37, 77
military greatness, 37, 96, 182, 187-188, 202-203, 215, 295 *et seq.*, 316 *et seq.*, 323
on war, 174
pacifism, 75 *et seq.*, 86
physical modesty, 25-26
political limitations, 115, 164, 275, 367, 390-391, 394, 446, 454-455, 457
reading, 45, 49
religion, 369-370, 499-500
second term election, 439, 440
smoking, 233, 320
Southern tour, 373-374
superstitions, 30-31
terms for Lee's surrender, 352
third term defeat, 473 *et seq.*

trip around the world, 457 *et seq.*
unpopularity, 23, 256
Grant, Ulysses, Jr. (son of U. S. Grant), 120, 123, 476
on the Grant genealogy, 466-467
Grant administrations, *Alabama* claims, 449 *et seq.*
appointments, 398 *et seq.*
Back Pay Grab, 418
Belknap case, 423 *et seq.*
condition of the country at time of, 404-405, 410
Credit Mobilier scandal, 405
Gould and Fisk financial scandal, 411 *et seq.*
legal tender money, 417-418
Motley affair, 447
opposition to, 438 *et seq.*
Panic of 1873, 452 *et seq.*
Sanborn scandal, 419
San Dominican affair, 441 *et seq.*
successes, 448, 454
whisky ring scandal, 420 *et seq.*
Grant and Ward, firm of, accounts analyzed, 491
failure, 486 *et seq.*
General Grant connected with, 479 *et seq.*, 486
Great Britain, *Alabama* case, 449
dependence on American wheat, 267
Greeley, Horace, a Liberal Republican, 438
attitude toward secession, 171
Greenback paper dollars, 273, 411

Halleck, Henry W., dislike of Grant, 212, 226
Halstead, Murat, criticism of Grant, 292
Hamlin, Hannibal, 176
Hampton, Wade, 156, 230
Helper, Hinton Rowan, on slavery, 148 *et seq.*
Hoar, E. Rockwood, 347, 400
Hoar, George F., on Grant, 261, 272, 446
Hood, John B., in Georgia, 335-336
in Tennessee, 336-337
Hooker, Joseph, 200, 313
Hunter, David, in the Shenandoah valley, 334

Inflation Bill, 453, 454

Jackson, Thomas J. ("Stonewall"), 40, 200, 238

Jefferson, Thomas, slavery and, 64, 111
Johnson, Andrew, accession to Presidency, 356
character, 363, 364, 387, 388
Grant and, 388, 393, 398
impeachment, 395
Johnston, Albert Sidney, killed, 253
Mississippi campaign, 217, 224, 245, *et seq.*
Johnston, Joseph E., advice to Pemberton, 295
and Sherman's march, 318-319, 335
surrender document, 357 *et seq.*

Kansas, John Brown in, 154
slave dispute in, 126, 153
Ku-Klux Klan, 380, 381, 383 *et seq.*, 434 *et seq.*

Lee, Robert E., 40
appearance, 351
at Appomattox, 349 *et seq.*
at Brown's raid, 158
at Cold Harbor, 30
at Richmond, 317 *et seq.*
battle of the Wilderness, 320 *et seq.*
character, 326 *et seq.*
Meade and, 352
Mexican campaign, 93 *et seq.*
military greatness, 200, 326, 328, 338
on Southern deficiency, 199
religion, 238
Legal Tender Act, 273 *et seq.*, 417
Liberal-Republican party, convention of 1872, 439
organized, 438
Li Hung Chang, 471
Lincoln, Abraham, character, 172, 277
compared with Grant, 27
czarism, 276 *et seq.*
dismissal of Butler, 271
Douglas debates, 162
election, 163-164
fictions about, 166, 176, 261
inaugural address, 166
in the Civil War, 189, 196, 202-203
letter of thanks to Grant, 300
negro emancipation, 278
on Grant, 256, 259
on saving the Union, 171-172
on slavery, 166

on the equality of the races, 163
reconstruction policies, 354 *et seq.*
reëlection, 307, 311
religion, 369
Lincoln, Mrs. Abraham, at the Richmond siege, 345
Mrs. Grant and, 346
Longstreet, James, 44
at Grant's wedding, 101-102
Lookout Mountain, battle of, 304
Louisiana, Grant in, 75
reconstruction, 433-434
Lowell, James Russell, on Grant, 471
on reconstruction, 435-436

McClellan, George Brinton, Grant and, 185, 225
nominated for President, 311
McClernand, John A., at Fort Donelson, 220, 221
at Vicksburg, 283 *et seq.*, 287, 297
McPherson, James Birdseye, 261, 297, 298
Massachusetts, financial resources, 142
Meade, George G., at Gettysburg, 201
in Virginia, 313 *et seq.*
Memoirs, Ulysses S. Grant, *cited throughout*
Mexican War, campaigns, 80 *et seq.*, 87 *et seq.*
causes, 62, 74
Mexico, French invasion, 367
Missionary Ridge, battle of, 304 *et seq.*
Missouri Compromise, 69, 70, 71, 97, 111, 112, 126
Monterey, battle of, 87-88, 89
Motley, John Lothrop, American Minister to England, 447, 449
Mount McGregor, N. Y., Grant's last days in, 501
Nashville, battle of, 246, 337
Negroes, attitude toward, 174, 434
"Black Codes," 372
legislative duties, 428 *et seq.*
free, 66, 67
post-war conditions, 366, 371 *et seq.*, 430-431
soldiers, 279
suffrage, 361
Newman, J. P., in Grant's home, 498
New Orleans, captured, 197, 263
New York City, disunion sentiment, 171

war riot in, 280-281
North, bounty system, 279
  business boom, 267 *et seq.*, 452
  finances, 142, 273 *et seq.*
  industrial collapse, 452 *et seq.*
  living conditions of laboring people, 150
  man-power, 199
  profiteering in, 269 *et seq.*
  secession sentiments, 68, 153
  tariff issues, 109 *et seq.*
  war debt, 273
North Carolina, negro rights in, 66

Paducah, capture of, 191-192
Parker, Theodore, 129
Pemberton, John C., 96
  at Vicksburg, 294 *et seq.*
Personal liberty laws, 114
Petersburg, Grant's advance on, 330
Phillips, Wendell, 129, 362
  on Lincoln, 276
  on negro slavery, 140
Pillow, Gideon J., at Fort Donelson, 218
Pittsburg Landing, Grant's forces at, 245
Polk, James K., 73, 78, 80, 87
Porter, David D., 284, 289, 293
Porter, Horace, 29, 104, 223, 261, 320

Radical party, chaos of rule, 435
  Grant and, 374
  Johnson and, 360 *et seq.*
Rawlins, John A., as Secretary of War, 401
  Grant and, 260, 266, 299, 323-324
  letter to Washburne, 213
  personality, 205 *et seq.*
Reconstruction, condition of South, 364 *et seq.*
  Georgia, 432, 434
  in South Carolina, 427 *et seq.*
  in Florida, 432
  Johnson's policies, 360 *et seq.*
  Lincoln's policies, 354 *et seq.*
  Louisiana, 433
Republican party, anti-slavery program, 153
  campaign of 1860, 162 *et seq.*
  Grant's alliance with, 394, 396
  organized, 131
  reconstruction ideas, 376-377
Richardson, William A., 419
Richmond, Va., bread riot, 237
  Civil War atmosphere, 233 *et seq.*
  evacuated, 348

Grant's advance to, 323 *et seq.*
  Union desire to capture, 202
Rosecrans, William Stark, 44
  at Chattanooga, 302, 303
Russell, W. H., 169, 171, 190

Sanborn, John D., tax collection scandal, 419
San Domingo, anarchy in, 442
Santa Anna, 91
Sartoris, Algernon, married to Nellie Grant, 437
Schofield, John M., on the negroes, 372
Schurz, Carl, opposition to Grant administration, 438
  Southern tour, 373
Scott, Winfield, 88, 158, 181
Secession, first proposals, 68, 153
  Northern opinion, 171
  opponents, 165
  vote in South, 170
Seward, William H., 107
  on the Constitution, 127
Seymour, Horatio, 397
Sheridan, Philip Henry, 261, 351, 372
Sherman, John, Presidential candidacy, 475
Sherman, William Tecumseh, 45
  at Shiloh, 249
  at Vicksburg, 286 *et seq.*, 297, 298
  character, 260, 358
  march through Georgia, 202, 318-319, 334 *et seq.*
  on slavery, 181
  surrender document, 357 *et seq.*
Shiloh, battle of, 245 *et seq.*
Slavery, abolition crusade, 127
  affected by the cotton gin, 64
  as an economic institution, 142-143, 148
  constitutional, 169
  fugitive slave laws, 113 *et seq.*
  Missouri Compromise, 69 *et seq.*
  public opinion of, 65 *et seq.*, 108
Smith, C. F., 53, 221, 225, 226
Smith, W. F., plan for relief of Chattanooga, 304
  removed from command, 346-347
South, characterized, 137 *et seq.*
  Civil War conditions in, 236
  conscription, 229 *et seq.*
  Confederate constitution, 169
  defense of slavery, 144
  draft-evaders and deserters, 231
  financial policy, 235 *et seq.*
  foreign policy, 168

Grant and, 137, 359
military government, 391-392
national organization, 228 *et seq.*
opposition to war in, 199, 233
post-war, 364 *et seq.*
reconstruction (*see* separate item)
secession sentiments, 68
states' rights claims, 112
tariff issues, 109 *et seq.*
war prisoners, 342
South Carolina, carpet-bagging in, 428 *et seq.*
reconstruction era, 427 *et seq.*
secession, 164-165
Sherman in, 338 *et seq.*
Specie Resumption Act, 418, 454
Spottsylvania, battles at, 322
Stanton, Edwin M., and Sherman's surrender document, 358
character, 277
removed from office, 390, 392
Stevens, Thaddeus, 356, 361, 362
reconstruction ideas, 375-376, 378, 389
Stewart, Alexander T., 399
Stowe, Harriet Beecher, anti-slavery activities, 129 *et seq.*
Sumner, Charles, 361, 362, 399
and the *Alabama* claims, 449
and the San Dominican affair, 444
assaulted by Brooks, 134-135
Grant's feud with, 446-447, 451-452
on Lincoln's death, 355
on reconstruction, 374-375
Supreme Court, 153
case of Hepburn *vs.* Griswold, 416-417
Dred Scott case, 152
Ku-Klux Act, 435

Tariff, Protective, controversies over, 109 *et seq.*
Taylor, Zachary, character, 107
described, 82-83
Mexican campaign, 78 *et seq.*, 80 *et seq.*
Tenure of Office Act, 389, 393, 395, 447
Texas, annexation, 70 *et seq.*, 96
in the Mexican War, 62

Thomas, George H., at Chattanooga, 303
Thomas, Lorenzo, temporary Secretary of War, 394
Twain, Mark, Grant and, 493 *et seq.*, 499

Underground Railroad, 113, 146
Union Pacific Railroad, building scandal, 405 *et seq.*

Vanderbilt, William H., loan to Grant, 487, 490
Vera Cruz, siege of, 88, 89, 91
Vicksburg, battle of, 77, 282 *et seq.*, 293 *et seq.*
Victoria, Queen, the Grants' visit to, 464 *et seq.*

Wade, Benjamin F., 356, 361
Wallace, Lew, at the battle of Shiloh, 246 *et seq.*
Ward, Ferdinand, business methods, 481 *et seq.*
financial speculation, 478
Warmoth, Henry C., 433
Washburne, Elihu B., Grant and, 189, 270, 475
Secretary of State, 399
Washington, George, contrasted with Grant, 99
Lee compared with, 327
Washington, Treaty of, 448, 451
Webster, Daniel, 104
Welles, on Grant, 309, 390, 393-394
West Point, 23
Grant at, 33 *et seq.*, 38-54
Whig party, 126, 163
"Whisky Ring," 420 *et seq.*
Whitney, Eli, invention of the cotton gin, 63 *et seq.*
Wilderness, battle of the, 320
Wilmot, David, anti-slavery bill, 97, 98
Wood, Fernando, 175
on disunion, 171
Wright, Marcus J., on the Confederate army, 198

Yates, Governor, Grant and, 185, 203, 368
Young, John Russell, 54
on Grant, 454, 463, 470